CONFESSIONS OF A CHANCELLOR

The Politics of Higher Education

G. DAVID GEARHART

Copyright © 2022 by G. David Gearhart

All rights reserved. No part of this book may be reproduced in any form or by any electronic or mechanical means, including information storage and retrieval systems, without written permission from the author, except for the use of brief quotations in a book review.

Cover and book design by Karen Long

Hardcover ISBN 979-8-9874075-0-9

This book is dedicated to Jane Brockmann Gearhart, my amazing wife of 50 years. We took this journey together and it would not have been possible without her.

CONTENTS

Foreword	xi
Preface	xvii

PART I
BEGINNINGS

1. Heritage	3
2. No Place like Home	18
3. Priesthood and St. Joe's	26
4. High School	30
5. Small College Experience	32
6. Law School	41
7. Jane Brockmann Gearhart	48

PART II
SOJOURN TO HIGHER EDUCATION

8. Westminster	55
9. Hendrix College	66

PART III
UNIVERSITY OF ARKANSAS, THE FIRST TIME

10. Back to Fayetteville	77
11. The New Boss and The Coach	80
12. New Boss – for an hour	87
13. On the Road Again	90

PART IV
PENN STATE AND HAPPY VALLEY

14. New Boss, New Adventure	95
15. Off Course	113
16. Another New Boss	123

PART V
A CONSULTANT

17. Raising Money for Me — 135

PART VI
THE UNIVERSITY OF ARKANSAS, THE SECOND TIME

18. Closing the Press — 145
19. University House — 149
20. Blame for Pepsi — 152
21. Historical Markers — 154
22. Saving Carnall — 158
23. Murder-Suicide — 162
24. 2010 Commission — 165
25. Football Games in Little Rock — 167
26. September 11, 2001 — 173
27. It's all Greek to me! — 177
28. Nolan Richardson dismissal — 182
29. The D Rule — 185
30. Retiring Frank — 188
31. Old Main Clock — 193
32. Volunteers and Towers of Old Main — 195
33. Second Book and CASE Conflict — 197
34. Driving them crazy! — 201
35. The Campaign for the Twenty-First Century — 204
36. Quantum: $300 Million — 215
37. Lawsuit — 236
38. Winthrop Rockefeller Institute — 241
39. High School for Sale — 244
40. Coach no Coach — 253
41. Harvard — 256
42. Hiring a New Athletics Director — 260
43. Fowler House — 264

PART VII
CHANCELLOR, THE EARLY YEARS

44. Ready or Not — 271
45. Budget Challenges and State Appropriations — 277
46. The Bucket List — 283

47. University Systems and the Flagship Campus	309
48. Into the Fray	315
49. The Razorback Foundation	330
50. Friends	334
51. President of Panama	342
52. Pressure to Move Our Nursing Program	345
53. No Tuition Increase	347
54. Out of State Students	349
55. Severe Budget Cutbacks	355
56. Alcohol	357
57. Expansion of the SEC	361
58. Walton Arts Center	364
59. Good National PR	369
60. Penn State, Paterno, Sandusky, Spanier	372
61. A Compact with the People of Arkansas	375
62. Food Pantry	380
63. Righting a Wrong	383
64. Veterans	385
65. Arkansas Department of Higher Education (ADHE)	387
66. Amendment 33	393
67. Milestone	396
68. Faculty Athletic Representative	398
69. Another Athletics Change	401
70. Open Door	407
71. Undocumented	414
72. Dalai Lama	431
73. Chancellor or President	435

PART VIII
CHANCELLOR, THE LATER YEARS

74. Division of Agriculture	447
75. Athletics Transfer to Academics	460
76. Governor	461
77. A New Conference Center That Never Was	463
78. Legislators	465
79. April Fool's Day—Say It Ain't so Bobby	476
80. Post Petrino	486
81. Bielema	492
82. Closing a Street for Campus Safety	495

83. Disloyalty	498
84. Hillary	532
85. Summer Vacation 2013	534
86. eVersity	543
87. Staff Retirements	557
88. White House Summit on Education	561
89. Finding a New SEC Commissioner	563
90. Crazies	566
91. Retirement Looming	570

PART IX
RETIREMENT

92. Some Things Done—Some Things Not	583
93. Retirement as Chancellor	590
94. Off to the Faculty	600
95. Qassim University	604
96. A New Chancellor	607
97. The Final Chapter	619
References	627
Acknowledgments	633
Index	635
About the Author	661
Also by G. David Gearhart	663

CONFESSIONS OF A
CHANCELLOR

FOREWORD

It's hard to know where to begin—a question with which Dave Gearhart never appeared to struggle. He just always seemed to know the first step to take or the first word to write—no time wasted in fear of the blank page or procrastination. It was always the season of action.

In the 17 years we worked together, I had the opportunity to see from the inside out how his vision, work ethic, willingness to listen to different points of view, and ability to get a job done manifested themselves in the transformational $300 million gift from The Walton Family Charitable Support Foundation, the $1 billion Campaign for the Twenty-First Century, and eight years of courageous and visionary leadership as chancellor.

Without question, he arose every morning and went to bed every evening thinking about how he could help to underwrite the success of Arkansas students and faculty. When I worked with students, faculty, staff, and alumni on his behalf, I often shared at least one of the four questions I believed he asked himself each day: (1) What if? (2) What does our best look like? (3) How can we get there? (4) How soon can we get there?

Although I did not know him—except by reputation—until 1997,

I imagine those four questions guided him and his work throughout the trajectory of his career—from Westminster College to Hendrix College to the University of Arkansas to Penn State, and ultimately back to the U of A. I see evidence of them throughout the text of this book and the curriculum and pedagogy of the classes he taught as a professor in his chancellor emeritus years.

Undergirding each question was a bold and pragmatic confidence in the university that ultimately brought about a transformation of Arkansans' faith in the institution we could become.

As the architect of the Campaign for the Twenty-First Century, he not only helped to put together the infrastructure of the campaign, he inspired the campaign steering committee to raise the goal not once but twice. When it became evident that $1 billion was in our sights, it was not in his DNA to walk away from the challenge. Thus, the University of Arkansas became one of 24 institutions at that time to have set a goal of 1 billion or more dollars. A bold and audacious move for a poor state!

No one—including Dave Gearhart himself—could have foreseen the impact the Campaign for the Twenty-First Century—which ultimately raised $1.046 billion and included 41,613 new donors—would have on the university and the State of Arkansas itself. The campaign made a profound difference in the number of scholarships and fellowships available to undergraduate and graduate students, the number of endowed professorships and chairs available to recruit and retain world-class faculty, the enhancement of academic programs across every college and school, an infusion of resources for University of Arkansas Libraries, an exponential increase in the number of honors students from across the country coming to campus to be part of the newly created and endowed Honors College, and in the rapid increase in new buildings, renovations, and capital projects that produced a building boom across campus.

Those of us who worked with him and for him always believed his extraordinary success as a fundraiser and his willingness to listen to all constituencies convinced the board of trustees to name him chancellor July 1, 2008.

And, in the minds and hearts of those close to the university, his tenure as chancellor—though more tumultuous—was no less successful than the Campaign for the Twenty-First Century, as evidenced by the explosive growth in student enrollment, the improvement of the university's six-year graduation rate, his remarkable stewardship of campus resources and facilities, and the exponential growth in online courses and enrollment.

Under his administration, the University of Arkansas entered the R-1 Carnegie status and was designated in the top two percent of universities in the U.S., thus raising the research profile of the campus as well as its *U.S. News & World Report* rankings. In the words of Dr. Suzanne McCray, vice provost for enrollment, "Dave was never content with good enough. He was always reaching higher."

Dr. Donald O. Pederson, vice chancellor for finance and administration in both the Gearhart and John A. White (1997–2008) administrations, believes much of this success emanated from Dave's long-term perspective on building institutional quality and strength in faculty and staff, facilities, and the finances to improve all aspects of the university.

Dr. Steve Boss, an esteemed professor in the university's Department of Geosciences, explains Dave's success this way: "He was truly the people's chancellor. He understood Arkansas and the people of Arkansas. And he understood the real mission of the university and worked to ensure we achieved that mission."

Certainly, his motto of "Students First" resonated with students, prospective students, parents, and alumni—especially when they saw evidence of it in every facet of student life.

Tori Pohlner Bogner, Associated Student Government president in 2012–2013, said that "Under Dr. Gearhart's leadership, the student body president was neither a mere sounding board nor a box to check to say that students were asked about policy decisions. If anything, the challenge during my term of office was not to get the administration to listen to students, but for me to acquire the variety of student feedback requested from Dr. Gearhart and his team."

His motto may have been "Students First," but he listened just as carefully to faculty members' suggestions and responded thoughtfully to their questions, and even their criticisms. For the most part, even the "most academic of the academics"—sometimes to their surprise—thought he was an amazing chancellor.

In the book that follows, Dave is honest about some of the challenges he faced with the board of trustees and the Arkansas State Legislature. Whether you agree with him on the issues he fought for or those which he fought against, I can say with full confidence that he did his best to make fair and equitable decisions, and his actions always aligned with the courage of his convictions.

In the words of former Associated Student Government President Billy Fleming (2008–2009), "Chancellor Gearhart was deeply committed to using his position and the power that came with it to elevate others, especially marginalized people and communities. He was a beacon in his support for undocumented students and LGBTQ+ students, faculty, and staff in a very conservative state—even when it came at a steep personal and professional price."

For me and many others, his stand on DACA and the DREAMers was heroic. Although he received threats to himself, physically and professionally, he carried on. The result: He fundamentally changed the relationship of the university with the Hispanic community and other minority groups. DACAmented students now have in-state tuition, in part, because of his work.

His success as a fundraiser and as a chancellor continues to reverberate throughout the campus today. The success of Honors College alumni is just one example. Dr. Lynda Coon, dean of the Honors College, says that "their collective success is stunning and ranges from CEOs of high-tech businesses, corporate leaders at companies like Amazon, resolute servants on Capitol Hill, attorneys representing farm workers, professors of medicine teaching at universities like Harvard and Duke, and architectural visionaries practicing in New York City. Thousands of alumni have benefitted from his vision."

And that is the sentiment many have shared with me both during and beyond his administration: His vision for the University of Arkansas changed my life, my child's life, or my grandchild's life.

I believe in the annals of the university's history, Dave Gearhart will be recognized as one of the institution's very best chancellors.

His indefatigable efforts to make the university work for everyone, his belief that Arkansas deserves a great public institution that can play at the top national level, and his ability to inspire others to give back to the U of A set a very high bar indeed.

Judy Gregson Schwab
Former associate vice chancellor
University of Arkansas

PREFACE

> *The politics of the university are so intense because the stakes are so low.*
>
> — WALLACE S. SAYRE AS QUOTED BY HENRY KISSINGER

Clark Kerr was one of America's great university presidents. He was chancellor of the University of California, Berkeley and later president of the University of California system from 1958 to 1967. He was known for clever witticisms. One of his quotes from 1963 sets the tone for this book:

> The university president in the United States is expected to be a friend of the students, a colleague of the faculty, a good fellow with the alumni, a sound administrator with the trustees, a good speaker with the public, an astute bargainer with the foundations and federal agencies, a politician with the state legislature, a friend of industry, labor, and agriculture, a persuasive diplomat with donors, a champion of education generally, a supporter of the professions (particu-

larly law and medicine), a spokesman to the press, a scholar in his own right, a public servant at the state and national levels. ... Above all he must enjoy traveling in airplanes, eating his meals in public, and attending public ceremonies.

You will find this book sprinkled with stories about my life in higher education. However, it is not meant to be solely about the author's life, but rather the many experiences I lived and breathed in higher education during 52 years in the academy, particularly when I served as chancellor of the University of Arkansas.

To be certain, some will find the stories I relate to be disturbing, and may even cause a few to revisit their thoughts about the "ivory tower" of higher education. As the late Toni Morrison once said, "I wrote this book because I wanted to read it." You will find reminiscences of good times and bad. Stories of academic challenges and athletics ones. You will read about trustee interference, system interference and legislative interference in our academic programs. Much will be said about the underfunded nature of the university. The book addresses the establishment of eVersity by the University of Arkansas System and policy decisions with little or no discussion. The book covers the firing of coaches, an athletics director and vice chancellor. You will also find comments on the resignation of a chancellor because of provocative photographs that emerged online.

The book also explores the good side of higher education, such as the phenomenal generosity of benefactors and amazing commitment of faculty and staff. I encourage you to go ahead and read between the lines if I have left something intentionally vague.

It is important to note at the outset that, although some of my experiences even disturbed me as I recount them here, I still have a very healthy view of the world of higher education.

You will find the good and the bad in the academy to be sure. You will find amazing presidents and chancellors who came into the profession to make a difference and commanded the respect and admiration from constituents. They gave of themselves unselfishly to make a difference in the lives of young and old that wanted to access the American opportunity system. Many of them are heroes to me. I have known and worked for several of them, and they made my life better and taught me that to be truly outstanding in this profession one needed to make sacrifices that used up the time they could have been spending with their own families.

To be a president is a way of life if you do it the right way. Good presidents cannot get away from the job, which is constant and unforgiving. So many groups vie for the attention of the CEO that it is simply impossible to do much of anything else but respond to their inquiries and attempt to provide the leadership necessary to make a difference in the lives of students, faculty, staff, alumni, parents, and others.

You will also find poor, even bad presidents who do not see the job as a calling. They enjoy the prestige and accolades but relegate the real work to subordinates, or just don't worry about making progress for the institutions they have been charged with protecting and advancing. I have worked for a few of those as well.

And you will also find faculty who obtain tenure, only to then get lazy and do the least amount possible, meeting classes but doing little else. They don't keep office hours, do little published research or scholarship, if any at all, and slide through to retirement believing tenure gives them some sort of entitlement. I have experienced that during my 23 years as a tenured professor. These faculty give the rest a bad name. These faculty fuel the pushback on tenure and create a skeptical public who sees higher education as a gravy train for washed-up teachers.

The important point is that good faculty who work hard to advance the common good of their schools and academic programs are in more abundance. Good faculty care about their students and make an indelible mark on their future. Good faculty are hardworking, engage in scholarship and contribute to society in amazing and important ways. It is the bad ones who hurt the reputation of the academy and cause legislators to question the efficacy of higher education and the entire system.

I still believe that higher education is the pathway to the American opportunity system. It is the great equalizer. Folks with a college education are happier, healthier, wealthier, and more likely to experience a life well lived. I believe passionately that four years (or more) of a college experience will make a person appreciate the world around them and open new and exciting vistas not realized by those who do not pursue college life. Just attending college for a few semesters will make a person more likely to appreciate the arts, literature, history, books, the classics, theater, and the overall human experience.

College graduates help increase tax revenues and decrease reliance on government handouts. They decrease crime rates and increase charitable giving to local communities. College graduates increase the quality of civic life and social cohesion. They appreciate the fervent need for diversity. College graduates improve the ability to adapt to and use technology and improved working conditions. They tend to have more hobbies and leisure activities.

It is not my intent to disparage people who decide a college education is not for them. Circumstances may prevent one from achieving a college education. Family needs, monetary issues, the need to work, the need to survive, all may contribute to abandoning college work. I get it. I understand that phenomenon. My wife of almost 50 years, Jane, and I have many dear friends who did not pursue college, and many have been very successful along life's path. Many have been extraordinarily successful financially. They live wonderful, fulfilling lives with great families and secure homes. Going to college just wasn't their calling. That's OK. They make great contributions to society and live respectable, wholesome, and honorable lives. But for me, a higher education changes a person and gives one a level of sophistication and worldly appreciation.

Growing up it never occurred to me that I would opt out of a college education. It was simply expected. My mom however, dropped out of college to marry my dad, but he used the GI Bill and graduated from the University of Arkansas in 1948. He was the first of his immediate family to achieve a college degree. Our parents absolutely insisted that their four boys get a college education. It was always in the cards. No other option existed. It was a given.

But I do understand it is not for everyone, and that it is a personal, private decision, which only the individual can and must make.

I do get very upset, however, when prognosticators proclaim that higher education is unimportant and a waste of time. Unfortunately, many current commentators cite statistics that seem to prove that getting a good job and forgoing a college degree is the way to go. They cite the outliers who have been very successful in life who did not get a college degree. Steve Jobs, Bill Gates and Mark Zuckerberg went from college dropouts to billionaire status in a few short years, as discussed in the Praxis article, *125 Successful People Who Didn't Graduate College*. Lack of a college degree didn't seem to deter them from making fortunes.

But they are a small group of outliers. Evidence is clear that there are numerous benefits to a college degree. Northeastern University lays out plenty of evidence for college graduation in their blog post, *10 Benefits of Having a College Degree*, including increased access to job opportunities, and college graduates seeing many more job opportunities than non-graduates. Preparation for a specialized career, increased marketability, increased earning potential, economic stability, networking opportunities, higher job satisfaction and personal growth, and improved self-esteem all come from a college degree.

A few years ago, Peter Thiel, a Silicon Valley entrepreneur, gave out grants of $100,000 to several young people with one caveat. Don't go to college. Thiel argued that young people who have an idea that could be world changing should not waste their time going to college. He also claimed college attendance will impose a huge financial debt for many young people, who will be paying on the debt for years and years.

I'm not buying it and few educators do. These are outliers and they have presented themselves throughout history. They are the exceptions not the rule.

I still preach to young people: Go to college. It will change your life for the better. However, according to a recent article in *Inside Higher Ed* not all Americans believe a college education is necessary:

Six in 10 American adults say that a college degree is worth the time and money, according to a survey released from the Association of American Colleges and Universities and Bipartisan Policy Center. The survey, which queried 2,200 American adults between March 3 and 5 of 2021, found that Americans' opinions on the value of a college degree vary greatly by political affiliation, age and income level. Wealthy and college-educated Americans are more likely to say a college degree is definitely or probably worth it, the survey showed. About three quarters of such adults endorse the value of a college degree. By comparison, only half of adults without a college degree or who earn less than $50,000 per year say the same. Republicans and Democrats showed a similar split in opinion. Seven in 10 Democrats say that a college degree is "definitely" or "probably" worth it, compared with only 53 percent of Republicans and 52 percent of independents.

I begin this book by relating my heritage and family background. I believe family helps to mold you and send you on your path in life. I then pivot to early schooling, St. Joseph Catholic School and then high school followed by the decision to attend Westminster College, a small school in Missouri.

The book spends some time relating how I got into higher education and the early days in college administration at Westminster and Hendrix College, including my experiences at the University of Arkansas the first time in 1982. Then later my time at Penn State University and then as vice chancellor at the University of Arkansas, with a brief time in private enterprise as senior vice president and managing director for a leading philanthropic management firm in Chicago. The final part of the book is dedicated to my time as chancellor of the University of Arkansas.

In the early days I never imagined my career would lead to a university presidency. I knew I didn't want to practice law, sitting behind a desk and doing law research in the library was of no interest to me. Truth be told I was lucky to get into higher education administration at a very young age. But things have a way of working out and I'm blessed beyond measure to have experienced a passion in higher education and at the highest level and to have lived a meaningful and full life.

Frank Broyles, football coach and athletics director at the University of Arkansas for almost 50 years, said late in life that he had lived a charmed life. I guess I know what he meant. At age 70 and on the cusp of old age, I feel blessed to have lived a very full life with amazing experiences and wonderful memories in higher education.

My dad never knew I became a college president. He died during my time at Westminster College when I was director of development. I think and I hope he would have been proud of me attaining that distinction.

In the following pages I will many times use "president" and "chancellor" interchangeably. At some institutions the CEO is called chancellor and at others called president. Some system heads are called chancellor and some president. Much of the reason depends on the historical context, but for this book they are interchangeable.

The American College President Study 2017 (ACPS) sponsored by the American Council on Education (ACE) was the eighth edition of the leading and most comprehensive study of the college presidency and the higher education leadership pipeline from all types of institutions, public and private, two- and four-year. The 2017 edition was produced by ACE in partnership with the TIAA Institute There were three main takeaways from the study:

Key takeaway 1: Diversifying the presidency will continue to grow in importance, especially as the nation's student body grows more and more diverse, and the presidency grays. Strategies and policies that diversify the presidency, senior administrative positions, the faculty pipeline, and the student body in parallel should be developed and implemented with fidelity.

Key takeaway 2: Dollars remain an area of primary focus. Presidents anticipate that state and federal funding will decline in the years to come, and nearly all spend most of their time on matters related to fundraising, budget and finance. Many are turning to revenues from private gifts, grants, and contracts; tuition and fees; and endowments to fill in the gaps left by receding public support.

Key takeaway 3: Data-informed decision making that prioritizes student success will continue to grow in importance, especially as funding and accountability pressures intensify.

You will see these themes develop throughout this book.

PART I
BEGINNINGS
1952–1977

My mission in life is not merely to survive, but to thrive; and to do so with some passion, some compassion, some humor, and some style.

— MAYA ANGELOU

CHAPTER 1
HERITAGE

> *People will not look forward to posterity who never look backward to their ancestors.*
>
> — EDMUND BURKE

Over the next chapters I will relate many stories that I hope the readers will find of interest. Most of them will come from the University of Arkansas, since my service there was paramount to the other institutions where I served. Some may be controversial, but all are true and factual as I saw them unfold. I hope it gives the reader an insight into the world of higher education. The good, the not so good, the bad, and the terribly bad.

Leading up to those experiences necessitates that I also describe a few of the happenings at other higher education institutions prior to serving as chancellor. The book would be incomplete without relating those items that molded my thinking prior to running a major public university. My time at Westminster College, Hendrix College, the University of Arkansas the first time in the early 1980s, then Penn State University and a brief stint in the consulting world and then the University of Arkansas the second time, all affected how I would respond to the many challenges as chancellor.

Those experiences all contributed to preparing me for a much bigger job as a CEO of a large institution. No doubt the 10 years I spent at Penn State University contributed the most to giving me a range of knowledge about how a university administration should operate and thrive. Penn State was a colossal, complicated, complex, and renowned institution, which educated me to the opportunities and perils that awaited me at the University of Arkansas. I learned much at Penn State, about life, professionalism, fundraising, politics, and the human condition.

When my wife, Jane, and I returned to Arkansas in 1998 to be vice chancellor, a dear friend of mine, Larry Bittle, told me that going to Penn State was a critical and important move to prepare me for what lay ahead. Larry said, "David, you needed to get your seasoning before returning home." He was dead right about that, and the time at a Big Ten University gave me an education and experience base for what was coming. No doubt I would never have been prepared to take on the job of chancellor without that time in the Northeast. It served as an important catalyst for me, and I am thankful for that experience. Life tends to repeat itself and I found that to be certainly true in my career. Many of the challenges at those other institutions prepared me for the future.

There are many reasons why a person makes it to a college presidency. One might even say it is a crapshoot, or perhaps a lightning strike! There are many fine academics that try their whole adult lives to prepare themselves for a presidency, but it never happens. For whatever reason, lightning doesn't strike. That is terribly unfortunate as higher education is in need of great leaders now more than ever. Many folks who don't make it would be superb presidents and their leadership as a CEO is lost to history.

Then, some fall into the job by happenstance, by being at the right place at the right time. Many people who do make it to that level of leadership have no business being a college president. As I mentioned, I have suffered through a few. They don't really have a genuine interest in making their institution better, nor do they work passionately for the students, faculty, and alumni. Perhaps it is a power trip for them or wanting the prestige that comes with the job. But I do know that if one does the job the right way, it is all encompassing. It becomes a way of life. It is a 24/7 job. And it wears you out, physically, mentally, and emotionally. For some it literally breaks them after only a few short years. Others love the recognition so much that they find it hard to give up the job and stay way longer than they should.

But why write this book? For self-aggrandizement? Hopefully that is not my intention. Many things happened during my years in higher education that are simply not known publicly, and this is my attempt to set the record straight for posterity. Will anyone really care? That remains to be seen. But here it is for the historical prognosticators 25, 50 or 100 years from now. It is not lost on me that my role in higher education is like a grain of sand when viewing the whole perspective. But it is my story and I want to tell it.

I begin this book, however, by relating my heritage and family background. Like most Americans, I'm the product of immigration. The blood in my veins is mostly Italian but also Swiss, English, Dutch and most likely a smattering of other European countries. My great-grandparents on my father's side immigrated from northern Italy through Ellis Island in the 19th century.

My wife, Jane Brockmann's clan came from Germany not too far from Dusseldorf. We visited the German Brockmanns when we were in Europe on a Fulbright Fellowship in 1992. That summer we must have been taken to every cemetery where a Brockmann was buried. Her relatives even took us on an outing that found us in the middle of a cow pasture to show us where her great-great grandfather was struck by lightning and died in the late 1800s. We still correspond with Jane's third cousin who is in his 90s and lives in Germany.

On Jane's mother's side were the McKennons. We don't have too much history on them but believe they immigrated from Ireland around Ulster in the Republic of Ireland.

My parents, George Anthony Gearhart, and Joan Inman Van Hoose met at the University of Arkansas. My whole family has been intertwined with the institution for decades. Aunts and uncles, grandparents, parents, brothers, cousins—some type of relationship between the University of Arkansas and the Gearhart family has existed since the early part of the last century. Added to that is Jane's family, the Brockmann clan, who have also been closely aligned with the UA for decades. My dad was originally from Ft. Smith, Arkansas, but lived in Fayetteville when it was time to go to college, and Mom was from Webb City, Missouri. Mom came to the university because it was closer to Webb City than the University of Missouri in Columbia, and known for being a safe environment. The two met in their junior year, dated, and subsequently were married in 1948. Dad was a member of the Sigma Nu fraternity and Mom a member of the sorority, Pi Beta Phi. Mom dropped out of college and never graduated. In those days, for a woman, unfortunately, getting married was more valued than a college degree.

My dad was a journalism major and an excellent student. From an early age he wanted to follow in his father's footsteps and work for a newspaper. At the time his dad was managing the Fulbright family paper in Fayetteville, the *Northwest Arkansas Times*. The Gearhart family had a small financial interest in the paper, but the controlling interest was held by the Fulbright family. Roberta Fulbright, Senator J.W. Fulbright's mother was the publisher of the paper and wrote a weekly column.

For many years my grandfather, Sam E. Gearhart, worked for the *Southwest Times Record* in Ft. Smith, Arkansas. In fact, my grandfather helped start the Ft. Smith paper in the early 1900s.

While information about my parents' college years is scant, I do know that my dad was well known for having a beautiful singing voice. He was invited by the Fulbright family to sing at Roberta Fulbright's funeral service in 1953. We have a letter from her son, Senator J.W. Fulbright complimenting him. He sang for many weddings and funerals in Northwest Arkansas and elsewhere, and I have an old record of him singing the Lord's Prayer. Wally Ingalls, the voice of the Razorbacks for many years, tried to get my dad to go into show business because of his amazing tenor singing voice. Mom was a beautiful and popular girl on campus and was known to be somewhat of a flirt.

Dad worked in the newspaper business his entire life, mostly in Fayetteville, but was dealt a bad heart in life, and died in 1977 at age 51 after suffering a massive heart attack. On October 13, 2022, Mom died at Butterfield Trail Village. She was 97 and had lived 46 years longer than our dad.

Mother could always be difficult to deal with sometimes, but it had progressed in recent years. She would be a lovely, caring person one minute and then devolve into her difficult mode. At Butterfield she could be absolutely charming to the nurses one second and then switch to being difficult and annoying the next. We thought it was a product of her dementia.

Joan Inman Gearhart Havens with her four sons, Van, David, Doug and Jeff.

Four years after Dad's death, Mom remarried. W.R. (Pat) Havens was a wonderful, thoughtful man. Pat did most of the cooking, cleaning, and taking care of chores around the house. He was very kind to Mother, and they enjoyed many wonderful years together in the large family home where I grew up.

Pat died from pancreatic cancer in 2006.

Pat went to Houston for treatment and was operated on using the Whipple procedure. I had no idea what that was and read everything I could about the Whipple surgery. Dr. Allen Whipple was an American surgeon who developed the procedure, and it is still used today. It is a tough surgery but seldom successful.

Four months after the diagnosis, Pat died. It was a very sad time for the whole family. Pat went through all the psychological stages of end of life. At one point he was absolutely convinced he did not have cancer. At another point in the illness, he would get very mad and upset about the cards he was dealt. But throughout the sickness he maintained a stellar composure and showed all of us how to die with honor and dignity.

The final days of Pat's life he was bedridden in their home. We had set up the first-floor den as a bedroom and brought in a hospital bed. He was non-responsive the last few days of his life. One evening when he was close to death, I was sitting by his bed holding his hand when all of a sudden, he raised up and said in a clear audible voice, "Well hello there young man" a phrase he used often when greeting me. I called out to the family to come quick, but when they got to the den, he was again non-responsive. Later his doctor told me that it was not uncommon for people on their deathbed to have a rush of oxygen and display an unusual outburst like I experienced. It had an indelible impact on me.

We never thought Mom would outlive Pat. He was so very strong and resilient, where Mother had her ailments. Brother Van even made legal preparations so Pat would be able to stay in the family home should Mother die first. We were certain he would outlive her. We were wrong.

Pat was a merchant mariner having graduated from the U.S. Merchant Marine Academy in Kings Point, New York. His job took him all over the world on a large commercial vessel. He was the chief engineer on the ship and had unbelievable handyman skills. He could make anything or fix anything, and was a perfect gentleman. In some ways I feel like I had the benefit of two fathers. Pat was a good man.

I do not know too much about my mother's heritage. The Van Hoose name is Dutch, and Inman is English, or at least that is what my grandmother Van Hoose used to tell me. My grandmother, Louise Inman Van Hoose—or Lulu as we called her—was a wonderfully warm person whom all the brothers loved very much. She was smart, caring, and had a marvelous sense of humor. Her husband died young of colon cancer. He had amassed a small fortune, but unfortunately the Great Depression caused him to lose most of their wealth. They lived in a large house in Webb City with four fireplaces, a butler, and a maid. The butler would arrive early in the morning at the house and light the fireplaces before the family awoke. The maid cleaned the house, did the laundry, and cooked the meals. They called their employees "the help" which was typical for that time. Mother has mentioned to me several times that, "Mother and Daddy always had help when I was growing up." No doubt this experience factored heavily on Mother's views of the world and issues of segregation and integration of the races.

All that disappeared during the Depression years when my grandfather lost a small fortune. Later, after her husband's death, Lulu found it necessary to find employment, moved to Fayetteville, and became a house mother at the UA campus. She served as house mother for numerous fraternities, sororities and living units, including Alpha Kappa Lambda, Zeta Tau Alpha, Phi Gamma Delta, and Carnall Hall. As a child I used to spend the night with Lulu at Carnall Hall multiple times, and she told me that I could tell people later in life that I spent the night at a women's dormitory! The students called her Mother Van, and she was a very popular house mother.

The last three years of her life Lulu developed dementia and died in 1994 at the age of 98. It was bizarre that her dementia happened literally overnight. She attended brother Jeff's wedding and during the reception she started acting strangely. We all noticed the rather dramatic difference in her that evening. She wasn't making any sense at all. It only got worse in the coming months. Her doctor said he thought she probably had some type of stroke that might have led to the dementia. Perhaps a vascular stroke that can cause problems with reasoning and judgment. The next three years she was essentially bed ridden with no recognition of her family.

But fortunately, my first cousin, Artie Berry, of Ft. Smith did an extensive search of my dad's family and we are the beneficiaries of much information about his heritage. My dad was Artie's uncle and Artie wrote a marvelous article about the family heritage which was published by the Ft. Smith Historical Society in 2008. Because of cousin Artie's hard work and determination, we have a valued record of Dad's family heritage.

A few interesting tidbits: My great-grandmother on the Gearhart side immigrated from Ireland in 1837. My great-grandfather fought in the Civil War for the Union and served under General William T. Sherman during his March to the Sea. My great-great-great-grandfather emigrated from Switzerland in 1758. My great-great-grandfather was a cigar maker. My dad and grandfather were inveterate cigar smokers and my brother Jeff, and I inherited that habit. I tell folks, "A man has got to have a hobby!"

On my grandmother's side we have even more extensive records. She was born in Krebs, Oklahoma, at Mine No. 10 in 1895. She was the daughter of Italian immigrants who came through Ellis Island in 1893. They were from Rivarolo, Italy about 20 miles north of Turin, Italy.

My grandmother was born Maria Theresa Constantino; we called her Grandmother Jeanne (pronounced Ginny). Apparently, the school children had trouble pronouncing her name and she became known as Jeanne. I loved her very much and spent a great deal of time with her in my younger years. Her parents found their way to an Italian settlement in Krebs, Oklahoma, where several Italian families were working the mines. In those days it was part of the Choctaw Nation. Krebs is still known as Little Italy and has several Italian restaurants that date to the late 1800's.

In 1896 the Constantinos moved to Ft. Smith, Arkansas, and started a general store and later a confectionery on Garrison Avenue, which was a popular area watering hole for several years. The building is still there.

My grandfather, Sam Gearhart moved to Ft. Smith from Circleville, Ohio, in 1907. He helped start the *Southwest Times Record Newspaper* in Ft. Smith. As Artie Berry points out, Ft. Smith was Indian Territory and boasted more than fifty saloons at the time!

The newspaper hired my grandmother as a bookkeeper and the couple were married in 1917. Grandad often told the story that when he laid eyes on my grandmother the very first time, he knew he would marry her—and he did. I have vague memories of my grandfather Sam. I was 7 years old when he died in 1959 of a cerebral hemorrhage. I remember the nuns at St. Joseph Catholic School taking me out of class and then being picked up by my mother and taken home. I also remember his funeral that was full to capacity.

Grandfather Sam was a gregarious fellow and well known in Fayetteville and Ft. Smith circles. Among newspaper people he was highly respected and served the industry in many volunteer capacities. He was chairman of the Fayetteville Progressive Committee and his advice and counsel was sought by the movers and shakers of our small mountain town. He was a rotund man in his later years and came across to me as almost jolly. He loved a good joke, the more off-color the better, and he had a wonderful smile and hearty laugh. At least that is how I remember him.

My grandmother Gearhart told me a story that stuck with me. *The Northwest Arkansas Times*, which Grandad managed for the Fulbright family, gave him a raise, and told him that he should share his raise with his son, my dad, George. (Dad had gone to work for *The Times* after working in Joplin and Jonesboro as the sports editor.) My grandmother was incredulous at the suggestion and thought the Fulbright family was being insensitive and downright cheap. She felt both Sam and George deserved a raise and wasn't about to share her husband's new compensation with anyone, not even her son, who by that time was really running the day-to-day operations of the paper.

Many years later, during my consulting years with the Chicago-based firm, Grenzebach Glier and Associates, I was assigned to make a call on the University of Miami in hopes of getting their business. I met with Dr. Tad Foote, the university president. During the meeting Dr. Foote asked me my background and we established a tie to the Fulbright family. He told me that he came very close to being the publisher and manager of *The Northwest Arkansas Times* after my grandfather died. I do remember my parents being worried if the Fulbright family would bring in someone new other than my dad to run their paper.

Foote was married to Senator Fulbright's daughter and apparently was available to run the paper for the family. He turned the offer down and my dad became the general manager and later publisher of *The Northwest Arkansas Times*. I have often wondered what might have happened to our family had Foote accepted the job to run the newspaper. He did hire me as the university's consultant, and I went to Miami every month for almost four years and got to know him well.

My grandparents had nine children. Two died shortly after birth, one had Down syndrome, one was killed in the Pacific during World War II, and the rest survived into adulthood. Only one, Sue, of the nine survives today.

My father was born in 1926 and Mother in 1925. Dad enjoyed a newspaper career until he developed heart problems four years before he died. He was playing tennis at the country club at age 47 and experienced sharp chest pains. His doctor prescribed a regimen of weight loss and healthy eating. He lost 40 pounds and cut back on cigars and alcohol. His doctor told us that he was trying to get him in shape to survive an eventual heart attack. My mother was an amazing caretaker for my dad, trying to cook appropriate foods to improve his cholesterol and keep his weight in a healthy range.

Unfortunately, his health took him into a deep psychological depression, and he left the newspaper business to run a weekly advertisement shopper until his death. *The Northwest Arkansas Times* had been sold to Thomson Newspapers, a United Kingdom and Canadian company owned by Lord Thomson of Fleet Street, which didn't seem interested in anything but making money. It was a tough time for my parents. Lord Thomson had met Senator Fulbright at an ambassadorial dinner party in London, and they struck up a conversation about their mutual interest in journalism. The next thing we knew was that the Senator had sold his family's controlling interest in the local paper to Thomson. The newspaper began a downward spiral and went through numerous owners, including the Walton and

Hussman families. Walter Hussman folded it into his statewide operations of the *Arkansas Democrat-Gazette,* and eventually closed the paper for good. It was a very fine paper and a sad day for Northwest Arkansas, which has no local newspaper today, thanks to Hussman interests. Of course, all newspapers across the world are struggling. One wonders how much longer Hussman's operations can survive with very few advertisements and reduced subscribers. Hal Douglas, manager of the Fulbright investments, told my mother that selling the paper was the worst decision he and the Fulbright family ever made.

Mom and Dad made a trip to Dallas, Texas, for the wedding of a close friend's son when Dad started feeling ill. He walked into the hospital at 11 a.m. that morning and died at around 6 p.m. The hospital report showed that eight doctors were working feverishly in a futile attempt to save him. It was not to be. His last words to Mother were that his feet were cold. At 51 he was way too young to die. My youngest brother Jeff was only 12 years old, with no father to raise him.

My dad's death at age 51 in 1977 affected me greatly. I wasn't particularly close to him but admired him from afar. Jane and I were at Westminster College when he had the heart attack. Mother and Dad had just been to visit us in Fulton, Missouri, a couple weeks earlier. We got a call from my mother that he had suffered a heart attack, and that we needed to get on a plane as soon as possible and head to Dallas. To say the least, it was a great shock to us. To this day when I walk up an airplane jetway I think of my dad. My mother was waiting for us at the end of the jetway and she was crying, and we knew immediately that something tragic had happened.

Dad was just dealt a bad hand when it came to health. In 1977 there were very few open-heart surgeries being performed in the United States. Medical technology had not advanced enough at that time to save him. No doubt he was a classic case for open-heart surgery, which might have given him several more years on this earth. I have often thought that, had he had the heart attack five years later, he very well might have survived and lived a full life.

Dad was a quiet person; really the best description is that he was modest, and perhaps even shy. He did have a remarkable sense of humor and a brilliant mind. On the initial trip to look at Westminster College we stayed at the Lodge of Four Seasons on the Lake of the Ozarks. The Lodge was having a contest to name a new entertainment area. As we got in the car to leave the lodge to drive to Westminster, he told us that he had entered the contest. He said that he had put in the name "The Fifth Season." My mother and I thought that was a brilliant entry, and lo and behold, he won the contest. He was notified of his success by a Western Union telegram that we still have today. That was Dad! He was a smart man, and a genius when it came to advertising.

Recently, Jane and I made a trip to the Lake of the Ozarks to visit a dear friend, college roommate and fraternity brother Randy Johnson and his wife, Kim, and stopped by the Lodge and saw the room that Dad named. It brought back many fond memories.

Unfortunately, as often happens in families, we had a break with some members of the extended Gearhart family around 1977, soon after Dad died. It was a colossal tragedy for me as I loved my dad's family, and particularly my Grandmother Gearhart, very much. It was all about money.

Shortly before my dad died, his mother had given him some money from the sale of *The Northwest Arkansas Times* newspaper owned primarily by the Fulbright family. My grandparents owned a small percentage of the closely-held stock, and had always promised the stock to my dad. It wasn't a lot of money in today's terms but a small nest egg that Dad felt would give him some semblance of protection at the newspaper if the stock was in his name.

After Dad died, grandmother asked my mom to return the money. It was a shock to all of us, as Grandmother Gearhart always seemed to me to be a loving and caring person. I enjoyed a special, close relationship with my grandmother, and this episode was most painful to watch unfold. Grandmother's surviving son, my dad's brother, tried to have the funds returned and divided among his remaining siblings. It all got very nasty.

I tried to maintain relations with that side of the family to no avail. My mother was extremely hurt, and then very mad and forbade her boys from having any contact with my grandmother or her surviving children. I still tried to stay in contact with my grandmother until my mother found out about it and went ballistic. In the end, grandmother backed down from the request for the money to be returned. My mother harbored extreme bad feelings and resentment against Dad's family for the rest of her life.

In July 2021, after 43 years of no contact with my dad's family, Jane and I attended a Gearhart family reunion of the surviving family members, all cousins by now. We got to see relatives we had not seen for so many years, and also meet their children and grandchildren for the first time. For years we had no contact with my dad's family—all over money. Tragic on so many levels.

George and Joan Gearhart family, circa 1964, at Jeff's baptism

I have three siblings. My oldest brother, Van, enjoyed a distinguished career as a lawyer and judge in Mountain Home, Arkansas. Van was a great country lawyer and superb judge admired by his constituents. He is a great writer and speaker, and judged law school exams for several years. His wife Candy was a salesperson for a novelty company. Jane actually introduced them during their college years. They are now retired and live in Bradenton, Florida.

Younger brother Doug had a distinguished career working for several prestigious clothing and merchandise companies in New York City for over 30 years. His last position was managing the American office of a Canadian women's clothing company called Lida Baday. Celebrity clients included Oprah Winfrey, Bo Derek, Brooke Shields, Jeanne Beker, and Sigourney Weaver, among others. He currently lives in Rogers, Arkansas, and is semi-retired. He is a wonderful uncle to our kids and grandkids.

My youngest brother, Jeff, practiced law before he went to work for Walmart. He rose through the company, made a considerable amount of money, and retired as an executive vice president at age 53. He was probably the smartest of the brothers, although I never tell him that! He and his wife Lisa recently moved to Naples, Florida, where he has a beautiful home, plays a lot of golf, and enjoys his 60-foot boat! (I refuse to call it a yacht). He named the boat the Fifth Season after the contest my dad won at the Lodge of the Four Seasons.

There is a 14-year gap between my oldest and youngest brothers. We love telling Jeff that he was a mistake. The doctor had told my mother after Doug was born that she should not have any more children. Surprise!

I think my brothers would agree that our parents were not particularly nurturing as we were growing up. Of course, I can only speak for myself, but during my younger years I felt many times that I was on my own. Alone to make my own way in the world. They never really tried to influence me or any of my major decisions in life, and I don't remember very many family discussions of importance regarding life's journey. Nurturing the kids just wasn't a priority for them. We were on our own from a very young age.

Most people don't know this about me, but I was a very shy youngster from my earliest age of remembrance. I never really shed my shyness, even to this day. I know now that some folks thought I was conceited, but not true. I was terribly, frightfully, awfully shy.

Jane was the exact opposite. She could make friends at the drop of a hat. Not me. Just too shy. I had a few very close, dear friends, but Jane was the one who carried me when it came to socializing and making acquaintances. Timid, bashful, and sheepish are not good attributes for a college president let alone a fundraiser!

CHAPTER 2
NO PLACE LIKE HOME

> *If the moderates of the white South fail to act now, history will have to record that the greatest tragedy of this period of social transition was not the strident clamor of the bad people, but the appalling silence of the good people. Our generation will have to repent not only for the acts and words of the children of darkness but also for the fears and apathy of the children of light.*
>
> — *MARTIN LUTHER KING JR., 1958*

I was born in Fayetteville, Arkansas in 1952. Life in the Ozarks was lazy, uneventful and a slice of Americana. I was one of millions of baby boomers who came along after World War II. Fayetteville was a sleepy mountain town of around 12,000 people. Walmart would not explode the population for many more years. It was a mountain town isolated from the rest of Arkansas and more closely identified with eastern Oklahoma and southern Missouri. Our television stations were all from Oklahoma, mainly Tulsa, and later one from Springfield, Missouri. In those days we were essentially cut off from the rest of Arkansas, which was in actuality being cut off from Little

Rock which was considered more sophisticated and worldly and the political and financial seat of Arkansas.

Ft. Smith was an hour and a half away before the interstate system and many of my dad's family lived there. We would visit often. We loved going to Cartwright Mountain above Winslow where my dad's family had a cabin with a magnificent view of Lake Ft. Smith and the surrounding Ozarks. Occasionally we would go to Little Rock or Hot Springs for press conventions and experience the big city life. I have memories of the slot machines and gambling tables in Hot Springs before Governor Rockefeller shut the illicit gambling down. I even remember throwing dice at the Southern Club in Hot Springs as people gambled. Don't ask me how that happened, but it did, and it is an early remembrance of the "old days."

In the year of my birth, 1952, The average home price was around $9,000, the average gallon of gas was 19 cents, and a new car could be purchased for $1,700. I remember when the filling station had a sale for 14 cents a gallon! People used to joke that the only thing exciting to do in Fayetteville was to watch the old clock at the McIlroy Bank on the square change hands. We did have at least one movie theater which costs 25 cents for a matinee. But, despite the lack of entertainment venues, it was as good a place to grow up as anywhere.

My earliest memory in life was when I was four years old. I remember vaguely going to the Safeway grocery store with my mother and getting lost for 45 minutes. I'm not sure how it happened but I got separated from my mother and she panicked trying to find me. After what seemed like an eternity, I was finally located and reunited with Mother. I had wandered into the back packaging area of the store and was watching the trucks unload. No one thought to look back there until the police arrived and one of the officers thought he should check it out. Of course, Mother thought I had been kidnapped, although in those days kidnapping young kids was not at all prevalent.

Not long ago, my mother, suffering from dementia and living at Butterfield Residential Care Center, exclaimed to my brother Doug during one of his visits, that "your brother David has been lost at Butterfield for four days and I can't find him!" I suspect the trauma of years ago had come back to haunt her. Mother was very comfortable at Butterfield and lived in the special care unit for persons with dementia. She recognized most of her family, at least her four sons, but her dementia was progressing. She would tell me every time I visited her in the last weeks of her life that she just spoke to her mother, and she was going to move back to her childhood home in Webb City. As mentioned previously, Lulu, Mom's mother, died in 1994. In some surreal way, maybe mother and daughter were communicating?

Mother could be a lovely person with marvelous social skills. She could entertain family and friends better than anyone, and always made people feel welcome in her home. I remember once a guest spilled a glass of red wine on her white carpet where a stain stayed for years. She calmly looked at the responsible person and said, "Homes are to be lived in, don't worry about it." She could make guests feel very comfortable in her home.

And speaking of her home, it was filled with antiques, silver service and objects of art, which never failed to make a very good impression on her guests. Her dining tables were a work of art with carefully placed knives, forks, glassware, china, and spoons always in the proper place. She knew how to entertain and did so with a masterful touch.

Mother always dressed to the nines. Doug made sure of that by giving her floor samples from his high-end clothing companies in New York City. Her thin waist fit perfectly in the model's samples and she was the best-dressed lady in Northwest Arkansas. Many of the articles of clothing retailed for well over $3,000 apiece and Mom had a closet full of them. I remember she had leather pants in four different colors! Dressing up and looking nice was a priority for mother and she always looked her best on every occasion. She went to what she called, "the beauty parlor" three times a week to have her hair styled and coiffed perfectly with enough hair spray to gag a horse. At Butterfield she still got her "hair done" twice a week at age 97.

Mother was what one might call, in her day, a prude. Webster's dictionary gives this definition of a prude: "A person who is excessively or priggishly attentive to propriety or decorum." That's Mother! She had Presbyterian social mores and her moral compass was very conservative and always proper.

Mother was somewhat disengaged from interaction with her four boys. She was much more social than my father and always enjoyed a great party and social event. Don't misunderstand me, she could be a lovely person and had many friends in the community. But she never had a nurturing element when it came to raising her sons. I suppose it wasn't all bad in that all of us turned out to be relatively successful in life, so perhaps she understood better than we that leaving us on our own might be the best medicine. She rarely attended any of our high school or college events, particularly sporting contests. She never came to track meets or our football or basketball games. It just wasn't her thing.

Perhaps the best way to describe her interaction with her four sons was that she felt we needed to attack life on our own. It did tend to make us quite independent thinkers. I don't mean to suggest she wasn't a good mother, but her priorities were different than you might find with other mothers of the time. Certainly, the helicopter mothers of today, being involved in all aspects of their children's lives, wasn't Mom's predilection. I do think she was more involved in brother Jeff's life after my father died. I suspect both needed each other after the tragedy of my dad's death at such a young age.

Mother and Dad had a domestic maid. Her name was Nelly Dart, Mrs. David Dart, and she worked at the house three days a week and on special occasions. My entire youth, all the way through college and law school, included the presence of Nelly Dart. She was a kind soul who helped raise the Gearhart boys. She did all the home chores, including cooking, on the days she was at the house. Nelly was an incredible cook. One of her specialties were sweet rolls and pies which were made from scratch.

Nelly had no children of her own, but raised multiple nieces and nephews. She lived in the African-American section of town behind the courthouse, known by the awful moniker of "Tin Cup." Nelly was paid less than minimum wages. Once I suggested that my parents give Nelly a raise. Mother answered that she did provide lunch for Nelly and my father would make her a cocktail before taking her home at the end of the day. Nelly's preferred cocktail was a mixture of milk and scotch! Mother provided Nelly with a white dress for special occasions and parties when she would prepare the meal and wait on the guests. Nelly would don a beautiful blond-colored wig to wear at such events.

Nelly told my mom that if she had any more children she would quit. Mom stopped having kids.

On one occasion, Nelly was babysitting my younger brother for a weekend while my parents were on an out-of-town trip. Nelly took him to a funeral of all Black attendees and relatives. When mother discovered what Nelly had done, she came unglued. She didn't ever want her son going to a Black church or attending a funeral with all Black attendees.

Those were awful times. Total racism and absolute prejudice were the order of the day. Mother, and probably Dad, certainly believed in the separation of the races, no doubt about that, and although kind to her domestic employee, "the help," she exhibited the prejudices of the times. She raised four boys who, no doubt, carried some of those prejudices forward in their early lives, but worked hard to overcome them and to understand that the attitudes of the past with regard to race and inclusion were plain wrong and unconscionable.

Unfortunately, Mother also harbored prejudice against people with different sexual persuasions. She doesn't understand people who are gay, and believes it is a lifestyle that they choose for themselves.

We can't excuse the prejudices and deep-seated segregationist views of our ancestors. They were wrong then as they are now. It is not likely that generation will change. Not too many of them are left as the so-called "Greatest Generation" is dying out at a very fast pace. They survived a massive Depression and defeated Hitler and made the world safer, but many were segregationists. All we can do is learn from their mistakes and promise not to carry forward those wrong-minded prejudices.

I must say, though, I am saddened that I lived in a family that took advantage of a wonderful, thoughtful, God-fearing person like Nelly Dart. She was like a member of the family to me. She was fun, clever, thoughtful, devoted, caring, proud, responsible, and loving.

I had a photograph in my bedroom of me with Ralph David Abernathy, the great civil rights leader. He had spoken at Westminster College, and I had my photo taken next to him. It never even occurred to me that Nelly might appreciate that photo. She told my mother that she was very proud of the photograph and that I had met one of her heroes. That was when I first realized that Nelly had aspirations, political awareness, and a political consciousness far beyond what she felt comfortable expressing around the Gearhart family.

Civil Rights leader Ralph David Abernathy with David Gearhart at Westminster College.

As I look back on Nelly's devoted service to my family, I realize that, at its base, her service, one might call servitude, was quite wrong. I grew up in a segregated south. Black people sat in the balconies of movie theaters if they were admitted at all. Black people did not use the city swimming pool, they sat in a segregated area of school and lived in a segregated area of town. Public bathrooms were for whites only, and most hotels prohibited Black people from staying in them. They were not on the Razorback football team or the cheer team or otherwise engaged in the social life of majority students. There were no Black people in a white sorority or fraternity. Greek social houses were for whites only. Certainly, no Black members at the country club. "Whites only" was the order of the day. They were denied professional and educational opportunities critical to advancement in our white society.

So, while my family provided some sustenance for Nelly Dart and her family, as meager as it was, we were complicit in an economic system that marginalized her and forced women like her to work menial jobs just to survive, but never flourish. Simply put, we took advantage of her circumstances and her lack of options. I have a sense of guilt that we exploited Nelly for our selfish benefit. We were indeed part of a bad system of segregation. It was and is repulsive and most Arkansans lived under those rules of life and made no attempt to change society. Dr. Martin Luther King, Jr. would describe it as the "appalling silence of good people."

Years later, tragically, Nelly Dart would die in a fire at her home along with one of her nieces.

Fortunately, the passage of time and the heroic efforts of people like King and Abernathy and many others, have changed the world for the better, but the system is far from perfect. Recent police shootings of Black people and the Black Lives Matter movement tell us that we have much more progress to make. It has taken decades to correct the worst of our society's offenses. We are not done yet.

For some time social advocates for Black justice had been advocating for the separation of a state holiday that honored both Martin Luther King Jr. and General Robert E. Lee on the same day. I was a strong proponent of the separation and advocated for it from my position as chancellor and wrote several legislators asking for them to pass a law separating the holiday. I didn't make any friends in the legislature, and got several nasty letters from members of the General Assembly. But the separation did not happen until 2017 under a Republican administration. The joint holiday had been established during Bill Clinton's time as governor in 1985. The only way to get King honored was to combine it with Lee's already existing tribute established as far back as the 19th century. It was a crazy pairing, a general in the confederacy and a civil rights leader honored on the same day.

CHAPTER 3
PRIESTHOOD AND ST. JOE'S

> *There was no known cure for a Catholic education.*
>
> — LISA SCOTTOLINE

During junior high and high school. I gave very serious consideration to becoming a Catholic priest. While my Catholic father encouraged that interest, my mother was very opposed. I should say extremely opposed! She was a Presbyterian and despite the urging of my Catholic grandmother on my father's side, my mother resisted converting to Catholicism. Mother would occasionally attend Mass but remained true to her Protestant heritage her entire life. Mother didn't encourage prayer in our home, except for saying grace at the dinner table on special holiday occasions. Formal religion was not all that important to her. We never read the Bible at home. Maybe she felt she shouldn't push it since she was not Catholic. Maybe she felt we got religious instruction at St. Joe, which we did. But, for whatever reason, she just wasn't into religion or spreading it to her sons.

All four boys were raised Catholic and attended St. Joseph Catholic School in Fayetteville. Meeting Jane in high school changed my mind about the priesthood and it became apparent the older I got that I simply did not have a calling for life as a man of the cloth.

I believe I received a fine education at St. Joseph. I attended the school from kindergarten through ninth grade. We were taught by Benedictine nuns who were very serious about their work and quite competent in their subject areas. Most of them came from Ft. Smith and the St. Scholastica Convent. For years after attending St. Joe I stayed in close touch with many of the nuns.

One person who I met in fourth grade at Saint Joseph was a kid named Ross Vivona. I thought he was the coolest person I had ever met, and our friendship has lasted for over 60 years and we still talk regularly. I guess Ross is my oldest friend dating back to primary school. His father worked for Springdale Farms, a chicken processing company, and they had moved from Kansas City to Northwest Arkansas.

The first date I ever had was a double date with Ross. My dad chauffeured us to a dance party at the country club. I was 12 years old. Dad, Ross and I picked up our dates, two girls from our St. Joseph class, and Ross and I sat in the front seat and the girls in the back. My dad laughed the whole trip.

David's oldest friend Ross Vivona and his wife, Deborah. David and Ross met in fourth grade at St. Josephs.

Later in life Ross began a construction company in Oklahoma and has been very successful. It is truly amazing that we have remained close friends all these years. I am the godfather of one of his children. Ross is a remarkably talented person.

Most of the nuns were amazing people dedicated to the church and the Catholic faith. I do remember a painful experience at St. Joe with one nun. She was the devil personified. Regularly she would use a ruler to slap her students—not for being difficult or acting up—but for not being able to answer a math, history, or other subject question accurately. Sister could be ruthless and mean spirited, and displayed terrible anger. She had her favorites and then her "others" that she treated with disdain.

One student, Gladys, was at the chalkboard trying to understand a math problem. Suddenly, Sister began slapping Gladys's face with her bare hand. The more Gladys tried to answer, the harder the slaps came. Gladys was crying, actually sobbing, but Sister kept slapping her harder and harder with considerable force. Then sister took out a ruler and hit Gladys repeatedly on the head and face. You could see the vein in sister's neck pounding as she hit Gladys over and over. Sister was on fire in an almost deranged way with spit coming out of her mouth as she shouted at Gladys.

Admittedly, Gladys wasn't the brightest student in the class, but no one deserved that kind of treatment. Finally, one of Gladys's friends leaped from her chair and answered the question to try to save Gladys from further injury. It was a despicable scene. The entire class was frozen in absolute fear.

The next day I decided the incident needed to be reported. I marched into the principal's office and related the story to the principal who was also a Benedictine nun. She simply listened and gave no indication things would change. The principal was stone-faced. At semester the mean, deranged nun was gone. No one knew where she went, but we were thrilled she left. Years later one of the nuns from that era told me that Sister had a very serious alcohol problem which manifested itself in anger.

Sister Benita was the head of the school and taught ninth grade. She was a very conservative nun, but I thought she was the best. She was dignified and stately, always with a smile on her face. She made you feel like she really cared about her students and was a marvelous conversationalist. She taught all subjects in ninth grade and was particularly proficient in English grammar and writing skills. I learned a great deal from her. I maintained a friendship with her for many years and would drive down to Ft. Smith and St. Scholastica Convent where she lived after retirement to visit her. She was thoughtful, kind and engaging until she began to suffer from Alzheimer's. I remember the last time I attempted to see her one of the nuns told me that she was incapable of having visitors. It was very upsetting to me.

I started taking piano lessons and did so for 7 years. Football and track finally put a stop to that. My teacher was a very thoughtful and patient nun, Sister Mildred, who taught many of the children in Fayetteville. I became somewhat proficient with the piano, mostly classical pieces, but gave it up cold turkey and today don't remember anything and couldn't play a note. I regret that I didn't keep it up and have thought about buying an electronic piano and trying again. Maybe after this book is finished! I did develop an interest in classical music and play it often on CDs I accumulated over a lifetime. Yes, I still use CDs and play classical music often. Usually, I have classical music playing in my car, much to the chagrin of my kids and grandkids, not to mention Jane.

President John F. Kennedy was assassinated on November 22, 1963 while I was in the St. Joseph school cafeteria. I remember the nuns gathered in a circle in the lunchroom and many of them were weeping. We had no idea what had happened until later, but knew it must have been something monumental. I was 11 years old, and it made a huge impact on my psyche. For the first time in my life I watched the news on TV continuously trying to absorb everything about the tragic event. I saw Jack Ruby kill Oswald and John Kennedy Jr. salute his father as the casket rolled by and was glued to the TV set for days. Now almost 60 years later I still remember that day as vividly as if it were still 1963.

CHAPTER 4
HIGH SCHOOL

> *True terror is to wake up one morning and discover that your high school class is running the country.*
>
> — KURT VONNEGUT

I attended high school in Fayetteville. It was a rude awakening. My graduating class at St. Joe was 14 students. Suddenly I was enrolled in a school with over a thousand students. I knew practically none of my classmates, except those from St. Joe, and the first semester I was totally lost. Fortunately, I was participating in sports (football and track) and ran for student government and that, plus my studies, kept me busy. But I must admit, my first year in high school was not much fun. I dated a little, one girl in particular, but she decided she liked someone else and went on a date with him much to my chagrin.

I started forming new friendships, but missed the days at old St. Joe when everyone was my friend. Two friends I met early in high school were John Stephenson and Joe Cogdell. John would become a first-class medical doctor and practiced in the New Orleans area. Joe became a distinguished corporate and tax lawyer in Charlotte, North

Carolina. They are retired but we have remained very close friends to this day.

Like most students, my senior year was enjoyable. I was very active and served on the student council. And, of course, meeting Jane in high school changed a lot for me. I liked her the minute I met her, and we started dating. She had an enormous circle of friends, most of whom I only knew casually, and they quickly became my circle of friends too. She was funny, popular, and very thoughtful and attractive too.

Prior to high school I had a momentary thought that I might want to be a physician. I can't really tell you why, perhaps I watched too many episodes of Dr. Kildare. When I took biology in high school those plans quickly changed after I dissected a frog. I didn't like chemistry or math either. I found them boring. The classes I did enjoy were history and anything having to do with humanities.

Mr. Krie was a very popular chemistry teacher in high school. He had a marvelous sense of humor and was good to the students that took his classes. I avoided chemistry until my senior year, but since it was a requirement in order to graduate, I had no choice but to sign up. Mr. Krie was very patient with me, but knew that I had no interest in the course. I was only taking it because I had to and had put it off till the last semester of my senior year. I was the only senior in the class and stuck out like a sore thumb. One day after class Mr. Krie said he wanted to speak with me. He said that if I promised not to come back to class, he would give me a D. It was the only D I received in high school, but I accepted his offer and praised the good Lord he offered it.

My senior year I served as president of the student body and enjoyed that experience very much. It was a tough time in our nation's history and young men were dying in Vietnam and college students were protesting the war all across America. Drugs had entered the spectrum and alcohol abuse was rampant. High school students were worried they would be sent to fight the Vietcong and the nightly news shows were filled with horrible war scenes.

CHAPTER 5
SMALL COLLEGE EXPERIENCE

> *A man who has never gone to school may steal from a freight car, but if he has a university education, he may steal the whole railroad.*
>
> — THEODORE ROOSEVELT

I decided I didn't want to attend a large institution like my older brother. I had grown up in the shadow of Old Main at the University of Arkansas in Fayetteville and was anxious to get out of town. I looked at several institutions, but decided to enroll at a small college in mid-Missouri called Westminster College. Winston Churchill had delivered the Iron Curtain speech, "The Sinews of Peace," there in 1946. President Harry Truman had appealed to Churchill to come to Truman's home state, Missouri, to deliver a lecture at Westminster College. Churchill's famous words "From Stettin in the Baltic to Trieste in the Adriatic, an iron curtain has descended across the continent," ushered in the Cold War. The small campus environment and this historical tie to Churchill and Great Britain appealed to me.

But the real reason was that my parents had met Missouri Governor John Dalton at a press convention. He was a member of the Westminster College board of trustees and encouraged them to look at Westminster. Governor Dalton made all the arrangements for us to visit the college and meet the president of Westminster, Dr. Robert L.D. Davidson. After two days of special treatment and a small scholarship, we were sold. My mother particularly liked the fact that Westminster had a load of fraternities on campus and that seemed very important to her. As the product of a sorority at the University of Arkansas, mother believed that Greek life on a campus was the social glue that was good for a student and provided instantaneous friends and associates. She wanted me to join a fraternity, and Westminster had plenty. That wasn't really a motivator for me, but it made Mom happy, and Westminster would be my home for the next four years.

Photo of burned out church, St. Mary the Virgin Aldermanbury, in London. It was brought piece by piece to Fulton, Missouri, and rebuilt as a memorial to Winston Churchill.

I arrived at Westminster a year after the dedication of a memorial to Winston Churchill and his 1946 speech in Fulton. The college had been pondering how to memorialize Churchill's historic Iron Curtain speech and decided to relocate a bombed-out church in London, England to the Westminster campus. It took years to obtain the proper approvals but finally came to fruition with the removal and relocation in the late 1960s. The church was hit by an incendiary bomb in World War II and had never been repaired. The church, St. Mary the Virgin Aldermanbury, seemed a perfect choice for a memorial. The campus had torn down its old chapel and needed a new one. Churchill was approached about the idea and he gave his enthusiastic approval. It is an interesting story which is captured in a book by Nancy Carver titled "The Inspiring History of a Special Relationship," published in 2020.

Top: Churchill Memorial under construction. Bottom: Completed memorial. Photos courtesy Dave Stinson

I packed my 1962 Volkswagen beetle and pulled out of Fayetteville at 4:30 in the morning for a five-hour drive and headed for Fulton Missouri, a sleepy town much smaller than Fayetteville. It was August 1970. My parents didn't even get out of bed to see me off. I was totally on my own. Five hours later I arrived at Westminster and Gage Hall in the freshman quadrangle.

Not long into the semester our suite of four rooms was raided by the police for suspected drug use. It made the headlines of the daily Fulton newspaper much to my parent's chagrin. I slept through the raid along with my roommate. Days after arriving on campus my suitemates had determined that I was more compatible with a fellow who seemed more conservative than my initial assigned roommate. Besides, the new roommate and I didn't smoke marijuana. We switched roommates. Their room, across the hall from ours, was the one raided! The police had received a tip that my suitemates had a large stash of drugs in their possession, but they didn't find anything. I suspect my suitemates also got a tip. I have no doubt that minutes before the raid they disposed of the incriminating evidence. Most evenings I could smell marijuana wafting from their room.

While I was not a partier in college, I did imbibe in alcohol beginning my freshman year. My parents had always served wine on formal occasions, so I grew up drinking small amounts of wine at home, even during high school. I suspect it was the Italian heritage. Neither Jane nor I drank liquor at high school parties, but there was plenty of that activity going around. Drugs were also an issue in high school, but we were too strait-laced to ever use any recreational drugs. To this day I have never smoked a joint or used any type of recreational drug. It just didn't appeal to me. Plenty of our high school buddies did.

Drug usage was a real problem during my college years. Alcohol abuse was too. During my junior year I was president of my fraternity, and about two in the morning one night I was awakened from a deep sleep. An anonymous caller told me that our frat house was going to be raided by police. I quickly went door to door and awakened my frat brothers letting them know what I had been told by the anonymous caller. Pretty soon about a third of the members were running to the bathroom flushing any contraband down the toilet. The raid never came. My classmates weren't very happy with me.

While drugs were strictly verboten by the dean of men and the college administration, the use of alcohol was another matter. In those days the college higher-ups seemed to me to just go with the flow. I even witnessed college staff drinking alcohol with students at our frat house on many occasions. The worst part of it was that many of my friends would drink too much and then drive to a local restaurant and get something to eat and sober up. A few times they would take off in their cars totally inebriated and drive 30 minutes to Columbia and hit the bars.

My sophomore year two students were killed coming back from

Columbia in a very inebriated state. I knew both of them, as everyone knew everyone at small Westminster. It was scary. But, in those days the penalties for driving while intoxicated were pretty light. Maybe a slap on the wrist but hardly ever any jail time even if someone was injured. Practically no one lost their driver's license. "Mothers Against Drunk Driving" would not be formed until 1980. I still remember some of my buddies driving back from a night out drinking and stepping out of their cars totally smashed and needing assistance walking into the house. It would be another several years before people woke up to the very real issues of binge drinking. But during those days just about everyone used alcohol and getting drunk on Friday and Saturday nights was just a rite of passage. Once a month a group of my fraternity brothers would have what they called J.C. Revivals. J.C. stood for Johnny Cash. They would put a stack of records on the hi-fi and drink until they passed out.

Of course, alcohol abuse on college campuses is a national problem. It is really an epidemic. I fought it aggressively during my time as chancellor and college administrators still do. In recent years a number of alcohol-related incidents have occurred. Especially vulnerable to alcohol abuse have been fraternities where some of the members have died after a night of partying or even abusive pledgeship.

One of my professors was a flaming liberal. Actually, most of Westminster's faculty members were liberal—but this professor was liberal on steroids. He was a very early proponent of smoking marijuana. Of course, it was illegal in all states at that time. Using weed for medicinal purposes was not on the radar. He simply believed that weed was no worse than alcohol and frankly most likely a better substitute than drinking hard liquor. One day he came to class with a joint. To the surprise of everyone he lit it up and took a few draws. I suspect he was trying to show the class that civil disobedience was a good thing. He saw it as a teachable moment. Some class members saw it as a heroic move. Some conservative classmates did not. Within two weeks the professor was gone. No explanations, no discussion, he simply disappeared from the faculty. I suspect the Westminster administration was informed about his actions and decided he was a liability, and dismissed him without fanfare. He was ahead of his time.

The early 1970s were a difficult time in our national history. President Nixon was winding down the Vietnam War, and in 1969 implemented the system of a lottery to determine who would be drafted. It all began while I was in high school, but was still active when I was a student at Westminster. (The first election when I became of voting age, I actually voted for Nixon).

The Selective Service allowed for deferments for those in college. Early on a person could avoid the draft and possible service in Vietnam by staying in college and even moving on to graduate school. The graduate school provision was eliminated, and the deferment only allowed for four years of college, and then a student was eligible to be drafted and possibly report for duty. I distinctly remember huddling around the TV with my fraternity brothers watching the Selective Service officials draw numbers in the lottery. Some of my buddies drew early numbers, which were tied to their birthdays. I was luckier and drew a higher number, which precluded me from being drafted after I completed college. I never had thought of myself as being very lucky, but thank goodness I won out that day.

I had a friend whose birthday was drawn in the lottery almost immediately, which made it clear he would have to serve in Vietnam. He was ordered to report for a physical within a matter of weeks. He was in his senior year and only had a few months left on his college deferment. He wasn't necessarily opposed to the Vietnam War like many were at the time, but he was scared to death of going to fight the Vietcong. He was already overweight and decided that he was going to avoid the draft by gaining an enormous amount of weight and being declared obese. He ate everything in sight. Bread, pasta, milkshakes, beer, everything he could to put on weight prior to the physical. Low and behold it worked. When he reported to the doctors for his exam, he was declared obese and escaped the draft. I guess it was a novel way to avoid service and fighting in Vietnam.

I suspect had I been drafted I would have served. Patriotism was embedded in me, and even though I was very much opposed to the war like most young people of the age, and thought it didn't make any sense, I would have done my duty. Most college students were opposed except for some in ROTC. Many students at the time were conducting demonstrations all over the country and holding Vietnam moratoriums against the war. The battle cries were, "Four Dead in Ohio," from the anthem by Neil Young after the shootings at Kent State in May 1970 and the chant "Hey, hey LBJ, how many boys did you kill today?"

Luckily, by the time I graduated from Westminster, the war was winding down and the draft was ending. I escaped serving in Vietnam by a close margin. I did, however, know two Westminster students who were killed in Vietnam. They were not in my fraternity, but one served on the student council with me. Sad and wasteful beyond description.

> *Some people get an education without going to college. The rest get it after they get out.*
>
> — MARK TWAIN

Another craze of the times was streaking. It became a national phenomenon. Men and women would shed their clothes and run butt naked across campus. At first it probably started as a way to protest the Vietnam War, but quickly evolved into a novelty. I remember watching the Academy Awards when a streaker ran across the stage on live TV. David Niven was on stage presenting an Oscar and got a huge laugh by saying something like, "Isn't it too bad that the only laugh that man will ever get is by stripping off his shorts and showing his shortcomings?" I thought the whole thing was crazy, but many of my good friends elected to participate. Strangely enough streaking still pops up even today, but usually a lone ranger trying to get attention. They usually end up in jail. But in the 1970s the police and administration just looked the other way.

Panty raids were also all the rage. Both males and females participated. They would come to a frat house or sorority house and steal everyone's underwear and parade it around. By the 1970s the panty raid was beginning to die out, but still going strong at Westminster. I think it had its genesis as far back as the 1950s. Westminster, being in the heartland, was a little slow to cast away old habits.

The 70's was what Tom Wolfe called the "Me" generation. Inflation was rampant and an economic crisis plagued the United States and many countries throughout the world as well as an energy crisis. The first microprocessor came along my freshman year, but wide use of computers was years away, and what I would have given for a cell phone in college. Life was simpler, perhaps more friendly, and it may be the last time that people in general trusted each other. The Vietnam War caused widespread mistrust of government by my generation. Mistrust of authority began a long journey and continues today.

I quickly fell in love with Westminster, which led to what would eventually become an academic career. Little did I know then that I would develop a keen interest in college administration that would evolve into a 45-year career in higher education.

At 18 years of age, I never thought my life would lead to a college presidency or chancellorship. I just knew that I enjoyed being around a campus and interacting with faculty, administrators, and other students. There was something exhilarating about a college environment. Four years at Westminster molded my deep feelings about the importance of higher education, and I left there in May 1974 with a bachelor's degree in political science and speech, and a general feeling that working for a college might be something I would enjoy someday. I had met many lifelong friends who I'm still very close to, and we will be celebrating our 50th college reunion in 2024.

My parents thought I would stay at Westminster for only two years and then enroll at the University of Arkansas to complete my undergraduate degree. After all, it was certainly much cheaper to attend the UA than Westminster, and I knew it was a financial burden on my parents. I had made a lot of friends at Westminster and wanted to remain a student and finish college there. I made a deal with my parents that I would work in the summers and dedicate those funds to tuition. I would also handle all of my own spending money. Things were very tight during my time at Westminster. I tried to live on $25 a month in spending money which didn't provide for much entertainment. Since I was still dating Jane, in absentia, I didn't have the need for dating money and that helped enormously. I lived three years in the Sigma Alpha Epsilon fraternity house and was the last senior living there upon graduation. All of my friends had moved out. I would have liked to have joined them in an apartment, but I just didn't have the funds to swing it. In those days it was actually cheaper to live in the frat house and have all meals and utilities paid on one remittance. We had a great cook, Vera, so the meals were decent.

My senior year I served as president of the student body as I had in high school. It enabled me to become acquainted with the senior leadership of the institution and further bent me toward a life in college administration.

CHAPTER 6
LAW SCHOOL

> *Mr. Hart, here is a dime. Take it, call your mother, and tell her there is serious doubt about you ever becoming a lawyer.*
>
> — HARVARD LAW PROFESSOR, CHARLES W. KINGSFIELD JR. AS PLAYED BY JOHN HOUSEMAN IN THE MOVIE PAPER CHASE

When I graduated from college in 1974, I had a real interest in going into university administration. But, for the time being, working for a college would be delayed by law school. My older brother, Van, was enrolled in law school at the University of Arkansas and it seemed right to follow in his footsteps. If it worked for my older brother it seemed it might be good for me. I had not followed him to undergraduate studies at the University of Arkansas. I just felt that heading to law school was the expected thing to do. I had a nominal interest in politics or government work somewhere, but if truth be told, I was more lost than having any idea what I wanted to do with my life or where I wanted to live. So, I enrolled in law school and followed my older brother's path.

Jane and I got married after my first semester in law school. She worked at Springdale High School as a journalism teacher and put me through law school, paying all the bills and giving me constant encouragement, which I sorely needed.

I remember my grandmother, Maria Theresa Constantino Gearhart, telling me that, while she loved Jane, she wished I would marry a Catholic! Jane and I were married by a Catholic priest and Methodist minister at Central United Methodist Church in Fayetteville in 1974, the first time that had been done in Northwest Arkansas. When Jane and I went to see the priest and Methodist minister, in separate meetings, the minister was not very supportive of a mixed marriage. He told us mixed marriages don't last. We were shocked by his attitude. On the other hand, the priest asked us one question, "Do you love each other? If so, that is all that is important, and I have no further questions." Nothing about raising our kids Catholic or do we plan to use birth control. Just the one question about being in love.

Two fraternity buddies served as best men in our wedding, Tom King and Chip Robertson. Sadly, we have not stayed in close touch through the years and that is something I regret very much. Chip was a Missouri Supreme Court Justice at a very young age, and Tom a college professor. Bob Feltmeier was another fraternity brother who was in our wedding party. I met him the first day I arrived at Westminster and we developed a close friendship. Bob was a lot of fun to be around, and the girls loved him. Bob was supposed to leave the wedding and drive to south Arkansas to become engaged to a William Woods College girl he had dated his senior year. He never made it to her house and stayed in Fayetteville with one of Jane's bridesmaids he had hit it off with while we were on our honeymoon. Nothing developed between them, but it was fun to see him when we got off the plane from our honeymoon in New Orleans. I also became good friends with Randy Johnson from St. Louis and have stayed in close touch with him through the years.

Most of my friends from Westminster days were from Missouri. Being from Arkansas and living out of state, I think the distance factor caused us to drift apart over many years.

I did not particularly enjoy law school. In fact, I didn't like it at all. I suspect few law students really do if truth be told. I had read the 1971 book, "Paper Chase" and then watched the movie that came out in 1973, and it made an impression on me. Acclaimed actor, John Houseman, as a law professor was ruthless. I had a few of those professors in law school too. While I made decent grades, I struggled to make sense of it all. I made the dean's list the first year but had to study harder than I had ever studied before. Memorization was a key factor to law school success, something that has never been my strong suit.

During my first year I competed in a moot court contest at the law school. We won the contest, barely. Minutes before the contest one of our close friends, Janet Estes Brown, asked me if I was wearing a new suit for the competition. I felt complimented and said yes indeed I had bought a new suit, and this was my first time wearing it. I thanked her for noticing. She immediately said that she knew it was new because of the tags on the sleeve! Yes, I had almost participated in the moot court competition with tags on my new suit all the way down the sleeve.

Up until I became chancellor Jane had always worked professionally. Through the years she has been a newspaper reporter, staff member of our church, public school educator and many other positions varied and diverse. Jane put me through law school teaching journalism in public high schools. During my second year of law school, Jane and I took a group of Springdale high school students to New York City for a conference at Columbia University. Jane was expected to take the journalism students as their chaperone. Law school wasn't easy for me and I was studying constantly. I didn't really want to take time out of my studies and class to make the trip, but Jane needed me to help her supervise the students. So, off we went to the Big Apple with seven students under the age of 18.

After our group settled into the Roosevelt Hotel, Jane and I went for a 5th Avenue walk. We told the students they could not walk more than a couple of blocks from the hotel, and must stay together if they ventured out. We thought they would be fine if they stayed close to the hotel. During our walk we heard several fire trucks coming down the avenue with sirens blaring. I commented to Jane what a catastrophe it would be to have a big fire in midtown Manhattan.

The trucks passed us, and we didn't give it another thought. When we arrived back at the hotel, we were greeted by two of our male students who were waiting in the lobby for us with a look of utter terror and shock. Firetrucks and police were everywhere, and a fire snorkel was outside the building spraying water toward the 16th floor of the building.

Our student's room on the 16th floor had been completely destroyed by a fire. The hotel management took us up to the room. When the elevators opened, we could smell the pungent odor of heavy smoke. We went down the hall to the room and opened the door, which was charred. On the inside was total devastation: Everything had burned—furniture, the walls, the bathroom fixtures, the boy's clothes and other belongings—everything. I will never forget the scene. Jane and I were totally aghast.

I immediately got in the face of the students while Jane called her principal to report what had happened. At first the students pleaded innocence as to what might have started the fire, but finally after much questioning one of them admitted that they had put a punk (a smoldering stick used mainly for lighting fireworks, cigarettes or marijuana) in the door jam and forgot it when they went exploring the avenues of New York City. They returned to what could have been an absolute catastrophe. The punk ignited the entire room and burned everything inside. All their clothes were lost, plus an expensive camera owned by one of the students. Of course, we were not totally certain it was the punk that had caused the fire, but it made sense.

At first the boys thought they should be reimbursed by the hotel for the clothes, belongings and an expensive camera. I thought otherwise! When we met with the hotel manager later, I told them to let me do the talking and keep their mouths shut. They complied with my request and sat silent during the meeting.

To my complete surprise the manager didn't ask any questions. He said that he was very glad no one was hurt and moved the boys to a new room. He told us the entire floor of guests would need to be relocated because of the smoke odor, but they luckily had plenty of rooms available to accomplish that task. They even planned to upgrade guests on that floor to a better room to compensate them for the inconvenience. No questions were asked about what might have started the fire. The principal, after speaking with the superintendent, allowed the students to stay in NYC and complete the convention. Jane and I would have preferred to return home after the calamity.

Some of my law courses were interesting, some boring, and a few I loathed. Two of my professors were Bill and Hillary Clinton. The future head of the free world was an easy grader, but Hillary was tough. She gave me a C in criminal law. I deserved worse. I was glad to survive her course with at least a passing grade. Bill Clinton taught constitutional law and admiralty law, or law of the high seas. Admiralty seemed a strange course to offer in Arkansas, but Clinton had taken the course in law school at Yale and apparently enjoyed the subject and offered to teach it.

Years later Clinton would come to the university while I was chancellor to dedicate a law school courtyard and I made a joke about his teaching admiralty when I introduced him. He responded with a long dissertation about the importance of the course much to the assembled group's delight. He gave me a B in the course, and I admitted to the crowd that Hillary had given me a lesser grade in her criminal law course. President Clinton remarked that she didn't realize at the time she would have a political career like the President and if so, she would have given me an A. It got a good laugh. President Clinton sat down after his speech, turned to me and said, "We have a good act together and should do this more often!"

The future President of the United States of America was almost always late to class but was a fair and interesting instructor. Both he and Hillary were smart as a whip. When he was elected attorney general of Arkansas, I mentioned to him that I might be interested in working for him in the AG's office after I graduated. He said to come see him and there might be a slot open. At that point I didn't have any other interests and thought it would satisfy an itch to work in government service.

It was not to be.

The first semester of my third year in law school, my life was about to change forever and steer me into higher education. On my birthday in 1977 I received a phone call from Westminster official Bill Stucker who had become the interim president of my Alma Mater, Westminster College. Bill had been a vice president of the college and I had become friends with him while a student. He asked me to come to the college and serve as his assistant. When he learned I was in my last year of law school, he revised the offer and said he would only hire me if I could complete my law degree. In those days there was no mechanism to finish law school remotely, and the University of Arkansas law school rules required a student to be in residency the final semester. I had taken classes in the summer to finish early and had 12 hours remaining and would graduate in December, a semester early. But, as Bill Stucker said, "no law school, no job at Westminster!"

The dean of the law school at the time was Wylie Davis. I went to him with my dilemma and job opportunity. He could not have been more helpful and supportive. I will always be most grateful to him for his help. He told me that he would waive the requirement of residency if I could get accepted to the University of Missouri in Columbia, Missouri, to finish the last 12 hours. My degree would still come from Arkansas and I would transfer the last hours back to the Arkansas law school. He knew the dean at Missouri and would call him to see if he would agree. He did.

Fortunately, I applied and was accepted to Mizzou, and finished the last hours there. Columbia was a short 30-minute drive from Westminster College, and I drove there three mornings a week for my final classes. It was a challenge to say the least. Driving to Columbia in the cold and ice was treacherous in our tiny red Chevrolet Vega. After class I would hurry back to Fulton, trying to handle a full-time job in addition to my studies.

With law school figured out, Stucker did hire me as his assistant. He paid me $6,500 a year and let me live in the elegant President's House as part of my compensation. (He had a home in Columbia, Missouri and didn't want to move to Fulton.) I studied for the bar exam from the beautiful oak paneled study at the President's House, and Jane and I got our first taste of living in a president's home! It wasn't always ideal as workmen and staff would constantly let themselves in the house without any notice. One night about 10 p.m. we heard a rattle downstairs. Someone had delivered light bulbs to the residence and just used their key to let themselves in. No telling how many people had keys to that house. We quickly determined that going downstairs partially clothed was not a good idea. I didn't realize it at the time, but that would be a good lesson later in life!

After a year serving as the interim president's assistant, a new president was elected. He opened a search for a director of development. I applied and miraculously was hired. Thus, solidified my journey into higher education.

All of us have regrets in life. I certainly do. But following my instincts and taking a job at Westminster isn't one of them. I literally loved working in higher education and would do it all over again, with a few caveats, and have never regretted my journey. A few times through the years Jane has jokingly said that she "thought she was marrying someone who would become a rich lawyer!" But, for the most part, our lives have been enriched by each institution where we have served.

CHAPTER 7
JANE BROCKMANN GEARHART

> *I would venture to guess that Anonymous, who wrote so many poems without signing them, was often a woman.*
>
> — *VIRGINIA WOOLF.*

I say *we* because Jane was the absolute perfect partner for a life in higher education. This sounds trite, but everyone—and I mean everyone—we became acquainted with fell in love with Jane. She has a knack for making friends easily. My shyness was always an impediment to making friends. Jane did it for both of us. She had a steel trap mind for remembering names and faces, and believe it or not, people's phone numbers, birthdays, and anniversaries. She is amazing with that rare talent and it has helped me my entire life.

College and university life all these years has been fun with Jane. She did more for my career than anyone with her amazing personality, sound judgment and winning ways. She still stays in touch with folks from each institution where we served. She is the absolute best. Meeting her in high school was the best thing that ever happened to me, bar none.

Jane and I are blessed with two amazing children and five grandchildren. We are very lucky that all of them are in Fayetteville. Our daughter Katy, a speech pathologist, married a wonderful, brilliant physician, Justin Hunt, and Brock married the sweetest person ever, Lindsey Vitale, a primary school teacher. Justin's parents, David and Sharon Hunt, are educators working in the local school system and the at the University of Arkansas. Lindsey's parents, John and Nancy Vitale, are also educators: John a high school football coach and Nancy a teacher. John and I play golf at least two days a week with a group of retirees. John is the humblest, most unaffected person I know, and always has a smile on his face. John Vitale has never had a bad day.

Back row: Katsy Brockmann, Jane's mother; Larry Wilkins, brother-in-law; David Gearhart. Front row: Beth Wilkins, Jane's sister; Bob Brockmann, Jane's father; and Jane

Brock went to work for Merrill Lynch in New York City and then came back to Fayetteville to work for a wealth management company, Greenwood and Associates. Later he would purchase the company and rename it Greenwood Gearhart. He has done extremely well and now is approaching $1 billion under financial management. Both Katy and Lindsey are stay-at-home moms raising our five grandkids, Ben, Caroline, Ellie, Lily Jane, and George. They live around the corner from our house, and we get to see them all the time. It is truly a blessing and we are very proud of all our kids and grandkids.

The grandkids: Ben, Caroline, Ellie, George, Lily Jane

After Katy got two degrees from Penn State, she came back to Northwest Arkansas to practice. That is where she met Justin.

Jane was an incredible mother and now grandmother GiGi. She raised the kids while I was trying to build a career. While I managed to attend many of the sporting events of the kids, Jane never missed one. She was a bounty of love and nurturing to our two children and gave them a loving upbringing. They turned out to be very responsible people in life, and that came from Jane.

I do have regrets for being an absentee dad. Jane raised them. I was around, but Jane raised them. I look back on it now and must admit that I should have been more engaged with our kids. It is a major regret of mine as I turn 70 years old. I've learned that nothing, not financial support, providing sustenance, telling them you love them, nothing says more than being there for them. Being available all the time and nurturing them every day. That is what is important. I regret that I wasn't there as much as I should have been. You cannot get back time with your young kids.

Gearhart family in Gulf Shores, Alabama. Celebrating 45 years at the beach.

Both Katy and Brock are amazing parents. Children are supposed to learn from their parents, not the other way around. I have learned a lot from my children, but mainly how to be a good parent.

Both of them spend quality time with their kids. I suspect they must have decided to be around more with their families because I was not.

Throughout our life together— we've been married almost 50 years at this writing—Jane has always been deeply involved in community service work. She has served on numerous boards and non-profits, and contributed to the welfare of every place we lived. She chaired the library campaign that passed a millage increase to build the new Fayetteville Public Library. She has been very involved in our church, the public schools and food insecurity. She gave her time and talent to so many endeavors it is impossible to mention all of them. However, food insecurity was, perhaps, her major passion. More on that matter later.

PART II
SOJOURN TO HIGHER EDUCATION
1977–1982

The highest result of education is tolerance.

— HELEN KELLER

CHAPTER 8
WESTMINSTER

> *This is a wonderful school in my home state. If you come, I will introduce you. Hope you can do it.*
>
> — PRESIDENT HARRY TRUMAN PENNED THIS NOTE AT THE BOTTOM OF THE COLLEGE'S INVITATION TO WINSTON CHURCHILL TO LECTURE AT WESTMINSTER COLLEGE

My first job in college administration was at my alma mater, Westminster College, in Fulton, Missouri. The president of the college had left somewhat abruptly, and the board of trustees had appointed an interim. Bill Stucker had taken over in a time of uncertainty, and he reached out to me to be his assistant. As previously mentioned, I was in my last semester of law school and he required that I finish my studies while working as his assistant.

Bill Stucker was an interesting person. He cared deeply about Westminster and, I believe, would have made a great permanent president. He just recently died at age 91 in September 2021 in Hot Springs, Arkansas, where he had retired.

My job was mostly administrative in nature, drafting letters and reports and some speech writing. I oversaw the president's office, making certain it ran smoothly, and I enjoyed the work very much, even though it was more clerical than anything. However, I did learn a great deal about the finances of a college during that time.

I became good friends with the vice president for finance, Roy Ruffner, and he was a great mentor to me. I was given some responsibilities in fundraising, which helped me to understand and appreciate the importance of development work. Trying to balance my work with law school was a real challenge, but it exposed me to many aspects of college administration. Stucker also allowed me to travel a few times with him on fundraising calls. I learned quickly that one of the keys to success in development work is making the ask. Stucker never shied away from asking for a gift and I got to watch him firsthand, and started honing my skills for my later career.

Westminster was involved in a capital campaign at the time to raise funds primarily for the endowment. The campaign was called the "Futures Campaign," and little did I know in my naïveté that the name turned out to be most confusing to potential donors. They likened it to the futures stock market, and no one really understood the reasons for selecting something that would confuse people wanting to make a gift to the college. It made it sound like the campaign was speculative. Despite the name, we did raise some funds and I particularly remember Stucker making a gift ask in the seven figures and landing the gift on one visit. That impressed me and served as an impetus to try my hand at fundraising. Stucker made it look easy to me, and I probably didn't realize that he was very skilled at asking for the order and getting results.

As I mentioned previously, part of my salary was living in the president's home. That was fun and exciting for Jane and me to live in a big, elegant house at such a young age, despite the considerable traffic in and out of the house at virtually all hours.

I worked for Bill Stucker for a year before a new president was selected, and I had hoped Stucker would put his hat in the ring for the permanent job. I was convinced he really wanted the job on a permanent basis, but preferred the board of trustees to come to him rather than applying himself. He kept denying he wanted the job permanently and the board believed him.

Dr. Harvey Saunders, who came from a small liberal arts college in Mississippi, Millsaps College, became the president of the college in 1977 and Bill Stucker resigned. Jane and I were quite unsure of our future when Stucker did not get the permanent job. We had no idea if Saunders would keep me in the role as his assistant, and had a few sleepless nights wondering where we would land with a new administration taking over.

Amazingly, Harvey Saunders invited me to be his director of development. I had practically no development experience and, quite frankly, was astounded that he selected me. I suspect many of the faculty and staff were shocked at the appointment as well. There I was, overseeing fundraising for my alma mater with little or no practical experience under my belt. I guess Saunders liked the way I parted my hair and gave me a chance, for which I will always be grateful. Westminster was starved for resources and I knew it would be a challenging job to say the least.

Westminster College has always had a bare-bones existence throughout its history. The college has never had a sizable endowment and has existed on a year-to-year budget. It is an excellent institution and I felt I got a superb education. The faculty were second to none during my time as a student, and I've always felt that I received paramount instruction. Several of the faculty had been at Westminster for decades and were renowned in their field of study. But, from a financial standpoint the college was suffering and still does today.

Of course, as a liberal arts institution in a small college town it is not alone. These types of institutions provide a wonderful educational experience, but do so with very little resources unless they are highly rated and enjoy world-class prestige. They are entirely dependent upon enrollment. During my time as a student at Westminster the enrollment was around 700 students. A few years ago, the enrollment spiked to over 1,000, but is currently down around 600 students today. Survival might be questionable, although the college does have a committed and distinguished alumni base which has kept it going since 1851.

Several years after I worked at the college and when I was at Penn State, I was elected to the Westminster College board of trustees. I was honored to be asked to be on the board, but, given my schedule, attending the meetings was difficult. It did give me the opportunity to see the finances of the college and realize that it was operating on slim margins. After a three-year term I informed the college I could not stand for re-election because of my responsibilities at Penn State. Later I would do some pro bono consulting for the college. An interesting aside: When I went on the Westminster board, I was invited to have dinner with the president and his wife the day before the board meetings. Jane accompanied me to the dinner for the four of us at the Fulton Country Club. During the dinner, the president's spouse told us that a few years earlier she had been kidnapped by aliens and taken to their spaceship. Jane and I sat there with our eyes wide open in disbelief.

After I retired as chancellor, I was asked again to come on the Westminster board, but turned it down. The president of the college at the time, Benjamin Ola. Akande, had been dismissed abruptly and I believed wrongly dismissed. Nine months before he was dismissed the board of trustees had given him an $80,000 bonus and then fired him a few months later. In my opinion he was only guilty of telling the truth about the poor financial situation at Westminster. Given my relationship with Benjamin and the way he was treated, I just could not accept a board position. The person serving as president at that time, and after Benjamin's dismissal, was a former Westminster president who had been fired from Westminster for having an affair with a staff member. I guess they brought him back thinking he was the only person who could save the college, even though he was dismissed several years before. I found the whole thing incomprehensible and very short on ethics and morality.

It would take a new president to bring me back into the fold as a donor in 2021. The new president, Donald Lofe, invited me to give the commencement address and I was impressed with him. I believe he will be a good president for my alma mater.

Westminster would approach me three times over the next several years to be president of the college, the last time in 2020. I did give it some thought each time, but concluded it was not for me and turned down the offers. In 2020 I felt I was too old, and just didn't have the passion for another challenge of that magnitude; in addition, I had decided I wanted to teach when I retired from administration. Jane and I had made a pact that we would live out our days in Fayetteville. Besides, if I wanted to remain a university CEO I would have stayed as chancellor at the University of Arkansas.

Jane and I met many distinguished people while at Westminster. Since Winston Churchill made the Iron Curtain Speech in 1946, it became a forum for world leaders and distinguished citizens to speak under the auspices of the John Findley Green Lectures. Among the speakers we met were the Rt. Hon. The Lord Harlech, former British ambassador to the United States during the Kennedy administration, and television executive in Great Britain; The Hon. Robert H. Finch, Counselor to the President, former Lieutenant Governor of California and Secretary of HEW; General Avraham Yoffe, Director, Nature Reserves Authority and general in the Israeli Army; Ardeshir Zahedi, ambassador to the United States from Iran; and Gerald R. Ford, President of the United States, to name only a few. Westminster has always been able to garner amazing speakers since Churchill made his historic talk on the campus.

Harvey Saunders started out being a good president, committed to doing the right things and working hard to bring in philanthropic dollars. He was likable, engaging, very smart and a true academic. He could make tough decisions, but didn't seem to have a real vision for the college. After a year working for Saunders, I felt his commitment was waning somewhat, and he seemed to spend a lot of time in his office reading his favorite books. I became disillusioned and started looking for job opportunities.

I liked Harvey Saunders very much personally, but he could be somewhat peculiar. Saunders seemed to have no filters and would later get in trouble with the faculty and the board of trustees over some comments he made that were deemed racist. I never felt Saunders had a racist bone in his body but the board tired of him and after many years he resigned.

Lady Mary Soames, Winston Churchill's daughter, with Chip Robertson and David Gearhart at Westminster College.

Saunders' legacy is somewhat mixed, but he did accomplish something tremendous for the college. We were in the car together on one of our fundraising trips when we started talking about the college finances. I told him that I thought the best solution was to go coed. Up to that point Westminster had been an institution for men only. We desperately needed more students, and the best way to do that was to open the college to women, which would hopefully give the college 100 percent more applicants to draw from. Saunders immediately told me he agreed, and he would set out to make the monumental change as soon as possible. It was not easy. Many alumni came out of the woodwork in opposition, but Saunders successfully navigated the substantial criticism and multiple issues, and the college went coed for the first time in its history. Presently the college is about 50 percent men and 50 percent women. I wonder if Westminster would have survived had that decision not been made. Saunders gets the credit for that regardless of any other issues that may have plagued him during his time as president.

Shortly after I became director of development at Westminster College, I was interviewed by a local newspaper reporter. I learned an early lesson about investigative reporting. The Fulton Sun Gazette was a tiny local paper owned and operated by the much larger Columbia Tribune. Jane was a cub reporter for the Fulton Sun Gazette covering the city council and school board.

During the interview the reporter kept focusing on the financial strength of the college. It was obvious to me that he had already written his story and was looking to me for confirmation. In my naïveté I made some comments that made him think the college might be having financial distress. The college had been losing enrollment and folks in the community were concerned about financial viability. It certainly was not my intent to supply him with fodder for his story. I tried to steer the conversation toward fundraising and the fact that development would be a major component of the Harvey Saunders administration.

The front page of the paper the next morning had headlines that made it appear as if the college was in serious financial trouble. I was misquoted, and the reporter had taken comments out of context. To say the least I was mortified, and quickly found my way to Saunders' office to apologize. He took the whole thing with a grain of salt and made me feel better than I deserved. I did learn a very important lesson about being very careful talking to reporters, and would keep my guard up in the future. It was my first experience with yellow journalism and the unfairness of reporters looking for a headline-grabbing story. During my career I would become jaundiced toward media which is rather ironic given my family's attachment to the newspaper business.

I will discuss this later in the book, but suffice it to say for now that I have lost all respect for the news media. The inaccuracies of news reporting today are unconscionable and dangerous to a democratic society.

Only one example is the terrible misinformation spread by the media about Covid 19. Fox News, and other media outlets like them, contributed to dangerous and unconscionable information that led to distrust and harmful messages about mask wearing and the vaccine. Someone sent me a statement that read, "Got polio, me neither, or diphtheria, pertussis, tetanus, pneumococcus or other life-threatening diseases. Thank Science." But many news outlets refused to trust science and instead spread lies that caused international havoc, resulting in multiple deaths worldwide.

Even the Arkansas Legislature enacted laws prohibiting mask and vaccination mandates, when the science was very clear that such measures saved lives. The governor of Arkansas at the time, Asa Hutchinson, signed the legislation that made those measures law. Then he attempted to walk back his action when things got very bad in the state due to the Delta Covid variant. The legislature refused to walk back the legislation, and demanded that citizens of the state should have freedom of choice to contract Covid and spread it to others, and possibly die.

Ironically, the Republican legislature was also against women having freedom of choice over their own bodies. As regards masks and Covid, many lawsuits followed, and one Arkansas judge ruled that the legislature could not prevent masking rules and they were unconstitutional on several grounds including equal protection under the law. Governor Hutchinson chimed in that the judge's ruling was well reasoned and he agreed with it, even though he signed the legislation that created the problem. Asa graduated from law school two years before me. A first-year law student had to know there were serious constitutional issues with the law he signed. But our governor signed the laws for purely political reasons. Unconscionable action for any leader.

I did learn a great deal at Westminster College and the role of a development officer, but it was mostly self-taught. Harvey Saunders did not have heavy major gift experience in his earlier academic college positions and relied upon me to set the tone for the development operations. We had some successes and many disappointments. Westminster College alumni were simply not accustomed to making major gifts, and it seemed an uphill battle for the year I served as director of development.

If you Google "fundraising," you get 250 million hits. Fundraising is big business in America and there is no shortage of materials related to the topic. During my career I have read hundreds, if not thousands, of books and articles about fundraising. Early on I tried to read everything I could get my hands on related to the profession. Personally, I have written two books on capital campaigns and one book of case studies on fundraising. I have also written a number of articles on fundraising that have been published in numerous journals. But in all of my research the best article I ever read about fundraising was written by J. Richard Taft. He runs an organization that provides fundraising consulting to colleges, hospitals, and social and cultural agencies in all areas of fundraising and development, including the capital campaign. Mr. Taft gave a talk in June 1974 at the Midwest Health Congress in Kansas City, Missouri. He titled the piece "When Development Directors Fail." Taft systematically laid out what he believes to be the most important issues to prevent failure in a development program. Those points are as follows, and I paraphrase:

1. Failure to establish immediate relationships with key volunteers and board members is a common problem among development professionals.
2. Lack of sophistication in developing marketing data for planning.
3. Not having a large enough operating budget to accomplish your goals.

4. Hiring low-cost people who do not have the requisite professional experience, just to fill slots.
5. Too many development directors do not keep records, do not send memos, and don't cover their tracks with a paper record.
6. Doing prolonged research in writing proposals and putting together brochures before they ever go to see a single prospect is the bugaboo of many development officers.
7. Many development officers fail because they lose their motivation quickly.

Taft concluded his speech by proclaiming that the rate of failure among development officers must be reduced. The turnover is debilitating and wasteful and no organization can afford that type of turnover. The phenomenon is still prevalent today. Development professionals move from one job to the next, and it is a problem all across the nation.

I have kept a copy of Taft's speech in my desk drawer my entire career and have given a copy to each president and chancellor I reported to. His comments so many years ago are still relevant today.

My disillusionment with the Westminster College leadership led me to apply for a job at Methodist-affiliated Hendrix College in Conway, Arkansas and I was selected for the position of director of development in 1978. It was very difficult to move from my alma mater to a similar college, but Jane and I thought it important to get closer to home after my father's death. In addition, all of Jane's relatives were Methodist, and they were ecstatic that we were coming to work for a Methodist institution in our home state. Besides, Hendrix College had a much more substantial endowment and a vibrant enrollment, and it just seemed a good move to make.

Harvey Saunders was not pleased, and initially made my move from my alma mater to Hendrix less than easy. I understood his disappointment in me as I'm sure he felt that he had given me an opportunity to move into college administration and I had abandoned him. Saunders even used the word "desertion" and I was made to feel as though I had been disloyal. It was a decision we labored on for days. I was very sorry that Saunders was so distraught over our move, but in the end Jane and I headed for Arkansas and a new job, albeit with mixed feelings.

The mixed feelings quickly dissipated as I went to work for one of the finest people I have ever known, Dr. Roy B. Shilling, Jr. president of Hendrix college. Roy taught me everything there is to know about development work and was an extraordinary mentor to me during those early years of college administration. Roy was an amazing person and marvelous college president, and I learned a great deal from him in the three years I worked for him. Roy turned 91 years old recently and we remain in close contact to this day. A couple of years ago Jane and I went to see Roy and his wife Margaret, and their lovely and talented daughter, Nancy, in Austin, Texas, where they are living. It was great to see them, and he is one of my heroes to this day.

CHAPTER 9
HENDRIX COLLEGE

> *We have all known a few Catholics and some of them are good people.*
>
> — FROM A BROCHURE TITLED, "SHOULD YOUR DAUGHTER WANT TO MARRY A CATHOLIC," FOUND AT A UNITED METHODIST CHURCH IN PINE BLUFF, ARKANSAS.

Hendrix had much better resources than Westminster College. Besides being very impressed with Roy Shilling, I thought the other members of the administration were first rate. The college had an enrollment of over 1,000 students, and seemed to be the institution of choice for Arkansas high school graduates who had high board scores and grade-point averages. The major competition for students came from the University of Arkansas in Fayetteville. But for a top student who wanted a small campus environment, Hendrix was the place. The college also enjoyed marvelous support from the Methodist Church. Westminster was loosely affiliated with the Presbyterian Church during that time but received no financial support of any kind from the Presbyterian authority.

I was a Catholic at the time, but that made absolutely no difference to Roy Shilling, who made it perfectly clear to everyone, particularly Methodist clergy, that one's religion should have no bearing on their capacity to do a good job for a Methodist-related institution. Not once did I feel like a second-class citizen for being a Catholic working for a Methodist college. My job required me to become acquainted with all the Methodist ministers around the state. When I would go on a fundraising trip, I would always make it a point to call on the Methodist preachers in the area. I got to know most of them on a first-name basis, and it was a real joy to work with them. Jane's family were strong Methodists, particularly her grandmother, whose father had been a Methodist minister. Many of the preachers I called on knew the family and that gave me instant recognition and opened a lot of doors.

At the time we were running a campaign asking for each Methodist church to sponsor one or more scholarships for Methodist students in their area. My job, along with another staff member, Dr. James Major, was to call on the ministers and convince them to sign on to providing one or more endowed scholarships. Of course, some of the smaller rural churches didn't have the resources to participate but many did, and the program was successful. I learned Methodists supported their colleges much more readily than the Presbyterians at Westminster.

I encountered only one incident of Catholic bashing, which I found to be quite humorous on my travels to visit Methodist preachers. I was in Pine Bluff calling on the minister at First United Methodist Church. I was waiting to meet with the minister and noticed a bin in the corner with several brochures. I started leafing through them out of curiosity. One was titled, "Should Your Daughter Want to Marry a Catholic." The entire brochure was dedicated to the perils of marrying a Catholic and how to handle raising your children as Catholics. One line stated, "We have all known a few Catholics and some of them are good people." I literally laughed out loud. I put the brochure in my pocket and still show it to Methodist preachers to this day. It always gets big laughs.

I think most people would agree that Hendrix enjoyed a reputation as the finest private liberal arts college in Arkansas and it has remained so for many years. I greatly enjoyed working for a prestigious college recognized for its academic prowess. Jane and I made many lifelong friends in Conway, Arkansas, and continue to be blessed with their friendship to this day. We met Steve and Susan Stoltz early on in Conway. Steve owned a manufacturing company and was a Hendrix benefactor even though he was a Notre Dame alumnus. Susan's family were huge supporters of the college. We have remained great friends to this day. I performed the wedding ceremony for his son, Drew.

The physical plant at Hendrix was first rate in every way. Roy Shilling had built new or renovated numerous buildings before my arrival. He was an extraordinary fundraiser and highly respected by benefactors and alumni in general. During my time at Hendrix we developed an extensive capital campaign, and it was much easier to appeal to alumni than my experience at Westminster. Not only did Hendrix alumni contribute generously to the college, but persons of the Methodist tradition also gave generously. I also found that parents of students contributed graciously, and it gave the college multiple sources from which to draw gifts. Many physicians, lawyers and business leaders were alumni of Hendrix and helped open doors to philanthropic resources.

Because of Roy Shilling's efforts early in his tenure, the college also benefited from foundation support. Many of the larger private foundations in Arkansas and beyond were contributors to the college. The Mabee Foundation of Tulsa Oklahoma, the Winthrop Rockefeller Foundation in Little Rock and many others had been cultivated by Roy for several years and they seemed eager to support the college.

Roy Shilling taught me fundraising skills that remained with me my entire life. I learned about major gift fundraising and the concept of moves management when dealing with benefactors. Roy was a tireless worker and always supportive of the people who worked for him. You always knew that Roy had your back and would do anything to make you successful. Simply put, Roy Shilling was a class act, and to this day I am deeply, deeply grateful to him for his stewardship of my career. His wife, Margaret, was a fully supportive spouse and lovely person. She was smart, energetic and the perfect partner for a college president. They were well respected in the Conway community as well as Methodist churches across Arkansas. They were quality people of high devotion and fortitude, and the political and corporate leadership of Arkansas recognized them as stellar leaders.

Roy B. Shilling, president emeritus of Hendrix College; Jane and David Gearhart; Margaret Shilling; Nancy Shilling

After almost 13 years as president of Hendrix College, Roy decided the time had come for a different challenge. I had worked for him for three years at this point, and they were literally the best years of my life. But regrettably, Roy was challenged by an unfortunate occurrence during his administration.

One of the senior members of the faculty was accused by students of sexual harassment and improprieties. The faculty member was very popular with alumni and some members of the board of trustees. Roy launched an investigation into the faculty member's alleged activities and determined that he had indeed been a predator. After an open and legitimate investigation, Roy dismissed the faculty member and the whole ordeal became a public matter. The board of trustees ultimately backed Roy in his decision to dismiss the faculty member, but there were a couple of board members who made his life miserable. I watched as it took a terrible toll on him, and I think he became discouraged and started looking for other opportunities. I was amazed at how well he handled the entire episode with grace and leadership. But ultimately, he decided to accept the presidency of Southwestern University in Georgetown Texas.

Jane and I were dismayed when he told us that he would be leaving Hendrix. But the dismay was somewhat short-lived when he asked me to come to Southwestern University as his vice president for development. We came very close to accepting his generous offer. We visited the college and met with members of the board of trustees, and found it to be a very tempting opportunity. The chance to continue working for Roy was the biggest motivation by far. But we would be leaving friends and family and moving to a similar type institution in south Texas. The whole reason we had come to Hendrix College in the first place was to be closer to family and we agonized for days about what to do.

Jane and I decided to stay at Hendrix, and it was the most difficult decision of my lifetime. I dreaded telling Roy our decision as I didn't want to disappoint him. I've often thought over these many years whether I made a mistake and should have accepted his kind offer. I suspect my life would have been much different had I done so. He ended up hiring a person as his vice president who succeeded him to the presidency of Southwestern University when he retired. It would be 25 years before I had the opportunity to serve as a university president. Perhaps under his tutelage that opportunity might have happened earlier in my life. I think about that quite often, and even though things turned out fine in the end, I always regretted not continuing my professional relationship with Roy Shilling.

Hendrix College hired a new president soon after Roy's departure, Joe B. Hatcher. He came from a small liberal arts college in Michigan, Albion College, where he was vice president for development. I missed Roy greatly in the early months of the new administration. It wasn't that I had any real problems with the new president, it was simply that he wasn't Roy Shilling. Looking back, I don't think I handled the situation maturely. I was never disloyal to the new president, but I found myself discovering his flaws and yearning for the old days with Dr. Shilling. After a year I decided it was time to make another move and started looking for new opportunities.

One of the major catastrophes at Hendrix College was the administration building fire on February 6, 1982. My phone rang at 3:30 a.m. waking me from a deep sleep. I was told that the college administration building was on fire, and I should come to campus. I immediately dressed and headed to campus. When I rounded the top of a hill overlooking Hendrix, I was shocked. The entire sky was ablaze. I was absolutely astounded how the fire lit up the surrounding area. The Conway Fire Department responded to the blaze. It was thirteen degrees outside, freezing fire truck water hoses. The fire could not be contained and the building was a total loss—when I arrived, it was obvious that would be the case. The next morning the only thing still standing was a fire safe, which had withstood the heat but not water damage. Some materials were saved from the safe, but it was a monumental undertaking to replace so many college records. Interestingly, a building standing in the same place had burned to the ground in 1928.

Fortunately, my office had moved out of the administration building before the fire and into the old president's home right next door. Thus, all the development and fundraising records were spared destruction. The major task before our department was to raise funds to replace the building. A major benefactor, Elbert Fausett, fortunately came to the rescue and made a considerable gift to help rebuild the facility.

One very tough regret I still harbor was my torn relationship with Dr. James Major. He had been vice president of the college before me and remained on staff to help me get acclimated to my new surroundings and introduce me to the major donors and clergy. He was an alumnus of Hendrix and a Methodist minister. He had been on the staff of the college for many years, and we became good friends. He even baptized one of our children.

The break in our friendship came when he got very upset with me for calling on a Hendrix donor after I went to the University of Arkansas. The truth was that the donor, Miss Lily Peter, was also a major donor to the university and had served on the development council. I tried to explain that to Jim, but he didn't buy it. It ruined our relationship, and we didn't speak after that. I wrote him a letter trying to explain and patch things up, but he never responded. Jim died in 2017 at the age of 101.

The position of director of development at the University of Arkansas became available and I was contacted by a headhunter and asked to submit my application. The university had just appointed a first ever chancellor for the Fayetteville campus. I received telephone calls from several members of the board of trustees of the university encouraging me to apply. I even got a phone call from Governor Bill Clinton who applied subtle pressure and encouragement for me to go to Fayetteville.

After much discussion Jane and I decided it was time to go home; I accepted the position and we moved to Fayetteville. It was not easy making the move, even though we were going to the place of my birth. We had met so many dear friends in Conway, and even though Fayetteville was only 2 1/2 hours away, we literally hated to leave our friends and the community. We had several tearful goodbyes.

I decided to go to Fayetteville earlier than Jane, and I moved in with my mother and stepfather and started my position at the University of Arkansas. I was going to come back to Conway on weekends. My plan was to leave Sunday evening and arrive at my parents' home to be ready for work Monday morning. I loaded up the car for the first trek, looked at Jane, and we both had tears in our eyes. It was at that moment I decided to leave early the next morning and be at my new job by 8 a.m.

It was a difficult move for both of us as we loved Hendrix, Conway and our many friends and associates. Hendrix College was a wonderful institution, prestigious, well-funded and a beautiful campus. Frankly, I can't really say I was overly excited about joining a large university, but I was not happy with the leadership at Hendrix and felt this was the best opportunity to make a move. On one of the rare occasions my dad gave me advice, he told me that, if I didn't like my boss, I should leave the position and find another job.

I have always found it difficult to work for someone who either, one, I did not like or, two, did not respect as a leader or, three, felt was not competent to hold the office. I suppose many people would just suck it up and try to get along, but not me. If I found my boss disagreeable, unlikeable, or incapable, then I was just unable to get past it. That was my problem and would hold me back a number of times in my career. I suspect it was a weakness that I was unforgiving when it came to the flaws of other folks.

I look back on my career and have no doubt my attitude was hurtful to my progression in academic life. Go along/get along did not work too well for me. I had to hold complete respect for the person I worked for, and was overly quick to see their flaws and foibles and form a negative opinion too quickly. It is simply a shortcoming of mine, which has haunted me my entire life. I suspect part of it was believing in my heart that I could do a better job than the person occupying the presidency. Not a good attitude to have. I simply refused to play the politics of "kiss ass" and I have no doubt it was detrimental to my career. I could have been nicer, more gracious and less antagonistic to people I worked for who I did not particularly like. But, alas, as one good friend told me, "Gearhart, it is in your DNA." I did not suffer fools gladly and would look for a new opportunity when I lost confidence in my boss. I may have even gotten a reputation for being a difficult person to get along with. I just could not bear working for people who I didn't respect. I had enough confidence in myself that I could get another job and always spoke up when I disagreed with the president or other staff.

Sometimes I spoke up too much and should have kept my mouth shut.

PART III
UNIVERSITY OF ARKANSAS, THE FIRST TIME
1982–1985

Pure as the dawn on the brow of thy beauty, watches thy soul from the mountains of God.

— UNIVERSITY OF ARKANSAS ALMA MATER

CHAPTER 10
BACK TO FAYETTEVILLE

> *My main home is in Fayetteville, Arkansas, a college town in the Ozark Mountains. I live on the highest hill in a quiet cul-de-sac, surrounded by friends.*
>
> — *ELLEN GILCHRIST*

In 1982 I interviewed at the University of Arkansas for the position of director of development. Again, I had mixed feelings about making the move and wasn't sure I wanted to leave a small liberal arts college for a major university. However, I felt my relationship had deteriorated with the president and a move was necessary. Many of the Hendrix benefactors had ties with the University of Arkansas and they spoke well of me to the search committee. I was hired for the job and headed to Fayetteville. It was the third time I had moved from Fayetteville and come back. The first being the trip to college in 1970, the second from law school to Fulton to work for my alma mater in 1977, and this move from Hendrix to the university in 1982. By this time Jane and I had two children, born in 1978 and 1982.

I went to work for Dr. Bill Nugent, the first chancellor of the University of Arkansas in Fayetteville. For most of its history the head of the Fayetteville campus also headed the entire university system. In those days it wasn't called a system but operated that way nonetheless. Chancellors of the other campuses were appointed by the university president and reported to the president in Fayetteville, after confirmation by the board of trustees.

The Fayetteville campus had never had a chancellor, as the president fulfilled that role. In some ways it was one university geographically distributed. It seemed to operate efficiently, and the president generally used a soft hand in dealing with his chancellors at other campuses. The concept was that the head of the flagship, major, research-based campus should also lead the way for the other campuses. Most of the resources and high-level staff were in Fayetteville where the university was founded on the old McIlroy farm in 1871. Fayetteville was the center of higher education for the entire state and most major decisions for all the campuses were decided there. Actually, I would learn later, that was the way Penn State operated. The nexus of higher education was at the main campus.

That arrangement didn't always sit well with the other campuses! It didn't always sit well with members of the General Assembly in central Arkansas either. For the most part, in those days, the center of economic and political power resided in Little Rock, the state capital. Jealousies were always apparent between Fayetteville and Little Rock, but the power of the state capital usually won the day. The economic power of Northwest Arkansas was just beginning with the founding of Walmart, and Fayetteville was still looked upon as a small mountain town. Walmart was in its infancy, having been founded in 1962 and not incorporated until 1969. Most major decisions, other than in the realm of higher education, were made in Little Rock. In 1969 Little Rock University became the University of Arkansas at Little Rock. LRU had experienced serious financial stress and its survival was in question so it joined the University of Arkansas as one of its remote campuses.

Dr. Robert Ross served as chancellor of UALR and accomplished many good things during his tenure. Unfortunately, he ran afoul of the university president, Jim Martin who did not appreciate Ross' relationship with the legislature and his end-run requests for legislative support for his campus. Ross was a popular chancellor with donors, alumni, and central Arkansas folks, but the board of trustees backed Martin and Ross was fired, an incident documented by the website "Encyclopedia of Arkansas." Sadly, Ross would die in a plane crash a few years later.

The clash between Martin and Ross precipitated a legislative movement to establish a chancellor position at the Fayetteville campus. Legislators and high-level University of Arkansas at Little Rock (UALR) alumni and supporters simply didn't like someone headquartered in Fayetteville telling their local UALR officials how to run the campus.

There had been rumors for many years that some legislators wanted the flagship campus in Little Rock. In fact, I discovered a letter written by Governor Faubus in my late father's papers where Faubus warned about the movement by members of the General Assembly to bring the main campus of the university to Little Rock. The Fayetteville versus Little Rock rift continues to this day. As Northwest Arkansas gained economic power with Walmart and the growth of other major corporations like Tyson Foods and J.B. Hunt, the area became more influential statewide. Years later the rift gained a fever pitch with the decision by Frank Broyles to move all Little Rock football games to Fayetteville. More on that contentious issue later.

Bill Nugent had a difficult time navigating all the politics. No one could decide who was supposed to crown the homecoming queen, the president or the chancellor. That sounds trite, but it best describes the issues after the establishment of a chancellor position on the Fayetteville campus. Who was really in charge? Nugent could formulate policy only to be countermanded by the president whose office was down the hall in the administration building in Fayetteville.

One of the worst decisions in higher education I believe was creating a chancellor position in Fayetteville and redefining the president's role. It was untenable and still is today. More on that later.

CHAPTER 11
THE NEW BOSS AND THE COACH

> *There is only one boss. The customer. And he can fire everybody in the company from the chairman on down, simply by spending his money somewhere else.*
>
> — SAM WALTON

Nugent was his own worst enemy. He wasn't a very good listener and thought he had all the right answers. From day one he fought the system president's office on many issues and did not endear himself to Martin or university vice presidents. He could be aloof and hard-nosed. To those of us in his administration, he constantly criticized the president and his staff. Around that time the terminology of a "system" started to be used. However, later when Ray Thornton became president, he chose not to use the term system, causing further confusion. Thornton wanted to be the president of *The University of Arkansas*, not president of a *system*.

Nugent called me to his office one morning, and said he wanted to start a campaign to benefit the library. He wanted to add 100,000 volumes to the library through private gift support. He reckoned it would require raising about $2.5 million to make it happen. At that time the University of Arkansas had a very modest fundraising program. It literally consisted of one staff member and virtually no fundraising operations in the colleges and schools. Planned giving, corporate and foundation giving was non-existent. The only program that was raising any funds to speak of was athletics and the Razorback Foundation and that program's success was built around ticket priorities exclusively. Every so often Frank Broyles, the athletics director, would land a major gift for a special building priority. The university endowment was minuscule, and no effort existed to raise funds for the endowment or any other priorities. Nugent's books campaign was one of the very first efforts to raise funds for academics.

Nugent concocted a most unusual name for the campaign. "The Campaign for Books, Incunabula to the Future." I tried my hardest to dissuade him from using the word "Incunabula," which no one would understand, but he was adamant. Incunabula was chosen! I had no idea what it meant, and quickly did some research to discover its meaning. Turns out that incunabula are early printed books, especially one printed before 1501 when the printing press came into widespread use. Who knew? I thought it was a terrible name and knew we would spend the first 30 minutes on a fundraising call explaining its meaning to a possible donor and making them feel ignorant for not knowing the meaning.

We made one embarrassing call on the owner and operator of the Arkansas Gazette, Hugh Patterson. Nugent looked at me and said, "Dave, I bet Mr. Patterson, as a knowledgeable newspaper man, knows what incunabula means?" Patterson, a refined, proud newspaper publisher of Arkansas' largest newspaper replied, "No, I have no idea." I was embarrassed, Paterson was embarrassed, and Nugent proceded to take 30 minutes to explain it. My memory is that we landed a very small gift. Patterson did agree to serve on our volunteer fundraising committee, pretty much in name only.

Frank Broyles served as our campaign chairman, and I had the privilege and pleasure to work with him for a full year, traveling and asking for gifts, literally across the country. One trip we took was to New York City on the Phillips Petroleum corporate jet to make calls.

An executive vice president of the company was an alumnus. Broyles was the ABC Collegiate Football commentator at the time, and we landed a meeting with the president of ABC and even received a nice gift from the company for our books campaign. I developed a friendship with Coach Broyles during that time and found him to be an absolute joy to work with. He was a true gentleman and a great spokesman for the effort. I do think it was a brilliant move that Nugent asked him to chair the campaign. It opened many, many doors for us.

David and Jane with Frank Broyles, UA Athletics Director

While traveling with Coach Broyles I experienced him telling many witticisms. Coach told me that he and his first wife, Barbara, had made a pledge to each other to always attend church on Sundays, if possible, and to always remain thin and not put on weight. "Nothing tastes as good as thin feels," proclaimed Broyles. On one occasion I told Coach that I needed to lose 20 pounds. He responded by saying, "Oh no, no David, just 15!"

Coach and I were going to a campaign event in Ft. Smith, Arkansas, about an hour's drive from Fayetteville. I called Coach and told him I would pick him up at a designated hour to drive to the event. Again, he exclaimed, "No, no, no, David. We will take the plane. Never walk anywhere you can drive and never drive anywhere you can fly," he said. That was Frank Broyles. We climbed aboard the Razorback Foundation plane to Ft. Smith which took about 11 minutes!

A few years later, after I had gone to work for Penn State, Coach called me and asked me to come back to Arkansas and serve as the head of the Razorback Foundation. It was hard to turn him down, but it just wasn't of interest to me. Besides, I was making a much larger salary than he offered, and we had not been at Penn State all that long. I wanted to stay in academic fundraising, but I was deeply honored he thought of me.

The Campaign for Books, despite the strange campaign name, Incunabula, was successful, and we raised all the funds in about seven months. It was a small campaign, but it did give alumni and volunteers a sense that the University of Arkansas could indeed raise funds for academics. The campaign has mostly been lost to history, but there is a plaque in Mullins Library as you enter the front door to the right that heralds the success of the first UA fundraising effort.

During my time at the university, the Arkansas Alumni Association controlled the annual giving program and kept all the funds for their operations. It was an outrageous system, and the academic colleges and programs received no benefit from annual giving from alumni. After much discussion and support from the deans, we wrangled it away from the association and started an annual giving program for the colleges, schools, and academic programs. The first year we raised $172,000 for the colleges and the deans were ecstatic.

It was the beginning of a very modest fundraising effort for the University of Arkansas. We were late into fundraising for public institutions, as many big ten schools had been doing it for many years with great success. The university relied on tuition, fees, and legislative support to pay the bills. After about a year, Nugent let me hire another fundraiser, but it was like pulling teeth. It would be many years until the university took fundraising seriously as an important and necessary function.

Jane and I invited Bill Nugent to our home for dinner one evening. After all, I reported directly to him and felt it was a courtesy to reach out and invite him to a social occasion in our home. Jane fixed a wonderful meal, I picked up wine and flowers for the table and when the agreed upon appointed hour arrived, Nugent didn't show up. I called his home but no answer. I had verified the date with his assistant a few days before the dinner. I suspect busy people forget, but found it unusual that a chancellor with a support staff would make such a faux pas. Jane was unhappy and felt slighted, but we both chalked it up to forgetfulness. However, the next morning I asked Nugent's assistant if it was on his calendar and she said, "Yes, and I reminded him when he left work. Why, did he not show up?"

One of Nugent's staff members was Clara Manning. She seemed to be everywhere he was. She would travel with us on development calls and involved herself in most of my activities raising funds for the university. One day I walked into my office and she was looking through my mail. I decided not to embarrass her by confronting her, but she was deep into my in box looking through my mail and papers when I walked in. I suspected she just wanted to see what I was working on, or just being nosy. Maybe she didn't trust me. In any event, I just let it go and didn't make it an issue.

Clara was an engaging person with a marvelous sense of humor, and I enjoyed being around her. She was very bright and extremely protective of Nugent. Rumors had been circulating for some time that Nugent and his wife were estranged. She occasionally came to university events, and then it seemed, suddenly, you didn't see her around anymore.

Most trips for fundraising Clara would accompany me and Nugent. It was standard practice. I thought it was odd that Clara always showed up when we traveled, but dismissed it as Nugent simply wanting staff around him when he was on the road. Even though I had heard the rumors being spread all over campus, I figured it wasn't any of my business and I chose to never ask Nugent or Clara about their relationship. Besides, Clara was sort of fun to be around, and we seemed to get along fairly well. I enjoyed her sense of humor. She was fun!

In time Nugent divorced his wife and married Clara, much to the shock of the university community. Unfortunately, his divorce from his first wife had not been finalized before he married Clara. The *Gazette*, the statewide newspaper, ran a story that Nugent was married to two women for a 48-hour timeframe.

Later he would resign as chancellor. He went on to have a long and successful career at the University of Illinois Foundation.

I don't think his resignation had too much to do with his matrimony issues, but more his inability to get along with the system administration. It wasn't all his fault, and I felt a little sorry for him.

I liked Nugent, but did not think he was a very effective chancellor. He didn't seem to have a plan or guiding mission for the institution and the two years I worked for him seemed like blind leadership. I never could quite understand what his academic objectives were, and he seemed to skip from one announced project to another with little or no follow-through.

I remember attending a meeting of faculty where he announced out of the blue that he wanted to build a bell tower on campus honoring former faculty and staff for their contributions to the university. He said he wanted to raise private funds to build the bell tower. He had never mentioned it to me before his speech and I was at a loss for words to understand why he wouldn't tell his chief development officer that he wanted private money to build the tower. Several deans asked me what it was all about, and I had to plead ignorance. Of course, the tower was never built and Nugent's idea fell into oblivion. That was Bill Nugent, flying from the seat of his pants without much direction or guidance. Somehow, he must have seen a bell tower on another campus, and decided it might be a good idea for the University of Arkansas. I really don't know where the idea came from.

It's not that I had anything against Nugent, I simply didn't think his leadership was good for the university. I guess the board of trustees and the university system president felt the same way, and

Nugent left the institution. Neither Nugent nor Clara ever said goodbye and just disappeared after his resignation.

Early in his administration Nugent had started a portrait of himself by a prominent artist to be displayed in Old Main upon his retirement, which was tradition. Since he left rather quickly the portrait was never finished until I became chancellor many years later. The artist was still living and had the unfinished portrait in his possession. For historical purposes we thought it important to have the painting finished and displayed in Old Main. I received a very nice telephone call from Bill Nugent thanking me for the gesture. It just seemed the right thing to do regardless of the circumstances surrounding his resignation.

In fairness to Nugent, I do believe his problems at the university were not all his doing. That was a time when the university administration simply could not decide who oversaw the Fayetteville campus, the president of the system or the chancellor. The problem would not be ameliorated until Alan Sugg became president years later and cleared up lines of authority. I will refer to Alan Sugg several times in this book, as he provided excellent leadership to the system. I'm reminded of a quote by Ralph Waldo Emerson, "Every great institution is the lengthened shadow of a single man. His character determines the character of the organization." Sugg made the university system work and provided good stewardship.

Immediately after Nugent's resignation, a search was begun for a new chancellor. From out of the blue emerged the name Dr. Ronald Carrier. He was the current president of James Madison University and had a lengthy Pedigree. Apparently, he was beloved at James Madison and had done a fine job as their CEO.

CHAPTER 12
NEW BOSS – FOR AN HOUR

> *The person who knows* how *will always have a job. The person who knows* why *will always be his boss.*
>
> — *ALANIS MORISSETTE*

James Madison University had seen extraordinary growth in student numbers and the physical plant during Carrier's time as president. He was not among the original candidates for our chancellor, but his name surfaced from University of Arkansas president Jim Martin. Carrier was chosen as the next chancellor. Shortly after the announcement Carrier came to campus to meet with staff and faculty. Accompanying him was his assistant and chief of staff, which many found peculiar that he would bring a staff member. The immediate reaction was that his staff member would be coming to the University of Arkansas also. Carrier gave a speech to the administrative council which was not well received. He started by criticizing the university and bragging about all the things he had accomplished at James Madison. Few people in the meeting were impressed by his words and I think shocked by his criticism of the University of Arkansas.

All of a sudden, the door opened abruptly, and a person entered the room and handed a note to Carrier. Carrier looked up with astonishment and announced that Jim Martin was leaving the university to become the president of Auburn University. There was a hush in the room and people were taken aback and surprised at the announcement. The Auburn search had been kept very quiet, and no one knew Martin was a candidate, or that he even wanted to leave the University of Arkansas. There had been much media attention about Carrier leaving James Madison, and that university's board members had worked very hard to convince him to remain there. In fact, students and faculty had signed petitions encouraging him to turn down the Arkansas job.

Carrier spoke up immediately and said that if Martin was leaving, he was not staying! He quickly left the meeting with his assistant and flew back to James Madison University. Apparently, the board of trustees of James Madison were quite eager to have him back, and he went on to serve that institution as president for several more years.

Thus, I witnessed the shortest tenure of a chancellor in perhaps the history of higher education. It was all bizarre. To this day I can't imagine that Martin would not have told his leading chancellor candidate that he was considering leaving for another presidency. That would seem the most appropriate way to proceed when starting a relationship of trust with one of your most important hires. Sitting close to Carrier, I did overhear him tell the finance VP that he had been promised first class tickets for his return flight. Carrier was back at James Madison by nightfall!

Having been burned in the search for the next chancellor, the decision was made to hire from within. A distinguished history professor, Dr. Willard Gatewood, was named chancellor. Gatewood was a highly respected faculty member and renowned scholar, and his selection was applauded by the faculty. Gatewood had no administrative experience, and after nine months in the job he decided administration was not for him and resigned as chancellor and went back to the faculty. Later, Gatewood told me that he did not like the pressure of being the decision maker and trying to solve all the university's problems. He felt it was affecting his health and just didn't enjoy the job. It was a blow to the university which had experienced turmoil in the chancellor's office from the very beginning.

The university went through a time when several officers of the institution were interim appointments. At an alumni and donor luncheon before a Razorback football game, I made a joke when introducing Jane that she was my "interim wife" after most of the staff had been introduced as "interim." Governor Clinton was in the audience as well as the new president of the university, Ray Thornton, and several staff, faculty and of course alumni. My comment got a huge laugh particularly from Bill Clinton. It probably was not the wisest choice of words, as I heard later that the president of the university was not happy with my comment. I guess he felt as though it reflected on his leadership, having so many staff members in interim positions. His dissatisfaction with my joke was told to me by a member of the board of trustees, who said it was one of the funniest comments he had ever heard. Probably it wasn't very smart on my part, but I have always liked a good joke.

Once again, I had become disillusioned with the leadership of the university and all the interim positions, and decided perhaps it was time to start thinking about another move. I had no idea where I might go, but felt that things at the University of Arkansas were not getting any better and the time had come to move on. Many universities across the country, during that time, had placed the university advancement operations under one vice president or vice chancellor. This was not the case at the University of Arkansas. I always felt that we had no coordination of advancement units that should be working as a team. Years later the university would make that change.

CHAPTER 13
ON THE ROAD AGAIN

> *Making a big life change is pretty scary. But know what's even scarier? Regret.*
>
> — ZIG ZIGLAR

It was quite frustrating to be going in different directions. It did not seem to me that the university was interested in pulling the advancement units together, and my frustration led to me to apply to Penn State University as the vice president for development and university relations. I knew it was probably a long shot, as Penn State was well known as one of America's great public universities. I wasn't at all sure they would hire a 32-year-old from Arkansas to be the chief advancement officer, but I applied for the job anyway.

Much to my surprise I received a telephone call from John Glier who was a fundraising consultant to Penn State and president of the Grenzebach firm in Chicago. John set up a personal interview with me and I thought the interview went well. Truthfully, I didn't have a lot of major gift experience, and felt that would be a real hindrance in taking my application seriously. I came to find out that Penn State had been searching for some time, and no one had emerged as the prime candidate. The current vice president had been dismissed and the advancement unit was somewhat in disarray.

I listed Governor Bill Clinton on my résumé as a reference. The president of Penn State was Bryce Jordan. Jordan called Governor Clinton and they had a long chat about my candidacy. I was told later by a Penn State vice president that Jordan came into his staff meeting elated that he could have a personal call with the governor of Arkansas. No doubt that call with Clinton went a long way to land me the job.

Jordan had come from Texas only a few months earlier and wanted to launch a major capital campaign at Penn State. He was looking for someone who would staff the campaign and get it moving. Much to my amazement, I was invited to campus for an interview. Arkansas was playing in the Liberty Bowl over the holidays, and Jane and I left Memphis and flew to State College, Pennsylvania for the interview. Unusual for Penn State they were not in a bowl game that year and Dr. Jordan thought it the perfect time for me to visit the university.

Jane and I landed in a snowstorm with several inches of snow on the ground. Since I was getting in late in the evening, the university had a car for me upon my arrival. As Jane and I left the airport we encountered a difficult turn on the highway and I came very close to sliding off the snow-covered road into a huge ditch. Fortunately, I was able to keep control of the car and inflicted no damage, but scared both of us to death. It would've been a terrible embarrassment if I had totaled the car or run it into a ditch.

I met all the senior staff members of the university, including, of course, President Jordan. Both Jane and I felt the interview went very well, but had no idea if the job would be offered to me. Jane told me the only thing she knew about Penn State was that Joe Paterno was the football coach.

Jane was a good sport throughout the interview process but when we met for lunch she immediately started crying. She had been with a realtor looking at homes, and couldn't find anything in our price range. In those days we were living paycheck to paycheck and had very little money in savings. I think Jane was sad about the possibility of moving, which was exaggerated by not being able to find a suitable home we could afford. I felt extremely sorry for Jane as I was having anxiety as well over the possibility of leaving our home and family in Arkansas.

A few days after the interview I received a telephone call from Dr. Jordan who offered me the job. We decided the opportunity to join the staff at Penn State at a vice president level at the age of 32 was something we could not pass up. We accepted Dr. Jordan's offer and prepared to move from Fayetteville, Arkansas, the home of my birth, hundreds of miles away to State College, Pennsylvania. I know it was very difficult on Jane to make this move as we were leaving family and dear friends behind. Our daughter Katy was five years old, and our son Brock was only two. It was a tough move to make, and I felt badly for Jane and our two kids. But move we did and never looked back.

PART IV
PENN STATE AND HAPPY VALLEY
1985–1995

May no act of ours bring shame, To one heart that loves thy name. May our lives but swell thy fame, Dear old State, dear old State.

— PENN STATE ALMA MATER

CHAPTER 14
NEW BOSS, NEW ADVENTURE

> *Would you tell me, please, which way I ought to walk from here?"* said Alice. *"That depends a good deal on where you want to get to,"* said the Cat. *"I don't much care where—"* said Alice. *"Then it doesn't matter which way you walk,"* said the Cat.
>
> — LEWIS CARROLL, ALICE'S ADVENTURES IN WONDERLAND

Moving to State College, Pennsylvania and joining the staff of the colossal Pennsylvania State University was a dream come true. Penn State was and still is a phenomenal institution. Today it is one of the finest major public research universities in the nation. The president of the university, Bryce Jordan, had come from the presidency of The University of Texas, Dallas and had previously been the interim president of the Austin campus. He was around 60 years old with major university experience.

I liked Bryce Jordan from the very beginning. He was kind, professional, and engaging. Most people at Penn State, including alumni, parents, members of the board of trustees and faculty also liked Jordan. He had a wonderful smile and amazing personality, and people gravitated to him. He could fill a room immediately upon entering.

The development program had gone through some ups and downs prior to his accepting the presidency. He was looking for somebody to restore confidence in the program. Penn State's development program was much more sophisticated than what we had at Arkansas. They had multiple staff members and were proficient in planned, corporate and foundation giving. Jordan wanted to launch a major multimillion-dollar capital campaign, the first in Penn State history, and made it clear to me during the interview process that he needed a staff person to lead the way.

We arrived in State College, Pennsylvania in March of 1985, and I remember getting a telephone call from Jordan's wife, Jonelle Jordan on Easter Sunday. It was snowing hard and accumulating on the streets, and she called to comfort the new guy from Arkansas, thinking we probably had never seen snow in April.

Jonelle was a lovely person who I would describe as a Southern belle. Everyone liked her, and she spread good cheer throughout the university. She and Bryce Jordan made a formidable couple, and his leadership elevated Penn State to new heights of achievement.

When I accepted the position, I expected to be compensated at a higher level than my salary at Arkansas. I was making around $50,000 a year at Arkansas and considered that to be on the lower end of comparable salaries of chief development officers. When Jordan offered me the job, he said he would pay me $60,000 a year. I was quite surprised that he was lowballing me from the outset. Penn State salaries were and still are confidential, so I was unable to determine the salary structure prior to accepting the job. John Glier advised me the offer was low in his opinion and that I should counter. I did counter with $75,000 and Jordan came back with $65,000—still lower than comparable salaries in the business. John still agreed it was a low-ball offer but advised I accept the salary which could be adjusted after I proved myself. It was a big disappointment, but I tried not to let it bother me and jumped into the job with enthusiasm.

Real estate in State College, Pennsylvania was much more expensive than Fayetteville, and we had a somewhat difficult time finding a home we could afford. With two children we struggled to make ends meet and pay a mortgage that was higher than we were used to. There were so many events at the university we were expected to attend that our babysitting costs were out of sight. But with Jane's incredible ability to stretch a dollar we made it work. It wasn't until years later that I became aware that most of the vice presidents at Penn State were being compensated at a much higher level than me. I don't really know why Jordan offered me such a low salary, but I suspect he felt I didn't have the requisite experience to demand higher compensation. It would be several years later at Penn State before my salary would be adjusted to a more appropriate level.

My first few weeks on the job were difficult ones. I was literally running with my tongue hanging out to try to put together the infrastructure for a big capital campaign. Soon after I arrived at the university, I contracted shingles. Jane and I believe that I was exposed to chickenpox a month or two before we left Fayetteville. Suffice it to say, it was a most unpleasant experience, and the shingles stayed with me for many months. I suppose the stress of starting a new job at an unfamiliar place contributed to my coming down with shingles. I was advised by my doctor to take a few days off and relax, but that simply was not possible. I was trying to prove to myself that I was capable of this job and I was literally working 12- to 15-hour days. On the weekends I would spend most of Saturday in the office and half of Sunday. I felt that was what it would take for me to be successful and show Jordan and others I could handle the job at age 32.

One thing that was much different from my time at any other institution was the abundant resources of Penn State. The physical plant was pristine and everything about the university seemed to suggest money was not a problem. Of course, Penn State had one of the highest tuitions of any public university, but it did not affect enrollment at all. Students flocked to the institution, as well as Penn State's two-year colleges throughout the commonwealth.

One of the first things I had to do at Penn State was to convince

Dr. Jordan that we needed more funds to run the campaign. John Glier was instrumental in helping me make the argument for a larger budget. My division managed the Parents Fund which was producing about $400,000 a year and Jordan allowed me to use those funds to help pay for staffing, travel, and other expenditures.

Bill Schreyer, chairman and CEO of Merrill Lynch, with Brock Gearhart and Coach Joe Paterno.

A major task was to choose a chairperson of the campaign as well as a team of alumni and friends who could help lead the way. After much discussion Jordan decided on Bill Schreyer who at the time was the president and chief operating officer of Merrill Lynch in New York City. Schreyer was a 1948 alumnus of Penn State and a passionate supporter of his alma mater. Jordan and I flew to New York City in the university airplane and met with Schreyer at his Manhattan office. Schreyer readily accepted serving as the chairman of the campaign and said he had only two requirements: First, he wanted to be certain that he would have maximum staff support. I had the feeling, at that point, he wasn't certain a 32-year-old "kid," as he affectionately called me, could provide the staff support he was used to.

He never said anything during that initial meeting about my Arkansas ties, but I suspect he was less than confident that a person from south of the Mason Dixon could deliver.

The second requirement was that Schreyer wanted the acclaimed football coach, Joe Paterno, to be heavily involved in the campaign. We had already decided to ask Paterno to serve on the committee and with Schreyer's persuasion skills he readily agreed to do so.

Bill Schreyer and his wife Joan would become very close friends of ours over the next several years. I could not have asked for a better chairman of the campaign, and Schreyer spent many, many hours working with us to garner financial support. We traveled together all across the country in the Merrill Lynch jet, and were accompanied many times by Joe Paterno. On one trip we went to the U.S. Open practice round at the Olympic Club near San Francisco. Jack Nicklaus was playing in the open and we had the opportunity to meet him. I remember several people waiting to get Nicklaus' autograph but the person the crowd really wanted to meet and get an autograph from was Joe Paterno. There were literally long lines waiting to shake Paterno's hand.

At that time Paterno was one of America's greatest football coaches. He had not only built winning teams, but he had graduated 98 percent of his players. That was unprecedented in college sports, and Paterno developed a reputation for doing collegiate sports the right way. Paterno and I got along famously and spent many hours together on behalf of the campaign. Of course, Paterno knew who he was and could occasionally flex his muscles on any number of issues. But he was a marvelous person who cared deeply about the university and its future.

I remember one call we made on a potential donor. We asked the alumnus to make a gift of $250,000 to an academic program. The person readily agreed to make the gift, but said that he wanted it to go to athletics in honor of Paterno. Joe told the donor that athletics had enough money, and requested he make his gift to an academic program. I was astounded by Paterno's promotion of academics over athletics, and I developed great admiration for him during my time at Penn State. He was the real deal and believed deeply in graduating players and supporting the university. Penn State would name its library after Joe and Sue Paterno and they made very generous gifts to the university over several years.

Often, we would have our campaign meetings in New York City. The conference rooms at the Merrill Lynch world headquarters were outstanding, and Schreyer always rolled out the red carpet when we met. On one occasion we were invited to the American Stock Exchange in lower Manhattan. When the brokers on the floor discovered that Paterno was there, they literally halted trading. Everyone wanted to meet and shake hands with Joe Paterno. He opened many, many doors for us during the effort and served as one of our vice chairmen for the campaign. It was simply fun walking on the streets of New York City with Joe Paterno. Almost everyone would shout out his name and he would always reply with a hearty smile.

Of course, years later it didn't end well for Paterno after the Sandusky scandal. Paterno would become embroiled in one of the worst pedophile scandals in higher education history when coach Jerry Sandusky was convicted of child molestation. Sandusky had been one of Paterno's top coaches.

Some of our campaign meetings were in Princeton, New Jersey, where Merrill Lynch had a training operation for employees. It was a magnificent facility employees called the Merrill Lynch Campus. I read somewhere that Governor Bill Clinton was planning on being in Princeton the very day we were meeting with our campaign committee. I called Clinton's office in Little Rock to see if he might be interested in appearing before our committee which was being held at Scanticon, an elegant conference center close to the Merrill Lynch Campus. To my surprise the governor agreed to stop by and meet committee members. He was accompanied by a couple of staff members and the New Jersey State police. I met his car outside the facility and all the way into the building he asked me questions about the members of the committee.

Governor Clinton had already started thinking about running for president and thought meeting some of America's top corporate executives serving on our committee could be beneficial. Clinton gave a marvelous 20-minute address to our committee and took questions. He opened his remarks by saying he was just in New Jersey checking up on Gearhart. During his speech he told the assembled group that he was not going to wash his hand after shaking hands with Joe Paterno, because his mother would want to shake the hand that shook the hand of Joe. He described his mother as a huge Paterno fan. I think Governor Clinton gained some support, or at least respect, that day from several highly-placed corporate executives.

The author with President Bill Clinton

Members of our campaign committee formed an extremely prestigious group. In addition to Schreyer the chairman, president, and by then CEO of Merrill Lynch, we had two top executives from Johnson & Johnson, a top executive from Goldman Sachs, the chairman and CEO of Saks Fifth Avenue, the chairman of Merck, the CEO of Hershey Foods, the CEO of Hershey Entertainment

Corporation, the CEO of Ameritech, the chairman of Metropolitan Life Insurance Company, the chairman of Stanley Works, the president of Marathon Oil, and many others. It was a great privilege for me to work alongside such a prestigious committee and one of the most gratifying experiences of my life.

David Gearhart, Bill Schreyer, and Jane Gearhart at a Campaign for Penn State committee meeting and dinner.

Bill Schreyer was known for his clever sayings, cliches and quotations. While all may not be original, the following are a few I heard him say, some on more than one occasion:

"Don't sweat the small stuff."

"It's a dumb dog that doesn't bury a bone."

"In my next life I want to be my wife Joan."

"May I have the other half of my first drink? Just add some ice and top it off."

"Let's have a pop. Special Perrier, please." (Cocktail time.)

"Here's to us, good people are hard to find."

"Gearhart, slow down; life's a journey, not a destination."

Bill Schreyer was a wonderful man. I still miss him every day. Our son applied for an internship at Merrill Lynch and Schreyer was helpful in getting him into the program. It led to an offer to work for the company, and eventually a career in wealth management. Before he died in 2011 at age 83, Schreyer had become the largest donor in the history of Penn State. His gift to create an Honors College at Penn State was the pattern we used a few years later when we created one at the University of Arkansas.

The opening gala of the campaign was quite an event. I remember the wife of one of our campaign volunteers commenting at the end of the evening: "Penn State is no longer a cow college." Donald Regan, President Ronald Reagan's chief of staff, was our keynote speaker. Earlier in his career he was the CEO of Merrill Lynch, and Bill Schreyer was able to secure him for our event. A few weeks before, Regan had made some disparaging comments about women, which made it into the media, and there was a small group of demonstrators outside the event venue.

On October 19, 1987, we were holding a campaign executive committee meeting at Merrill Lynch world headquarters in New York City. I could tell something important was happening, as Schreyer was repeatedly interrupted and was asked to step out of the meeting multiple times. After the third time he was called out, he returned and informed us what was happening. The stock market was declining in value by an almost unprecedented level. It would later be called Black Monday, and it became known as one of the worst days in financial history. The Dow Jones Industrial Average lost 22 percent in a single day. By the end of the month, most major exchanges had dropped more than 20 percent. From August 1982 to its peak in August 1987, the Dow Jones Industrial Average rose from 776 to 2,722, including a 44 percent year-to-date rise as of August 1987. Looking back on it today, the market was certainly due for a correction.

Throughout the events of that day, Schreyer remained extraordinarily calm in the face of a market catastrophe. He excused himself for about 30 minutes and when he returned informed us that he had just recorded a video, which would be broadcast on all three networks to calm the waters. Merrill Lynch would also run full page ads in multiple newspapers asking for the public to stay calm and ride out the collapse. It would take two years for the Dow to recover completely, and by September 1989 the market had regained all of the value it had lost in the 1987 crash.

But, of course, that wasn't at all helpful to our multimillion-dollar capital campaign. Gifts slowed during this time, and a few donors asked for an extension on their pledge payments. A very small number canceled their commitments. Not a prime time to be running a major fundraising campaign!

At one of our campaign meetings Bryce Jordan left the meeting early without excusing himself to attend a Mellon Bank board of directors meeting in Pittsburgh. Our campaign meeting included an elegant dinner that evening with additional meetings the next morning. Of course, Schreyer noticed Jordan was not in attendance at the dinner and subsequent meetings and thought he had become ill. When he found out that Jordan left for a Mellon Bank board meeting, he went ballistic. He was upset that Jordan had not told him and upset with me that we had not rescheduled the meetings for a time when he could attend. Of course, I knew nothing about the fact that Jordan had to leave, but it was still most embarrassing. Paul Critchlow, Schreyer's senior staffer, told me it did damage their relationship and I should call Jordan and have him come back to the meetings. Trying to be a good soldier, I did make the call, which made Jordan upset too. He informed me the Mellon meetings were part of his compensation and he would not return. Not too much fun being in between two powerhouses!

The campaign ended up being very successful, despite the events of October 19, 1987, and we went over our goal by several million dollars. We had many multi-million-dollar gifts and even a few $10 million gifts which was unusual for the 1980s. We had naming gifts for two of our colleges, the College of Science and the College of Business.

I suppose I worked harder than I had ever worked on any effort up to that point during my Penn State years, and I look back on those days with much pride and accomplishment. We added substantially to the endowment, in addition to endowing multiple chairs, professorships, and scholarships. Jordan was very pleased with the results and wrote me several notes of congratulations, as did campaign committee members.

Toward the end of the campaign, we started planning for a concluding gala to honor our benefactors and volunteers. This happened when the economy in Pennsylvania was going through hard times, and the senior vice president of the university told Jordan that he didn't think we should spend funds on what he described as a "big party." His name was Steve Garban and he liked to throw his weight around. Of course, my view was that we needed to do something to thank our many volunteers who had worked very hard on the campaign. We also needed to herald the university and gain some high-level public relations benefit from such an event. I had appointed a committee to plan an evening celebration to thank and congratulate our donors and volunteers, and they had been working for many months to put together an appropriate program. Everything had been planned out to the letter. We had set aside private funds to pay for the concluding gala.

One month before the event Jordan, influenced by senior VP, Steve Garban, pulled the plug on our plans. He called me to his office with Garban present and told me that he didn't like the optics of spending money for a "party." I knew where that language came from and was furious. The senior VP had not lifted a finger during the campaign, and I knew him to be jealous of my relationship with trustees and benefactors. I made it crystal clear that I thought he was interfering unnecessarily with my division and thought he should mind his own business. He told me that I just wanted a big event to shine the spotlight on myself. I was furious and, unfortunately, showed my anger in front of the president.

Jordan was not happy with my reaction. What bothered me most was the timing of the decision. We had caterers lined up, as well as many other plans that had come to fruition through months of planning and all of it was to be canceled. I guess my disappointment resonated with Jordan as he agreed to allow us to produce a much smaller event than we had planned. It worked out OK, but certainly not what we had hoped for. Some of our contracts with caterers could not be canceled and it ended up costing wasted dollars.

It was a lesson in bait and switch, as well as a lesson on the real importance of private gift support for a major university by the old guard. That same senior VP who disrupted the concluding campaign event, told me many weeks later, and in front of a benefactor, that endowment was not all that important to a public university. I was incensed. What a stupid, ignorant comment.

Steve Garban would retire from Penn State and run for a board of trustees slot. He would later become the chairman of the board of Penn State, and held that position during the Sandusky fiasco. He was the chairman of the board when his friend and mentor, Joe Paterno was fired. His former boss, Graham Spanier, was also fired on his watch. Garban was highly criticized in the media for the way he handled the scandal and his omission in keeping the full board informed of the Sandusky tragedy. Many commentators believed it was a gross conflict of interest to have a board chair who had worked for the university president. Garban would later resign from the board under intense pressure.

Several people were heroes in the Campaign for Penn State. One of them was Roger Williams, one of the best writers and communicators I have ever known, with a brilliant mind. He oversaw university relations at Penn State and handled all our campaign communications. After I left the university, he went to Georgetown University to be a vice president. Our paths would cross again when I invited him to come to the University of Arkansas to do some consulting. Eventually I was able to convince him to work for the University full time, and he became our associate vice chancellor for university relations for five years. More about that later.

Another person who has remained a very close friend is Dave Lieb. I met Dave when he was a graduate student at Penn State in his early 20s. After he got his graduate degree, we hired him full-time, and he eventually became the chief development officer at Penn State and is still there as of 2022. Dave is a class act and one of my dearest friends. We've stayed close for over 25 years. He knows development better than anyone, and has been recruited by several major universities to be their vice president for development. He loves Happy Valley and turned down all the offers. He and his lovely wife, Sharon, have three beautiful children, and they made a conscious decision to keep them in State College close to family. I admire Dave greatly for putting family first.

I also had an extraordinary assistant during my time at Penn State who managed my office. Sandy Thompson was efficient, thoughtful, caring and very savvy. She was one of the best assistants I ever had in any job. She made my appointments and kept my calendar and handled all the voluminous mail. This was before email had become commonplace and it required much more work by the office staff. Sandy worked for Penn State for over 30 years. Jane and I still stay in touch with Sandy and her husband, Jeff. Classy people.

Another person who was critical to our campaign success was Bernie Prince. Bernie handled all the logistics for the campaign and was a godsend. Unfortunately, I have not stayed in touch with Bernie through the years, and last I heard she lives in Washington D.C. When I consulted for the American Farmland Trust she was working there, and I got to spend some quality time with her during that time.

Two other people critical to the success of the Campaign for Penn State were Clay and Sandy Edwards. Years later I would recruit the Edwards to the University of Arkansas and benefit from their collective leadership and wisdom.

Another person involved in the campaign was Peter B. Weiler. Jane and I became close to him and his wife Karen during our time at Penn State. He was the head of the Alumni Association, a position I hired him into. Peter would go on to be vice president of several universities, Ohio State, New Hampshire, and Maryland. He was an Iron Man competitor and participated in several of those competitions in Hawaii. The last one was when he was in his late 50s. He was athletic, engaging, an excellent public speaker and very presentable, and we developed a close friendship. Years later and most tragically, he had a horrible, life-changing biking accident that left him a quadriplegic, and he subsequently died of those injuries in 2019. He was only 64.

Bill Clinton had announced for president and we invited him to come to campus. His schedule did not permit a visit at that time, but Jane and I did travel to Philadelphia to hear him speak. He gave us a big hug and suggested we invite Hillary to campus. We did and she came. I introduced her to a huge crowd in front of Old Main. One of her advance people told me later it was the largest crowd Hillary had enjoyed up to that time. Her brother played football at Penn State for Joe Paterno and he accompanied her to the event. It was a great day for the university, although some of our Republican benefactors and volunteers expressed slight annoyance. Hillary gave a rousing speech to loud cheers from the assembled crowd, mostly students and liberal faculty. Joab Thomas, university president at the time, did not attend Hillary's speech. He told me he was busy and besides, Bill Clinton did not have a ghost of a chance to win the presidency. I learned later that Thomas was playing golf.

We were in Washington D.C. in 1991 for a capital campaign steering committee meeting. We would hold committee meetings in Washington D.C. or New York City as well as State College. First Lady Hillary Clinton invited us to the White House to take a tour. Most of the campaign committee members decided to go, even the Republicans. We funded a scholarship in honor of her father who attended Penn State, and presented it to her that day at the White House. Hillary was very pleased and most gracious. One person who decided to sit out the tour was Bill Schreyer. Bill had been a huge contributor to George Bush's campaign, was on his re-election committee, and was also slated to be the Ambassador to the Court of St. James had Bush defeated Clinton. Bill was his usual thoughtful self about our venture to the White House, but just couldn't stomach the adventure to see Hillary.

Penn State had a sizable alumni base of Jewish heritage. Coming from Arkansas, that was new to me. Jane and I developed close friendships with many Jewish alumni and attended a few bar mitzvahs and Jewish ceremonies during our time at Penn State.

On one occasion I was asked to come to a dinner that would be a major fundraiser for a Jewish philanthropy. I was told I would find it to be a little different from fundraising dinners I was accustomed to.

That was an understatement. After dinner a person stood up with a microphone and said, "My friends, it is time to lock the doors and raise some money and see your generous spirit." He started calling out names as person after person rose to pledge a major gift to the project. That evening the assembled group raised over $3 million. I was absolutely astounded. I had never witnessed anything like it before and it was an education on how some Jewish groups raise money. I was shocked at the total generosity by many, many folks in attendance that evening.

In the middle of the campaign Penn State went through a terrible public relations issue, which I thought could have been handled much, much better. Penn State has always had a very small Black enrollment, 3.6 percent in 1988. At the time Penn State was under a federal court order to reach 5 percent as quickly as possible. The Black students were becoming frustrated with the administration, believing it to be disinterested in the African-American population and just giving lip service to their complaints.

Jordan agreed to meet with representatives of the Black students, and then reversed himself. It was reported to me that the university's general counsel convinced Jordan that such a meeting was unwise and might even be personally dangerous for Jordan. I advised in the strongest possible terms for Jordan to accept the meeting which seemed to be the only way to calm the waters. I could tell Jordan didn't like my "interference" and shut me out of any further meetings on the issue. Even though I was supposed to be in charge of public relations, that seemed to be in name only to Jordan and the senior leadership. I was selfishly very concerned that such poor publicity would hinder our efforts to raise funds, particularly from minority alumni. It seemed to me the president of the university had a duty and obligation to meet with Black students and hear their issues.

On April 8, 1988 a large group of Black students engaged in a sit-in in the administration building, Old Main. They occupied the president's office and stayed there overnight. Negotiations by senior officers broke down and Jordan never did agree to meet with the students.

To this day I believe he was afraid for his safety. At one point there were close to 150 Black student protesters in the building, most crammed into the president's office. They defecated on the floor and sink and soiled the furniture. Then the decision was made to call in the state police and multiple arrests were made.

Over 75 police participated in the arrests of students. The police were decked out in riot gear, batons, shields and helmets. It looked like the storm troopers had arrived in Happy Valley. Some of the students left peacefully when the police arrived but dozens had to be dragged out of the building forcibly by state police. At one point over 300 students, Black and white were standing outside the building shouting jeers at the police. Some faculty joined them. It was an awful scene that was played out on national and statewide media for weeks. The students were also told that, besides being arrested and facing potential charges criminally, they could also face charges under the student code of conduct and potentially be expelled.

In the aftermath a number of senior faculty were extremely critical of the administration for using what some called Gestapo tactics. The state newspaper editorial pages were not kind to Jordan and criticized him for not agreeing to meet with the students and hear their demands. He pushed back, saying other officers had met with them to no avail.

I believed in my heart the entire ordeal could have been prevented had cooler heads prevailed. The truth was, the decision to forcibly remove the students was made by a very small number of senior staff, none of whom had ever had any dealings with the demands of Black students—or dealings in general—had never met with them previously, and did not know the first thing about their sincere issues and concerns. The general counsel was mostly concerned about appearing tough-minded before the trustees and convinced Jordan that the use of force was required.

I learned that day a president should always have the benefit of his or her lawyers weighing in on any issue of substance. However, the president should not always take their advice if he or she truly believes the advice is in error. Lawyers have a way of weighing in on matters that are not always of a legal nature, and use the law to their advantage. A president needs to know when the general counsel has overstepped the boundaries of legal advice and common sense.

I have always thought the use of force in a situation like that should be the absolute last resort. Jordan should have met with the Black students, and I personally lost some respect for him that day. I also think he should have involved his entire cabinet in the decision making rather than two or three people—all white males.

Years later Penn State would face another very serious crisis when a former football coach, Jerry Sandusky, was accused of pedophilia. Having witnessed a closed-minded administration in the past, being run by good old boys who had been in their positions since the beginning of time, I can truly understand how that fiasco could happen. While certainly different circumstances the same scenario played out. All of the decisions were being made by a very small number of senior folks who had been at the institution for years. Most of them, other than the president, Graham Spanier, had been at the university for over 30 years. Their advice was introspective and did not have the clarity of judgment that people who had been at other schools would surely have. Their experiences were defined by a career at one place, which really was no experience at all. Spanier relied on their expertise and closed-minded thinking to his demise.

After the conclusion of the major capital campaign, we decided to launch an effort to build a basketball arena and convocation center. The existing basketball facility was woefully inadequate for the alumni and student base. We were charged with the responsibility of raising $25 million to match an appropriation from the Pennsylvania legislature. We used some cutting-edge techniques in fundraising, including video mailings to major donors, followed by visits or phone calls.

We also got Pepsi to make a major gift for the arena, in exchange for signing a contract for the exclusive use of Pepsi products on campus and support for multiple projects from the Pepsi Foundation. It was one of the earliest Pepsi/Coke bidding wars in soft drink history. Several institutions would follow our lead throughout the country, including Arkansas many years later.

One dean who was very much opposed to the effort to build an arena was James Moeser. Moeser spoke against the project, and made it difficult to navigate getting approval to begin the fundraising. I resented his opposition and it hurt our relationship. He believed other campus projects were more important than what he characterized as a basketball building. Perhaps he was correct, but the decision had been made that we would proceed with the project. I tried, unsuccessfully, to convince him we had just finished a massive campaign for academic programs and Penn State desperately needed a new activities facility. Moeser would go on to become chancellor of the University of Nebraska and later The University of North Carolina. For a brief moment he made my job very difficult. The campaign was most successful, due in large part to the Pepsi gift.

CHAPTER 15
OFF COURSE

> *Adventure is worthwhile in itself.*
>
> — AMELIA EARHART

About midway through the campaign, something happened that soured me to some extent with Bryce Jordan. I look back on it now and realize that I was probably immature in how I handled the situation. The campaign was going along very well, and we had raised several major gifts. I felt Jordan was happy with my leadership and our relationship seemed quite strong. I liked him very much and I think he enjoyed working with me. He would brag about the campaign in every speech he gave.

Penn State was in a football bowl game almost every year during the campaign. Jane and I had been invited to be a part of the official party for the bowl games each year, and it was an exciting time to be at the university. We held many development events at the bowls, and used it as a cultivation time for prospective donors, alumni, and friends.

One particular year Penn State was asked to participate in a bowl game that didn't provide as many resources to pay for the trip as other larger bowls provided. I received a memorandum from President Jordan, which informed me that I would be excluded from the official party, even though Jane and I had been included in all previous years. Jordan did say we could attend the bowl and have our expenses handled by the Penn State Alumni Association, but would not be official party members, and needed to handle our own arrangements. Basically that meant we would not be invited to official bowl functions or events. He asked me to talk with the leadership of the alumni association to find my own funding.

Both Jane and I were very surprised by the memorandum and, quite frankly, I was disappointed and even hurt. We'd had a great deal of success in the campaign, and I knew Jordan was pleased with my commitment to the university. I simply could not understand why he would decide Jane and I were not worthy to be a part of the official party like other officers of the institution. He did, of course, give us permission to attend the bowl, but I had to find my own financing to make the trip. I was embarrassed, angry, and felt like a second-class citizen. As I look back on it now, it was perhaps childish, immature thinking on my part, and I should have just sucked it up and kept quiet.

During those years the athletics department reported not to the president but to the senior vice president for finance and operations. The person who held that job was a former football player for Joe Paterno. It was the same Steve Garban who had interfered with our concluding campaign event. It was a strange arrangement: At most institutions the athletics director reported to the president. My intelligence told me the senior vice president made all the decisions on who would be members of the official party, and advised Jordan that we should be excluded. The official party would fly in a jet with the team to the ball game and be entertained at the official functions. Jane and I would have to find our own way to the bowl and were not invited to participate in any of the official functions.

I didn't handle our exclusion with grace. I went to see Jordan and told him of my disappointment. He did not handle it well either and told me I was being childish. Perhaps he was right. But I was so hurt that he did not consider me one of the senior people at the university that I simply couldn't get over what I considered to be a real slight if not a slap in the face. Our campaign had been most successful, and I felt certain Jordan had been pleased with my leadership. I enjoyed a very good relationship with the board of trustees and major benefactors.

Benefactors began to call me with questions about official events at the bowl game. I had no information, and had to tell them we were not a part of the official party. I was embarrassed.

I told Jordan that Jane and I had decided we would not attend the bowl, and instead we would return home to Arkansas during the holidays. Jordan was very upset with me and told me so. No doubt I had damaged my relationship with my boss. I did believe the financial officer of the university made the actual decision, and Jordan just carried it out. I was told by another highly-placed trustee that the senior vice president was jealous of my relationship with trustees and didn't want me around trustees at the bowl.

But that didn't make it any better in my mind. I had been a loyal trooper for Jordan and helped make him a great success in fundraising. I had built strong relationships with donors and members of the board of trustees, and developed close relationships and friendships with many of them. To rub salt in the wound, several leadership trustees assumed I would be in the official party and reached out to Jane and me to have dinner or lunch while attending the bowl. In addition, if you are a member of the official party, your children of high school age and below also could attend at no cost and ride on the charter plane. No bowl game this year for our kids. If we attended, we would have to pay their way or leave them behind and find sitters for Brock and Katy, especially difficult during the holidays. My kids had been excluded from the bowl game this year. That angered me even more.

We did not attend the bowl game and spent the holidays in Fayetteville. Not long after returning to State College from Fayetteville I got a telephone call from a headhunter. The person wanted to know if I had any interest in leaving Penn State and becoming the vice president for university advancement at Rice University in Houston, Texas. The salary was three times what I was making at

Penn State and the perquisites very appealing. Rice was and is a very prestigious private institution, heavily endowed, and I was flattered my name came up. I agreed that I would explore the position.

On the invitation of the president of Rice University, I visited the campus and met with senior officers. If offered the job, Jane and I would have to move to Houston. We really had no interest in doing that, and truly loved Penn State. Jane was very much opposed to my considering a move, especially to hot and humid South Texas. While Jane was also hurt at being excluded from the official party for the bowl game, she has always been much more capable of handling those kinds of disappointments than me. She would've preferred that I just let the matter go, but that was not part of my DNA. I thought to myself, maybe Rice University would appreciate my talents more than Penn State.

I was made to believe by the Rice University president that I was their first choice. I came home and told Jane it looked like I was going to be offered the job at a considerable increase in salary. Jane was not happy. She loved State College, and our kids did as well and she did not want to move. But I was prepared to move if need be.

I went to see Jordan and told him I was giving serious consideration to moving to Houston and working for Rice University. He was taken aback and quite angry with me, and he asked if the bowl decision had anything to do with seeking another job. I told him I was over the issue but, yes, it did make me wonder if another institution would appreciate me more. I was becoming too bold with my boss.

Even though I wasn't sure I would accept the Rice offer, I decided to play it out and see how Jordan would react. I was taking a big gamble, and knew it might mean moving to Houston, Texas. Again, I think it hurt my relationship with my president. We were in the middle of a capital campaign, which was going very well, and he could not understand why I would want to abandon the effort. I also told Jordan I felt like a second-class citizen. At Penn State there were vice presidents and senior vice presidents. I never really thought there was much difference until the bowl episode when it occurred to me that I was definitely a second-class citizen. That made me even angrier. Jordan asked me what it would take to keep me, at Penn State and I told him the major consideration was my status as a vice president as opposed to senior vice president. I also told him I was underpaid and the salary at Rice was three times what I was making at Penn State. John Glier had also told me about the salaries of development personnel at other Big Ten universities. They were considerably higher than my current salary. At the meeting Jordan made no promises, and I left there thinking that moving to Houston might just become a reality. Mainly, I felt Jordan had been taking advantage of me by not paying me what I felt I was worth, and what the market bore out.

Bill Schreyer had become a dear friend. He was also on the board of trustees. I had listed him as a reference, and he got a call from the Rice president. I had decided not to tell him he might get a call from Rice or that I had applied. He expressed great disappointment, and said there was no way I could leave in the middle of the campaign.

About two days after my conversation with Schreyer I was asked to come to the president's office. Jordan was upbeat and expressed none of the disappointment in me that he had during our previous meeting. It was like he was a different person. He said he had decided to give me a salary increase and change my title to senior vice president for development and university relations. I was very gracious and thanked him for his consideration, and he said he would give me a contract, in addition to the title change and the increase in salary.

Bill Schreyer never told me he had called Jordan and other board members about my potential exit from Penn State, but I heard from another board member that he had done so. Apparently, several board members called Jordan at the behest of Schreyer.

When I talked to Schreyer next, I alluded to his involvement, and all he would say was he didn't want me to leave Penn State. He also said he did not think that the higher administration had treated me very well regarding compensation. He fessed up that my salary was much lower than other officers, and when he discovered that, he was upset and told Jordan and other trustees he thought I should be better compensated.

I suspect he put a great deal of pressure on Jordan and I always felt from that day on that my relationship with my president had been badly damaged. I completely understood why, and maybe I should have kept my mouth shut. I had not asked Schreyer to intervene, but in my heart of hearts knew that he would probably do so.

Interestingly, Jordan decided he had to make two other people on the staff senior vice president if he made me one. Title inflation was rampant. I got what I wanted, but at a tremendous cost. From that day forward, some of the other senior vice presidents looked upon me as an intruder. Particularly the finance senior VP who had excluded me and my family from the bowl game. The only one who was kind, thoughtful, and supportive was the senior vice president of the Hershey Medical Center: Dr. Mac Evarts was genuinely happy for me and I appreciated his reaction.

About halfway through my tenure at Penn State I had a personnel issue, which affected me greatly. I had recruited a development officer who worked for me, both at Hendrix College and the University of Arkansas, and offered him the job of associate vice president at Penn State. We had developed a friendship during our time at those previous institutions and I considered him to be a close friend. When I left Arkansas for Penn State, he went to the University of Missouri as associate vice president.

I was looking for people who I could trust to help me launch the major campaign at Penn State. As I look back on it now with the benefit of hindsight, I probably made a serious error in recruiting a close friend to come work for me for the third time.

He and his wife, and Jane and I further developed our friendship while at Penn State and socialized together frequently. Probably not a good idea. After working for me for three years at Penn State, he was recruited to be the vice president of another institution. Because we were close friends, I don't think he knew how to extricate himself from Penn State and maintain our friendship. For some reason, unknown to me to this day, he went to my president and told him that I was difficult to work for, and he was leaving because of me. President Jordan called me to his office and told me I needed to get rid of him immediately because he was not loyal. Jordan made it clear he wanted the staff member out as soon as possible. I complied with Jordan and sent my associate packing.

I suppose everyone wants absolute loyalty from their staff members and it was very hard for me to understand why this friend and colleague would badmouth me to my president. To make a long story short, it ended our friendship and bothered me for many months. I take some of the blame, and perhaps I was too hard on him during the time we were trying to get the Campaign for Penn State up and running. I regretted losing my friend and still do. It taught me a lesson that hiring your friends may not be the best policy. It was a painful time for me, and it would take a later similar episode before I would learn not to hire friends.

We had so many major gifts during our campaign. One gift, though, was unique and particularly stands out. Thomas Hallowell was a wealthy gentleman from Philadelphia. He was on the Penn State board of trustees. Although he was a Swarthmore graduate, he adopted Penn State and was a benefactor. He owned a steel manufacturing business and made a lot of money. Hallowell owned an estate in Philadelphia he called Deerfield. He had planted 10,000 azalea plants on the estate which included a beautiful home and 50 acres of prime real estate. He was a dear man.

Mr. Hallowell and I became good friends and I started cultivating him for a large gift to the university. I visited him multiple times over the next two years. One thing I came to realize in my time at Penn State was that major gifts require months and even years of cultivation. Building trust between the development officer and the prospect is the absolute key to success. Our modus operandi was to head to lunch after I arrived at his mansion at Deerfield. We would load into his huge Mercedes and he would speed to the nearest McDonald's. At one point I noticed he was going 80 miles an hour on the backroads of Philadelphia! He scared me to death with his driving. He would always order the same thing and duplicate it for me: small hamburger, diet coke, and an ice cream sundae.

Hallowell wanted to give Deerfield to Penn State as an arboretum for use by our substantial College of Agriculture. The senior officers of the university, as well as the general counsel, did not want the gift to be kept by Penn State in perpetuity, and wanted to be able to dispose of the property when the need arose. Hallowell agreed to that stipulation after many months of negotiation. He made the gift along with an endowment for its upkeep. His wife was opposed to the gift but signed the deed of gift under pressure from Mr. Hallowell.

Later, after Hallowell died from a long bout with cancer, and much to my regret, the university decided to sell the property back to Mrs. Hallowell for a considerable amount. The proceeds were placed in an endowment for scholarships in the Hallowells' name. I never felt comfortable about the transaction, as I knew it was not what he wanted. But owning and keeping the property as an arboretum was impractical, at least in the eyes of the administration.

In those days the university contracted with a local law firm to handle all the legal work for the institution. Some trustees had called for the creation of a general counsel's office so the university would not experience such exorbitant legal fees. It wouldn't happen for several more years. I always found it curious that every member of the firm drove a BMW or Mercedes and lived in pricey homes! The general counsel was not an employee of the institution, but attended all the president's staff meetings and was involved in every major decision of the university. Seemed a little bizarre to me that a private citizen would attend confidential policy meetings. That arrangement would change many years later, when a new president decided to end the relationship with the local law firm and hire an in-house general counsel.

In 1990 Bryce Jordan decided to retire. Before he left, he renewed my contract for another five years to protect me should the new president want a change. I learned later that Bill Schreyer orchestrated that decision.

At the time I admired Bryce Jordan very much. Except for the bowl issue, we got along well, and he would confide in me on university issues that were bothering him. I thought he had been a great president and my views were similar to most everyone else's. However, he was more like a Texas politician, as Bill Schreyer said to me one day. I could see that too. Jordan always took care of himself first and foremost!

After he left the presidency, his wife developed Alzheimer's. The disease was fast moving, and Bryce Jordan decided to institutionalize her. They had moved back to Dallas and built a home. It was a tragic situation and very sad time.

I was at home in State College one evening watching TV with a big roaring fire and glass of wine when the phone rang. It was a prominent member of the Penn State board of trustees. The board member asked me if I was sitting down, and then proceeded to tell me that Bryce Jordan was getting remarried. I didn't know Jonelle Jordan had died, and I was told she hadn't. Jordan had come to the realization that his wife, Jonelle, was not getting any better and had severe dementia, and he should find a way to live his remaining years to the fullest. He decided he would divorce Jonelle and remarry. Naturally, he would pay all the bills for his wife's institutionalization, but he felt there was no reason he shouldn't live a full life, just because his spouse was suffering from dementia.

I suppose a lot of medical experts would advise such a course of action, and Jane and I have certainly known other cases similar to Jordan's. It is not for me to judge, but my old-fashioned concepts of marriage left me disappointed in Jordan's decision. My conscience would have never allowed me to take such an action, but then again it is hard to stand in someone else's shoes.

Then the board member told me Jordan would be marrying his former assistant, Carol Herrmann. She was a very competent person and had served Jordan as his administrative assistant. Carol was married to Bob Herrmann but would be seeking a divorce. Carol was one of the people who Jordan had made a senior vice president at the same time as me. She was really an office manager who handled the president's correspondence, appointments, and speech writing. Just a few years earlier she was a proofreader in the office of university relations. She had a meteoric rise.

Apparently, the marriage of Carol and Jordan did not move forward because of the objections of her children, who were dramatically opposed to the divorce and marriage.

Jordan did divorce his wife and remarry someone other than Carol, a reporter for the local State College newspaper.

As I just said, not for me to judge. But it did make me realize that your heroes can have feet of clay.

The whole episode reminds me of the Bible passage in Daniel 2:41-43: "Just as you saw that the feet and toes were partly of baked clay and partly of iron, so this will be a divided kingdom; yet it will have some of the strength of iron in it, even as you saw iron mixed with clay. As the toes were partly iron and partly clay, so this kingdom will be partly strong and partly brittle. And just as you saw the iron mixed with baked clay, so the people will be a mixture and will not remain united, any more than iron mixes with clay."

CHAPTER 16
ANOTHER NEW BOSS

> *Take lack of candor. ... I'm not talking about boldface lying, but a tendency to withhold information. That behavior is far more common, and it frustrates teams and bosses to no end.*
>
> — JACK WELCH

The search for a new president operated efficiently and rather quickly. The board of trustees took total control with very little input from the faculty, staff, or students. Jane and I heard rumors that Jay Oliva, chancellor of New York University at the time, was being considered and was the front runner. Shortly after the rumor circulated Oliva accepted the higher office of the presidency at NYU. The board of trustees went to its next candidate, Joab Thomas. Thomas was Harvard educated and had served as chancellor of North Carolina State University and then president of The University of Alabama. He had made headlines with his replacement of Bear Bryant as well as the athletics director; neither appointment lasted very long. He apparently got in trouble with his board over issues in athletics.

The first time I met Joab and Marly Thomas I was not overwhelmed. They were interesting people. As first lady of Penn State, Marly wasn't the warmest of people. I remember on one occasion she became very upset with the staff because she didn't like the holiday card they had created for her use. It was hard to satisfy Marly. I didn't think she had much of a sense of humor.

There were a lot of rumors that followed Thomas to Penn State from his time at Alabama. Most of the rumors had to do with athletics and the replacement of Bear Bryant. That seems to be standard procedure when a new sheriff is in town and I discounted the rumors as merely gossip.

Shortly after the Thomas's arrival, one of the trustees of the university told me Joab Thomas had been hired to be a laissez-faire president after the phenomenal growth years under Bryce Jordan. I found that comment to be incredulous, as I knew very well that institutions that don't move forward will most assuredly move backward. The Jordan years had built so much goodwill and incredible institutional progress; the thought of taking the foot off the pedal was counterintuitive to me.

Early in the Thomas administration I concluded that the comment was accurate. While I seemed to get along reasonably well with Thomas, he was more interested in the status quo than continuing to build the institution. We had five years of passive growth, but apparently that was what the board of trustees may have asked for.

Penn State had operated administratively as a good old boy network. The institution was run by three or four senior folks, alumni of Penn State, who made all the decisions. They had all been at the university for over 30 years. It was very much a closed environment. If you did not graduate from Penn State, you were looked upon as an outsider. All the major decisions were made behind closed doors by the same long-standing administrators. I often thought perhaps Jordan, and then maybe Thomas, might change things but they both fell into the same old pattern, allowing these few officers to control most everything. It was very much a syndrome of "you scratch my back and I'll scratch yours." Nothing much changed during the Jordan era. Nothing was going to change during the Thomas administration.

I remember a conversation with the provost at the time, Dr. Bill Richardson. He was overlooked to be president after Jordan retired. He would later go on to a very distinguished career as president of Johns Hopkins University. He told me one day that he completely agreed with my feelings about the mentality of the "insiders" grip on the institution, and he had experienced it throughout his time at Penn State. He was supposed to be the number two person at the university, but it didn't work that way. He had become frustrated as well, and believed in-house breeding had greatly hurt the university for many years. I feel confident that the in-bred senior vice presidents had a lot to do with his not being offered the Penn State presidency and subsequently leaving the university for greener pastures.

I worked for Thomas for five years, and even though we never had a sour word during that time, I really didn't enjoy working for him. Thomas was a terrible communicator and you never knew where he stood on a particular issue. He played his cards very close to his chest and it was difficult to make any progress on his watch. Just like his wife, he also had an air of superiority about him. I suspected it was his three degrees from Harvard. He was "sour and dour" as one trustee told me.

Joab Thomas was a scratch golfer. I've only known a few. To be that good you must play and practice all the time. Thomas did! Most days he would head to the golf course in the late afternoon to play nine holes by himself or practice at the driving range. I think he had an addiction to golf. On one occasion he was playing in a university sponsored golf tournament and won an automobile by hitting a hole-in-one. I was asked by the tournament sponsors to ask him to turn down the car as it would look like a conflict of interest. I debated what would be the right thing to do. I concluded that he should not accept the car. Then I chickened out and never said anything to him. I figured "not my rodeo!" He kept the car.

When Joab Thomas decided to retire after a five-year stint, I was gleeful. He and his wife had peculiar personalities. Besides, I didn't feel the institution was really progressing under his leadership. My saving grace was my close personal relationship with several trustees, including Bill Schreyer who had become chairman of the board.

Another trustee who I was close to was Mimi Barash Coppersmith. She owned a local advertising agency and was the first female board chair. Mimi had a marvelous sense of humor and was very outgoing. She always told the truth no matter what, even if some of her male counterparts didn't like it. She won election as chairperson by one vote. With some secret politicking, I assisted measurably with her election. She didn't let the "good old boys" push her around and naturally I loved that about her. As of 2022, Mimi is still going strong and almost 90 years young. She recently wrote a book about her many life experiences. We still exchange holiday cards.

Perhaps, looking for an escape from the humdrum leadership in 1992 I applied and was selected to be a Fulbright Scholar. My assignment was the UK, working at Merton College, Oxford University. It was a four-month Fulbright, and I was given a leave of absence from Penn State and headed off to Oxford, England.

Oxford claims to be the oldest university in the English-speaking world. Merton claims to be the oldest college at Oxford and formed the model for other colleges, both at Oxford and Cambridge alike. At that time, Oxford University was engaged in a capital campaign which was to include all the colleges. My task was to assist the college in firmly establishing a development program. I left State College a month early and the family followed a month later. My friend, David Lieb, came over before my family and we did a dry run to European capitals before the extended family arrived.

The experience at Oxford University was wonderful for our entire family. Merton College gave us a flat to live in, which was plenty large enough for the family as well as guests who visited us during our time abroad. Pat and my mom and Jane's parents, along with my brother Doug visited us in Oxford and we toured Europe. The kids were exposed to the European capitals at a very young age. Brock was 10 years old, and Katy 13, and they remember our sojourn very well. We explored Rome, Paris, London, Naples, Berlin and took side trips to see Stonehenge and other places of interest. We visited Runnymede and saw where the Brits had donated an acre of land in memory of John F. Kennedy. We also saw where the Magna Carta was signed and Jane was particularly enamored with that trip.

Bill Schreyer, of course, knew we were spending a summer at Oxford university and invited us to the tennis tournament at Wimbledon. I later learned that each ticket cost $10,000 where we had prime seats watching the tournament. As always, Bill and Joan Schreyer were the perfect hosts and we had dinner at several of the top restaurants in London.

The headmaster at Merton College was Dr. John Roberts, a distinguished historian and educator. One of his many books was "The History of the World." Who writes a history of the world? He gave me a signed copy and I even read it. I found it interesting but laborious. It was painful at more than 800 pages! We invited Roberts to come to Penn State and give a lecture which was attended by a huge crowd of faculty and staff, as well as local alumni.

After five years of Joab Thomas's leadership I was getting restless. I knew I would not progress any further at Penn State, and started thinking about new opportunities. A new president, Graham Spanier, chancellor of the University of Nebraska–Lincoln, had been elected by the board of trustees and I thought it a good time to make a break.

I was very, very proud of the accomplishments at Penn State. For the most part my team and I had built a powerhouse advancement program. We had been recognized nationally by our trade organization, the Council for Advancement and Support of Education (CASE) in three different years as the best advancement program in the nation! We had quadrupled gift support in a short time frame, and I felt good about my contributions. A Pittsburgh newspaper ran a very complimentary editorial about the campaign, as did the local paper.

We competed against some of the biggest advancement programs in the nation. The University of Michigan, The Ohio State University, and the University of Florida all had first-class advancement programs. But it was our program at Penn State that won the grand award three times in a row. CASE would later do away with the grand award, most likely because of jealousies that cropped up because we had won it so many times. That put our program on the map nationally, and Penn State appeared on the cover of several trade magazines heralding our advancement prowess.

The recognition for our excellent staff was well deserved, but it did lead headhunters to recruit many of our top producers. We began losing some of our staff members who became the chief development officers at many top universities. For a few years it seemed as though we had become the training ground for future vice presidents. Former Penn State staff members became vice presidents at The University of Texas, The Ohio State University, the University of Maryland, Arizona State University, Iowa State University, Emory University, Gettysburg College and Villanova University to name a few.

During my last year at Penn State some of my friends encouraged me to start thinking about a university presidency. I had completed my doctorate degree and my first book, and had also published a few articles in national journals. I also taught a course at Penn State in the higher education program and had been named an adjunct professor. I knew that I didn't have the academic credentials to aspire to a college presidency easily, but decided to put my name in the hat at a few institutions. I was only 43 years old, but felt I was ready for a presidency. I had gone back to school to get my doctorate, the union card, hoping the combination of a law degree and doctorate would help me attain the goal. I had been in higher education for 20 years.

I applied for the presidencies at The University of Tulsa, Hendrix College in Arkansas, and Arkansas State University in Jonesboro, Arkansas, and the University of Arkansas, Little Rock (UALR).

I was very interested in the chancellor position at UALR and thought it would get me back into the UA System. Alan Sugg was president of the University of Arkansas System, but at that point in my career I had never met him. I appealed to a person who I respected greatly, and had become acquainted with while at the University of Arkansas in the early 1980's. Carl Whillock was a former UA vice president and served as president of Arkansas State University for a period. He and his wife, Margaret, were well known throughout Arkansas. Carl was serving on the board of trustees for the UA at the time of my application. He was most supportive and gave me excellent advice, but I never got an interview. Later I would serve as a consultant at Baptist Health, as Margaret was their chief development officer. Jane and I would share a wonderful friendship with the Whillocks for many years. They were good, solid citizens and later both would serve in important positions in President Clinton's White House. Carl passed away suddenly in 2005. We still see Margaret regularly.

While I never got an interview for the UALR job, I did get a phone call from Alan Sugg thanking me for applying. I suspect Carl Whillock made that consolation call happen.

I felt confident that I would do well in the search for the presidency of Arkansas State University. The search got down to the final two candidates and I was one of them. I went to the interview and Jane and I spent three days on the campus and met with many officials as well as the board of trustees. My session with the board was public, and I remember distinctly three members of the board falling asleep during the public interview. That gave me a pretty good idea that I was not the leading candidate.

Out of the blue the board hired someone who had not been in the selection process, and it was obvious to me the person they selected had been in the wings the entire time. Unfortunately, my candidacy was reported in the newspapers both in State College, Pennsylvania, and Arkansas. It had the effect of making me look disloyal to Penn State and was not well received by the Penn State board of trustees. I started getting a reputation of being always a bridesmaid, but never the bride, and I feel certain it hurt me with folks at Penn State.

I did apply for a presidency at a regional institution in Kentucky, Murray State University, and felt confident I would be offered the presidency. Jane and I visited the campus, but decided during the process that it was not a place we wanted to be. It was located many miles from a commercial airport and practically isolated from the rest of Kentucky.

In the final days of the search, I pulled out of the running and decided I needed to stop applying for presidencies. It looked as though lightning was not going to strike for me at least at a place that was of interest to both Jane and me. I began to think that being a college president might not be an option for me. Of course, the truth was, I did not have heavy academic credentials, did not come up through the faculty ranks, and had never served as a dean or provost. I was a fundraiser, plain and simple, and at that time fundraising just wasn't considered to be all that important, especially to search committees.

At that time there were very few people in the advancement world being considered for major university presidencies. Although painful, I had to accept the fact that my lack of credentials was holding me back. I began thinking I had gone the wrong way with my career and should have started as a faculty member and worked myself up the academic ladder. On top of that, I wasn't at all sure that I really wanted to be a president, and for the first time in my career I felt lost. I just didn't know what was in store for me. Was being a vice president for advancement all I would achieve in life? It caused me to question my career and wonder if I had already achieved the pinnacle of my professional life. It wasn't an easy thing to admit to myself that, in my mid-40s, I had gone as far as I could go. I began thinking that being a senior vice president of Penn State was all I would achieve in my life. Did I peak too soon?

Bill Schreyer called to tell me the new president, Graham Spanier, had told him that he wanted university relations to report directly to him. While I understood Spanier's thinking, I wasn't happy my division would be broken up. I also learned from Schreyer that Bryce Jordan may have soured my beginning relationship with the new president as retribution for demanding I be made a senior VP years earlier. A trustee told me that Jordan had told the new president that he almost fired me over the matter. Of course that would need board of trustees approval under Penn State board rules begun many years earlier.

I was offered a very lucrative position as the senior vice president of Children's Hospital in Philadelphia at a phenomenal salary. During that time John Glier explored with me the possibility of joining his firm as a managing director and senior vice president. I had done some limited consulting while at Penn State and enjoyed it very much. I turned down the job at Children's Hospital, as we didn't want to live in Philadelphia, and went to work for John at the Grenzebach Glier consulting firm in Chicago. Since I would have clients across the country, I could live anywhere if there was access to a good airport. State College had an airport with flights to Chicago, Pittsburgh, Philadelphia, Washington D.C., and elsewhere. Those were the days of lax security measures, and I could arrive at the University Park Airport, owned by Penn State, minutes before my flight.

As mentioned, Jordan had asked John to interview me prior to inviting me to campus. He had been hired by Penn State to take a close look at their development program. John would later become the president and chief executive officer of his firm, and it would be renamed Grenzebach Glier. John Glier continued to work with Penn State throughout my tenure at the university. He has become a dear friend, and I believe him to be one of the best consultants in the business; he has worked with Penn State for over 40 years. John is also one of the brightest people I have ever known. He is beyond astute and knows the ins and outs of development work. John has an international reputation, and has advised colleges, universities and other philanthropic endeavors as they conduct capital campaigns for billions of dollars. We have remained good friends to this day. Jane would like to spend an evening with John Glier over just about anyone. He's funny, high energy and very, very savvy. His principal business partner, Martin Grenzebach, son of the founder, is equally engaging and a marvelous person as well.

PART V
A CONSULTANT
1995–1998

I'm a creative consultant, whatever that means.

— JIMMY KIMMEL

CHAPTER 17
RAISING MONEY FOR ME

> *Consultant: any ordinary guy more than fifty miles from home.*
>
> — ERIC SEVAREID

In 1995 I joined the Chicago-based consulting firm, Grenzebach Glier. I knew very little about consulting and a traveling consultants' life, but quickly learned by jumping in feet first! The first few weeks I missed Penn State greatly and certainly missed having a staff I could rely on for all my administrative needs. But that quickly faded as my plate became very full almost overnight.

It was hard work, as I had 20 clients spread across the United States. Some of my clients were the University of Washington, American University in Washington DC, the University of Miami, Brigham Young University, The University of Alabama, the University of Pittsburgh, the University of Connecticut to name only a few. It was very different from my time at Penn State. Basically, I had no staff other than the very competent central staff in Chicago. I made all my own appointments, kept my consulting calendar, and wrote all my reports myself. I lived through email and a cell phone. The World

Wide Web was just getting started, and widespread use of cell phones was relatively new, too. Email was being used mostly by academics and not at all widely. Before I was issued a cell phone, I had to pull off the road many times to use a pay phone! What I would have given for Google, and especially Google Maps.

My modus operandi was to try to leave home early Monday morning and fly to either Pittsburgh, Philadelphia, or Washington D.C., all cities where I had clients. I generally would not get home until Friday evening. Immediately when I arrived home I would repack my bag and get ready to hit the road again on Monday or maybe even Sunday depending upon my schedule. I loved my weekends, though short, but without any college functions to attend or any personnel problems to deal with.

We had decided to remain in State College because our son was in high school and our daughter was at Penn State, and we had built a house in 1992 that we were quite fond of. I suppose it would've been easier to move to Chicago where the firm's headquarters resided, but keeping the kids in State College schools seemed the best thing to do for their welfare, and was a major appeal to Jane in signing on to consulting work. John Glier said I could live anywhere close to an airport.

I had no shortage of work as the firm provided me with tons of clients, and I recruited a few myself. I had built something of a reputation from my time at Penn State, so getting clients was never a problem.

John Glier paid an adequate salary, which took care of all the monthly bills, and then I earned a bonus that was paid in February based upon consulting activity. For the first time in my life I was able to build a substantial nest egg, as we were able to save most of the bonus and it could be sizable. We put most of those proceeds into the stock market and my time with the firm was quite lucrative. Investing heavily in the stock market would pay off years later.

John Glier was a good boss. If I was producing billable hours, he left me alone. He was always supportive of me and took my side if I had a difficult client, and we developed a great friendship and extraordinary relationship. He would tell me that no one should have to work for a discourteous person, and we could always get more clients who were respectful. The entire 3 1/2 years I worked for John, I don't believe we ever had a bad word. He was one of the brightest people I had ever met. I liked his brilliance and management abilities, and also developed a friendship with Martin Grenzebach who was the chairman of the company.

Other than John and Martin, I was the highest biller in the company during my time there. After about a year on the job, John and Martin invited me to assist them with a feasibility study at the University of Hawaii. After we conducted multiple interviews in Hawaii we went to the island of Lanai, stayed at the incredible resort on the island, and played golf. It was a thoughtful gesture by John and Martin and much appreciated by me.

On my first trip to Hawaii to participate in the feasibility study for the university I remember asking John if we should wear a coat and tie or dress like Hawaiians in an aloha shirt. He expressly told me that we were professionals and should dress in suit and tie. When he appeared the next morning ready to conduct our interviews he had on an aloha shirt. I wore a coat and tie as instructed. I stuck out like a sore thumb and quickly went to a men's store and bought three aloha shirts. I only ever wore them on my visits to the University of Hawaii, but I still have them in my closet today. Jane has never been to Hawaii and I've been trying for several years to get her to make the trip with me. Hopefully we will make the sojourn soon and I'll pull out those Hawaiian shirts, which will probably be too small to wear!

Glier had a very competent staff. Much of my work I did remotely by electronic dictation or email back to the home office in Chicago, where they would prepare documents for me for my signature. Mary Sorrentino and Maggie Leroux were my go-to people and made life much easier for me during my time with the firm. I considered them good friends and they were extraordinarily helpful in my work.

I really enjoyed my time with Grenzebach Glier. I only had to go to Chicago three or four times a year for firm meetings, and those were enjoyable as well. We always stayed in high-end hotels and got to know all the other consultants very well. I found all of them to be extremely competent and engaging. I felt like I was a star at the firm as I was billing at a very high rate and John tended to defer to me during our firm meetings. Of course, I didn't like being away from home and the kids and Jane most of the week, but I must say the experience of working for one of America's great consulting firms was most enjoyable. I would try to bring t-shirts or sweatshirts with college logos to our kids from all the places I was consulting. I remember son Brock commenting, "I'm going to like this new job of Dad's."

On one of the calls I made for a feasibility study for the University of Connecticut, and one of my last appointments with the firm, I went to see an elderly lady in Hartford who had been a donor to the University. My job was to gauge if she might be a possible donor to the campaign the institution was planning. I arrived at her home on time and rang the doorbell. No one answered. I noticed her newspapers were piling up in her driveway, as if she was away. Come to find out the lady had died a few days previously and no one was aware that she was lying dead in the house. I informed John Glier of the death and he said just write down on the feasibility report that the prospect was unavailable due to circumstances beyond her control. That is what I did!

During my time as a consultant for the American Farmland Trust I got to know Peggy Rockefeller, who was on the board of trustees. She was a marvelous person and very generous to the trust. I got to spend time in her home in New York City, as well as in upstate New York. Her husband, David, was a wonderfully generous man, and it was a privilege to spend time with him. I had the opportunity to tour the old John D. Rockefeller 3,400-acre estate, Kykuit, 25 miles from New York City. Their brownstone in NYC was a lovely, old-money home with famous paintings and sculpture throughout the house.

Time with the consulting company helped sharpen my skills as a fundraiser. I was exposed to the cutting-edge techniques of the profession, and met some of the top development officials in the nation, as well as their presidents. I was also exposed to some of the wealthiest people in America who served on the institution's boards of trustees where I was consulting. I met countless major gift benefactors, including major corporate leaders, during my consulting years. I had an extensive network at colleges and universities across the country, many of whom I still remain in close touch with.

But, more than that, I really felt I was making a contribution to the profession. Most of my clients were easy to work with and accepted the advice I would offer them. It was fulfilling to see my counsel being put into action at a number of institutions, but it was even more gratifying that I did not have any of the personnel issues or other problems of running a development team. My job was not to implement but to advise. I would do my two or three days at an organization, send them a confirming letter of our discussions and decisions, but it was up to them to make it happen. Sometimes they did, sometimes not so much.

In 1998 I received a telephone call from a headhunter. The University of Arkansas was looking for a new vice chancellor for university advancement, and my name had been mentioned. I wasn't really interested in leaving the firm, but Jane and I felt that I should at least listen to their proposition. I arranged to meet the new chancellor of the university, Dr. John White, in Washington DC. We had dinner at 6 p.m. at the Marriott Hotel just outside the district, and the evening lasted for five hours. I found Dr. White to be most engaging and was excited about the plans he had for the University of Arkansas. I did have some reservations about going back to the University of Arkansas as my last stint there was less than fulfilling. Had things changed? Would it be any better after 13 years?

White had been the dean of the College of Engineering at Georgia Tech University and had phenomenal credentials. Alan Sugg had pleaded with him for several weeks to allow himself to be considered in the search, and he finally relented. He told me he wanted to undertake a massive capital campaign and tossed out a figure of $1 billion. I later told Dr. White that I thought he was crazy to think the university could achieve a figure that colossal. At the time the university was only raising about $20 million a year including athletics gifts. How could Chancellor White think he could jump to that level of giving? But I listened intently and found him to be a breath of fresh air when compared to some of the other CEOs I had worked for at previous institutions. He was polite, engaging, and thoughtful during our initial conversation and I went back home and told Jane it was something we should probably consider. Dr. Sugg called me and applied subtle pressure on me to give strong consideration to the job.

Dr. White offered me a lucrative salary, more than I had been making at Penn State when I left, but far less than my consulting revenue. I didn't jump at the job immediately and told him I really needed more time to consider his generous offer. A couple of days later he called to tell me that he would give me tenure in the College of Education and Health Professions if I would agree to come on board. That was a clincher. I had done some teaching of graduate students at Penn State and enjoyed it very much. I had in the back of my mind that I would perhaps go on the faculty as my last professional position. I thought I might work as the chief advancement officer for seven or eight years, maybe ten, and then take up my full tenured professor position to round out my career. It seemed to Jane and me to be a safeguard should I decide that I didn't want to be in development any longer. I had pretty much given up on being a college president by that point. I had applied for a number of presidencies, but nothing came my way to interest us.

Becoming a tenured full professor at a major university was appealing to me, to say the least, and it was really the catalyst that helped make up our minds to return home to Fayetteville, Arkansas. I knew that I would miss the Grenzebach Glier firm and all the people I had built strong relationships with, particularly John Glier and Martin Grenzebach. I would be jumping back into all the issues that had led me to leave Penn State, like personnel problems and navigating the politics of a complex institution. I wasn't certain I was ready to jump back into the fray, but the salary and the tenured position was something I just couldn't turn down. On top of that, we would be going home, closer to family and friends who we had left behind in 1985 when we headed to State College.

The deal was struck, and we decided to move back to Fayetteville in 1998. It would be the fifth time I had left Fayetteville and moved back, and I knew this move would be the last.

With best friends from State College, John and Karen Walizer at the Greenbrier Resort in West Virginia.

Leaving State College was very difficult, even though we were heading home. Jane and I had so many very dear and close friends who would make this move difficult, if not excruciating. One couple we had become very close to was John and Karen Walizer. John was our insurance agent, and we hit it off well with them the first time we met. John was also a volunteer for our fundraising program, particularly the new athletics and convocation center, for which he raised considerable funds in a short period of time, about $30 million. John and Karen were Penn State donors themselves, and had three boys around the age of our kids. We have remained very dear friends for almost 40 years and try to see them at least once a year.

Another person was David Lieb whom I already mentioned. I had hired him at Penn State in an entry level position when he was in his early 20s. We became close friends and still are to this day. I tried to recruit him to Arkansas, but he was a Pennsylvanian through and through and wanted to remain closer to family. He now runs the development program at Penn State.

Another one we found very difficult to leave was the person who took care of our house cleaning and lawn. Mark Modaffare had become like a member of the family. I don't think I have ever seen Jane so upset or cry as much as she did when she said goodbye to Mark. We have stayed in close touch with him for all these years.

We had so many dear friends in State College after having lived there for 13 years. Leaving was going to be tough.

PART VI
THE UNIVERSITY OF ARKANSAS, THE SECOND TIME
1998–2008

It's déjà vu all over again.

— *YOGI BERRA*

CHAPTER 18
CLOSING THE PRESS

> *A word after a word after a word is power.*
>
> — MARGARET ATWOOD

When I interviewed for the vice chancellor position at the University of Arkansas in 1998, I walked into a firestorm. At the very first meeting I attended during the interview process, a member of the search committee asked me if I had an opinion on closing the University of Arkansas Press. Of course, I had no idea what she was referring to. Those were the days before Google or other search engines were in operation, and Jane and I were not taking the Arkansas newspapers or keeping up with University of Arkansas news.

The University of Arkansas Press was established by the board of trustees in May 1980 as the publishing arm of the University of Arkansas. Well-known poet and author Miller Williams was named the first director of the Press, and history professor and former chancellor, Willard B. Gatewood Jr., was named the chairman of the first Press committee. (Miller Williams' daughter is acclaimed country music star Lucinda Williams).

Its mission is to publish peer-reviewed books and academic journals. For several years, the Press received accolades from the academic community and published a few pieces by well-known writers, including civil-rights activist Daisy Bates, President Jimmy Carter, and National Book Award winner Ellen Gilchrist. It had become a well-established program of the university, and many believed it brought prestige and acclaim to Arkansas. The only problem was that it was operating at a deficit of around $250,000 a year, which had accumulated to a sizable amount for the university to carry on its books.

From the perspective of the academics that was not a huge price to pay for such an important operation. Besides, they reasoned, most academic presses are operating at a deficit. That's just the price you pay for the prestige of a University Press and being able to publish books. Mounting financial pressure had closed many university presses around the country, and the trend seemed to be going that way. Administrators concluded that if the Press cannot generate enough income to remain viable, that tells you it may not be as popular as some proponents believe it to be.

A few months before I arrived on campus for my interview for the vice chancellor for university advancement position, Chancellor John White had closed the Press because of the mounting deficits. There was an immediate outcry from the academic community. Literally hundreds of letters arrived at the chancellor's office demanding that the Press be reinstated. Former President Jimmy Carter even got in on the action by writing a letter supporting the Press.

The media aggressively beat up on White for closing the Press, in an almost daily tirade of damaging headlines. Academic purists came out of the woodwork. White had decided to close the Press based on financial information given to him by his staff, and was reluctant to withdraw his decision.

The most verbal dissenter was the former chancellor, Willard Gatewood. Gatewood was an amazing historian and teacher, and was highly respected on campus and throughout Arkansas. Although he had been chancellor for only one year, realizing administration was not to his liking, he was one of the most respected academic voices in Arkansas. Gatewood came unglued and vowed to get the decision reversed. He wrote letters to the board of trustees and President Sugg.

It is certainly true that White was trying to be fiscally responsible in cleaning up a sizable deficit, considering the many urgent needs of the university. But he found himself in a growing outrage among prominent faculty members. It didn't help matters that he was not a liberal arts graduate but an engineer. His detractors used the fact to berate his decision, telling people that someone interested in the humanities would never have closed the Press. Things got ugly. The faculty senate weighed in on the decision against White.

The real truth was the university had no money. The state was not living up to its obligation to provide adequate funding, and White was looking for every penny he could find. He saw it as a simple matter of cleaning up a substantial deficit that was harming the financial position of the institution. I completely understood his logic. But others didn't care about logic. This was a war against poetry, publishing and the prosperity of the humanities. I contend to this day that White was just trying to do the right and responsible thing by closing a program that had a negative balance.

The evening after my day of interviews on the campus I was at my mother's home on Washington Avenue where I was staying. I was telling my mother and Pat about the day and my thoughts about the job. Suddenly the doorbell rang. It was 9 p.m. and dark outside. We were not expecting any visitors. My mother went to the door and called my name saying I had a visitor. It was John White. After exchanging pleasantries and discussing my day he launched into the issues he was having with the Press. He related how he was advised to close the Press by a staff member, and he wasn't sure how to extricate himself from the catastrophe. He asked if I had any advice. At first I thought he was testing me but then decided he was genuinely asking for help.

I recommended that he appoint a blue-ribbon committee to do a full review and advise him as to future action. I thought he needed to change the discussion and dialogue from White versus the Press and involve more people in the decision making. I learned later that he did follow some of my suggestions, but I'm not sure my advice really did much good. I really felt sorry for Dr. White, as I'm not at all sure he was overly committed to closing the Press. He was trying to be a good steward of resources and follow his staff person's recommendation. The problem was that the recommendation was terribly flawed and never considered the public relations outcry over the closing. I never quite understood how a PR person could recommend something that would have had such enormous PR consequences and be such a major controversy for the chancellor. John White got very bad advice!

In the end, White was saved by a benefactor. Don Tyson, chairman and CEO of Tyson Foods, stepped forward and gave the university $1 million to keep the Press open and operating.

Ironically, the University of Missouri Press had assisted the University of Arkansas Press in its early years of establishment, and had served as mentor to the UA in the early days of the Press's formation. In 2012, the University of Missouri Press would attempt to close as well, only to reopen a few months later after a huge outcry from faculty. I told the Chancellor of Mizzou he should have called me, and I would have saved him a lot of headache and heartache.

CHAPTER 19
UNIVERSITY HOUSE

> *Old ideas can sometimes use new buildings. New ideas must use old buildings.*
>
> — *JANE JACOBS*

When I arrived at the University of Arkansas the second time, we had limited staff and resources, and the staff we did have were spread across campus—and even off campus. As we began hiring staff, we desperately needed a place to house them. As I was driving down Maple Avenue one afternoon, I noticed a For Sale sign in the front yard of the Delta Gamma sorority house. I could not understand what was possibly going on with selling the Delta Gamma house on the central campus. I immediately investigated the matter and determined that a group of local investors had offered to buy the property from the Delta Gammas and were planning to make it an apartment house for students with a bar on the first floor. Was this potential sale even legal? I assumed the house was on university property and might have even been owned by the university as were most sorority houses.

I brought the matter to the attention of the chancellor and our

CFO, Don Pederson. We got our attorneys involved, and found out there was a major problem in the purchase. The house and the grounds were not owned by the sorority but by the university. The sorority had a long-term lease on the house and the real estate it was sitting on, but title was held by the University of Arkansas. That tended to cramp the style of the investors, all of whom I knew well. One I had known since kindergarten! They were not happy when they found out the DG house could not sell the property to outside investors.

The Delta Gammas had closed their house many months previous, as they had difficulty filling the house and getting new members. There were probably many reasons the house was not faring well, but a major reason was too few students and too many sorority houses. The number of female students could not support the plethora of houses. The fraternities were having the same issue, and many of the frat houses were in peril as well.

The Delta Gamma house sat empty for some time with grass growing to an unsightly mess. The DGs wanted out from under the house and decided to put it on the open market. No one seemed to ask the question as to whether they actually owned it.

The DGs did have a long-term lease that had some equity and we offered to pay them for the remaining life of the lease. The question was what to do with the property? At that time, we were not seeing growth in student enrollment and had closed several of our residence facilities, and no other sororities or fraternities came forward to take the property over. Besides that, the DG house was in a state of disrepair and needed major renovations and general refurbishment. Since we urgently needed a place for our growing fundraising staff, I approached John White to allow our division to take over the facility. He agreed.

We would put our annual-giving telephone call center in the basement, and staff on the top two floors. The first floor would be reserved for university events. At that time the only facility we had for university events was the Alumni Center. We had not opened the Carnall Inn yet, and the Chancellor's House at the time was totally inadequate for large events. Many, if not most, campus events were being held off campus. We agreed to raise private money and totally renovate the facility for our advancement and development needs.

When completed, the new building was a godsend for our staff. Just as important, it provided high-end space for numerous events on campus, which the colleges and schools needed for entertaining purposes. We held countless events through the years in the facility. The building was elegantly decorated by a volunteer committee staffed by Sandy and Clay Edwards. While the offices were small, they were nicely furnished, and the downstairs event space was decorated in an elegant style. We held literally hundreds of events in the facility and the deans were ecstatic to have new space for their many events that were previously held off campus.

We named the facility University House and provided coffee and doughnuts every morning for faculty and staff who wanted to stop by. We even held a few special lunches for faculty on a reservation basis, and faculty could walk over for a light and inexpensive lunch. Some of the areas in the building were named for major gifts to the project.

Tragically, in 2021 the development office surrendered up the building so it could be used as unrelated office space. Apparently, the change happened so quickly during the Steinmetz administration that the staff occupying the facility had no place to go, and were told to work from home. Some of them ended up at the Hembree Alumni House in overcrowded conditions. Just recently it was announced that the fundraising central staff would be moved off campus. The decision was hard for me to understand.

CHAPTER 20
BLAME FOR PEPSI

> *They do what they do for money—that's all. I don't even know why you're listening to me. I've done commercials for both Coke and Pepsi. Truth is, I can't even taste the difference, but Pepsi paid me last, so there it is.*
>
> — DAVE CHAPPELLE

While at Penn State University in 1993, we orchestrated a beverage contract with Pepsi-Cola. I believe it was the first time a university entered into an exclusive agreement with a beverage provider. This was during a time that the Pepsi and Coca-Cola companies were competing heavily for the soft drink market. Both companies were eager to get Penn State business and were willing to put several million dollars on the table. We had those two companies bid for our business, and ended up getting a commitment from Pepsi for $15 million. We used those funds to build a new basketball facility later named after Bryce Jordan.

Because Penn State had a centralized administrative structure, we were able to include all 17 campuses of the university in the deal.

After we consummated the contract, several other colleges and universities around the country followed our path.

When I arrived at the University of Arkansas in 1998 after serving at Penn State, we approached both Pepsi and Coke to bid for our business. At the time Coach Broyles was not interested in changing the athletics soft drink provider from Coke. Later, when Jeff Long became athletics director, he had athletics join our contract. Pepsi won the bid with an offer of $10 million. Several different offices, including athletics, benefited from the contract. Naturally, we were criticized by Coke drinkers but held the line for much needed additional revenue.

When I was asked why we decided to switch from Coke to Pepsi I would generally answer that we had 10 million reasons to do so. Pepsi remains the provider for the University of Arkansas and it has brought in several million dollars of additional, much needed revenue.

Jane is an inveterate Coke drinker first thing in the morning. I drink a Diet Coke every morning. We get our caffeine fix from Coca-Cola as we don't drink coffee and never have.

I told Jane that I really could not tell the difference and gave her the blind Pepsi/Coke test to see which one she would choose as the better tasting product. She tasted both products and chose Pepsi! To this day she says I tricked her.

Then, in 2022, the University of Arkansas decided to change the soft drink contract back to Coke. Little information about the deal was released, so it is difficult to compare the two providers.

CHAPTER 21
HISTORICAL MARKERS

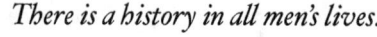

 *There is a history in all men's lives.*

— *WILLIAM SHAKESPEARE*

One of the projects we had accomplished at Penn State was to place historical markers around the campus grounds lauding various accomplishments of national renown by faculty and the university. Roger Williams spearheaded the effort at Penn State and my recollection is that it was his brilliant idea. I asked him to implement the same thing at the University of Arkansas and many of them were unveiled in 1999, with some following later. If you walk the campus today you will see almost 20 markers related to major accomplishments. A few of them are quoted here:

THE $300 MILLION GIFT

"On April 11, 2002, the University received the largest gift in the history of U.S. public higher education—a $300 million challenge gift from the Walton Family Charitable Support Foundation. The gift established and endowed an undergraduate honors college and the graduate school. Its express purpose was to elevate the University and the State of Arkansas, placing an aspiring flagship public university on a level playing field with the best public universities in America. The gift was the fifth largest ever to any American university, public or private. The Walton Family Charitable Support Foundation was established by the family of the late Sam M. Walton, creator of the world's largest corporation, Wal-Mart Stores, Inc. of Bentonville, Ark."

This marker is located at the northwest corner of Maple Street and Lindell Avenue.

ADVANCES IN NUTRITION

"Agricultural Chemistry Professors Barnett Sure (1920–51) and Marinus C. Kik (1927–67) made major advances in nutrition science during their long tenures at the University of Arkansas. Sure co-discovered vitamin E, and extended knowledge of how vitamin E, amino acids and B-vitamins function on reproduction and lactation. Kik developed the process for parboiling rice to increase retention of vitamins and shorten cooking time. He documented benefits of adding fish and chicken to rice and grain diets to provide adequate protein for a growing world population. Sure and Kik were Agricultural Experiment Station scientists and professors in the UA Department of Agricultural Chemistry, which merged in 1964 with Home Economics, now the School of Human Environmental Sciences."

This marker is located at the south entrance to the Human Environmental Sciences Building.

CAMPAIGN FOR THE TWENTY-FIRST CENTURY

"The Campaign for the Twenty-First Century, considered the most ambitious fund-raising effort undertaken by an organization in Arkansas, spanned 3/1/1998 - 6/30/2005. The $500-million Campaign's objective was to raise funds for scholarship and faculty endowments, capital improvements, program support and annual giving. The goal was reached, then raised to $900 million. That goal was attained and raised to $1 billion, placing the University among 24 other institutions in America actively engaged in such drives. The Campaign finished by raising more than $1 billion, significantly augmenting the institution's endowment. Commemorating the Campaign's *transformational impact and symbolizing that the University's 'time has come,' the Campaign Steering Committee gave gifts to add a clock to Old Main's south tower, a part of the structure's original design, finally realized 130 years later."*

This marker is located near the northwest corner of Maple Street and Lindell Avenue next to University House.

CHI OMEGA

"The Chi Omega Greek Theater was built in 1930 as a gift from Chi Omega, the national women's fraternity (sorority) that was founded at the University of Arkansas in 1895 when four coeds and a faculty adviser chartered the mother chapter, Psi. Since then, Chi Omega has become the largest women's fraternity in the nation, with 240,000 current members and alumnae in 172 chapters. The Psi chapter house is located at 940 Maple Street. The Greek Theater is a replica of one built at the foot of the Acropolis in ancient Athens to honor Dionysus. It has been used for commencements, concerts, and many other events."

The Chi Omega marker is located on McIlroy Avenue north of the Chi Omega Greek Theatre.

CLINTONS ON LAW FACULTY

"The nation's 42nd President, William J. Clinton (1993–2001), and First Lady, Hillary Rodham Clinton, were faculty members of the University of Arkansas School of Law in the mid-1970s. Mr. Clinton started in 1973, teaching Trade Regulation, Admiralty, Criminal Procedure, Federal Jurisdiction, and Constitutional Law. Ms. Rodham came in 1974, teaching Criminal Procedure, Criminal Law, Trial Advocacy and Prison Project. She also founded the Legal Clinic program and taught it every semester. They were wed at their home at 930 California Blvd. on Oct. 11, 1975. The couple left at the end of 1976 so Mr. Clinton could begin work as Arkansas' new attorney general."

This marker is located on the north side of the School of Law, on Maple Avenue.

CREATIVE WRITING

"The Master of Fine Arts in Creative Writing, a 60-hour program begun at the University of Arkansas in 1966, has grown into one of the most productive and highly ranked programs of its kind in America. Founded by English professors William Harrison and James Whitehead, and later joined by Miller Williams, the program was in the vanguard of a revolution to transform the traditional study of literature into a demanding training ground for young writers. The writer-teachers and writer-students in the program, many of whom have won national fame and honors, have produced hundreds of works of fiction, poetry, creative non-fiction, and translation."

This marker is located on McIlroy Avenue at the middle entrance to Kimpel Hall.

EARLY INTEGRATION

"The University of Arkansas became the first major Southern public university to admit a black student without litigation when Silas Hunt of Texarkana, an African American veteran of World War II, was admitted to the University's law school in 1948. Roy Wilkins, administrator of the NAACP, wrote in 1950 that Arkansas was the 'very first of the Southern states to accept the new trend without fighting a delaying action or attempting to ... limit, if not nullify, bare compliance.' Silas Hunt Hall, across from the law school, was dedicated in his honor as the student admissions center in 1993."

This marker is located along Maple Avenue on the north side of Silas Hunt Hall.

CHAPTER 22
SAVING CARNALL

> *We are the only country in the world that trashes its old buildings. Too late we realize how very much we need them.*
>
> — *JACKIE KENNEDY*

One of the oldest buildings on campus was Carnall Hall, a women's student housing facility. It was one of the dormitories where my grandmother served as house mother, and an iconic building that had become an eyesore in teardown condition. The board of trustees had slated it for razing. In fact, a local advocate for saving old Fayetteville buildings had come forward as a staunch supporter for renovating the building. She actually was invited to make a presentation to the board, made possible by a member of the board who was an acquaintance. Her presentation went on for what seemed forever, and the chairman of the board had to finally intervene and ask her to stop her presentation. The board came away from the meeting all in unity of thought to raze the building as soon as possible.

I toured the building with Mike Johnson. It had a fence around its perimeter and signs saying "Danger, Keep Out." It was in horrible shape. Windows broken, dead rats and birds all around, and warped and missing wood flooring. The plaster was virtually nonexistent where you could see the lumber sticking through the walls. It was in a sad state of total demise.

Carnall Hall in teardown condition. Notice the fence around it.

As I toured the worn-out former women's residence hall, I couldn't help but think of my Grandmother Lulu who served the university so well as a house mother so many years ago. I remembered being with her for dinner at Carnall Hall and the bell ringing signaling us to walk down the hall from the housemother's suite to the entrance to the dining room where we would stop before going in so the women could sing grace. They would all congregate on the two circular staircases. The dining tables all had pressed tablecloths and silver and glassware set expertly. Meals were served by house boys and no one ate until Mom Van was served. After dinner and dessert no one got up until Mom Van got up and exited the dining room. As a young boy, I thought it was the neatest thing I had ever witnessed. I felt like my grandmother was a queen and I a prince.

Of course, those innocent days are long gone, never to be again. I hated to see Carnall in such a deteriorated state. It really broke my heart and so many good memories came flooding back of visiting my grandmother and spending the night in such an elegant building. Tearing it down would be too bad, but perhaps necessary. That's what the trustees wanted.

Then we came up with a possible solution. For some time, we had known the university needed a hotel on campus. While there were plenty of hotel facilities in relative proximity to campus, we didn't have one actually situated on campus grounds. We thought Carnall Hall might be suitable for such an idea. A local developer expressed interest in partnering with us to renovate the hall and build a topflight hotel. It would need to be a boutique hotel as there were not enough rooms in the facility to make it larger unless we added on, and lack of footprint made that very difficult.

Carnall Inn renovated as a hotel and restaurant. Photo by Russell Cothren.

We developed plans for renovation as well as a sizable addition. At the next board of trustees meeting, John White made a phenomenal presentation of transforming Carnall Hall into Carnall Inn. The presentation had been put together by university relations under Roger Williams' supervision. It was so well done the trustees approved the idea at the meeting. Only one trustee voted against it, only because at the break he wasn't in on the private discussion among trustees that they were going to reverse their earlier decision to tear the building down.

Carnall Inn has served the university for many years as a place for alumni, faculty, and students to congregate. It has been highly successful, especially on game weekends. I only wish it was larger.

We donated some photographs of my grandmother's time as housemother at Carnall Hall, which are still on display.

CHAPTER 23
MURDER-SUICIDE

> *Strumming my pain with his fingers, singing my life with his words, killing me softly with his song.*
>
> — ROBERTA FLACK

Monday, August 28, 2000 was a day nobody wants to remember. On that day, the university experienced a murder-suicide in Kimpel Hall.

I was headed to the airport to catch a plane for a consulting job in Miami, Florida. I had kept a few clients as John White allowed me to do some private consulting on the side, actually up to 50 days a year. My cell phone rang, and it was White informing me of the tragedy on campus and two people dead from gunshot wounds. I immediately turned my car around and headed back to the university, canceling my consulting trip.

Tragically, Dr. John R. Locke, associate professor of English and head of the comparative literature program had been murdered. The perpetrator was James Easton Kelly of Marianna, Arkansas. Kelly had started in the PhD program in English at the University of Arkansas in 1990. In 1996 he moved to the PhD program in comparative literature, and Dr. Locke was his faculty advisor. By the late 1990s, Kelly had enrolled for several consecutive semesters and in each case he subsequently withdrew. Based on his record, he was ultimately dismissed from the program on August 21, 2000, but was allowed to continue taking courses as a non-degree student. Kelly was 37 years old.

Apparently, Kelly believed his advisor, Dr. Locke, had voted to remove him from graduate school, but that was not factual. Locke had actually refrained from voting against Kelly, but all of the other professors did vote to remove Kelly from the program. Kelly shot and killed his former professor and then turned the gun on himself.

At approximately 12:14 p.m., a 911 call was received by the Fayetteville Police Department. The caller alerted the police to an incident involving gunshots in Kimpel Hall. Such calls are routinely monitored by the University of Arkansas Police Department, and officers were on the scene very quickly. University officers secured the area around room 231 and began the evacuation of the building immediately. Kelly used a .38-caliber handgun to kill himself and Dr. Locke.

The tragedy became national news. The incident even prompted a statement from President Bill Clinton who, of course, was a former professor at the University of Arkansas law school. Telephone calls started flooding into the university from parents and concerned citizens.

The police report indicated there were three shots fired. The first officer on the scene attempted to make contact, when he heard a voice inside the room yelling, "Don't come in!" Not long after the verbal exchange there was a sudden bang coming from the room.

Our head of university relations, Roger Williams did his usual outstanding job in working with the media and keeping them totally informed. John White appeared before the media several times that day, and several days following the incident, to inform them of everything that was happening. He was superb in front of the cameras.

We all believed from the beginning this was an isolated event on our campus. Nothing of the sort had occurred at the university for more than 20 years and we all trusted that the campus was a place of safety, security and respect. But the shooting caused much concern among parents, and some students even left the university because of a perceived notion that it was not a safe campus. The murder-suicide shocked the community, and it would be several months before anything approaching normalcy returned to campus.

CHAPTER 24
2010 COMMISSION

> *The production of too many useful things results in too many useless people.*
>
> — KARL MARX

Around the year 2000 John White began a new effort to try to convince the Arkansas legislature to pay more attention to higher education in general, and the flagship in particular. He called it the 2010 Commission and asked the provost, Bob Smith, to chair it. The 2010 Commission—a group of 92 dedicated business, government, and academic professionals, plus students—were charged with studying and presenting reports that lauded the state's major higher education resources and our state's future. The commission's reports were designed to:

1. Demonstrate that Arkansas' economic future demanded a comprehensive research university ranked among the nation's top 50 public institutions.
2. Define the University of Arkansas' role in driving the

intellectual, economic, and cultural imperatives of the state.
3. Identify and assess the financial support necessary for us to reach our goals, based on wise stewardship of current resources.

White would spend hours and hours creating the various reports to be released to the legislature and the public. Bob Smith was probably not the best person selected to chair the effort, as John ended up doing much of the work. I don't want to suggest it was a failure, but most people were not quite sure what it was trying to accomplish. The legislature did not appropriate any more funds to the university and the media didn't appear too terribly interested in promoting the effort.

The commission did meet a few times, but mainly to hear reports from White, which could border on boring and redundant. I do commend White for trying to change the legislature's mindset, but members of the General Assembly just didn't seem to have much interest in higher education. Except for West Virginia, Arkansas had the lowest percentage of its citizenry with a college degree. It still does to this day. I never saw much benefit come out of the commission's work and after a few years it was abandoned.

Later, Smith wrote a piece on the commission's work and suggested that the Campaign for the Twenty-First Century, our billion-dollar capital campaign, was an important part of the commission. Nothing could have been further from the truth. The two efforts were completely separate, and Smith's claim was upsetting to me and my dedicated staff. At one of White's cabinet meetings, I unloaded on Bob Smith. It was not pretty and perhaps I was a little too harsh on him. However, I just could not stomach his taking credit for something he had little to nothing to do with. Luckily White never reprimanded me and Smith refrained from using that language in the future. Later I noticed in Smith's vita that the language he used made it seem as though the billion-dollar campaign was organized by him under the auspices of the 2010 Commission.

CHAPTER 25
FOOTBALL GAMES IN LITTLE ROCK

> *Some people think football is a matter of life and death. I assure you, it's much more serious than that.*
>
> — BILL SHANKLY

Around the year 2000, coach Frank Broyles decided he wanted to move all of the Razorback football games to Fayetteville. For years he had been an advocate for playing three games in Little Rock as he felt it helped to unite the state behind the team. The University of Arkansas was one of the last institutions to play a split schedule. Due to SEC rules, it was impossible to recruit at the Little Rock games and really ended up being tantamount to an away game. Broyles had improved the stadium at Fayetteville and added substantially to the number of seats. Little Rock had done practically nothing to improve their stadium and had not added substantially to seating capacity.

Broyles started telling people of his plans and the media got hold of it. The next thing was an uproar in Little Rock, which caused a dramatic pushback from Razorback fans in central and south Arkansas. Two business leaders in Little Rock were highly critical of the plan, and were close friends of Broyles. The first was Jack Stephens and his son Warren of the investment banking firm Stephens Inc. While the Stephens clan had lost some of their political power as Northwest Arkansas blossomed, they still packed a punch. While Jack was opposed to moving the games, his son Warren vigorously led the fight.

The second person was Joe Ford who was the chairman and chief executive officer of Alltel Wireless, later acquired by Verizon. The fight became nasty and filled the newspapers. This, of course, got the attention of the board of trustees who decided it was really their decision to make as to where we played the games, and not Frank Broyles decision, or the chancellor's or system president's.

At that time, Frank Broyles was still very much a powerhouse in Arkansas. Generally, he always got anything he wanted, and the board tended to follow his decision making. After all, Frank had been highly effective as a coach and later athletics director, and had built successful intercollegiate athletics programs at the university. But this time the stakes were too large and the outcry so loud that the board was not going to let Frank make this critical decision all by himself.

Broyles started out wanting to move all of the games to Fayetteville. It made good financial sense to do so—since the Little Rock community did not put forward resources to renovate and add capacity to War Memorial Stadium, Broyles concluded that he had no choice but to move the games. To him it was purely a financial decision and in the best interests of football, the athletes and coaches.

Dr. Sugg, along with the chairman of the board of trustees, decided to hold a board meeting in Fayetteville and allow faculty, staff, and students to voice their feelings about moving the games. Sugg invited anyone who wanted to speak to do so and suggested they form two lines, one in favor of moving the games to Fayetteville and one in favor of leaving the games, or some games in Little Rock. The majority of those who gathered in the lines were students. The line in favor of moving the games to Fayetteville was enormous and literally went down the hall and out the door. The line for keeping games in Little Rock was quite small. It was an orderly meeting, and people attending were very impressed by how thoughtful and polite our students were in front of the trustees. It was obvious, though, that students at the University of Arkansas wanted all of the games in Fayetteville. Their arguments were rational and well-reasoned, and several members of the board commented on how impressed they were by the students.

One student was a little caustic, nothing really that bad, but he came off with an edge for keeping the games in Little Rock. The chairman of the board was not going to allow him to speak because of his mild belligerence. Sugg intervened and asked Clark to allow the student to speak despite his attitude. I gained even more respect for Sugg's leadership that day.

At the next board meeting the trustees decided to move one game to Fayetteville. Most of us in the administration thought it was a huge fight to only get one more game in Fayetteville. We lost a lot of support in Little Rock and central Arkansas that day to only get one game moved. A number of south Arkansas benefactors were miffed, and many stopped contributing. Many letters to Broyles and White were mean-spirited and downright nasty and profane. The university had created a huge uproar and upset many Razorback fans for very little payoff.

Not long after the meeting, Jack Stephens resigned from our campaign committee and Joe Ford made a seven-figure gift to the University of Arkansas at Little Rock, even though he was our alumnus. It would be years before we were able to patch things up with the Stephens family. The Fords and the Stephens felt that Frank Broyles had lied to them, and it didn't seem they could get past what had happened. Broyles said that he didn't mean to lie, but times had changed, and lack of resources required a change of mind on playing in Little Rock. Sadly, it basically destroyed a close friendship between Jack Stephens and Frank Broyles. Jack had been a huge supporter of Frank's and enabled him to become a member of Augusta National Golf Course, a prized membership among the golfing community.

Personally, I liked the Stephens and Fords very much, and hated to see the damage done because of football games. It was sad on so many levels.

The entire ordeal was unfortunate, and I feel certain it hurt the University in Little Rock and South Arkansas; there are still reverberations to this day. It would take many years to rebuild damaged feelings. I felt that it most likely caused our campaign a minimum of $100 million in gift support.

Even today we still play football games in Little Rock.

> *You can't be a real country unless you have a beer and an airline. It helps if you have some kind of a football team, or some nuclear weapons, but at the very least you need a beer.*
>
> — FRANK ZAPPA

I have been asked several times about my thoughts regarding playing games in Little Rock. When I was chancellor, I told Jeff Long I wanted to let sleeping dogs lie and not get back into a battle over Little Rock football games. Like Broyles, Jeff believed all of the games should be played in Fayetteville. Now that I am retired, I can say that I wholeheartedly agree with him and the late Frank Broyles. Here are my reasons, and I know that many people will disagree with them:

1. Intercollegiate sports are supposed to be the social glue for the student body. I realize that over decades that has changed, and many people may think that football games are played for alumni and fans. College sports have become a sports industrial complex and far more than a competition for the students and alumni. But that isn't the way it was originally conceived. Playing home games away from the students just doesn't make good sense. Maybe it's the same sentiment that caused me to use the phrase "students first," but to my way of thinking it should be all about the students, first and foremost.
2. Playing games in Little Rock is a definite hindrance to our

recruiting opportunities. That hurts our football program immeasurably.
3. The University of Arkansas is the only program in the nation to play a split schedule. Yes, we are the only one left standing. Should that tell us something?
4. It makes absolutely no financial sense to play games in a much smaller stadium. We give up several million dollars a year in revenue when we play games in Little Rock. Since we do not have a student athletics fee and we do not get any revenue from the state for our athletics program, it doesn't make any sense to leave money on the table.
5. The people of Little Rock have refused to improve War Memorial Stadium through the years. While some improvements have been made and a few seats added, there has been very little action taken to make a difference financially. There's an old saying, "put your money where your mouth is." War Memorial Stadium is an old, worn-out venue that doesn't deserve to hold games for one of America's finest football programs.
6. Finally, some will argue that if we don't play games in Little Rock, we won't get financial support from people in central and south Arkansas. Well, here is the truth of the matter and the truth may hurt. For the most part the University of Arkansas, Fayetteville athletics program has been built by people in Northwest Arkansas. The Walton, Tyson, Hunt, Bogle, Walker, Billingsley families have done much of it. That's not to claim that the University of Arkansas has received no support from central and south Arkansas, but suffice it to say that the lion's share of major gifts for athletics have come from Northwest Arkansas. If you seek evidence of that fact, just look around at the named athletics facilities. Practically all are named after benefactors in Northwest Arkansas.

In 2021 the athletics department made the decision to begin playing Arkansas State University in football in 2025. The game will be played in War Memorial Stadium. The Fayetteville campus also began playing the University of Arkansas, Pine Bluff in 2021. Coach Broyles was always opposed to playing in-state teams in football. His rationale was that the Razorbacks are the state's team and may be the only thing that unites the citizens of the state. He felt the Fayetteville campus could not benefit in any way by playing in-state teams in football. I won't weigh in on the decision but suffice it to say that Coach Frank Broyles was a smart man. Watching local sports news in October 2021, I heard Sam Pittman, Razorback's head football coach, relate the difficulties of playing games in Little Rock.

CHAPTER 26
SEPTEMBER 11, 2001

> *We didn't crumble after 9/11. We didn't falter after the Boston Marathon. But we're America. Americans will never, ever stand down. We endure. We overcome. We own the finish line.*
>
> — JOE BIDEN

I was scheduled with a full day of appointments in Dallas, Texas on September 11, 2001. For some months we had been working hard to establish a presence in Dallas, which has one of the largest concentrations of UA alumni. Unfortunately, we had not previously done a very good job calling on our alumni in Dallas or in Texas generally. Many of our prominent, wealthy alumni resided in Dallas because of the favorable income tax treatment in Texas. Since there is no state income tax in Texas, it became a tax haven for a number of well-to-do Arkansas alumni. I suppose it did save some persons a lot of money, but personally I would be hard-pressed to leave Arkansas. The same tax loophole exists in Florida and my brother moved there a couple of years ago; one reason among many, was due to the avoidance of income tax. He told me it would save him a considerable amount of money on an annual basis. Also, he is an avid golfer and enjoys boating, and can enjoy those activities 12 months out of the year.

I was staying in a hotel in central Dallas and getting ready for my first appointment at 9 a.m.. I was listening to the Today Show when the commentators said an airplane had hit one of the twin towers in lower Manhattan. At first, they thought it was an accident, but then within a few minutes a second plane struck the towers, and they were baffled. I remember one of the commentators saying, "What is going on? This can't be an accident." I finished getting ready to face a long day of appointments while listening intently to the television.

The commentators on the *Today Show* had no idea what was going on. A plane hit the North Tower of the World Trade Center complex in Lower Manhattan at about 7:45 a.m. About 15 minutes later the World Trade Center's South Tower was hit while my eyes were glued to the TV. Of course, at that point, the world knew America was under attack. The commentators, while not knowing for absolute certainty, believed the planes must have been hijacked.

I began telephoning all of my appointments for the day to see if I should still come to their home or office in light of what was happening. Much to my surprise, everyone I called wanted to keep the appointment, so I got in my rental car and headed out for the first appointment of the day.

When I arrived at each of the appointments, the prospects and donors—mostly alumni—were all glued to their television sets. If they didn't have a TV in their office, they went to another office where one existed. Naturally, we didn't talk about the university but stayed glued to the television, trying to get any news we could about what was happening. I witnessed both 110-story towers collapse which led to the collapse of the other World Trade Center structures including 7 World Trade Center, and significantly damaging surrounding buildings. I was very familiar with downtown New York City, because it used to be my stomping ground when I worked for Penn State. Many Penn State alumni had offices in one of the buildings in the World Trade Center and surrounding buildings. I had been in several of them many times in past years. In fact the Merrill Lynch World Headquarters was just across the street from the twin towers and was badly damaged that day. While watching the television we learned a third flight crashed into the west side of the Pentagon, causing considerable casualties and damage to the building. Later in the car I heard that a fourth flight crashed in a field near Shanksville, Pennsylvania. It was perhaps the most somber day of appointments I had ever experienced. Everyone was shocked and dismayed, and literally speechless and filled with emotion.

Luckily, I had a rental car and quickly called the company to see if I could extend the time period of the rental. I was scheduled to fly back to Fayetteville the next day but learned all flights nationwide had been canceled. I finished my last appointment late in the afternoon and drove back to Fayetteville. I was lucky in that regard as I learned later that many acquaintances got stranded all across the country.

The next week I learned several Penn State alumni were presumed dead, as they were in the World Trade Center buildings when they collapsed. It was a tragedy of Herculean proportions and one of the saddest days in the history of our nation. I then learned that a member of our campaign committee was in a hotel in downtown Manhattan when the Trade Center buildings collapsed. Fortunately, she was able to get out of the hotel prior to the collapse and made her way across the river to New Jersey. It would be several days before she could get back to Northwest Arkansas.

For another member of the campus community, alumna Sara Elizabeth Low, the events of that day ended her life. Low, who grew up in Batesville and earned business degrees at the University of Arkansas, was a flight attendant on American Airlines Flight 11, the plane that crashed into the north tower of the World Trade Center. Of the nearly 3,000 people who were killed, 7 were born in Arkansas, including Sara.

The world changed that tragic day.

Not long after September 11 and as the public phase of our campaign was heating up, we wanted to try to bring the local community together as closer partners with the university. We decided to hold a series of luncheons and invite community leaders from across Northwest Arkansas. We billed the luncheons as "Town and Gown." We invited local mayors to speak and a few legislators, and filled the athletics practice facility with over 500 citizens of Northwest Arkansas. At the right moment cheerleaders and the Razorback marching band flowed into the facility, and the people present loved it. I do believe it helped solidify good relations with the local community for several years.

CHAPTER 27
IT'S ALL GREEK TO ME!

> *True friends, like ivy and the wall, both stand together and together fall.*
>
> — FRANCIS BACON

In 2002 it became obvious to those of us at the university that Greek life was failing. In most cases, women's Greek life was holding its own but not flourishing. In past years about 800 to 900 male students would participate in rush every fall. Through the years that number had declined precipitously and the men's Greek houses were having trouble paying their bills with so few students living in the houses. In 2002 only 160 men pledged a fraternity. Greek life was sinking fast and most of the houses were having financial difficulties.

Some of the sororities had closed as well. We simply had too few students to support so many houses. On top of that, juniors and seniors were moving out of the fraternity houses at an alarming rate, making it even more difficult for the Greek houses to survive.

Complicating the situation for the men were a couple of factors: First, students would show up a week or two before classes began to participate in rush. After they pledged a fraternity they would move into the house immediately. For those young men who were not selected by a fraternity, they would have to find housing—which was sometimes very difficult as most on-campus rooms were already taken. Many times the student not selected to be in a fraternity or sorority they wanted did not get a bid, as it is called, and would simply leave, and go home or to another institution. This was a problem not only for the fraternity houses but also for the female sororities. I remember my son telling me that, as a member of Sigma Chi, he was designated as the person to inform students when they did not get a bid to be in any house. He said it was one of the hardest things he ever had to do. One of the students who he informed that a bid was not forthcoming from any house, said to him, "You mean nobody wanted me." Heartbreaking on any level, particularly for an 18-year-old student just enrolling in the university. Female students would go through rush before classes even started. There were many instances where a girl who didn't get the sorority bid she was hoping for would just leave the university for good.

The other problem was that, once the freshman students would move into the fraternity house, upperclassmen would move out. Therefore, only a few older students lived in the fraternity houses, which made it difficult to exercise much discipline under the guidance of the more senior students. The biggest problem, however, was that we had more fraternities and sororities than we had students to fill them.

I went to John White and discussed with him the problems, and suggested he appoint a Task Force for the Enhancement of Greek Life and he did so in April 2002. He asked me to chair the task force and put together a group of students, alumni, and administrators to make recommendations to him.

Unfortunately, many people felt that Chancellor White was opposed to having Greek life on campus at all. I believe those opinions were unfounded. White was a member of Sigma Nu fraternity when he was a student, and I did not detect any malice on his part against Greek life. I do think he was very concerned about alcohol consumption among fraternity members which, of course, had become a national issue and still is.

I do know, however, that his chief student affairs officer, Johnetta Cross Brazzel, was diametrically opposed to Greek life and said many times she wished we would close all the houses, fraternities, and sororities. As a Black woman I certainly understood her feelings. Many of the Greek houses still did not recruit Black members, and some of them were very much opposed to taking Black pledges. Some of that awful thinking came from older alumni who harbored racist views. My son experienced several alumni who said they would absolutely prohibit a Black person from accepting a bid from his house. He was shocked and dismayed. Many of the northern and eastern universities had crossed that horrible divide many years ago and all Greek organizations nationally allowed and accepted Black members. At my fraternity at Westminster College, we integrated the fraternity in 1971 and some houses long before. Southern fraternity and sorority houses were unconscionably slow to change, and some institutions in the south are still resistant to Black members.

I was a member of Sigma Alpha Epsilon fraternity at Westminster College. I even served as the president of the house my junior year. However, I cannot say with accuracy that I am a huge enthusiastic supporter of Greek Life. I participated and belonged in college and made lifelong friends, but, frankly, the whole concept of frat life was never that appealing to me. I thought the rituals were silly and hazing downright stupid and childish. I lived in the house for three years because it was cheaper at the time than living in an apartment and buying food and paying for utilities.

But I do know that membership in a Greek organization is very important and special to a lot of students and alumni. In fact, it is well known that alumni who belonged to Greek houses are much more likely to be philanthropic than non-Greek alumni toward their university. For me, the decision to try and help the houses was an exercise in financial management and simply good for fundraising, plain and simple!

The primary charge of the Greek task force was to forge a mutually beneficial partnership among students, alumni, and university administrators who would be committed to the long-term success of fraternities and complement the mission of the fraternity's national member organizations, as well as the university's mission as a student-centered institution. At least that was the formal charge. The real reason the task force was launched was to save the fraternities and help the sororities fill their houses.

Two members of the task force who were extremely helpful were alumni Gary George and Charles Whiteside. They worked very hard to establish new guidelines that could be implemented to save Greek life on the campus. We knew we had to do something to appeal to more students to go through rush, and we had to get it done quickly or the entire program would be in jeopardy.

After a six-month review of the University of Arkansas Greek system, the task force proposed several recommendations for improving the quality of Greek life at the institution. Perhaps the most important recommendation was to not allow men to move into the fraternity house till their sophomore year. They would live in the freshman dormitories and move into the houses in their sophomore year. Hopefully this recommendation would keep upperclassmen in the houses much longer than was the case at the present time. More upperclassmen in the houses would help with maturity and discipline. An important side effect would be more students living in residence halls.

The task force was also deeply concerned about the condition of the chapter houses and knew something had to be done to improve them and maintain them in proper order. We were particularly concerned about safety issues and adherence to fire codes.

Within two years of adopting the task force recommendations, over 1,000 men were going through rush. It looked like a bright future for Greek life on campus. Charlie Whiteside, Kappa Sig alumnus and chapter advisor called me one day all in a huff. "Where are we going to put all of these people who want to join the house!" I just laughed out loud and said what a great problem to have. The fruits of unintended consequences had come home to roost. Many of the houses were not prepared to take in so many new members and a few refused to increase their quotas. The first year 300 men did not receive bids, which caused much criticism from parents and students. We lost several students who left the university when they did not get a bid due to availability of space in the houses. I wasn't happy. It seemed to me that our student services folks had been asleep at the switch and were not carefully monitoring the situation and allowing the houses to dictate the numbers. We made a lot of folks unhappy when they could not get bids. It would take a few years for everything to iron out and the houses to start taking more students.

CHAPTER 28
NOLAN RICHARDSON DISMISSAL

> *A lifetime contract for a coach means if you're ahead in the third quarter and moving the ball, they can't fire you.*
>
> — *LOU HOLTZ*

Coach Nolan Richardson was an icon in Arkansas sports history. He came to the university in 1985 from The University of Tulsa. He won a national basketball championship in 1994. He began his coaching career at Bowie High School in El Paso, Texas, his hometown. His mother died young, and he and his two siblings were raised by his grandmother, who had a major impact on his life.

I did not know Nolan all that well, but had been around him a few times. I liked him. He was direct and suffered no fools. You always knew where he stood. Unfortunately, he had an abysmal record in graduating students, one of the worst in the nation. I overheard him make a comment about his players: that they don't come to the university to study but to play basketball and chase women.

The fan base loved him because he won games ... until he didn't. For most hardened fans winning is all that counts. Graduating with a degree was not—and in some quarters still isn't—seen as important.

But, as educators, it is our duty to graduate students and is the final culmination of the reason one attends a university. Most athletes will not go on to play in the pros; for those who cannot aspire to play in the big leagues after college a degree is paramount. That didn't seem to be of any importance to Coach Richardson.

Frank Broyles was unhappy when Nolan started losing games. Their relationship deteriorated. Nolan would rail about the negative stereotypes Black coaches were subjected to. When things turned sour for Nolan, Frank was giving consideration to making a change. He seemed to have the support of the board of trustees. Then Nolan miraculously won the conference title, and he was back in good graces for the time being. Later Nolan went through another losing streak and no doubt felt his job might be in jeopardy.

In 2002 he began criticizing the university administration, and made a comment to the media, saying, "If they go ahead and pay me my money, they can take my job tomorrow." Athletics director Broyles was livid. He came to see John White and said that Nolan must be dismissed immediately. I always believed in his heart that White really didn't want to fire Nolan and was placed in an untenable position. The board of trustees put their usual pressure on White to act. The board always had a position when it involved athletics.

The pressure mounted and White decided that Nolan had to go, primarily due to his comments to the media—which became a national story—and pressure from Broyles and the board leadership. I had hoped perhaps White and Nolan could somehow reach a compromise and Nolan could keep his job. I believed that at heart Nolan was a good person who got caught up in the moment and said something he later regretted. Maybe he could be asked to apologize and not suffer dismissal, but it was not to be. Nolan was fired before the end of the year.

Nolan Richardson filed a lawsuit against the university, the board of trustees, and the Razorback Foundation in federal court almost immediately, citing racial discrimination. He hired the firebrand attorney, John Walker, a civil rights advocate well known for a long-running court battle over desegregation of the Little Rock schools.

While I was a bit player in the trial, I was called to testify as a witness to actions taken by White and the university that I had seen firsthand. The judge was William R. Wilson. (Interestingly, Judge Wilson changed his name to Billy Roy Wilson in 2011 to reflect his actual supposed birth name). Years before Judge Wilson had been my professor for the law school bar review course many law students take just before the bar exam. I found him to be an excellent teacher, and he used a good deal of humor—for which he was well known—during the course.

At the trial, Judge Wilson asked me about my background and I told him that I had taken the bar review course from him. He asked if he had been a good instructor and I said, "Well I did pass the bar exam." He laughed and we had a good exchange.

Nolan Richardson's lawyer, John Walker, was a tough cross examiner and frankly, rude to me and other witnesses. But that was his modus operandi: intimidate and try to scare the witness into saying something incriminating. He asked me in a condescending manner if I had become a consultant because I had been fired from my last job. I decided to list for him the 20 clients I had during my consulting years until he stopped me after hearing about 10 of them.

A member of the board of trustees was asked on the stand if he had ever told any racist jokes in his life. He calmly replied, "Yes, I told one yesterday." Our lawyers just dropped their chins in agony.

The lawsuit was dismissed in July 2004—but not before Judge Wilson slapped the university's wrist for practicing discrimination in general.

Years later we would make a concerted effort to patch things up with Nolan. In 2019 the basketball court in Bud Walton Arena was named for Coach Nolan Richardson. I believe Nolan does indeed love the university and the whole episode was most unfortunate.

CHAPTER 29
THE D RULE

> *It's kind of hard to rally around a math class.*
>
> — BEAR BRYANT

One issue that raised its ugly head in the fall semester of 2003 was the controversy over the so-called "D rule." While strictly speaking the issue did not apply solely to athletics. The media cast it as an athletics problem. For some time, the transfer of academic course credits from other colleges and universities to the University of Arkansas had been receiving a great deal of attention in the news media and talk radio shows. The discussion centered around the minimum grade allowed in a course for it to count toward the requirements for an academic degree.

Some institutions allowed the transfer of a D grade to their university while others, like the University of Arkansas, did not. Coaches and athletics benefactors suggested that it did not make for a level playing field and if an athlete cannot transfer a D grade they will go somewhere else to play sports. Several members of the University of Arkansas board of trustees believed the rule to be too restrictive and that the university was in fact losing talented athletes because of the rule. That belief was never verified on any scale that would have really made a difference. The board wanted changes, and told the system president, Alan Sugg, as well as Chancellor White that they wanted less restrictive rules.

Typically, degree requirements have been left to the faculty, and boards of trustees rarely become involved in those decisions. While it is true that the board of trustees of an institution generally has the final say in all matters, it is standard practice to leave academic issues such as transfer credits to the faculty. Faculty tend to guard their prerogatives with added zeal.

Chancellor White found himself in the middle of the controversy, trying to pacify the faculty and the board at the same time. The faculty senate made it clear that they were not in favor of board interference in this matter. In fact, the university faculty expressed disapproval of modifications of grade transfer policies by the board of trustees.

The board, at its November meeting in 2003, voted to amend the transfer of credit policy to allow a D to transfer into the UA as well as apply to a degree credit. After that board action the faculty expressed no confidence in the board, accusing the board of trustees of basing its decision on the recruitment of athletes to the university. Faculty members were quoted as saying the board of trustees had placed the well-being of the men's athletics programs ahead of the academic mission of the university. One renowned professor even suggested that the policy change promoted the university as a school for jocks. Many felt the policy changes undermined faculty authority to set academic standards. Faculty were heard to say that the board of trustees didn't care about anything but the welfare of the athletics program. There may have been some truth to that charge.

Basically, what the board did was to authorize the chancellors of each campus to make exceptions to the D rule. Unfortunately, Chancellor White was browbeaten, both by the faculty and the board, for trying to find a compromise. I admired his position but some just thought he was being stubborn. I feel certain he was attempting to stand up for academic integrity.

During my time in higher education, I have witnessed many

instances when governing boards tried to do the work of the faculty. Faculty guard their academic prerogatives and are not at all happy when those prerogatives are dismissed by boards of trustees. The furor over the D rule was kept on the pages of the media for some time, but then seemed to dissipate after a few months.

One thing this episode taught me was that the University of Arkansas faculty tend not to be very rebellious against the authority of the board. That is certainly not the case at many other institutions across the country. I have found our faculty at the University of Arkansas to be rather passive when it comes to board decisions. I have thought about the issue quite a bit, and believe most faculty at this campus are happy with their situation, like living in Fayetteville, and typically won't do anything that might jeopardize their position on the faculty. Through the years there have been many issues I could have sworn would cause the faculty to stand up to the board. Rarely does our faculty make waves after an initial voicing of concerns.

CHAPTER 30
RETIRING FRANK

> *I am not going to be a star. I am going to be a legend.*
>
> — FREDDIE MERCURY.

In the summer of 2003, I was asked to attend a meeting with John White, Alan Sugg and the chairman of the board of trustees, Bill Clark. The meeting would be held in Little Rock at the system office. Bill Clark told us Frank Broyles had lost the support of the board of trustees. He said everyone's time comes, and that retirement is always inevitable. While he very much appreciated Frank's legacy, he thought Frank had stayed too long.

Clark believed it was important that Broyles make the transition to retirement while he was still vigorous, so that we could ensure a smooth and seamless transition. He further explained that Broyles should retire while the current university leadership was in place because John White and Alan Sugg would ensure that Broyles would be treated fairly and substantially. Clark, who had a construction company and lived in Little Rock, believed it was time to heal wounds across the state from the issue of moving Little Rock football games to Fayetteville. He believed these wounds were more serious than people thought, and the only way to patch up the differences was for Broyles to retire.

John White commented that it is always wise to retire while a person is still at the top of their game. The athletics program at the university was in great shape and now would be a good time to go out as a winner. White also mentioned that Frank's wife, Barbara, had been diagnosed with Alzheimer's and that had to be a major concern for Coach Broyles. He himself was almost 80 years old, and some felt that he was losing his edge. It would be a few more years until Broyles would be diagnosed with Alzheimer's as well. Some administrators had noticed Broyles would oftentimes fall asleep in meetings and his attention span had declined.

After a long discussion, a decision was made that John White would give Frank Broyles a letter outlining the terms of retirement as athletics director and forthcoming transition. Frank would retire as athletics director on or before December 31, 2003. Everyone present agreed Broyles should be treated with the utmost dignity, and that his perquisites should be extended into his retirement. He was to be given an office at the Razorback Foundation as well as a substantial salary to continue for a period of years, which would be paid by the Razorback Foundation. It was a pretty sweet deal for Broyles. He would have a salary, office space, clerical assistance, an automobile, benefits, and club memberships for seven more years.

We ended the meeting deciding that Sugg and Clark would call all members of the board of trustees to inform them of what was about to happen. White would schedule a meeting with Coach Broyles as soon as possible. We made a list of persons who should be personally notified prior to White's meeting with Coach Broyles.

I left the meeting with doubts about the plan. Was it accurate that the board of trustees wanted Broyles to retire? I knew very well that Jim Lindsey saw Broyles as almost a father figure and I could not imagine he would be in favor of such a move. Lindsey was still on the board. Every time I was around Lindsey, he would praise Broyles and quote him incessantly. They were big buddies with years of friendship and loyalty to each other. Could Clark be wrong about the perception he had regarding all of the trustees wanting Broyles out?

I was driving to Bentonville to meet with the Walton Foundation when my cell phone rang. It was John White's assistant telling me that the media were calling the chancellor's office claiming they had knowledge that Frank Broyles was going to be fired by Dr. White. John White was not in the office and his assistant wanted to get my thoughts on how they should react. The first thing I told John's assistant was to reach John White as soon as possible and tell him to be very careful in his statements to the media. We needed to try to determine how the media got ahold of the story and exactly where their information was coming from. We didn't want to get caught in a lie if the full story was in the media's hands.

Later we determined that someone unknowingly had mentioned Frank would be retiring to a person associated with the university and athletics. That person told someone else who told someone else ... and there you have it.

Apparently Sugg and Clark had not gotten around to notifying the board of trustees of the pending action. The three University of Arkansas trustees who lived in Northwest Arkansas were livid. Gary George, Charles Scharlau, and Jim Lindsey were extremely upset by the media reports. Lindsey considered himself a very close friend of coach Broyles and one of his major protectors. Bill Clark may have misjudged the reaction from Northwest Arkansas trustees. I suspect Clark felt he would have unanimous approval among the trustees to move forward but that was certainly not the case.

After the trustees in Northwest Arkansas heard about the contemplated action in the media, they became even more protective of Broyles, and started calling the other trustees to put together an alliance of support. Unfortunately, John White became the enemy in their minds. They believed White had initiated the plan to remove Coach Broyles, when it actually came from Central Arkansas and the chairman of the board, specifically Bill Clark. But John White bore the brunt of the criticism, both by trustees in Northwest Arkansas and the media. I do believe that White thought it was time for Broyles to retire, but didn't see him pushing it until Clark interjected himself. Many people across Arkansas shared those feelings. Many did not! However, White was not the ringleader, but he bravely and courageously took the blame.

The uproar was so loud that Clark, Sugg and White had no choice but to back down. It was apparent other trustees might join with the Northwest Arkansas trustees to fight the action against Broyles. Strangely, the media also rallied to support Broyles. He won the fight to attempt to oust him. Broyles was still the powerful AD. Coach Broyles would remain athletics director for almost four more years.

In 2007 Coach Broyles would indeed retire. The board of trustees had changed, and a number of Broyles supporters had retired from the board. I remember it like it was yesterday when Coach Broyles called me and told me he was going to retire. He said he wasn't necessarily wanting to step down but that he had lost the support of the board of trustees for the first time in his history with the University of Arkansas. He didn't put up much of a fight this time. Jerry Jones, owner of the Dallas Cowboys did make a few phone calls and actually came to the board of trustees meeting where the retirement was announced and made glowing comments about Broyles. But the die was cast, and the sports icon of Arkansas retired.

Broyles had come to the University of Arkansas in 1957 after having coached at the University of Florida, Georgia Tech, and the University of Missouri. He had amassed a record of 144 wins, 58 losses and five ties. In 1964, in his seventh season, Broyles led the University of Arkansas to its only national championship in football. In 1973 he became director of athletics, which he balanced with his head coaching duties until 1976 when he retired as Razorback head coach. Soon after his retirement from coaching Broyles made a move to the broadcasting booth, working alongside legendary sports anchor Keith Jackson on ABC's college football coverage. He would continue that for nine years. He was often criticized for being a sitting AD as well as a national sports broadcaster, something that would never happen today. But Broyles was an amazing talent and was as good on ABC as anyone.

Frank accepted the fact he had to retire, and did it with the utmost dignity. He took an office at the Razorback Foundation and would remain in an advisory position at full salary for another seven years.

In 2014 I recommended to the board of trustees that Broyles be awarded an honorary degree. They agreed and on May 8, 2015, Frank became Dr. Frank Broyles.

CHAPTER 31
OLD MAIN CLOCK

> *Time is money.*
>
> — *BENJAMIN FRANKLIN*

Former President Bill Clinton was on campus and took a nighttime stroll across the Old Main lawn. He looked up at Old Main and didn't see the clock. He turned to one of his staff members and asked where the clock was? Did someone steal it? He told the staff member to call me and tell me that we needed to put the clock back in Old Main.

Of course, Old Main never had a clock.

The initial plans for Old Main outlined an actual clock for the south tower, but the hard economic times prevented the university from purchasing and installing it. In 1928, a dial was painted on the tower to give the impression of an actual clock. The painting remained on the tower until the 1970s.

I thought President Clinton had a good idea and I approached our campaign steering committee with the idea.

In 2005 the Campaign for the Twenty-First Century steering committee elected to have a clock installed in recognition of the successful fundraising campaign by UA students, faculty, capital projects and programs, which raised more than $1 billion dollars.

More than $250,000 was raised for the Old Main Clock Fund by the efforts of the campaign steering committee. Enough was raised to begin a fund that helps maintain and preserve the clock to this day.

On October 27, 2005, the clock was publicly dedicated, 130 years after Old Main's construction. The clock was custom-made by Balzer Family Clock Works, located in Freeport, Maine. The company is the only one in the U.S. that manufactures clocks of this type. It is also registered with the National Association of Watch & Clock Collectors. The clock is located on the fourth floor of Old Main, with the mechanism encased in glass. The driving rods go from the fourth floor up to the top of the tower. The 1,000-pound workings are decorated with apple blossoms, a Razorback, and cardinals, the U of A's original mascot.

Also, the original Old Main bell is located in the clock room in Old Main. The bell, made of solid brass, was cast in 1879.

A computerized bell mechanism chimes every 15 minutes. The mechanism can produce the sound of 318 bells in six voices across six octaves. The carillon plays the Westminster Chimes every hour from 8 a.m. to 8 p.m. and plays the U of A Alma Mater after the 5:00 p.m. chimes.

The person most responsible for getting the new clock up and running was the late Jerry Homesley who worked in the College of Arts and Sciences and was a clock aficionado. He worked tirelessly with Judy Schwab to be certain the clock chimed accurately. Admiral Mike Johnson also was instrumental.

The original bell and clock are still located on the fourth floor of Old Main and are worth a visit. See if you can find the Razorback and Cardinal (UA's former mascot) on the clock.

CHAPTER 32
VOLUNTEERS AND TOWERS OF OLD MAIN

> *We make a living by what we get, but we make a life by what we give.*
>
> — *WINSTON CHURCHILL*

The University of Arkansas had used volunteers for fundraising in the past, but we were about to rev that up to a whole new level. We ended up engaging over 300 volunteers in all aspects of a new campaign we called the Campaign for the Twenty-First Century.

Soon after I arrived at the university John White asked me to call on alumnus Jim Faulkner in Little Rock. Jim had an idea he wanted to explore with me. We had lunch at the Little Rock Country Club, and he told me the university needed a gift club like the Razorback Foundation. He felt strongly that it would be a catalyst for people to aspire to reaching new heights of giving. He also told me no one had ever asked him for a major gift for academic purposes, nor had anyone ever called on him from the university. I was surprised. It would be a chorus I would hear throughout our campaign. Another alumnus, Gaston Gibson, told me the same thing. He had never been asked to make a gift to his alma mater, other than for athletics.

Jim was a well-known advertising executive having founded James H. Faulkner Advertising which grew into Faulkner and Associates one of the largest and most respected marketing firms in the Southwest. Later, he and his wife Joyce would become major donors to the university, making a gift that funded The Jim & Joyce Faulkner Performing Arts Center. Through the years they would become dear friends to Jane and me and marvelous benefactors to many causes across Arkansas.

I agreed with Jim Faulkner that we certainly did need a major gift club or society that would get alumni thinking of making sizable gifts to the university. I asked him to chair a committee to establish such an organization. We asked another alumnus and former board of trustees chairman, Lewis Epley, to serve on the committee.

At Penn State we did have such an organization called the Mt. Nittany Society. We used that as the model for our new Old Main Society. A person became a member of the Old Main Society by having a cumulative giving record of at least $100,000. That amount would increase over the years.

During the years of the campaign, we literally inducted hundreds of people into the Old Main Society at an annual black-tie dinner. It was most interesting to encounter alumni and friends who wanted to be a member of the group and would make gifts and pledges so they could participate in the new giving club. Today there are 964 Towers members. The late Jim Faulkner would be thrilled.

CHAPTER 33
SECOND BOOK AND CASE CONFLICT

> *I think I did pretty well, considering I started out with nothing but a bunch of blank paper.*
>
> — STEVE MARTIN

My first book was published in 1995 while I was at Penn State. The trade organization representing all college and university business officers, the National Association of College and University Business Officers (NACUBO), contacted me in 1993 and asked if I would write a book on capital campaigns at institutions of higher education. I agreed to do so.

The book was well received, or I guess well received with such a limited audience. In 2005, NACUBO contacted me again and asked that I write a second book, sort of an update to the one in 1995 on the tenth anniversary of the first publication. I suppose they caught me at a weak moment, and I agreed to their request. This book would be more comprehensive with an appendix of several tools development officers could use in their approach to campaigning. The second book would also be published by NACUBO in 2006.

The book was to be a collaboration with the Council for

Advancement and Support of Education (CASE) just like my first book. NACUBO would publish the book and CASE would promote it.

In 1994 CASE asked me to serve on a blue-ribbon committee to create guidelines for counting gifts to a capital campaign. That sounds like an easy task, but it was actually quite complicated. No standards existed and institutions were all over the board in what they counted in their gift totals. That had the effect of skewing the totals in campaign reporting so no one really knew what was actually being raised by colleges and universities in campaigns. Comparisons from one institution to the next were impossible. We also discovered that some places were misreporting government gifts or estate gifts that had never come to fruition. In short, it was a mess and CASE wanted us to clean it up. Big Ten institutions were putting enormous pressure on CASE to come out with solid guidelines that all would be expected to follow. I was a prime author of the first iteration of the guidelines CASE would adopt. I would serve on the committee a second time a few years later to iron out a few areas that some found confusing.

In an effort not to bore the reader I won't go into dramatic detail, but the biggest controversy was how to count estate gifts and charitable remainder trusts (CRT) that had not yet materialized to the institution. (Basically, a CRT pays an income to a benefactor for a lifetime or period of years and when the donor dies the trust comes to the organization).

In the 1995 book I had actually included in the appendix the new CASE guidelines we had promulgated. However, around 2005 CASE formed another committee made up of a whole different set of development officers to make serious revisions to the guidelines created over the past decade or so. I did not agree with the revisions, nor did the SEC or Big Ten schools. We held several conference calls with my colleagues in the SEC and Big Ten and decided to lobby CASE leadership to change the guidelines back to where they were originally promulgated.

In my new book I wrote about the revisions and pointed out that many professionals were not happy with the changes. I urged CASE to revise the most recent rendition and put the guidelines back as they were originally prescribed.

My book came out in 2006 and the president of CASE, John Lippincott, reneged on our handshake agreement that they would promote the book. I wrote John a letter asking why he reneged, and he wrote me back simply saying that CASE was under no legal duty or obligation to promote my book and because I disagreed with their new guidelines, promoting my book would be confusing to their members.

I called my contact at NACUBO and she was equally shocked, but did not want to get involved in battling the issue as she feared she might upset NACUBO's new president and possibly damage her relationship with him. John White even wrote a letter on my behalf to the NACUBO president, but it went nowhere. I was livid. I was being muzzled for disagreeing with my trade organization. A national organization had just tromped on my first amendment rights and kept me from expressing a different viewpoint.

Lippincott did not come out of the fundraising genre. He had been the public relations officer for a small college before becoming CASE president. He knew very little about fundraising and less about how to count gifts. He was the product of small liberal arts colleges and had no understanding of multimillion-dollar capital campaigns at major institutions. Because of his limited knowledge and level of campaign ignorance, he allowed the old guidelines to be revised.

I did not make it a secret with my colleagues around the country who wrote numerous letters supporting me. In fact, a few of them resigned from CASE over the issue, including the vice presidents of Big Ten and SEC institutions. One point I should make is that it had nothing to do with money. I had signed away the profits from the book to NACUBO before it was published. That is common for a book of this type with a limited audience. I wasn't trying to make a profit, but to contribute to my profession.

CASE never promoted the book or mentioned it in any of their publications. But, a couple years later CASE revised the reporting guidelines back to where they had been a decade before. I guess that is some sweet justice. I had been very active in CASE and my division at Penn State had been honored with the top advancement CASE award three years in a row, signifying the best institutional advancement program in the country and internationally. I never again participated in CASE programs. I believe CASE has lost its way and no longer represents the interests of major public institutions.

CHAPTER 34
DRIVING THEM CRAZY!

> *By all means don't drink the last cold Diet Coke.*
>
> — JUDY SCHWAB

I have no doubt that through the years I have driven the staff who have worked for me absolutely crazy. Jane used to joke with the staff that she was going to put out an APB (all-points bulletin) when I headed to the office. She was glad to get me out of the house but felt sorry for my staff.

I demanded a lot from the staff and expected them to dedicate themselves totally to our goals and objectives. For the most part, I enjoyed very competent staff members who worked hard and worked smart. My office staff was extraordinary in their commitment to a strong work ethic.

Leading the team was Judy Schwab who ran my office on a day-to-day basis. She has a master's degree in English, which was extremely important to me as she edited all my writings and speeches to ensure I used the proper Queen's English. When I first came back to the university as vice chancellor, Judy was being recruited by the Fayetteville Public Schools to be an assistant superintendent. I called John White to get a read on her and he told me she was one of the ones I should work hard to keep. He wasn't kidding! Judy Schwab is the definition of competent. Not only is she extraordinarily intelligent but people enjoy working with her and she is able to deliver bad news with a smile.

Judy worked with me in the vice chancellor's office and then came with me to the chancellor's suite. I simply could not have done the job without her marvelous support. Judy was involved in every major decision during my time as both vice chancellor and chancellor. She was indispensable in so many respects and deserves much of the credit for our many successes.

I also had four highly competent assistants, on and off, as VC and chancellor. They handled my mail and appointments and kept the office running smoothly. Both Laura Cate and Gloria Sutherland were first class members of the team and provided me with extraordinary support daily. Marcia Overby was also an important member of the team and was our liaison to the system office and board of trustees. Marcia has served several chancellors and her institutional memory was very important to me during my time as chancellor. In addition to her hard work as a member of our team, she was able to get her doctorate in higher education, not an easy task for a full-time staff member. Marcia is good as gold. And Sally Adams was the other member of the team who was indispensable. She handled all of my correspondence and did an incredible job for all the years she worked with me. She quickly learned my writing voice and could create letters that sounded exactly like my voice. She would give the correspondence I would later sign to Judy who would check them off and then deliver them to my desk. It worked like a well-oiled machine clear through my time as chancellor.

One morning when I arrived at the office, I found an index card on my desk entitled "Survival Code for Working With Dave Gearhart." It was signed "Anonymous." Here is the survival code:

1. Follow up.
2. Live by the axiom, "No time like the present."
3. When Gearhart says no rush, don't believe him.

4. Check and double check everything, be certain all information given to Dave is current and accurate because he will catch any errors.
5. If you make a mistake, admit it. Don't try to cover up. Tell him what steps you've taken or will take to be certain it won't happen again.
6. If he asks your opinion, give it to him as straightforwardly and succinctly as possible. There is no reason to be timid.
7. Follow up some more and some more.
8. Don't bring him problems without also proposing solutions.
9. Know you can ask for his assistance and counsel any time.
10. By all means, don't drink the last cold Diet Coke.

I suspect that little ditty was orchestrated by Judy. Truth be known I loved it and I guess I lived it.

CHAPTER 35
THE CAMPAIGN FOR THE TWENTY-FIRST CENTURY

> *It is more blessed to give than to receive.*
>
> — ACTS 20:35

For much too long, Arkansas had languished at the bottom of national rankings of educational and economic indicators, and its people had not prospered as they deserved. While Arkansas was struggling, other states were rapidly building economies that threatened to widen the prosperity gap between Arkansans and the rest of America.

Many believed high-quality research universities were the very foundation of these new economies that other states were witnessing. The University of Arkansas was the only major research university in the state as defined by the Carnegie Foundation for the Advancement of Teaching. The University of Arkansas is unique among the almost 50 institutions of higher learning in the state. The University of Arkansas is charged not only with teaching undergraduate students, but also with inventing new knowledge through research to improve the human condition. We believed the University of Arkansas was poised to become a nationally competitive, student-centered research university that could be the engine of Arkansas' economy. But it could do so only by increasing its resource base substantially. Increased private gift support was the best hope for doing so. We believed the Campaign for the Twenty-First Century was the vessel for that hope. We wanted the university to be the undisputed, preeminent leader in Arkansas in teaching and research, and take our place among the world's great, model, public universities.

While we were already nationally competitive in many areas, we wanted a global vision in which we embraced more students and faculty in our community who have a global impact on the quality of life. Our tangible mission became one of primarily serving the citizens of Arkansas, as well as the global community through the further integration and advancement of teaching and learning, research and discovery, and outreach and engagement. If we could accomplish that through philanthropy, we would improve the quality of life in the state, and help elevate Arkansas among the nation's leaders in social, economic, intellectual, and cultural development and opportunity.

Many citizens of Arkansas did not understand why a major research university was at all important to the state. With a small number of citizens in the state earning college degrees, a major research institution did not hold much clout in the collective mind. We worked very hard to show the populace, as well as the legislature, that the economy of the state would be increasingly based on technology, science, and knowledge, and we needed to foster new products, processes, and discoveries for economic progress. It became most evident that we were not going to be able to rely on the General Assembly to provide the much-needed resources to make progress on these fronts. Too many legislators didn't appreciate the importance of a research university in their midst. It was imperative that we bring in private philanthropy if we were going to progress.

But we knew the economy of Arkansas in the future would be based on technology, science and knowledge. Our research was spawning new products, processes, discoveries, insights and interpretations necessary for economic and cultural progress. New start-up businesses would be based on a knowledge-based economy and would transfer technology from the classroom and lab to the marketplace. UA research was fostering a vibrant entrepreneurial climate and enhanced venture capital availability, and educating a scientifically and technologically trained workforce for our state's future. We were bringing in increased dollars to the state from outside sources for research projects, and having an overwhelmingly positive impact on the Arkansas economy. We were positioned to deliver profound economic benefits to the state with our research programs. We believed, as UA research continued to grow and develop, it would provide the scientific, technological, and intellectual infrastructure the state needed for the economy moving forward.

Most people have no idea that public universities educate over 85 percent of undergraduate students and 70 percent of all graduate students in the United States. They produce more than 50 percent of the doctorates granted in this country in the national needs categories, including 92 percent of doctoral degrees in agriculture and 90 percent in natural resources and conservation, and 80 percent in computer and information sciences and engineering. We knew Arkansas could not sustain a competitive economy and provide adequate and well-paying jobs without developing new technologies and products, as well as enhancing productivity.

We strongly believed the fortunes of our state were deeply and inextricably connected to the quality of our universities, our ability to produce Arkansans with bachelor's degrees, and the amount of state, federal, and private investment in university-based research and development.

According to the Arkansas Department of Higher Education's funding formula, which the Arkansas General Assembly passed, the state's public four-year colleges and universities were underfunded by the state by approximately $250 million when we launched the Campaign for the Twenty-First Century. Our campus was underfunded by over $40 million and that is on an annual basis!

John White had made fundraising a key component of his administration from day one. As mentioned earlier, he wanted to raise over a billion dollars and appeal to alumni, corporations, and foundations as never before. While there was a professional program in place, much better than when I was at the university in the early 1980's, there was still much work to be done to build a solid program that was sustainable on an annual basis.

I could feel from the start that he knew fundraising, having been a dean at Georgia Tech, and came into the job as chancellor with a very good base of knowledge on what it would take to raise that level of resources. John was a pusher. He knew what he wanted and was completely cognizant that to get there he could not rely on public resources or tuition income to make it happen. His dreams and aspirations for the university would require private resources and lots of it. I could also tell from the very first that John trusted me to know how to get results, and he would follow our plan to launch a major capital campaign.

In 1998 our first order of business for the Campaign for the Twenty-First Century at the University of Arkansas was to build an infrastructure of new staff and volunteers. When I arrived back at Arkansas, we had a modest staff and a very small operating budget for our division of advancement. I knew I would have to bring in some very competent staff members and started thinking about people I knew in the business who I might be able to recruit.

I thought immediately of three people who had worked for me at Penn State, Clay and Sandy Edwards and Roger Williams. They had all done a superb job with the Penn State campaign and had developed a national reputation as top-flight advancement officers.

The Edwards were both excellent fundraisers and I knew that I would have to recruit them as a team if I was going to convince them to make the move from State College, Pennsylvania to Fayetteville. I wasn't at all certain they would be interested in moving to the southwest. Fortunately, both expressed interest in coming to Arkansas and I was able to offer them jobs as associate vice presidents. It was the smartest decision I ever made, and bringing them to Arkansas made all the difference in the world for our ability to get the Campaign for the Twenty-First Century up and running quickly.

Sandy, the face of the campaign, had an extraordinary and uncanny ability to establish close relationships with our volunteers and potential benefactors. Clay was also a great fundraiser but also had an amazing ability at organization and running a development operation. Clay ran the internal operations of the campaign while Sandy focused more externally. It was a match made in heaven, and they did more to make the campaign successful than anyone.

Sadly, at the end of the campaign Clay Edwards would pass away suddenly and unexpectedly. I will never forget the phone call I received on a cold day in January: Sandy had found Clay sitting in his chair in the lower level of their Fay Jones house having suffered an apparent heart attack. The day before Clay had appeared healthy and vibrant. His father had lived into his 90s and Clay thought he would as well. He was only 59 years old when he died, and it was devastating to everyone. Clay and Sandy were highly respected in Northwest Arkansas by our staff, faculty, deans, and vice chancellors. Sandy was inconsolable and had difficulty going back into the office where they had worked so closely together. I was asked to speak at the funeral service, and it was extremely emotional. The Presbyterian church was full to capacity.

Soon after Clay's death, Sandy determined that it was just too difficult to remain at the University of Arkansas without Clay, and was recruited by the Walton family to be the deputy director of the new art museum Alice Walton was launching. She became a key member of the staff at the Crystal Bridges Museum of Art. Losing Sandy was a devastating blow to our program and the university in general, but I knew she simply could not remain at the university without Clay. They did everything together, coming to work in the morning and leaving after a long day, usually around 7 p.m.. Sandy needed something new and different in her life that wouldn't be a constant reminder of losing Clay. She told me she found it difficult to even go into her office without Clay by her side. It was heartbreaking. While I was bereft at her leaving, I certainly understood her decision. It would be a loss that would reverberate for many years to come.

Sandy will conclude her professional life at Crystal Bridges, and was one of the early members of the staff at the museum who was responsible for much of their success. Jane and I have remained close friends with Sandy. She is a gem.

Clay Edwards, Sandy Edwards, Susan Stoltz, Jodi Melhorn, Mel Melhorn

Sandy and Clay deserve the credit for much of the success of the Campaign for the Twenty-First Century. They were hard workers, intelligent, and knew how to raise funds and establish relationships. They recruited many of our best staff members, some of whom are still with the University of Arkansas.

The other person was also a Penn State staff member. Roger Williams had been the associate vice president for university relations at Penn State. He was superb. He left Penn State shortly after I did and was in private consulting. I convinced him to come to Arkansas and work with me. He did so for five years, flying back to State College on most weekends to see his wife. Roger is one of the smartest people I have ever met and a brilliant writer. He would later go back to Penn State as head of the Alumni Association and enjoyed a distinguished career until his retirement. Jane and I have stayed in close touch with him all these many years.

Mark Power, Dan Hendrix, Jim Harris, John Tolleson and Harley Lewis were staff members and amazing fundraisers during the campaign. Mark was well liked by staff and donors, Dan headed up our corporate and foundations office and garnered phenomenal support from those benefactors and would go on to be the distinguished founding president of the Arkansas World Trade Center. Jim was a tax attorney and ran our planned giving office. He knew planned giving backwards and forwards and assisted me on numerous large gifts to the university. John was extraordinary in asking for the gift. One of the best I ever encountered. Harley was a former athletics director and accomplished fundraiser before arriving at the university. He knew how to ask for the order and raised millions of dollars for the campaign, in particular our Greek houses and for scholarships.

Mike Macechko was head of the Arkansas Alumni association and did an extraordinary job; he was a key factor in the success of the campaign. His wife, Kris, handled all of our constituent relations work and was amazing in donor relations activity. Proposal writers Anne Green and Jim Taylor cranked out hundreds of superb proposals. Much of the campaign's success is due to their important work.

And, of course, Judy Schwab, who contributed immeasurably to success in the campaign. I'm not sure we would have been successful without Judy. She was an absolute rock!

At an early meeting of the campaign steering committee, we invited former Arkansas governors and United States senators Dale Bumpers and David Pryor to speak at a dinner following the meeting. They were joined by former Senator Kaneaster Hodges. They challenged their colleagues to make the campaign an unprecedented success. "As Jack Kennedy used to say, 'We can do better.' We can do better by this university …. It's more than a matter of pride. It's doing our best for future generations, this state and the nation," said Bumpers.

Added Pryor, "If not us, who? If not now, when? If we don't do this now for Arkansas, who will."

It was a magical evening. The campaign had begun in style and class.

In the early days we needed to find a source of revenue for our

THE CAMPAIGN FOR THE TWENTY-FIRST CENTURY   211

development operations. I knew we could not expect the university to foot the entire bill for the campaign, as the budget was very tight. We explored a number of ways we could finance the effort. We would use unrestricted gifts; we would charge a small fee to administer annual giving and we would use basis points off of the endowment.

Many institutions charge a small percentage of the income off of the endowment to pay for fundraising costs. The average among institutions was 100 basis points (1 percent) to be used to defray costs of operations. The head of the University of Arkansas Foundation, David Malone, was giving us 40 basis points for operations. I appealed directly to him to increase that amount, but he refused. He claimed he already had too many expenses running the foundation and we would have to remain at 40 basis points. I tried to explain to him that we were attempting to dramatically increase the size of the endowment, but we needed resources to bring in new dollars. I didn't move him one inch.

Many, if not most, private university foundations are under the control of the fundraising staff. Sometimes the fundraising staff are considered university employees, and sometimes they are employees of the foundation. At Arkansas, the vice chancellor in charge of fundraising had no control whatsoever over foundation business.

Because of confidentiality issues, I could not tell Malone that we were working on a very large gift that would make revenue projections much better, as I was sworn to secrecy about our negotiations with the Walton Foundation. I had worked well with Malone up to that point and liked him very much. I suppose he was only doing his job in his mind, but it put much pressure on our ability to finance the campaign. I had a tough time understanding how he could be the sole determiner of the basis points on our funds. Shouldn't we have some input into how we divvied up the earnings on our campus endowment.

Years later, when I was chancellor, one of our benefactors, Tommy Boyer, a former basketball star and businessman, objected to having basis points from his endowment used for development operations. Tommy and I had a broken relationship as he had been pushing aggressively to have basketball Coach Mike Anderson fired. He also wanted athletics director Jeff Long dismissed. I ignored his demands.

I believed he used the issue of bonus points for operations to get back at me. He took his battle to the system president at the time, Dr. Don Bobbitt, who allowed an exception to be made. I was close to retirement and decided to just keep quiet but didn't like the precedent for other benefactors who might want to do the same thing, making it impossible to finance fundraising operations. Boyer's attitude over a relatively small amount of money seemed petty and silly, but he wanted the meager few dollars from his alma mater returned to him. They were funds that came from interest earned on the endowment fund he had established and were not even very significant. He had even been a co-chair of the Campaign for the Twenty-First Century.

Boyer would later become a university trustee.

One of the major jobs ahead of us was to recruit volunteers to our campaign steering committee. John White and I traveled across the country to recruit our top volunteers, and we only had one person turn us down for membership.

We decided we would have multiple cochairs for the campaign that would rotate over the term of the effort. We were fortunate to be able to recruit Rob Walton and Jim Walton to serve as cochairs. We also invited coach Frank Broyles to serve as a cochair. For the volunteer position of treasurer of the campaign we recruited Johnelle Hunt of the Hunt Transport Services Company. Lee Bodenhamer, an alumnus and investment banker from Little Rock was another big player in the campaign. Lee would go on to establish the Bodenhamer Fellowship program, which recruited some of the brightest students to the university. His early multimillion-dollar gift to establish the program set the bar for other members of our committee. Lee showed the way for others to make very sizable gifts to the campaign and he established a serious tone for philanthropy. Julian Stewart, a former IBM executive, was another early volunteer and supporter. He and his wife, Nana, were generous donors to the university for many years. The Tyson interests also were major donors and John Tyson a volunteer.

When the University of Arkansas publicly announced the Campaign for the Twenty-First Century on October 26, 2001, the campus community was invited to a pep-rally-style event on the steps of Mullins Library. At that time, $270.3 million had been raised in gifts and pledges during the silent phase beginning in 2001. Fast forward to June 22, 2005, when the university announced the campaign had surpassed its $1 billion goal. Eight days later, the campaign ended, and the total amount raised was $1.046 billion in gifts and pledges. That was unprecedented for any organization in Arkansas by large margins. The Campaign for the Twenty-First Century forever changed the University of Arkansas, as well as the state itself. Thousands of generous benefactors contributed and supported key investments in faculty positions, student scholarships, and much needed capital improvements. As a result, those benefactors helped elevate the U of A's quality, affordability, and accessibility, and helped position us for even greater academic success and service to the people of Arkansas. The campaign would improve our national rankings and enhance the reputation of the faculty and students.

Outcomes of the Campaign for the Twenty-First Century included the creation of the Honors College and endowments for the library and graduate school, 162 endowed faculty chairs and professorships and 1,936 endowed scholarships and fellowships. When we started the campaign, we had only 19 endowed faculty positions, which had accumulated throughout the entire history of the university. The new endowments enabled us to hire many faculty away from some of the most prestigious institutions in the world.

More than 41,600 new donors participated in the campaign, and the total number of individuals who contributed reached 72,641. In sum, benefactors made 304,328 gifts and pledges to the campaign. My heart swells with appreciation when I look at the sheer numbers of individuals who participated—and participated multiple times—throughout that seven-year effort. $39 million went to the libraries, and almost $300 million to facilities, including the Pat Walker

Health Center, Willard Walker Hall, J.B. Hunt Transport Services Building, Bev Lewis Women's Center, a law school expansion, the Fred and Mary Smith Golf Center, Donald W. Reynolds Razorback Stadium, University House renovations and literally hundreds of classrooms and labs.

APPA (formerly the Association of Physical Plant Administrators) claims that there exists in this country a backlog of $112 billion in facilities needs at institutions of higher education. The Campaign for the Twenty-First Century carved into that figure measurably as far as our campus was concerned. More would come later when we decided to undertake a huge renovation program of our iconic buildings.

Advancement staff celebrate after achieving $1 billion in the Campaign for the Twenty-First Century.

CHAPTER 36
QUANTUM: $300 MILLION

> *A billion here, a billion there, and pretty soon you're talking real money.*
>
> — EVERETT DIRKSEN

Of course, the largest gift to the campaign came from the Walton family. John White and I had been discussing a strategy for engaging the family in what we hoped would be a game-changing gift from the Waltons. Since both Rob Walton and Jim Walton were members of our campaign committee and alumni, we believed and hoped they would be interested in doing something special.

Early in the campaign the family had already contributed $50 million to the College of Business. The College was subsequently named for Sam Walton. Doyle Williams, dean of the college at the time, was mostly responsible for that gift. I'll never forget when he called me to let me know of the gift—he said that would be a good start for the campaign we were planning. It certainly set a good tone for the future of philanthropy at the university. Of all the deans I had worked with during my tenure in higher education, Doyle was one of, if not, the best. He was gracious, professional, caring, thoughtful and determined to make the Walton College into one of the finest business schools in the nation. By the time he retired, he had managed to climb in the rankings to number 25 among undergraduate public business schools. Quite a feat, and he deserves much of the credit for making it happen. I'm certain the Walton family knew they were backing a real winner when they made the $50 million gift.

We knew that we had to have a program that would appeal to the Waltons if we were going to engage them in something much larger, we just didn't know what it could be at that time. We were certain they would not just give to a "capital campaign" without some real definition, and we needed something to appeal to them. We were also aware that they would be most interested in economic development and quality of life for Northwest Arkansas and its citizens. At that time, we did not know what the size of a gift might be, or if it would even be possible to interest the family in making another major gift after the $50 million gift to the business school. However, we started thinking about what might be possible as early as 1998.

John White had spoken to Mrs. Helen Walton soon after he arrived on campus in 1997 about the possibility of doing something epic. John told me that he tossed out a figure of $1 billion. That was John, going for gold from the git go! Apparently, Mrs. Walton replied to him, "Don't kill the hen that lays the golden egg." So, we had an idea that a figure of that size would be a reach too far. I admired White for going for broke. He had an amazing passion for wanting to improve the University of Arkansas across the board and a gift of that magnitude would do it.

I was still receiving information and literature from Penn State and read that my friend, Bill Schreyer, had made a $30 million gift to Penn State to establish an honors college. I immediately called him to congratulate him on the gift, which was one of the largest ever made to Penn State. He sent me all the details on how the college would work and how it would fit into the fabric of the established academic programs. Something clicked that perhaps the model at Penn State might be used by Arkansas to appeal to the Waltons.

Penn State hoped to use the funds to recruit high caliber faculty and students.

Maybe we could do the same thing here at the University of Arkansas. I immediately went to see John White to get his reaction to establishing an honors college. He loved the idea, but added an important component. He also wanted to do something that would benefit our graduate school, library and research initiatives. I showed him the Penn State literature on their new honors college concept, and he decided we should pursue that path to engage the Waltons. So, the idea initially came from Pennsylvania State University, and we used their model for our purposes. I was proud of that fact, which would probably be lost to history but for this writing.

A few years after the Waltons made the $300 million gift, Bill Schreyer called me and said, somewhat jokingly, that he would make a nice gift to our campaign and the Honors College if we could convince the Waltons to donate to his honors college at Penn State. I laughed and said, "Bill, I don't think it works that way!"

One person critical to our success was the individual who managed the Walton philanthropy, Stewart Springfield. Jane and I were fortunate to get to know Stewart and his wife Yvonne early in our tenure at the university. Stewart took no prisoners and could be very direct, but we liked both of them from the beginning. They were real people who had a wonderful sense of humor, and didn't mind socializing on a personal basis. They invited us to their home around 1999 and came to our house a few times too. We grew to be good friends in a very short time.

Tragically, Stewart was out jogging one day and when he came home, he told Yvonne he wasn't feeling well. He said that perhaps he might need to go to the hospital, so they loaded up the car and started off to emergency care. By the time they arrived at the hospital Stewart had died. We assumed that he was the victim of the heart anomaly known as the widow maker. He was only 50 years old. I remember it like it was yesterday when I got the call from Rick Chapman, of the Walton family office, that Stewart had expired. I had seen him only a week before and he seemed so vibrant. I was in total shock. To honor Stewart's leadership and commitment to fostering educational outreach, the U of A created the Stewart T. Springfield Professorship in Educational Administration in the College of Education and Health Professions, and named a primary conference room in his honor. We announced the naming at a special luncheon on campus.

Buddy Philpot, an Arvest banker, would replace Stewart as head of the Walton foundations. Buddy too was a wonderful person who was easy to communicate with, and most helpful to me in those early years. He would be a big player in Walton giving over the coming years.

The other person connected to the Waltons who I had already met and grown fond of was Rick Chapman. Rick managed the Walton Enterprises office, colloquially known as the family office. He would also become a huge player in the $300 million gift. The Walton family had total confidence in Chapman, and he was their senior advisor and ran their home office.

We decided to approach the Waltons in 2000 through Rick and Buddy, and float the idea of a major gift to the campaign. My job was to feel out the situation and thoughts on the size of the ask and the programs it would be used for. I had lunch with Rick and tossed out our ideas of an Honors College, library and graduate school endowment. He asked what seemed like a hundred questions. That was Rick, incredibly astute and street smart, but always protective of the Waltons. He raised the issue of gift size. I told him that we did not feel we could accomplish all we needed unless the potential gift approached $300 million. John White had come up with that figure from calculations that I never quite understood. John had an engineer's mind and often I just listened to his rationale and didn't try to question his thinking. If it sounded good, go with it. That was my way of dealing with White's intelligence. He was absolutely brilliant. Rick looked at me and didn't flinch and immediately said that was a figure that was certainly on the high side and further commented that he had no idea how the family would react.

I didn't realize that my brother, Jeff, had been on opposite sides in a business deal with Rick Chapman. Jeff was practicing law at the time with the firm Kutak Rock in Little Rock. Jeff had previously been at the Rose Law Firm, but had been wooed away by Kutak. Both Rick and Jeff were understandably trying to protect their client's financial interests. At one point in my early relationship with Rick he asked me if I was related to Jeff Gearhart. He laughed at my response. I said, "Well it depends!" Later Jeff and Rick would become friends and colleagues, but not until Jeff joined Walmart as general counsel. They worked together on many projects and developed an admiration of each other's business prowess. But, for a time, I thought I might have to disown my baby brother.

Campaign funds were raised for six critical areas of need: faculty positions, scholarship funds, improving existing academic programs, creating new ones in key areas, strengthening University of Arkansas Libraries, constructing new academic facilities, and increasing annual giving to enhance a variety of university programs. The size and success of the Campaign for the Twenty-First Century helped people understand how private gift support could transform an institution —and how that transformation would ripple through the state, cementing the University of Arkansas' role as a partner, resource, and catalyst in advancing the state's economic, cultural, social, and educational needs and potential.

Private support would become even more essential, considering economic conditions that had seen flat or declining financial support from government appropriations. This factor, combined with the aspirations of our students and our state, underscore the importance and necessity of private giving to the University of Arkansas.

One hurdle we had to climb was the feeling on the part of the family that they did not want to fund anything the state should be funding. We hit that head on and attempted to show that the state legislature was not going to put any resources into the endowment. Of course, the family was certainly cognizant that the General Assembly was underfunding the flagship campus by at least $40 million on an annual basis. We held our breath that the poor support from the legislature would not hurt us in the eyes of the Walton family.

While we were working with the Walton family on the gift, Chapman told us that the family would like us to keep it strictly confidential until a decision had been made, when they would then allow us to announce the gift. So, we decided we had to come up with something to call the proposal for confidential purposes, even for referring to it around the office. Roger Williams came up with the name, "Quantum." Therefore, from the very beginning we named the proposal "Quantum" and referred to it that way leading up to the announcement.

One bright and sunny day in 2001 I received a call from Rick Chapman asking John White and me to attend by telephone a Walton family meeting. Rick told me that, at the meeting, the proposal for the $300 million gift would be discussed. When the day came for the meeting John and I gathered in his office and waited for White's private telephone line to ring.

Our part of the call lasted about one hour and the Walton family, including members of the third generation, asked a number of questions. We were then dismissed from the call. About 30 minutes later my cell telephone rang and Rick asked if I could get with John White and call him back. I was in the parking lot by the administration building getting ready to go to a campaign committee meeting on the Fayetteville square. I immediately went to John's office and we called Rick. He informed us that the family had approved our request for $300 million, but that we should keep it confidential for the time being. John and I gave each other a big hug and proceeded to the meeting.

We had told Clay and Sandy Edwards, Judy Schwab, and Roger Williams that we would give them an agreed-on signal if the news was good. We arrived late to the campaign committee meeting and Clay, Sandy, Roger, and Judy were waiting for the appropriate signal which John gave them with a big grin. We were all beyond pleased. The largest gift ever made to a public university and the fifth largest contribution to a higher education institution, public or private, had just been given to the University of Arkansas. Never before had an institution of our scope received a gift of this magnitude. The ivy schools and major public institutions had garnered many large gifts before, but this was unprecedented for a school in the southwest to land such a remarkable commitment. It was indeed epic.

About $200 million of the donation was used to create an undergraduate Honors College and to support its research, faculty, scholarships, and study abroad programs, in addition to library and technology support. The rest would be used for other academic needs, including endowing the graduate school and doubling the size of its enrollment to 5,500 students by 2010. The university libraries received a significant chunk as well.

We would publicly announce the gift several weeks later in the International Connections Lounge in the student union. We had a packed crowd as Roger had done a beautiful job drumming up a good crowd to attend.

The donation was contingent upon the university raising another $300 million for academic and support programs by June 30, 2004. The donation would more than double the size of the university's endowment, valued at that time at about $200 million—a small sum compared to most major universities.

After the gift was made, Rick Chapman told me the family was in favor of allowing us to use the gift as an incentive match, to entice other benefactors to make gifts of faculty chairs, professorships, fellowships and student scholarships.

What the Waltons allowed us to do was to appeal to a potential donor by telling them that their gift would be matched 100 percent by the Waltons. So, if an endowed chair had a price tag of $1.5 million the Waltons would allow us to use their gift to match a $750,000 commitment, which would then form a fully endowed chair. That decision by the Waltons was an absolute godsend, and enabled us to appeal to hundreds of people who wanted to make a significant gift. Essentially their gift commitment would be doubled and would allow benefactors to achieve a major commitment of an endowed chair or professorship that might not otherwise be affordable. It literally made all the difference in the world for our campaign. We were able to procure matching funds for the entire $300,000 million; basically, it had the impact of doubling the Walton gift to the university.

The Waltons even allowed us to match a gift from Tyson Foods of an airplane. In 2001 Tyson Foods acquired IBP Inc., the largest beef packer and number two pork processor in the United States. When Tyson Foods merged with the beef company, they had a surplus airplane that they wanted to give to the university. It was a Beechcraft King Air and a very nice airplane. Tyson asked us if it could be matched by the Waltons and the Waltons agreed. So, the university got a nice King Air, and the Tysons got their name on a professorship.

Before we received the gift from the Waltons, Rick Chapman called me and made a request. He wanted a letter from John White saying that John would stay as chancellor through the end of the campaign. The family obviously had great faith in John and wanted to be certain that the gift would be implemented properly and under the guidelines that we had agreed to.

The Campaign for the Twenty-First Century raised the bar for the University of Arkansas. The university was selected for inclusion in *The Best 331 Colleges* by *The Princeton Review*. The schools constitute the top 8 percent of the nation's 4,000 institutions of higher learning. Further, *The Princeton Review* ranked the University of Arkansas third in academic quality of the universities of the Southeastern Conference, behind only Vanderbilt and Florida. The venerable *Fiske Guide to Colleges*, the original college guidebook and still one of the most popular and respected, upgraded the University of Arkansas academic quality rating from two to three stars on a five-star scale. Inclusion in this guidebook among 294 other institutions placed the University of Arkansas in the top 8 percent of American colleges and universities.

And by the time the campaign was over, the University of Arkansas was the only American college or university, public or private, with the following array of national scholarships and fellowships won by undergraduates: a Rhodes scholar, Marshall scholar, two National Science Foundation fellows, three Barry Goldwater scholars, a Morris Udall scholar, and a James Madison fellow.

In 2009 I wrote the Walton family informing them that, directly related to their gift support and many others during the Campaign for the Twenty-First Century and beyond, we had achieved a number of milestones:

- The School of Architecture recently was ranked 20th in the nation in the Annual Survey of America's Best Architecture & Design Schools, a study conducted by the Design Futures Council. This marks the first time that the School of Architecture has been included on the top 20 list.
- The School of Architecture also was cited with a rank of "notable distinction" in a new, comprehensive list of America's World-Class Schools of Architecture.
- The School of Law tied for 48th place among the nation's public law schools. In the category of "Specialty Rankings: Legal Writing," the School of Law ranked 9th in the nation among all public law schools.
- *The Atlantic* designated the university's creative writing program as one of the top five programs of its kind in the country.
- Other graduate programs that ranked nationally, per *U.S. News & World Report*, were rehabilitation education and research (15th); biological engineering (16th); and industrial engineering (26th).
- The Sam M. Walton College of Business once again placed in a tie for 24th among the nation's top public undergraduate business schools, according to *U.S. News & World Report's* 2009 rankings. Since the 2005 ranking, the Walton college had consistently stayed in the top 25 public business schools, as well as in the top 45 public and private schools.
- *U.S. News & World Report* has ranked the Walton college supply chain program 13th among all undergraduate programs nationally.
- The university was now among the top 50 colleges and universities in the country as measured by the number of national merit scholars in attendance.
- The university was now ranked ninth nationally in the number of Goldwater scholarship recipients over the last decade—this scholarship is awarded to the top

students in math, science, and engineering in the country.
- The state of Arkansas awarded 75 state undergraduate research fellowships; the University of Arkansas received 51 of the 75.
- For his pioneering research in manufacturing high-quality nanocrystals, faculty member Xiaogang Peng (Scharlau Endowed Professorship in Chemistry) was one of two researchers to receive a Recognition of Excellence in Innovation certificate in 2008 from the Under Secretary of Commerce for Standards and Technology.

The Campaign for the Twenty-First Century would have a monumental impact on both students and faculty, and provided the funds needed to recruit and retain top achieving students and world-class faculty. The campaign provided funds to endow scholarships for undergraduates and fellowships for graduate students. It also provided endowed chairs and professorships to recruit and retain faculty who are both superb teachers and researchers.

Here is a breakdown of where most of the Walton's $300 million gift was initially allocated:

ENDOWED DEAN'S CHAIR, $3 MILLION

An endowed dean's chair allowed the university to attract and recruit a highly qualified individual to lead the Honors College and provided the resources to further the dean's contributions to teaching, research, and public service. A minimum of $3 million dollars was required to endow a dean's chair. The chair holder had to be a full-time member of the University of Arkansas faculty with the academic rank of distinguished professor, university professor, or professor. Income from the endowment supplemented the dean's salary and provided funds for graduate assistant salaries, secretarial assistance, course development, essential equipment, and scholarly travel.

ENDOWED CHAIRS, $30 MILLION

It was necessary to supplement the excellent faculty already at the University of Arkansas by attracting additional scholars to develop the program and reputation of the Honors College. These 20 endowed chairs were used to recruit faculty to enhance areas where strength was needed, as well as to recognize and retain key current faculty. Income from the endowment supplemented the chair's salary, and provided funds for secretarial assistance, course development, essential equipment, scholarly travel, and other related needs. These chair holders had joint appointments in the Honors College and the school or college of the university in which their discipline was based. Endowed chairs were placed strategically in fields having the greatest potential for enhancing economic competitiveness and quality of life in Arkansas and for elevating the university to international prominence. The oversight committee was particularly cognizant of the needs of business and industry when making determinations.

ENDOWED DISTINGUISHED PROFESSORSHIPS, $10 MILLION

Endowed professorships provide the opportunity to recruit or retain renowned professors and young assistant professors with proven potential for greatness; they play a special role in working with honors students. This funding enabled the faculty members to pursue new lines of research or innovative teaching methods for working with this select group of students. These distinguished professors served as mentors, and provided intellectual guidance to the honors students. A named professorship enabled a scholar to spend more time in direct contact with students. Income from an endowment provided salary supplements, funds for graduate assistants' stipends, support staff, and travel expenses. As with the endowed chairs, the distinguished professors held joint appointments. These Endowed Distinguished Professorships were also allocated across the university in areas of strategic importance to the Arkansas economy and quality of life.

MATCHING FUNDS FOR ENDOWED FACULTY POSITIONS, $15 MILLION

As with the gift to the Sam M. Walton College of Business, this fund provided incentives for other benefactors to invest in the Honors College by having their gift matched 100 percent to establish an endowed faculty position in the Honors College. This applied for both chairs (for which a benefactor gave $750,000 to be matched by $750,000) and professorships (a $250,000 gift matched by a $250,000). This strategy allowed the university to leverage a pool of $15 million into $30 million, which created as many as 20 new endowed chairs or 60 endowed professorships, or any combination thereof. The resulting endowed positions were named for the benefactor making the match.

ENDOWED HONORS COLLEGE STUDENT FELLOWS, $75 MILLION

A scholarship or fellowship is the passport to higher education for many bright, hard-working students. Such talented young people will become tomorrow's leaders for our state and nation.

The success and reputation of the Honors College depended on the quality of its students. Attracting to this program the most highly recruited, sought-after students in the state, nation, and world required competitive awards. This allowed the university to attract the top one percent of graduating seniors. The infusion of these students into the overall student population produced a marked effect on the overall quality of the campus experience for all students. A special emphasis was placed on recruiting high-achieving minority students from Arkansas and the mid-south for this very bright cadre of students.

Students who held Honors Fellowships were among the highest achieving students in Arkansas and the United States—on a par with

Bodenhamer and Sturgis Fellows, which require an ACT score of 32 or higher. This cadre of superb students were essential in setting the highest possible standard for the Honors College. This endowment produced about $12,500 per year in spendable income per student, covering the full cost of attendance. We expected that sum to increase annually to keep up with any increases in the cost of attendance. The growth of the endowment helped to underwrite those annual increases in support.

ENDOWED HONORS COLLEGE ACADEMY STUDENT SCHOLARS, $24 MILLION

One of the unique features of the Honors College was the emphasis placed on recruiting very good, hardworking students without the top-tier credentials of Bodenhamer Fellows, High Honors Fellows, Sturgis Fellows, and Chancellor's Scholars. This was accomplished by incentives designed to attract students whose ACT scores fell within the band of 27 to 30. They were enrolled in the Honors College Academy as freshmen. If they earned an appropriately high grade point average and met other criteria, they were offered admission as sophomores to the Honors College, and their scholarship continued.

At the time, the university was losing too many of these very good students to other colleges and universities. The Honors College Academy provided an excellent avenue for attracting them to the university, rewarding them for their academic talents and motivation, and providing them the opportunity to succeed at the highest levels nationally, through admittance to the Honors College after their freshman year.

To establish the University of Arkansas Honors College Academy, an endowment of $24 million was needed to generate annual earnings of $1.2 million. These funds were used to create $4,000 annual scholarships for freshmen who qualified for the honors academy. (The $4,000 represented approximately a full tuition scholarship for in-state students and a half tuition scholarship for out-of-state students.)

These scholarships were renewed annually, assuming the students qualified for the Honors College and continued in good academic standing through graduation.

The honors academy would attract 75 entering freshmen annually. As they moved through their college years, and succeeding classes followed, those students who enrolled in the Honors College through this portal numbered an additional 225 (75 sophomores, 75 juniors, 75 seniors). At full strength, the number of students in the Honors College who enter through the honors academy totaled 300.

STUDENT RESEARCH GRANT ENDOWMENT, $10 MILLION

Increasingly, undergraduate teaching is being carried out in a "hands-on" manner through participation in faculty research projects. Accordingly, expectations and opportunities have increased for undergraduate students to prepare and publish research, working closely with their faculty mentors. Research and creative projects required specialized equipment and material for the primary research, as well as travel funds to perform research and present the results of the research at scholarly conferences. The undergraduate research portfolio was the defining measure of quality for graduates of the Honors College, resulting in better opportunities for employment or graduate study.

There are numerous national competitions and opportunities for recognition for students who conduct outstanding research projects. Such competitions are a major part of building reputation and drawing attention to the quality of undergraduate instruction at a given university. The University of Arkansas intended to be a perennial winner in such competitions. To qualify for funds from this endowment, honors students went through a formal application process and had their proposals judged by Honors College faculty members.

The added bonus of this endowment was that faculty members stood to do better in the competition for federal grants by engaging undergraduates in research. As undergraduate research increased across the board, federal research grants increased accordingly, with an economic benefit accruing to the entire state.

INTERNATIONAL EXPERIENCE ENDOWMENT, $4 MILLION

As education and industry have become global, students expect, and must have, access to international educational experiences to be competitive in employment or for graduate school. Following the tradition of the J. William Fulbright College of Arts and Sciences, the Honors College had a focus on international experiences. As a result, a significant number of honors students had the opportunity to study internationally at some point in their four-year experience. These opportunities ranged from fieldwork studying hunger in impoverished nations to research projects at partner universities in distant lands, as well as the more traditional semester-abroad programs. This endowment supported 40 honors students studying abroad per semester, assuming costs associated with such an experience amounted to $2,500 per semester or $5,000 per year.

LIBRARY ACQUISITION FUND AND ENDOWMENT, $24 MILLION

Supplementing the holdings of the University of Arkansas Libraries established the standard of excellence required to support the special scholarly needs of honors students and faculty. An immediate acquisition fund of $5 million was established to update and acquire critical serial publications, journals, books, and information materials in various technological forms. The remaining $19 million created an endowment to be used by the university libraries to purchase journals, publications, and electronic media to support the specific ongoing scholarly needs of honors students and faculty. Support at this level moved the university libraries much closer to membership in the prestigious Association of Research Libraries, the criterion by which all top-tier university libraries are judged, and an essential part of the university's strategy to work its way into the top-50 public universities in America.

TECHNOLOGY UPGRADE FUND, $5 MILLION

Technology in the classroom has been the most dramatic and expensive development in higher education in the last decade. It promises to remain at the center of research, classroom instruction, curriculum development, and the extended learning process beyond the classroom. Electronic communication between students and faculty, access to remote databases, and the ability to use other digital resources were essential elements of the Honors College experience.

Students at this ability level expect access to the highest quality digital network available. An initial sum of $2 million was used to improve access to Internet2 for all students in the Honors College. This occurred through improved technical infrastructure at Mullins Library, the university's various schools and colleges, and in key facilities available to honors students throughout campus including residence halls. With the remaining $3 million, certain classrooms used for Honors College courses were technologically upgraded into state-of-the-art instructional environments. Dedicated computer labs for Honors College students were created and equipped, and other technological services were provided.

GRADUATE FACULTY ENDOWED RESEARCH CHAIRS, $24 MILLION

Top graduate students choose their universities based on their desire to work with particular faculty members who have established a reputation for excellence and innovation in their disciplines. While the University of Arkansas had an excellent faculty, it needed to increase their number to facilitate the planned growth in graduate enrollments. More importantly, it had to attract world-class scholars and researchers in order to attract world-class graduate students.

The establishment of new endowed faculty chairs was the key to making that happen. Accordingly, the university used $24 million to endow eight new Graduate Faculty Endowed Research Chairs in strategic disciplines—particularly in science, engineering, business, and technology—which would have special relevance for improving economic competitiveness and quality of life in Arkansas. Each chair was endowed at a level that was twice as much as the standard $1.5 million endowment principal. A research chair endowed at $3 million would generate about $150,000 annually in endowment earnings to support the chair holder.

This special endowment was used exclusively to recruit eight world-class researchers, men and women who had been elected to the The National Academies of Sciences, Engineering, and Medicine or equivalent organizations worldwide. These faculty members focused exclusively on developing or enhancing the research programs in their areas of expertise and worked with graduate students and honors-level undergraduates in their research programs.

These eight research chairs had a tremendous impact on the university and, by extension, the state. Their work enabled the university to rise quickly in quality and reputation in select graduate programs, and to become a major force in producing the advanced-degreed leadership Arkansas needs for the 21st century.

DISTINGUISHED DOCTORAL FELLOWSHIPS, $24 MILLION

For this new program, the university established 60 Distinguished Doctoral Fellowships, each funded by an endowment of $400,000, which in turn would generate usable earnings of about $20,000 per year. This level of stipend—to be matched up to an additional $10,000 by the university departments enrolling the student—would allow the university to compete successfully for the best doctoral students in the nation, particularly in the high-cost areas of science, engineering, technology, and business.

The chancellor, upon the recommendation of the provost of the university and the dean of the Graduate School, strategically apportioned these prestigious fellowships in areas where they were needed to build nationally competitive programs. In this manner, the university rose quickly in quality and reputation in select graduate programs, and became a major force in producing the scientists, engineers, business leaders, and intellectual leaders for Arkansas and the nation in the 21st century.

GRADUATE ASSISTANTSHIP ENDOWMENT FUND, $40 MILLION

To move the university to the next level in terms of attracting top graduate students—and greater numbers of them—the university allocated an endowment of $40 million. This was used to supplement, on a selective basis, the existing number of graduate teaching and research assistantships across the university. The annual earnings from this endowment—roughly $2 million—was used to increase the number of stipends for graduate students, while also creating additional new stipends where needed.

Most doctoral programs attract graduate students by providing full support for tuition and a stipend for living expenses. At the University of Arkansas, these stipends tended to be extremely low, in the $6,000 to $13,000 range, which was well below the range provided by top private and public research universities. The endowment allowed the Graduate School to supplement those existing stipends on a selective basis, getting them up to $15,000, $17,000, even $20,000—depending on the tipping point in each respective department that was required to attract top-flight students.

Across the university, academic departments identified the single greatest barrier to increasing the size and quality of their graduate programs to be the lack of competitive stipends. This endowment enabled them to compete with the top research universities in the nation for the best students.

GRADUATE STUDENT RESEARCH FUND, $8 MILLION

For graduate students to be competitive and successful, they must travel to regional and national conferences to learn from leaders in their disciplines and to present their own research papers. In addition, they often need to travel to distant sites, here and abroad, to conduct research, to work in specialized laboratories and facilities, and to visit libraries and archives. To begin research projects, especially their dissertation work, they often need start-up money to pay for related expenses.

The university set aside $8 million in endowment for these purposes. This generated about $400,000 per year to provide support on a selective basis to graduate students across the university. It was not enough merely to attract the best and the brightest of these students to the university; they must also be given the support and tools to succeed, as this endowment ensured.

LIBRARY SUPPORT ENDOWMENT FOR GRADUATE SCHOOL, $4 MILLION

The $100 million investment in the Graduate School, attracting greater numbers of higher quality graduate students and research faculty, placed additional stress on the university libraries. Thus, $4 million was allocated as an endowment to support library acquisitions and other services related to graduate studies. Demand increased greatly for new scholarly journals and periodicals in particular, and this fund helped to make their purchase possible. The $200,000 in annual income from this endowment was also used partly to support new library staff to serve certain highly specialized scientific and technical graduate disciplines.

Just before the announcement of the $300 million gift, we approached the governor's staff about the possibility of matching funds from the state. We had discussed this with the Walton Foundation staff and they agreed it was worth a try. Our first task was to invite the governor to the announcement of the gift. Unfortunately, he was unavailable. A few weeks after the announcement we approached the governor's office with the matching idea, but it never went anywhere, and we never received a reply. We just assumed that the funds were not available and that perhaps the governor did not want to deliver bad news. Had it happened it would have been a wonderful public–private partnership that would have resonated throughout the country. We also approached a major national foundation to match the $300 million gift, but we were unsuccessful in that attempt as well. Perhaps we were dreaming, but as they say, nothing ventured, nothing gained.

The first dean of the Honors College was Bob McMath, and he would serve brilliantly for nine years, providing the vision and framework that made the college nationally prominent. Under his leadership the Honors College was ranked 17th in "Overall Excellence" in the first national study of the top 50 public honors programs, and ranked third out of 50 in "Excellence Impact."

The second and current dean as of 2022 is Lynda Coon. She has been terrific in every way. Her doctorate is from the University of Virginia, and she brought a deep commitment to honors education, academic excellence, and a fresh vision for the future. She has done an outstanding job.

Several years later, while I was serving as chancellor, a candidate for governor, Bill Halter, approached me about asking the Waltons for another large gift to match scholarship funds from the state. He had no authority to make such an offer but wanted to make it a signature part of his campaign. I told him that I didn't think it was a workable idea, but he asked me to think it over and get back to him. I did not call him back. I was not about to get involved in a political campaign and one candidate's idea to tap the Waltons. Halter lost the election but did manage to get a lottery established in Arkansas while he was Lieutenant Governor which has benefited thousands of Arkansans in getting a college degree. He more than anyone deserves credit for making that happen.

The Campaign for the Twenty-First Century would be the tool for building the university's endowment, which, compared with other major institutions, was quite small. Our goal was to at least double the size of the endowment and move close to $1 billion by the end of the decade. If it had not been for the economic downturn in 2008, we would have easily reached the $1 billion level.

Years later, in 2020, the Walton Family Foundation, primarily being run by the third generation, commissioned an outside agency to undertake a study to determine if the $300 million gift had accomplished what we had promised it would accomplish for the region, state, and nation. The agency interviewed numerous people, including myself and John White. I had contacted John to alert him to what was happening, and to be ready with plenty of ammunition. I also spoke with Lynda Coon, dean of the Honors College at the time to compare notes and information. The day of the interview I was worried that the new generation might be trying to prove that the gift had not done what it was supposed to do, and it could affect future support of the university. The interview was relatively non combative, and I answered questions and did most of the talking. I gave the interviewer tons of data and believe I showed them that the gift had indeed accomplished exactly what we had hoped. I suspect John White made an even better case for the $300 million gift's outcome. None of us ever heard another word from the agency and never received their report.

CHAPTER 37
LAWSUIT

" *Be suspicious of the litigious.*

— STEWART STAFFORD

Immediately after we announced the $300 million gift, the *Arkansas Times* newspaper in Little Rock filed a freedom of information request to see all of the documents related to the gift, including the proposal that we used.

The proposal included addendums that were literally thousands of pages long. The Walton family requested we show proof that their gift would have an economic impact on Northwest Arkansas and the state in general. We produced a number of reports that would prove such an investment in the university would have a cascading effect. The Walton Foundation also hired outside counsel to prove that such a gift would have a major impact on the region and state.

There really wasn't anything in the proposal that would have been earth shattering, and I didn't have a problem with sending it to them. I was mildly concerned about other institutions seeing our work product and using it in a competitive manner. We had spent hours and hours on the proposal and did not really want the rest of the world to discover our methods and secrets to success.

I called Rick Chapman to discuss releasing it, and he said he would just prefer not to have the proposal in the hands of others. He suggested that we not release the proposal under the competitive advantage clause of the Arkansas Freedom of Information Act.

Our attorneys felt we should release the document and pushed hard to have us do so. I called Alan Sugg to discuss the matter with him and he said that he thought we should do exactly what the Waltons preferred. The university attorneys report to the system president, and Sugg was the only person who could overrule them. John White also agreed we should hold firm and not release the document. Dr. Sugg said that he would run interference with general counsel.

Max Brantley, editor of the *Arkansas Times* was not happy. He immediately filed a lawsuit against the university asking that the Walton proposal be released under the Freedom of Information Act. With the Walton backing we decided to go to court over the matter. Our attorneys weren't at all certain we would win the argument in court, but Dr. Sugg agreed that we should go to court and get a definitive determination.

The Arkansas Freedom of Information Act (FOIA) requires public agencies to preserve and maintain public records. Under Arkansas FOIA, public records include "writings, recorded sounds, films, tapes, or data compilations in any form," which would include electronic content like social media. There are however a number of exceptions to the act requiring disclosure. One clause says that files do not not need to be disclosed if they would give an advantage to competitors or bidders. This is the clause upon which we based our refusal to release the proposal. We did give the *Arkansas Times* all of the information as to how the gift would be used. That didn't satisfy Max Brantley. He wanted everything, and beat us up mercilessly in his newspaper. Day after day he would comment on our decision and claim that the Waltons were "buying" the university.

We asked John Brown III, Former president of John Brown University to testify on our behalf and he readily agreed to do so.

John's testimony was a key factor. At the time he was serving as the executive director of the private Windgate Foundation, and his comments were obviously well considered by the judge. Our basic argument was that if we released the proposal it would give a competitive advantage to our competition, other institutions that wanted support from the Walton family.

I testified as well. The court proceedings lasted about two hours, and at the conclusion of all of the testimony the judge ruled from the bench in our favor. It may have been the first time a public institution in Arkansas had beaten the media on the competitive advantage part of the FOIA law.

Max Brantley was not happy. He decided not to appeal, because he said it would cost too much and he had limited resources, but he did comment in his column that he would have won the case on appeal. I'm not so sure.

I always felt Max harbored ill will against me and the university from that point forward. For years after the lawsuit, and the ruling in our favor, Max would comment on his blog about how unfair he thought the ruling had been. He would also criticize me and the university for a variety of issues during my time as chancellor. Max just wasn't able to get past the defeat, and is no doubt still angry about the ruling to this day.

I'm certain that Max Brantley thought we had sold the university to the Waltons. He kept asking questions as to what we gave up in order to get a gift of such magnitude. After all, it was the largest gift ever made to a public university, and he felt certain the university must have sold its soul. Personally, I just don't think he could get his arms around a gift of that magnitude as being pure philanthropy. There had to be a catch somewhere. What was the university hiding? What had we given the Waltons in return for such a colossal gift?

Surprisingly, I identified favorably with a lot of what Max wrote on other issues of the day in his daily blog. A good bit of it seemed to be common sense and resonated with me. I regretted that he had taken issue with the Walton gift and had sued us.

The truth of the matter is that the Waltons put no restrictions on the gift. The only thing they asked of us was to submit an annual report on the progress being made at the university because of the gift. They wanted nothing else from the university in the form of restrictions. They didn't want any naming rights whatsoever. Judy Schwab was in charge of preparing the annual report which was a work of art. For the first few years the report was quite large and voluminous and then the Waltons told us that it did not need to be quite as big. I suspect they got tired of reading through all of the materials Judy submitted to them.

The only time I lost my patience with Rick Chapman was after the campaign concluded and I took him on a brief tour of the offices of the Honors College. John White wanted to put the Honors College on the fourth floor of the administration building to show its importance to the university. We renovated two spaces and provided a lounge for honors students in close proximity to the chancellor's office. That way we could come in contact with honors students who came to the fourth floor. Our long-range plan was to provide larger quarters as soon as funds became available.

As I took Rick to see the new honors quarters, he paused and looked at a new flat screen TV installed in the honors lounge. The new Honors College Dean had purchased the screen as a novelty to attract students to use the lounge. At the time flat screens were quite expensive, and few people owned one due to the price. I recall that the TV cost $4,000. Rick paused and turned to me and asked me if the Walton money had purchased the TV? I told him, yes, probably so since the gift did have a component for equipment purchases. He was not happy. He said he wanted me to reimburse that amount to the Walton funds; they had no intention of paying for such an extravagance. I tried to explain the dean's thinking, but Rick was not buying it. He was adamant. So, we replaced the funds with other private money. At the time I thought Rick was being cheap if not silly. Out of $300 million it seemed like a pittance. But it was their money, and I didn't say too much at the time.

A few days later I was in Rick Chapman's office going over the Honors College budget and Rick began questioning every line item. He had never done that before, and I felt like I was at the inquisition. After several minutes of pretty direct questions, I finally lost my temper. I raised my voice, which I had never done before in front of Walton representatives, and said "Rick, at some point you have to trust us." The meeting did not end well. I was embarrassed and mad at myself that I had let my temper flare. I guess I thought Rick was a friend who respected our accounting for the funds and that I was being questioned unnecessarily. Later I told Rick I should not have raised my voice and he was a perfect gentleman and laughed it off. Rick was a tiger when it came to protecting Walton money. I guess that was his job!

CHAPTER 38
WINTHROP ROCKEFELLER INSTITUTE

> *I have enjoyed the personal use of money, but I have gotten the greatest satisfaction from using it to advance my beliefs in human relations, human values.*
>
> — *WINTHROP ROCKEFELLER*

In 1953, Winthrop Rockefeller, then 41, and fourth son of the world's richest family, left New York City and came to Arkansas. It shocked the world. Rockefeller had been described as the black sheep of the family, but would go on to become the progressive 37th Governor of Arkansas. The state was purely democratic, but Rockefeller pulled together a coalition as a Republican, including Black voters, and won the governorship. He was a builder and early supporter of civil rights. He was a good governor and many of the reforms he implemented still resonate today.

When he decided to come to Arkansas, he purchased almost 1,000 acres on top of Petit Jean Mountain, built a cattle farm and a home with a magnificent view. He literally built a city on top of the mountain and lived there for 20 years before his untimely death from pancreatic cancer in 1973. He was only 60 years old.

Besides family bequests, Rockefeller let the bulk of his estate to charitable foundations, including Winthrop Rockefeller Foundation and the Winthrop Rockefeller Charitable Trust, which included Winrock International, an international nonprofit organization headquartered on his family estate atop Petit Jean. Winrock decided to relocate to Washington D.C. and abandoned the substantial physical plant on the mountain.

The trustees of his charitable trust were all former supporters and employees of his during his lifetime. They had at their disposal well over $100 million dollars, and possibly more, in the trust. The trustees decided they wanted to turn the Petit Jean property into an institute and think tank with a hotel and meeting space.

The trustees first approached the Fayetteville campus to be the caretaker of the property and move the idea forward. We were interested. I was dispatched to speak with members of the trust board about our interest. Pretty quickly after my initial meeting, I learned the trust had decided to make the property a University of Arkansas System project. All of a sudden, our campus was out of the running for implementing the project.

The system and the trust hired David Davies to get the project up and running. Davies was the former executive director of Garvan Woodland Gardens in Hot Springs and became executive director of the Winthrop Rockefeller Institute. Around 2006 Alan Sugg asked me to be the chairman of the institute board. I didn't really need another job but didn't feel I could turn down Dr. Sugg, and I accepted.

It was two years of hell. The only saving grace was David Davies. David was a first-class administrator who was responsible for building the new facilities and did a marvelous job. I grew fond of him from the very beginning. He was honest, forthright, and very competent. The problem was that the trust board, which was funding the effort, didn't really know what they wanted the institute to become. They had very heady ideas that were not necessarily rooted in reality. The push and shove between the trust, administration, and the voluntary institute board I chaired was not always a happy time. As hard as David and I tried, we didn't seem to be able to satisfy the trustees of the Rockefeller trust. I held several meetings with Rockefeller trustees but was unable to pacify them. They seemed to always have a complaint about items that were either ridiculous or petty. For some reason they had soured on Davies' leadership which I suspected came from an employee at the institute who fed them made-up information and innuendo. Davies built the institute and needs to be credited for doing a fabulous job under difficult circumstances.

When I became chancellor, I suggested to David he should come to work for our campus in Fayetteville and stop beating his head against the wall working with the trust board. In 2010 he did so, and retired from the university in 2021. At his retirement event David was lauded by multiple administrators for his incredibly effective work. The Institute's loss was our gain.

CHAPTER 39

HIGH SCHOOL FOR SALE

> *Dear Fayetteville High, our Alma Mater true. Dear Fayetteville High, all hail to you. Our colors wave, the purple and the white. Our spirits brave, for great your might.*
>
> — *FAYETTEVILLE HIGH SCHOOL ALMA MATER*

Sometime around 2007 the university was approached by the superintendent of schools, Dr. Bobby New, to purchase the Fayetteville High School. The property was somewhat contiguous to the University, only a block away, and the school board and Superintendent New had decided that they wanted to build a new high school on property they had purchased for that purpose. The decision to build a new high school was very controversial in the community. Some folks felt that they should simply refurbish the existing facility, add on to it and leave it at the same location. Others felt that a new high school should be built at the place where the school board had acquired property, while another group still wanted to tear down the existing high school and build at the same location. All three groups were quite vocal. It had become something of a flashpoint for community leaders.

Dr. White was favorable toward acquiring the property. He began negotiations with the school board and Superintendent New while he was still chancellor. New and the school board wanted $60 million for the property. The only way the university would be able to purchase the property would be to raise student fees to pay for a bond. At that time the university had very little in reserves, and did not have near enough cash to make the purchase. Borrowing the funds would require the board of trustee's approval, as well as legislative approvals. Putting the purchase on the backs of the students was the only viable option, and legislators and trustees were already worried about the rising tuition costs that might exclude poorer families from affording a higher education. Tuition had risen every year for decades.

The property consisted of 40 acres and multiple buildings, including the high school, superintendent administration building, Bates Elementary School, and a host of athletics facilities. Dr. White moved quickly to indicate to the school board that we were a willing buyer. Many people had questions about the purchase. We were suspicious about the condition of the facilities on the property, particularly the high school. The high school was a cinder block building built in the 1960s. It was not a particularly attractive facility and none of the buildings on the property were in prime condition.

During the negotiations, Dr. White retired as chancellor and the purchase became an immediate issue for me as the new chancellor. One of my first priorities as chancellor was to determine if we wanted to move forward with the purchase. I knew that there were many people on campus and in the community opposed to the purchase. The folks who wanted to redo the existing facility were quite vocal, and did not want to move the high school to a new location. They made their feelings very well-known to me and to the media.

We worked very hard to remain neutral during the discussion and debate on location, believing that was the province of the Fayetteville Board of Education. We maintained the position that the board of education needed to decide where the high school would be located separate from our purchase and that we should not try to influence their decision. It looked to me and my senior staff that the school board was trying to make the decision by getting the university to purchase the property and therefore locking out the dissenters who wanted the high school to remain at its existing site. I felt from the beginning that Superintendent New was using us to make a tough decision for him and the school board. I didn't like being in that uncomfortable position.

Our position was that the land was much more valuable than the buildings. We had all the buildings inspected and appraised and the result was that the facilities needed major renovation, which would be quite costly. HVAC systems were in disrepair or in need of immediate replacement. The useful life of some of the facilities was very short. While we would be able to use some of the space in the buildings and perhaps the athletics fields, we knew that we could not utilize all the space in the immediate future and the acquisition would need to be viewed as a long-term decision.

While the purchase of property so close to campus was seen to be desirable, that would depend to a large extent on our ability to grow our enrollment and expand our research and public service capacity. We knew that if we were going to purchase the property, the acquisition had to be viewed as a 15- to 25-year term before its benefit could be fully realized and even then, I had some reservations.

The appraisal indicated that the land was worth approximately $6 million. The Bates Annex, formerly an elementary school, was over 50 years old and the high school over 60 years old. If we kept the buildings, we would have to do major renovation as the spaces were not designed and configured optimally for immediate university use. We might even need to raze some of the buildings or replace the building systems.

Our physical plant folks thought that we would have to invest somewhere around $25-$30 million to make the property usable for our needs. This would put our investment in the project close to $90 to $100 million when added to the $60 million purchase price. On top of that, we did not really know how we would utilize the property. My team and I began discussions on how we might use the considerable space. We did have some need for additional classroom and research space, including wet labs for teaching and research, but only if our enrollment grew dramatically. And, of course, the buildings sat up on a hill not easily traversed by our students. It would be a long uphill walk to class for most of our living units.

One idea that came to mind was the possibility of starting our own two-year institution as a feeder to the main campus. The Northwest Arkansas Community College had filled that need for several years but we did not believe that their students were adequately prepared for the rigors of our curriculum. Could we do a better job preparing students for their sophomore or junior year? Many felt we could. Of course, we would need state approvals for such a move, and we were not at all sure that approvals would be forthcoming. We had also grown weary of hearing that NWACC wanted to become a four-year school in direct competition with the UA. Many were just tired of fighting with NWACC president, Dr. Becky Paneitz.

Not to digress too much, but I never felt that the establishment of a two-year community college so close to our institution made much sense. NWACC was established in 1989 after citizens in Bentonville passed a three-mill property tax to support the new institution by a 65 percent margin. It opened its doors in 1990 with a headcount of 1,200 students. A few years later the student enrollment headcount obtained the level of 8,900. Recently, however, enrollment has declined to around 6500 students. In 2021 enrollment had declined another 8 percent. Administrators claim that Covid 19 has been responsible for the heavy decline.

It might have been preferable to launch a two-year program at the University of Arkansas instead of building an entirely new campus just 20 minutes away. To me that would have been the less costly solution and much more expedient in the short term. Dan Ferritor, former UA chancellor, told me that he was a major proponent for starting NWACC. I'm certainly not opposed to two-year institutions, but it would have been much more workable if NWACC had been under the UA, Fayetteville's control. I would not have been supportive of a new college 25 minutes from our campus.

The state simply cannot afford such a proliferation of colleges across the state.

More on other conflicts with NWACC in a later chapter. For now, back to the high school purchase.

Since I was a new chancellor and Dr. White had been negotiating the sale for some time, I felt that I should not make a unilateral decision abruptly to scrap the project in deference to his leadership. If we could get the property for a more reasonable amount, then perhaps it made sense to move forward with the purchase. I personally felt that the property was probably worth around $25 million. I spoke with President Sugg and several members of the board and we decided to make a counteroffer to the school board of $50 million, still too high in my estimation. I had major qualms about that price and had several sleepless nights wondering if I did the right thing. That was much more than I thought the property was worth, but the negotiations had been going on for so long that I felt we should exercise good faith in trying to conclude them favorably to everyone involved. Sugg had also polled the board and the majority at that time supported his idea to move forward at that time. However, I could sense that the board also had questions about the sale amount.

We also discussed with the UA board of trustees the possibility of implementing a student facility fee that would pay for the purchase of the property. I really hated to tack on a fee to student's already high tuition but that was the only way we could swing the deal. If we were going to buy the property, we would need it to be on the backs of the students. As previously mentioned, we had literally no reserves when I became chancellor.

A few days after my appointment as chancellor, Don Pederson, our chief financial officer, and I traveled to Little Rock to meet with Dr. Sugg at the system office. I had been studying our financials closely and knew that we had very thin margins. Before I was appointed, I knew we were not flush with resources, but had no idea of the gravity of the situation. If we had a financial catastrophe we could have been in serious financial calamity. When Don and I met with Dr. Sugg and showed him the financials, his very first comment was, "Your campus is broke!" Indeed, we were.

The board of trustees agreed that we should make a counteroffer and I met with Bobby New and told him of our decision. I could tell during the meeting that he was not pleased that we were countering with a lower figure than the original $60 million. He told me that he might be able to get the board down $1 or $2 million dollars but did not think that $50 million would buy the property. I must say that I was somewhat relieved with his revelation that $50 million would not work. From the beginning I had reservations about purchasing the property. Days turned into weeks with no word from Bobby New.

I decided to ask the deans and vice chancellors to tour the property along with, Admiral Mike Johnson, who headed up our facilities management. During the tour it became obvious to everyone that we might be buying a pig in a poke. Virtually everyone on the tour was negative about purchasing the property and I don't remember anyone stepping forward and telling me how they could use the facilities. One dean did say that it would be nice to have the property for parking but everyone else on the tour was quite negative about the purchase. Buying it for parking didn't seem to make a lot of common sense to me. That would be a long walk to classes for students and offices for faculty. We were already planning to build three new parking decks that would relieve some of our rather serious parking issues. If we used the property for parking we would likely need buses or vans to transport students and faculty due to the distance. I could not help thinking of the Disney World transports that picked people up from the parking lot and deposited them at the admission gate!

I had and still do have great respect for Mike Johnson who had retired from a career in the Navy as a two-star admiral. He was an engineer and managed many of the facilities for the Navy as Chief of Civil Engineers as well as Commander of Naval Facilities. He was a member of the National Academy of Engineers, one of only 5 in Arkansas. Mike accepted the invitation to be head of facilities a few years before I took over as chancellor and commanded the respect from everyone. Few people know that he was offered a different job for three times the salary within hours of committing to the University. Because he had made a commitment to the university, he did not accept the other job that would have compensated him at a much higher level. That is Mike, a good, honorable and very talented person.

Mike Johnson knew his business better than anyone. He had serious questions about the purchase of the high school and felt it was way overpriced and would need very serious and costly renovations. He even suspected some of the buildings might need to be razed.

Then, out of the blue, I received a telephone call from a high school classmate that was close to Bobby New. The classmate and Superintendent New attended the same church together and were good friends. This classmate proceeded to tell me that he had a buyer from New York City that was going to purchase the property for $60 million and turn it into a large hotel and ballroom complex. He said that he knew these investors personally and knew they were legitimate, and that the university was about to lose the sale.

I knew this classmate well and also knew that he didn't always have legitimate and sound business practices. I was extremely skeptical that he really had another buyer. I felt certain that he was just trying to scare me into purchasing the property and never really had another buyer in the wings. I called him back a couple of days later and told him that if the school board had a better offer, they should take it. Besides, it would be very nice to have a hotel and convention center so close to the university. I surmised that was not the reaction he thought he would get.

Several weeks went by with very little contact from the school board. I received a telephone call from a member of our board of trustees who felt strongly that we should conclude the negotiations and withdraw our offer. Since so much time had elapsed, I wasn't even certain if our counteroffer was still active or valid. The trustee told me that it wasn't good business practice to have an offer of that magnitude outstanding for such a long period of time.

I told the trustee that I agreed with him and that I had been giving the project much consideration and felt that we should inform the school board that we were not going to purchase the property. I told him that all the deans and senior officers were negative on the purchase and we really didn't have a solid plan on how to utilize it. He wholeheartedly agreed. I called Dr. Sugg and asked him how he felt about the project. He agreed with me and surveyed the board of trustees for input. All the trustees agreed we should withdraw the counteroffer and get out of the project.

One thing that helped me make up my mind was a conversation I had with our Director of Athletics, Jeff Long. Long told me that he had no use for the athletics fields or gymnasium. I asked him why and he said that he would be criticized both in the media and by other SEC teams proclaiming that Arkansas practiced on high school fields and used high school facilities for intercollegiate sports. He felt that could be a death knell for recruitment. Frankly it had not occurred to me that could be a problem but after Long related his concerns I understood completely. I suspected the trustees, who always wanted to do everything and anything for intercollegiate sports, would have sided with Jeff Long.

I relayed our decision that we were withdrawing our offer in writing both to the superintendent of schools and the chairman of the school board. I received an immediate telephone call from one of the superintendent's senior staff members who told me that he did not think I had the authority to make that decision. I was polite but frankly his comment offended me, but I decided to just let him find out himself that I had the backing of the system president and the board. I guess he must've thought I was so ignorant that I would not have done my homework with the president and the board before making the decision.

I never received a call from either the school board president or the superintendent. I thought that was very strange.

A few weeks after the media carried our decision to the world, I got a telephone call from the same high school classmate that had claimed he had a $60 million offer from a New York City buyer. He told me that he wanted me to pay him $75,000 for all the work he had done in securing another buyer. I was astonished at his boldness and basically told him, in a not so polite way, that he was crazy. I didn't owe him a single cent. I never heard from him again.

I'm very glad that we did not purchase the high school. The amount the school board wanted was way more than the property was worth and we would have difficulty paying for all the renovations and improvements. To this day I believe the school board thought they had a cash cow on the line and tried to take advantage of the University. The school board would go on to tear down most all the facilities on the property and build a new high school at that site. I received numerous letters and telephone calls from community citizens thanking the University for not purchasing the property so that the high school could remain at the same location. Even to this day I run into people that were pleased with the decision and very glad that the high school remained at the same location.

As for the University I believe we came out much better. We were able to convince our board of trustees that we wanted the facility fee, that would have paid for the high school purchase, to be used to renovate numerous buildings on campus. The facility fee, when matched with private gift support, allowed us to totally renovate multiple facilities on campus as well as build a few new ones. The facility fee is still in use to this day and has enabled the university to renovate many of our iconic buildings. In the end I believe it was the smart decision and I'm not sure we would've been able to use any of the buildings on the high school site and it would have burdened our students with much higher facility fees for the long term. Besides that, we would not have been able to renovate existing facilities had we purchased the property.

CHAPTER 40
COACH NO COACH

> *There will be no whining or complaining from us.*
>
> — DANA ALTMAN, AFTER A GAME

April 3, 2007, was not a good day for Razorback Athletics, or the University of Arkansas. That was the day that Dana Altman decided he didn't want to coach Razorback Basketball after accepting the appointment and appearing publicly in front of the media and Razorback nation.

I was at my desk in the Administration Building when my phone rang. It was my brother, Van, who follows all things Razorback sports. He told me Altman was going back to Creighton, and the blogs were overheating. I argued with my brother telling him not to listen to that nonsense. After all, Altman had accepted the invitation to be the next basketball coach the day before, and appeared before a crowd and called the Hogs. Van swore that it was true, and said Altman was behind closed doors that very moment at Bud Walton Arena with John White.

I immediately called White's assistant and she told me something was going on but wasn't sure exactly what. She confirmed he was with Altman behind closed doors. I smelled a public relations catastrophe of epic proportions and hightailed it down to the arena. Sure enough White and Altman were behind closed doors. Rarely do I try to insert myself into a private discussion with the chancellor, but this time was different. I pushed my way in to find them both huddled in a corner of a room with absolutely sullen and ghostly faces visibly flustered. I asked White what was going on and he told me in a very frustrated voice that Coach Altman was not staying, and was headed back to Creighton.

The day before at the public announcement, Altman's performance was less than satisfactory. He was lackadaisical and very tentative. I actually commented to Jane that I didn't think he was happy about taking the Razorback job, and might go back on his acceptance of the head coach. During the public announcement he had put on a Razorback cap and then immediately had taken it off. When calling the Hogs, he made what can only be described as a half or quarter effort. He wasn't into it at all. You could tell it was painful for him to be standing there while John White made the announcement of our next coach. But I must admit, I was still shocked when John told me in that room at Bud Walton that Altman wasn't staying.

I looked at Altman and asked him what his intentions were from this moment forward. He said a private plane from Creighton was coming to pick him up, and he was headed to the airport immediately. I asked if he was planning on making any comments to the media and he said he wasn't. He thought it best to get out of town as fast as he could. I looked at White and said that I really thought Coach Altman needed to explain to the media and Razorback fans why he was leaving.

Rumors had been flying that Altman was not happy at all with the fact that so many of our players were ineligible to play, and drug usage and academic grades might be the reasons they couldn't. I point blank asked him why he was leaving and was it the rumors that had been flying around. He said, no, he was going back totally because his family did not want to leave Creighton. I pushed him on that reason, and he confirmed it again. I looked at both White and Altman, and said that Altman needed to share the reason behind his decision to leave with the media and Razorback fans. He paused for a moment and I thought he might say he was leaving and would not do it. I spoke up again and said he owed it to Dr. White to explain his sudden reversal. Finally, he said he understood and agreed to go before the media.

Altman and White appeared before the media outside the Bud Walton Arena loading dock, and Altman did what he said he would do. He said something like he had "deep regret" and that "his decision was completely due to his family." He apologized to the Razorback fans profusely. Then he got in a car and headed to the airport to catch the Creighton booster's plane.

It was an embarrassment for certain. Where does the blame lie? Squarely with Dana Altman. Why in the world would someone accept a major coaching job only to reverse himself less than 24 hours later. The media played it up big. The 24-hour coach, they said, much to our chagrin.

I felt badly for John White. Frank Broyles was at the Augusta National Golf Club attending the Masters Tournament. John had to cover the whole debacle without an AD! Dana Altman would probably have been a good coach for Arkansas. He has certainly been successful in his career, just not in Fayetteville!

CHAPTER 41
HARVARD

> *It might be said now that I have the best of both worlds. A Harvard education and a Yale degree.*
>
> — JOHN F. KENNEDY ON RECEIVING AN HONORARY DEGREE FROM YALE.

In 2007 a headhunter contacted me about the vice president for alumni affairs and development position at Harvard University in Cambridge, Massachusetts. The headhunter was someone who I had known for a number of years, and had worked with on projects at Grenzebach Glier. Manny Berger and I had become friends through the years, and he told me that he would like me to interview with the President of Harvard, Dr. Drew Gilpin Faust. Apparently, the university had not settled on anyone for the position, and he mentioned my name to her, and she was amenable to an interview.

While Dr. Sugg had talked with me about the possibility of becoming chancellor of the University of Arkansas, nothing definitive had happened. I thought this might be a potential opportunity if the chancellor position did not come my way. Frankly I wasn't terribly interested in moving to Boston, and neither was Jane, but the allure of Harvard did have some appeal. I had been vice chancellor for 10 years and needed a new challenge.

A couple days before I was to leave for the Harvard interview Alan Sugg called me about another matter. During the conversation I told him that I would be interviewing with the president of Harvard University. He told me that he still had plans to talk with me about being the chancellor at Fayetteville, and he hoped I would hold on and not accept a new challenge until all of the particulars had been worked out at Arkansas. I told Dr. Sugg that I had committed to the interview in Boston but I certainly did still have interest in discussing the chancellor position.

I arrived in Cambridge to a snow-covered Harvard Yard. I stayed in a hotel adjacent to the campus. Promptly at 9 a.m. the next morning I was escorted to the president's office to meet with President Faust. I knew a little bit about Dr. Faust as I had done some preliminary research on her background. She greeted me very warmly and we sat in her office under a famous painting of Harvard alumnus President Theodore Roosevelt. I remember thinking how small I thought her office was as the head of the glorified Harvard University. It was actually quite small compared to the offices of major university presidents I had been in during my consulting years.

She asked me many questions, particularly having to do with coming to Harvard from Arkansas. I had a little bit of an impression that she might think we Arkansans are not as sophisticated as her Harvard brethren, but she was gracious and thoughtful.

After my hour-long interview with Dr. Faust, I met with several other members of her team. I was then taken over to the development offices and met with some of the staff. I went to lunch at the rarified Harvard Club with members of the faculty. The faculty asked me very few questions and we talked mostly about some of the controversial issues happening at Harvard. One distinguished professor mentioned Harvard was having some funding issues, which I found surprising and amusing that it would be mentioned in an interview.

After lunch I met with some other university officials and alumni. At the end of the day, I was given a tour of the university which I found extremely interesting. I was taken to the rooms where FDR lived during his four years at Harvard as well as the room used by JFK. Both rooms were being renovated so I was only able to stick my head in the door, but found it to be an enjoyable experience. I left the next day and returned to Arkansas.

As soon as I was back in my office, I got a phone call from Dr. Sugg. He told me John White was giving very serious consideration to retiring as chancellor, but he could not give me a definitive idea when that might be. He asked me if I was going to pursue the job at Harvard and I told him that I didn't know if they were going to pursue me, but that I would leave my options open.

Sugg asked me if I had told John White about the Harvard interview; I replied that I had not, but felt I probably should. Sugg agreed that I should inform Dr. White as soon as possible. I made an appointment to see Dr. White that same afternoon to tell him about the interview.

Much to my surprise, Dr. White said immediately that I should stay at the University of Arkansas and be the next chancellor. He told me that he and Sugg had discussed the matter and while nothing was for certain, he thought the board of trustees would be wholeheartedly supportive of my candidacy. He said that he wasn't certain that Sugg would have an open search and might name me as an internal candidate. White told me that he and his wife had discussed his tenure at the university and felt it was time for new leadership. He further told me that he was tired, and that he had had too many battles that had worn him out. The average college CEO served for only four years, and John White had stayed for eleven. He particularly was concerned about the support he was receiving from the board of trustees. While he did not feel any pressure to retire, he said he thought the time had come for someone new to take the job. He reiterated that he was ready to step down.

The next day I received a telephone call from the headhunter. He asked me about the interview and if I had any interest. I told him it looked like things were going to open up at the University of Arkansas and that I had a shot at being the next chancellor. I have no idea if Drew Faust had any interest in my candidacy at Harvard, but I suspected not. I told Manny I did not want to pursue the position, given the possibility of being chancellor at Arkansas, and he didn't argue with me. I thought perhaps Faust might be thinking about going a different way with the appointment at Harvard.

Sometime later she did make an announcement that she had hired an internal candidate to fill the position. I don't regret having the interview with Dr. Faust and it was a wonderful experience to be able to meet somebody of her stature. I would follow her career over the next several years. I noticed that even a person of her breadth of accomplishment could have issues with her governing board. Not too many years later she retired as president.

CHAPTER 42
HIRING A NEW ATHLETICS DIRECTOR

> *I'm pretty upset, but I know how the world works. I'm just sick because I tried to do everything the right way with high ethics and morals and doing the right thing for young people. That's the only thing that disappoints me.*
>
> — *JEFF LONG*

Because I was scheduled to be named chancellor, I was asked to be a member of the high-level search committee for the replacement of Broyles as director of athletics. It would be a daunting task. Broyles had reigned over Razorback athletics for almost 50 years and was an Arkansas icon. How do you replace someone like that? It was decided that a small search committee composed of the chairman of the board of trustees, Stanley Reed, president of the system, Alan Sugg and chancellor John White would perform the task. I was asked to round out the committee as a fourth unnamed person to sit in on the meetings and offer advice. My selection was kept quiet since I had not yet been named by the board.

John White was focusing on the athletics director at Notre Dame. White told us the candidate did have a legitimate interest in coming to Fayetteville and wanted to wait to present him to the committee until a commitment was firm. Then the committee would interview him. We waited. And we waited! It became obvious that White's candidate was not going to commit, much to White's regret. We had wasted valuable time on a candidate who may have been using Arkansas to sweeten his deal at Notre Dame.

The next candidate who came forward was the AD at the University of Missouri. We interviewed him and were impressed. Then he decided to stay put at Missouri. John White was not happy. We had a cancellation in our schedule, and I floated the name of Jeff Long, who was AD at the University of Pittsburgh. I knew Long from a consulting job I had done for him a few years back. He had an excellent reputation for graduating student-athletes and was a stand-up guy. White checked him out with our search consultant who told us he really didn't know him that well but had heard good things about him. We had several potential candidates in the mix at that point but none on our schedule to see that day. We were in the university jet and could fly just about anywhere in the country in 2 to 3 hours and the group decided we should go see Long in Pittsburgh, probably out of support for me, the upcoming chancellor.

We landed at the Pittsburgh airport and were spotted by a reporter who relayed our trip back to the media in Arkansas. White had taken numerous precautions to hide our search escapades as most of the candidates did not want their names released for fear for their current positions. White had even required the pilots to wear unidentifiable shirts without Razorback logos. He even thought about repainting the plane and taking off the Razorback identification.

We interviewed Long and his wife, Fanny, for three hours in a conference room at the Pittsburgh airport. All of us came away from the interview highly impressed with Long and Fanny. We told Long we would be back in touch very soon after doing our due diligence. On the flight back to Fayetteville we all agreed that we were extremely impressed with Long, and, if he checked out, he could very well be the next AD.

One thing I remember distinctly was when Long said he was not an AD who believed in winning at all costs. He wanted to win, but the right and honest way. He also said that he believed in graduating student-athletes, and that would be very important to him in all sports. Our current graduation rate among athletes was abysmal. He went on to say that obeying SEC and NCAA rules was most important to him. We all thought we had found our person.

In his more than 20-year career in intercollegiate athletics, Long had served as an athletics administrator at The University of Oklahoma, Eastern Kentucky University, Virginia Tech University and the University of Michigan. He had also held coaching and administrative positions at Rice University, Duke University, and North Carolina State University.

Jeff Long, athletics director at the University of Pittsburgh, was named director of men's athletics at the University of Arkansas, effective Jan. 1, 2008. Later he would be named director of women's athletics as well, a commitment made to him by White before he accepted the job. Merging men's and women's programs under one AD was a move that was overdue. They had been split by Chancellor Ferritor as a way to better spotlight women's programs, but the budget and resource allocation had remained with Broyles. It was a constant battle to get more revenue for the women's efforts. Bev Lewis was serving as the women's AD and doing an excellent job. I know it was very difficult on White, who had to tell her that he was merging the programs. White and Lewis were close friends and he had been a major supporter of women's athletics. He made it as easy as possible on Lewis by giving her a healthy compensation package and making the merger as painless as possible. Bev accepted the change with dignity.

One minor hiccup in the hiring of Long was that White had not told him that he would be retiring soon, and that I would become the new chancellor. To this day I'm not entirely sure why, but I suspect White didn't want to spook him. I decided unilaterally that Long needed to know and I told him on the ride from the executive airport when he was coming for the announcement of his new job. White was not happy with me. I must say it did spook Long, and he was caught off guard. Neither White nor I handled it very well. Long should have been told from the very beginning and I should not have spilled the beans on him at the 11th hour.

In the announcement White made the following comments:

"Finding a successor to a legend is a daunting responsibility, especially when the person sought is entrusted with a state treasure such as Razorback athletics. In conducting the search process, I sought input from dozens of respected individuals in college athletics, and one name kept coming up: Jeff Long. Jeff is an established leader with a track record of success with honor. He understands the role of intercollegiate athletics at major public universities, and is positioned to raise the bar even higher for Arkansas athletics—inside and outside of competition"

Coach Broyles was equally thoughtful in his remarks saying:

"The University of Arkansas and the men's athletics department are extremely privileged to welcome Jeff Long, his wife Fanny and their two daughters, Stephanie and Christina, into the Razorback family. Jeff brings a wealth of knowledge and experience from some of the most successful athletics programs and institutions in the Big East, Atlantic Coast Conference, Big 12 and Big Ten.

CHAPTER 43
FOWLER HOUSE

> *Sandy and I will begin the process of moving out of Fowler House promptly.*
>
> — JOE STEINMETZ IN HIS RESIGNATION LETTER. HE LIVED MOST OF THE TIME IN HIS PRIVATE HOUSE IN SPRINGDALE.

During the Campaign for the Twenty-First Century we had approached a few individuals to build a Chancellor's residence on campus. The university owned a parcel of land on the corner of Maple and Razorback Road. It was a wooded lot and had always been reserved for a chancellor's residence should funds become available. At one time the Tri Delta sorority owned the property, and before that the dean of the college of education, Dr. Henry Hotz. There actually used to be a president's residence on campus where Brough Commons dining hall is located. That facility was torn down many years ago. The next president's home was on Mount Sequoyah overlooking the city and campus. When a chancellor position was created on campus and the president was still remaining in Fayetteville there was no chancellor's residence.

When John White became chancellor, a small house on Razorback Road was purchased for his use. While it was a nice home, it was totally inadequate for entertaining purposes. The Whites were able to have small functions at the home, but never more than around 12 to 15 people. We started looking for a benefactor who might provide the funds to build a larger chancellor's residence.

At that time the largest private residence in Arkansas was situated in Jonesboro and owned by Wallace and Jama Fowler. The Fowlers were very successful businesspeople who owned several food and hotel franchises and banks. I started calling on the Fowlers during the early days of the campaign. I have met many fine people during my career, but the Fowlers are some of the best. Both of them are lovely people, thoughtful and supportive. They were huge Razorback fans and benefactors. I approached them about the possibility of providing funds for a chancellor's residence. Initially they did not say they would do it, but remained somewhat interested.

Toward the end of the campaign, I approach them again for a gift. Both of them were serving on the campaign steering committee and had attended most of our meetings. I began to think that the residence was not a project they were interested in, so I approached them to do something major for the library. We had submitted another proposal to a prospect for a chancellor's residence, but had not received an affirmative answer.

When I spoke to the Fowlers about what they might want to do for the campaign, they asked me if the chancellor's residence was still available. I asked them to give me 24 hours to see if the other individual we had approached was interested. We needed $3 million in order to build the facility. The other prospect offered $1 million, and I told him that we could not build it for that amount. I made an appointment with the Fowlers to show them architectural plans and they were sold. They signed a pledge for $3 million, but said they would pay it off more quickly than the three years they had agreed to. They ended up paying it in 18 months.

Unfortunately, the other prospect who offered $1 million began telling people that we had offered the house to him, and then went to someone else. The truth was, that prospect simply did not offer adequate funds. That prospect never made a significant gift to the campaign.

The Fowler House residence was completed the first week I became chancellor, and Jane, and I were the first occupants. At the dedication I told John and Mary Lib White that they could stay at the Fowler House anytime they wanted, and we would even give them the master bedroom. Then I said, "It might be a little crowded in the master bedroom with the four of us." It got a nice laugh.

Mrs. Judy Snowden of Little Rock and her daughter were the interior designers of Fowler House and chose all of the furnishings. They did an extraordinary job. The interior furnishings were elegant and warmly inviting. On top of that, she brought the furnishings in on budget and did not charge a single penny for the work. They were marvelous people to work with and did everything with professional flair.

When I became chancellor, toward the end of my administration, I approached the Fowlers to add a dining facility to what we were now calling Fowler House. It would be a facility that could seat over 100 people for dinner. The thought was that we could have a cocktail function in the main residence, and then walk over to what we would call Fowler Conservatory. We estimated that, in order to do all of the site work and prepare the property for the conservatory, it would cost another $3 million.

In the last days of my time as chancellor the Fowlers generously agreed to provide the resources for that new facility adjacent to Fowler House. With the Alumni House, University House, Carnall Inn and now the Fowler facilities, it would give us four venues for entertaining alumni and friends. The university was growing by leaps and bounds, and we needed more places for our deans and vice chancellors to entertain our constituents.

After the Fowlers committed an additional $3 million, I decided to retire as chancellor. I called to inform Wallace of my decision and he immediately said that he wasn't sure he wanted to move forward with the Fowler Conservatory. After much discussion I told him that I really hoped that he would move forward on the project and in the end, he agreed to do so.

The conservatory was completed after I retired, and chancellor Steinmetz held a dedication of the new building. Jane and I attended the event. We had tried to be invisible in the first days of a new chancellor's tenure, wanting to stay out of his way. But, since I had worked very hard to obtain the gift and was proud that it was now coming to fruition, and because Wallace and Jama were such good friends and asked that we attend the dedication, we felt we should make an appearance.

I thought perhaps Steinmetz might introduce Jane and me at the dedication, and maybe even mention that we had been involved in obtaining the gift. He did not. He made no mention that we were even present at the ceremony. His vice chancellor for advancement, Mark Power, who I had worked with very closely, did not acknowledge our presence either. Jane and I stood at the back of the crowd as seating was limited.

I was disappointed that he did not have the wherewithal to even mention we were in attendance. During my time as chancellor, I always made a point of introducing previous chancellors who attended university events. It just seemed the right thing to do. It wasn't so much that I was seeking recognition, but I just thought it was a courtesy that I afforded former chancellors. After all, Steinmetz had come from a major institution (The Ohio State University) and certainly had learned by now how to be gracious. I knew at that very moment that Steinmetz did not have much southern hospitality, if any. During the 5-plus years of his administration, Jane and I were rarely invited to any university events and never included in the chancellor's box for football or basketball games. We were persona non grata as far as Steinmetz was concerned. More on that later.

When I took the reins as chancellor, Jane and I used Fowler House for entertaining purposes and events extensively. One month I counted 14 consecutive events in the house. We held celebrations of faculty, students, alumni, and athletics achievements almost continuously. The first week the house was opened, we invited the media for a site visit. I had been worried that the media might write disparaging articles about the project, even though it was built and furnished with private money. Luckily, we did not get any negatives from the media. We would hold 144 private dinners in the house during our seven years in the job. We had what we called "Dinners for 14," which became special evenings honoring benefactors and prospects. The beautiful dining room table held 14 and they became important functions for raising private funds.

PART VII
CHANCELLOR, THE EARLY YEARS

2008–2011

Whatever you are, be a good one.

— *ABRAHAM LINCOLN*

CHAPTER 44
READY OR NOT

> *Don't let the fear of striking out hold you back.*
>
> — BABE RUTH

For some time, Alan Sugg had been discussing with me the possibility of serving as chancellor once John White retired. White was having a tough time with the board of trustees his last year or so. The board had changed rather dramatically and liked to meddle in issues that should have been left to the administration. Most of the issues had to do with athletics. It actually seemed that very few trustees cared for anything academic. But if it had to do with athletics, they were front and center telling the chancellor and president what to do.

In 2004 the Association of Governing Boards (AGB) adopted a "Statement on Board Responsibilities for Intercollegiate Athletics." The statement made it clear that boards should delegate direct responsibility for the conduct and control of the athletics department to the institution's chief executive. When a president or chancellor makes a controversial stand regarding an athletics matter, the governing board was expected to publicly support and defend the president. AGB even recommended boards not form an athletics committee of the board, because it gave too much cause for interfering with presidential duties. Boards should stay away from trying to manage athletics and leave that duty and responsibility to the CEO. Unfortunately the board tried to meddle with athletics decision making many times during White's tenure. Little did I know that I would experience the same interference years later. It continues even today, but isn't all that different from other big-time universities.

Sugg told me he was not going to conduct a national search but would interview several stakeholders about my leadership abilities. If he got negative feedback from vice chancellors, deans, donors, students, legislators, alumni, or others, he might have to change his mind. Sugg went on to say he had spoken with the board of trustees and all of them were favorable toward my candidacy.

On January 25, 2008, I was elected chancellor of the University of Arkansas by the board of trustees on the recommendation of President Alan Sugg. I was asked to make comments in the open session and at the executive session and Jane was invited to join me.

I began by thanking Dr. Sugg and the board for their consideration of me to be the next chancellor of the University of Arkansas. I told them that I was honored, flattered, and completely humbled and truly grateful for the opportunity. In some ways, I felt my entire adult life had prepared me for this moment, while at the same time realizing the daunting task that lay ahead of me. I thanked the board for allowing Jane to accompany me to the executive committee meeting. It was important that she be there, as she would be a real partner in this venture—every step of the way, as she had been for all of my adult life. It would truly be a partnership.

I then made a few short comments about my philosophy, vision, mission and plans for the future. I believed then, as I do now, that the ultimate success of the University of Arkansas depended to a large extent on its capacity to demonstrate its usefulness to society. That meant the institution had to not merely be "in the world," but also "of the world." The university, at root, exists to serve the larger society, not itself.

I told the board that, of all of the rich contributions America had bestowed on the world, American higher education was among the most important. Our colleges and universities had become, perhaps, the most vital expression of the American political and social philosophy—a philosophy based on pluralism, inclusion, opportunity, merit, and, of course, an abiding faith in the power of education to improve the human condition. The last two decades had made it abundantly clear that the American opportunity system was increasingly difficult to access without a college education. Thus, it was the mandate of American higher education to find ways of expanding access to our higher education system, and to ensure that the education we offered at the University of Arkansas was one of high quality.

I told the board my overriding philosophy was to give the people of Arkansas a superb university, both at the graduate and undergraduate levels. My hope was to construct a learning environment, one in which the community of scholars, teachers and researchers actually functions in a way that crosses disciplinary boundaries and works toward a collegial environment that rewards research, teaching and service.

I increasingly favored the emerging view of research as scholarship—it needed to be more broadly defined than, perhaps, the traditional view. More than ever, we had to view our faculty as individuals, some of whom had greater proclivity for basic and applied research and some for teaching. Research and teaching were not incompatible.

I relayed to the board that I wanted to dramatically improve our student centeredness and make our institution much more student friendly. Once having made the decision to accept a student into the university family, we should do *everything* in our power to make that student successful and launch them on a meaningful pathway in life.

There were indeed serious challenges facing higher education, and perhaps the most serious was the ability of our students to afford a University of Arkansas education. Far too many low-income and minority students were denied a college education at their flagship institution because of financial barriers. I wanted to be very engaged in our admissions process. I firmly believed we had to continue to increase the size of our student body—perhaps even to 28,000 or 30,000 to take advantage of economies of scale—and I promised to work very closely with our staff and faculty to propel us forward. We had made good progress, but we needed to continue to emphasize planned growth.

I would have a strong interest in legislative relations. My sense was that we had to go beyond the requisite appearance before the state legislature at appropriations time and emphasize the development of relationships with key members of the General Assembly.

We had to explain to the public the value of higher education's essential services and products, and what it was that we did best, I told the board. We had to be able to demonstrate that we were not only a valuable road to personal opportunity, but also a solution to many of society's problems, the wellspring of innovation and creativity, and the foundation for economic growth and competitiveness.

We had worked very hard to make a compelling case for diversity at the university, but while making progress, our efforts still fell far short of expectations. I didn't believe this would change until we could find a way to reward those who practice what they preach. I proposed we look very carefully at providing financial incentives to deans and vice chancellors to hire people of color and expand the number of faculty and staff with diverse backgrounds. I believed we had a duty and a responsibility to effect change in this area, and place resources where our mouth was.

Intercollegiate athletics play a key role in American colleges and universities. Athletics played an important role in providing the social glue, if you will, on our campus. They created excitement that translates into support and recognition for the university. But we all agreed they had to be based on integrity and intimately engaged in the educational mission and life of the institution.

I assured the board of trustees that my management style would be straightforward, clear and compelling, with frequent communication as a necessary ingredient for leadership. The faculty and staff needed to know and buy into the goals, objectives and strategic direction of our institution, but they also had to be trusted and empowered to devise the best means of getting us there. My administration would be open, inclusive and transparent.

We also needed to renovate several of our more iconic facilities. That would be a huge undertaking, as we had millions of dollars of deferred maintenance since the General Assembly was not giving us support for capital improvements.

We now had one of the finest Honors Colleges in the nation, thanks in large part to the Walton gift that endowed scholarships, fellowships and professorships. Keeping that important and vital component of the university strong and viable would be a priority.

It was also imperative that we made our university libraries the best they could be, and continued to provide adequate funding for this lifeblood of our programs.

I thought we could do more to spread the news about the university—statewide, nationally, and even globally. This could potentially involve a comprehensive marketing program and an investment in emerging media opportunities.

As the university continued to grow, I feared our technical infrastructure would fall behind the curve. We needed to ensure our technical operations were in tune with emerging technology to advance the campus. We had to remain on the cutting edge of technology. I also hoped to provide leadership in expanding our telecommunications and distance learning capabilities over the next decade, to bring a University of Arkansas education to more homes, more citizens, and to increase our overall reach and visibility. Expanding online course delivery would be most important.

Faculty and staff salaries would need to be at the top of our list if we were to remain competitive in the years ahead. It could be said that we had built the university on the backs of our faculty and staff. Salaries at the time were running anywhere from 15 percent to 40 percent below the market—and I was talking about the market of similar institutions in our backyard.

And, at some point, we needed to think very seriously about another major capital campaign. Private gifts would forever be a most important ingredient to our success. I concluded by saying that I hoped to put a team in place to continue to appeal to our very generous alumni and friends to make an investment in their university. I thanked John and Mary Lib White for their years of dedicated service and John's stable leadership.

White was an excellent chancellor. He brought in superb students and faculty. He raised millions in private funds. He substantially increased our research funding. I was there and witnessed his leadership. There was no doubt he had put the university on the map.

When one of his friends and a university volunteer developed prostate cancer, White changed his calendar, got on a plane, and flew down to be with him and his wife during the operation to remove the cancer.

I knew the road ahead would not be an easy one. It would take critical resources, both private and public, as well as a careful allocation of budgeted funds, but I pledged to work very hard—and hopefully very smart—to lead our university into the future.

CHAPTER 45
BUDGET CHALLENGES AND STATE APPROPRIATIONS

> *No man's life, liberty, or property are safe while the legislature is in session.*
>
> — MARK TWAIN

In 2008 the latest Arkansas Poll under the auspices of the Fulbright College revealed that Arkansans were overwhelmingly concerned about the economy. The overall mission of the poll, according to its website, was to supply timely, accurate, and impartial public opinion information on matters of policy and politics to public officials, researchers, students, and the public. The first year of my administration saw a huge downturn in the economy and people were more than concerned. The Arkansas Poll indicated economic concerns were at their highest in the 13-year history of the poll. During the first year of Governor Beebe's first term in office, he worked to get a sizable increase in higher education's appropriation. However, it was a one-time increase. Many of us in higher education were hoping he would continue to provide increases every year, but that was not to be.

When I became chancellor, Arkansas's universities and colleges were yearning for more public support through an increase in their state appropriation. We had experienced many years of unavoidable cost increases, including utilities, fuel, insurance, software, transportation, scientific and lab equipment, library materials, and deferred maintenance on literally thousands of square feet of educational space. Many institutions had not given salary increases for some time or very modest increases, if at all. In 2008 alone, the University of Arkansas had more than $17 million in cost increases, including more than $5 million in higher premiums for health insurance and another $2 million for utility increases, not to mention hiring the new faculty needed to meet the demands of record enrollment as we started growing by leaps and bounds. All of the public universities in Arkansas were experiencing serious financial issues.

As a result of no state appropriation increases, we were struggling mightily to adequately pay faculty and staff. Our faculty continued to be among the lowest paid in the country when compared to benchmark institutions. Among all flagship universities across the United States, professorial salaries at University of Arkansas were ranked 43rd. Hundreds of our university employees received wages below the national poverty level.

Within a matter of days of beginning my tenure as the new chancellor, I made an appointment to see Alan Sugg in Little Rock. I asked Don Pederson, our CFO, to accompany me. Don Pederson had served in both the White and Ferritor administrations as the chief academic officer and later as the chief financial officer. I asked him to remain as CFO when I became chancellor, and he did a superb job. He was hard working, smart and loyal. When he retired, he had been at the university for over 45 years.

The purpose of the meeting was to inform Dr. Sugg of our precarious financial position and the fact that we had very little in reserves should we experience something catastrophic. Within weeks of my start we came very close to not being able to meet our payroll obligations. Some of our short-term investments had been frozen since they were under water, meaning invested funds were worth less than the price paid for it at its current market valuation. We literally had to hand carry a check to Little Rock to avoid defaulting on our payroll obligations.

Don and I laid out our financial situation to Sugg, and he sat back in his chair and exclaimed, "You folks are broke!"

And indeed, we were. I had inherited practically no reserves during a major downturn in the economy and the freezing of our investments due to being under water. We had to build back our reserves as quickly as possible. The only way to do that quickly and successfully was to increase our student enrollment and do so as rapidly as possible. I stayed up night after night worrying about how we were going to pay our bills. The UA had always been in a precarious financial situation from its very beginning, but the economic downturn in 2008 had strained us to a breaking point. We were indeed broke!

There are only a very few sources of revenue to run public universities. The bulk of a public university budget comes from three primary sources: tuition and fees, state appropriations, and private gifts and grants. We had been working very hard to make sure private support was increasing, and had made huge advances in this area with the Campaign for the Twenty-First Century. Over the past several years, the percentage of state support in our overall budget had declined more than 20 percent. That percentage decline was now being paid for by our students and their parents through higher tuition and fees. While scholarships paid for by the state lottery did indeed help students to avoid some debt, the pressure on students to bridge the funding gap between what state appropriations provided and what it actually cost to run a university was widening at an unacceptable rate. We were not unique. Most public universities across the nation were experiencing the same financial issues.

To be sure, we did everything possible to dramatically cut expenses and I asked Don Pederson to lead an effort to reduce costs. Through his efforts and that of the deans and vice chancellors we experienced cost savings of over $40 million annually. But we still were building the university on the backs of our students and faculty.

High tuition and fees and a low salary scale were the only ways we were able to meet budgeted needs.

Since becoming chancellor, I had the privilege of visiting several high schools across Arkansas to proclaim the importance of getting a college degree. The amazing thing was that most of those school's facilities were absolutely first rate. I remember a visit to a high school in south Arkansas and was simply flabbergasted at the top-shelf facilities in the school district, which were much better than we had on our campus.

Having quality facilities is certainly a good thing for secondary education and good for Arkansas in general, however, we would have been proud to offer the same quality of the state's high-school buildings on our campus. But support for higher education compared to primary and secondary education continued to be elusive. Perhaps one of the primary reasons for the lack of support from the General Assembly was the simple fact that a relatively small percentage of Arkansans had college degrees. It just didn't seem to be a priority for Arkansans or the Arkansas legislature. It still isn't. Most members of the General Assembly have absolutely no concept of the importance of higher education to the state's economy. Many couldn't care less about supporting the state's colleges and universities, except for athletics. The amount of funding they appropriate to the University of Arkansas is less than 15 percent of our total budget.

But we knew, and I believed very strongly, that the fortunes of Arkansas are deeply connected to the quality of our universities and our ability to produce Arkansans with bachelor's degrees. I approached Governor Beebe and asked him to consider a very modest appropriation increase equal to the rate of inflation, a little more than 2 percent. That would amount to approximately $14 million in new revenue for all of higher education statewide. I told the governor, if he would make that commitment, we would keep tuition increases at 2 percent as well. Two percent for 2 percent seemed to be very reasonable in my mind. That did not seem too much to ask from our students and their parents.

A modest increase in state appropriations to match the rate of inflation for our colleges and universities would help tremendously to keep tuition increases down. Increasing the number of college-educated citizens was a high priority for our governor and should have been for our legislature. It is the only way we would see truly lasting changes in our economic outlook as we stimulated business growth the way only an educated workforce can. It's just 2 percent. Not much to ask for the future leaders of Arkansas and the nation.

I presented my thoughts to the other presidents and chancellors in Arkansas and got a show of support from most of them. Two percent for 2 percent seemed to be a plan that made sense to me. Of course, one never gets unanimity of thought from all the state's presidents and chancellors on any subject. Most of them are working side deals with their local legislators for funding opportunities and the Higher Education Coordinating Board was too weak to make any decisions at all.

I asked our vice chancellor for government relations, Richard Hudson, what he thought, and he agreed it made good fiscal sense. Richard had been a lobbyist in Arkansas for many years and knew all the legislators personally. He was highly respected by the General Assembly and the governor and had his pulse on state politics.

Unfortunately, it was not to be. We did not receive any increases in our state appropriation during the seven years of my tenure as chancellor. None. Not a penny. Increasing the number of college educated citizens was a high priority for the governor. But it's almost impossible to do that without the funding to make it happen. The governor was certainly right in wanting us to increase the college-going rate, but he was wrong in not funding an effort to make it happen.

Talk is cheap. It is easy for a politician to say he or she wants to increase the number of citizens with a bachelor's degree. But, with no funds to make it happen, it is virtually impossible to make progress.

Personally, I liked Governor Beebe very much. I think generally he was a good governor for Arkansas, and his favorable ratings remained high throughout his administration. He retired as a highly respected government servant. But he was a politician. Politicians don't like controversy. They shun it at all costs. The status quo is what reelects politicians. Don't rock the boat, keep things on an even keel. Except for his first year, we received no new state funds for our general budget during his time as governor.

CHAPTER 46
THE BUCKET LIST

> *Some people want it to happen, some wish it would happen, others make it happen.*
>
> — MICHAEL JORDAN

When I took office, I believed the first order of business was to conduct interviews with stakeholders on and off campus. I had my own personal ideas of what needed to be accomplished and how to prioritize those ideas, but at an academic institution the worst thing one can do is to impose ideas from the top down. It is most important to get maximum buy-in from faculty, deans, vice chancellors, staff, students, and alumni, and show those various constituents they have a voice in governance.

With Judy Schwab's excellent assistance, we created "Priorities for the Gearhart Administration—The First 100 Days." We immediately established a new committee on improving diversity. We began a rigorous review of the curriculum, and looked closely at our scholarship programs, both merit and need based. The most important item for me was substantially increasing enrollment and retention.

That was an absolute priority. We also knew we would need to launch another major capital campaign.

Cost saving was another priority. Don Pederson took on the challenge by looking at everything with an eye to cutting costs and eliminating waste. At the same time we wanted to make the campus more pleasing aesthetically. Improving faculty and staff salaries was a huge priority. As simplistic as it sounds, improving parking for faculty, staff and students would improve morale.

Renovation of a number of facilities was staring us in the face. The state was not giving us any new funds for capital improvements, so we would have to devise a way to renovate and refurbish several iconic buildings on campus. We also needed more classroom space, and would need to build new facilities as well as renovate old ones.

Getting more funding from the state was most likely a lost cause, but that didn't stop us from trying.

We held a series of meetings to gain maximum input on the priorities of the university going forward. Some of the meetings spanned two days and were held at the Winthrop Rockefeller Institute on Petit Jean Mountain.

After much work and deliberation, we created a list of 15 priorities, which the academic and administrative community viewed as the top items of importance going forward. There would be additional items over the next 7 years, but the 15 that were set at the many meetings we held would be a road map for us in the coming years. It would be our strategic plan. I called them verifiable objectives providing transparency and accountability to the people of Arkansas.

I long believed that hollow, lofty prose without real objectives does not allow an institution to measure progress. I wanted to prove to the university community—and beyond—that we intended to make real progress, which could be measured to objectively show the world we were actually meeting milestones on a number of fronts. We published the first report that was based on the multiple meetings in 2009 and called it "Providing Transparency and Accountability to the People of Arkansas" (TAP). The document was one way to hold ourselves publicly accountable to the people of Arkansas and to the students and families who made the university their institution of choice.

We established 15 institutional goals and showed how we planned to meet our aspirational goal of becoming a top-50 public research university by 2021. John White had clearly made a part of his administration his desire to be a top 50 public university as ranked mainly by *U.S. News and World Report*, but also other ranking guides. Achieving the top 50 goal would mean the University of Arkansas ranked among the top 8 percent of all public research universities in America.

I followed his lead and all of our deans and vice chancellors bought into the goal of becoming a top-50 public institution. It would be a challenge, but we believed it was doable by 2021. By the year 2015 we had reached 62 in the rankings. I believe we could have made it to 50 if we had stuck to it and focused on our goal. But the chancellor who replaced me, Joe Steinmetz, was not interested in what he referred to as chasing rankings. In 2021 we had fallen to 78.

By 2015 we had shown very impressive gains in the rankings in *U.S. News and World Report*. The College of Education and Health Professions' graduate education programs moved up nearly 50 places in the overall rankings; the Sam M. Walton College of Business MBA program moved up 11 places in the rankings—but even more notable—it continued to lead the nation in the number of full-time Master of Business Administration graduates employed at graduation. The School of Law, meanwhile, improved its overall ranking by seven places and had climbed 47 spots since the 2008 rankings.

One particular ranking that made me very proud was a new survey of college leaders across the U.S, which gave the University of Arkansas top-ten ranking among national public universities for having made "the most promising and innovative changes" to advance academics and the student learning experience. The survey was conducted as part of *US News & World Report's* annual college ranking, "Best Colleges 2013." Hundreds of university and college chancellors, presidents, provosts and admission deans took part in the survey.

Each participant was asked to nominate up to ten public and

private colleges and universities that have made noteworthy advances in their academic quality and student life. The University of Arkansas was ranked ninth among public universities. Tim Kral, chair of the Faculty Senate, made a comment to the media that was much appreciated: "Around the nation universities are laying off faculty and cutting budgets. The University of Arkansas is hiring additional faculty and providing support—financial and professional support—for our teachers and researchers. It's not surprising that our colleagues at other universities have noticed and are impressed."

Along with the University of Arkansas, the other top public universities in the survey included Arizona State University, Clemson University, George Mason University, Indiana University—Purdue University Indianapolis, North Carolina State University, Portland State University, Ohio State University, the University of Central Florida, and the University of Maryland.

To get to the top 50 we established the following verifiable objectives and published them in our TAP report:

GOAL 1) PUT STUDENTS FIRST BY ENHANCING ACADEMIC PROGRAMS, CREATING AN ENGAGING CAMPUS LIFE, KEEPING COSTS AS LOW AS POSSIBLE AND REDUCING OBSTACLES TO STUDENT SUCCESS.

I had long felt that, as an institution, we were not very student friendly. We were order takers. If a student wanted to attend the University of Arkansas, fine, but we were not going to make it as easy as possible to do so. We were not hungry for students and our recruitment efforts were abysmal. As vice chancellor I heard many horror stories about throwing up roadblocks to students and refusing to help them achieve success.

A story was told to me by a faculty member that curled my hair. Apparently, a student got a serious illness three weeks before the end of the semester. She was so sick that she had to miss class those last three weeks. She dutifully had a classmate take notes so she could have all the materials from class lectures, and emailed the professor to allow her to take the final exam late when she recovered. In the meantime, she asked the teacher to give her an incomplete until she took the test, which the student hoped would be within days of the last class. Her professor refused. She needed the class to graduate, but the professor was telling her she had to come back in the summer session and retake the class. She already had a job in a tough job market and would have to delay the job she had already accepted, or possibly be in peril of losing the job altogether. I called the professor's dean and the dean intervened and got it fixed. I found the professor's attitude absolutely unconscionable. I wanted a university that helped students achieve their dreams and aspirations, not one that put up roadblocks to success.

Those kinds of stories frustrated me greatly and I wanted to change the culture and climate, and make it much more friendly for our students and prospective students. We could no longer be order takers. The competition for students was intense all across the nation and particularly in Arkansas.

One example of putting students first was the case of Raymond Walter. He was a brilliant student who had graduated from Mountain Home high school at the age of 14. My brother Van, who lived in Mountain Home at the time, made me aware of Raymond's interest in attending the University of Arkansas. Raymond had Duchenne muscular dystrophy, which is a severe, progressive, muscle-wasting disease leading to difficulties with movement and, eventually, to the need for assisted ventilation. My brother hooked me up with Raymond and his devoted father, Hal, and they came to visit me in my office in 2009. Raymond was in a wheelchair, but my initial impression was that I was witnessing a remarkably intelligent young person who was dealt a bad hand as concerns his health. Hal explained his son wanted to pursue three simultaneous degrees in physics, math and economics.

Raymond would need some accommodations due to his disability, but mainly his dad was asking to be allowed to live in his dorm with his son and help him navigate the campus during his college years. We sprang into action. Our chief student affairs officer, Danny Pugh, was a huge advocate for Raymond and made all of the necessary arrangements for a living space that would accommodate his father.

We gave him an oversized room so his dad could be with him and provide all of the necessary personal care assistance. On Mondays the two, father and son, would drive to Fayetteville from Mountain Home in time for his classes and return on Friday after Raymond's last class of the day. Hal had to be home on the weekends to tend to their farm. During the week Hal would take Raymond to his classes and to dining and be certain he had all the elements he needed to be successful.

In 2013 Raymond earned his bachelor's degree and went on to pursue his masters and Ph.D. which he received in 2014 and 2019 respectfully. It is a story of courage, responsibility and love and I am very proud of the university in stepping up and putting students first.

I decided to have lapel pins created that read "Students First" and distributed them to anyone who wanted one. (Later, when we were not faring too well in football, my brother Van made up a lapel pin and sent it to me. It said, "Students first, football last." He laughed uproariously. I didn't think it was funny).

The "Students First" pins were a big hit with our students and their families, and I got multiple letters complimenting the pins and asking for them. However, there are always a few people who don't appreciate something new and different. Some faculty objected to the pins as they felt it denigrated faculty. After all, weren't the faculty the life blood of an academic institution? Shouldn't faculty be first, followed by students?

This minor pushback angered me. But it was the same few faculty who could be counted on to complain about anything they possibly could. It was suggested perhaps I should say "Students First, Faculty Always" to pacify those few faculty who were somehow offended.

Most faculty were wonderful people—supportive and helpful and striving to do all they could to assist our students. I always felt I had excellent relations with faculty and deans throughout my entire career. But then there were a few who, well, could be difficult.

Students, faculty and staff across the campus worked very hard to make the University of Arkansas a first-class institution, as well as a top-50 public research institution. We tried to look at every decision

—academic, financial, and administrative—and to ask how we can best enhance academic programs and engage campus life, while keeping costs as low as possible. The main thing we wanted to accomplish was to reduce obstacles to degree attainment and academic success.

It was also important to continue to assess performance in intercollegiate athletics. We had earned considerable progress in the Learfield Directors' Cup, given annually by the National Association of Collegiate Directors of Athletics. But more progress needed to be made.

We also looked to the Carnegie Foundation for the Advancement of Teaching. Our hope was that we could enter into its highest research classification, which is based on the number of doctoral degrees awarded, grants received, and level of research activity. We would achieve that goal in 2011 by offering incentives to faculty to ramp up research and publishing. We also beefed up our research office and provided more professionals to assist faculty in writing grants.

That same year we would finish in the top 20 in the Learfield Directors' Cup.

I do believe the university had always been a good steward of its resources, but we had more work to do to try to keep costs as low as possible, by carefully monitoring expenses and finding ways to reduce costs at all levels. To maintain our reputation as one of the best college buys in the country, the university had to find a way to contain costs. Dr. Don Pederson, vice chancellor for finance and administration, led our efforts at cost containment.

The first year I was chancellor we created a task force to become a veteran-friendly campus, and ensure the university provided a welcoming environment for veterans and would support their progress toward a degree. As a direct result of the task force recommendations, the university established the Veterans Resource and Information Center within the Division of Student Affairs. The center helped veteran students find their way around the university and supported them with information about educational benefits, scholarships, and other forms of financial aid. It also provided details about campus, community, state, and national resources for current and former military personnel.

While I never served in the Armed Forces, I have always had a special place in my heart for those who have served their country. My uncle, Sam Gearhart, Jr. was killed in World War II. He was just 20 years old, and his B-24 bomber was shot down in the Pacific theater. His body was never recovered, and even though I never knew him, the fact that he was killed while providing service to his country was very meaningful to me. He married just before heading to war, and his wife bore a child who my uncle never met. I wanted to do everything I could to support veterans and persons serving in the military.

We also beefed up our Center for Educational Access as a way to support those with disabilities. I met a young student named George Turner from Dallas. He was born with spina bifida. He helped me tremendously in making our campus more accessible to wheelchair-bound students. George even helped us raise funds for the Center for Educational Access. He is an amazing young man and we have continued our friendship with him and his engaging younger brother, Quip, and lovely and successful sister, Maria. It has been such a pleasure to get to know them and remain in close contact. George advised us on removing physical barriers and providing extensive accommodations for students with disabilities. University of Arkansas remained in compliance with the Americans with Disabilities Act, and we committed ourselves to supporting students throughout their college careers. While much more needs to be done, George was extremely helpful. He is a person who was dealt a bad hand in life but has risen to the challenge, and through his efforts, helped other students with a disability.

On one occasion George sponsored a challenge where persons could use a wheelchair for a day to experience what it is like to be wheelchair bound and navigate all of the barriers on campus. It was quite revealing to me and senior officers of the university. We had much more work to do to make the campus truly accessible to students with disabilities.

We also added considerably to scholarships for needy students.

We made a pledge that we would not deny any student a University of Arkansas education because of their financial circumstances. But unfortunately, it wasn't enough and still isn't.

By 2014 we were having solid success with three major scholarship awards: Truman, Goldwater and Rhodes. We were first in the SEC for the number of Goldwater and Truman awards. We were 38th in the nation in the number of Rhodes scholarships.

GOAL 2) BE TRANSPARENT AND ACCOUNTABLE TO THE PEOPLE OF ARKANSAS IN ALL DECISION-MAKING

Early on I wanted to communicate to our students, faculty, and staff, as well as alumni, in a transparent and accountable way. In the first couple years of my administration we produced and posted online more than 30 videos and email communications on topics ranging from the institution's facility renewal stewardship plan to its economic impact on the state of Arkansas. I was hoping that by being transparent it would make an impression on the legislature.

Don Pederson created a program called Open UA. The whole purpose was to provide transparency on how we spent our funds. Open UA created a searchable database of expenditure records. It contained expenditure records for the university and all of its accounts. Our hope was that the legislature would appreciate our quest to be as open as possible about how we were spending our legislative appropriation. I learned early on that not very many of our legislators read the materials we sent to them, and our records indicated very few legislators were accessing Open UA. That was discouraging.

GOAL 3) INCREASE OVERALL ENROLLMENT WHILE REMAINING THE SCHOOL OF CHOICE FOR THE STATE'S MOST GIFTED STUDENTS; PROVIDE A CONCOMITANT INCREASE IN FACULTY AND STAFF

In our first year, 2008, the university set goals for enrollment growth. We wanted to be at 22,000 students by 2015 and 25,000 by 2021. Our enrollment at that time was about 18,000 students so the goals seemed ambitious. We hired a new vice provost for enrollment management, Dr. Suzanne McCray. I believe it was one of the best decisions we ever made. Previously the administrative areas involved in enrollment management all reported directly to the Provost. We amalgamated those areas and put them under Dr. McCray. She performed unbelievably well in her role of managing growth. The first year she was operating as our enrollment manager the new freshman class steadily outpaced predictions, propelling the university past our 2015 goal. We then felt we could reach a goal of 30,000 students within the next few years.

There were three main reasons enrollment grew dramatically at the university: increased scholarship funding through the lottery, our enhanced academic reputation, and the incredible work of Dr. McCray and her staff in building a professional recruitment base. At one point we became the seventh-fastest growing university in the nation. The quality of the professional staff under the leadership of Dr. McCray was absolutely phenomenal.

Because of her work, we were able to right-size the university. Throughout our history we had more programs and more faculty than we had students. It had been a systemic problem for dozens of years. It was imperative that we grow our student body so we would have additional revenue to support our many programs. Our ability to create a sizable fiscal reserve was due to the increase in enrollment.

Of course, with the increase in student numbers came a concomitant need to increase the size of our faculty. We also knew that more students were placing a strain on student services, as well as our ability to house students on campus. We began an effort to build new residence facilities and renovate those that had been out of commission for some time.

After I retired as chancellor, the next administration slowed down our growth. Had that not happened I firmly believe we would have hit 30,000 students by 2019 or 2020.

One benchmark we looked at to determine how large our enrollment should be was the size of peer institutions. The University of

Arkansas at the time was still one of the smallest of the universities in the Southeastern Conference. While Mississippi State and The University of Mississippi had smaller numbers, most SEC schools were well over 30,000 students. With more than 200 program offerings, the University of Arkansas needed to continue to grow its enrollment. We had far too many academic programs for the relatively small student body. Our new provost, Dr. Sharon Gaber, did a magnificent job monitoring the faculty needs by benchmarking against other major research universities to be certain we had enough faculty as we grew our student body. We were going to need additional classroom space, especially laboratory teaching space in the hard sciences, and Sharon worked hard in planning to bring new facilities online. She instituted a planning effort to build smart and provide the facilities needed for our growing student population. I was very fortunate to have Sharon as our provost. She was smart, engaging and easy to work with. We formed a great partnership. I shared with her an anonymous line about provosts: "The faculty's role is to think for the university. The chancellor's role is to speak for the university. The provost's role is to keep the faculty from speaking and the chancellor from thinking!"

Sharon would go on to be a highly effective president of The University of Toledo and later chancellor of the University of North Carolina at Charlotte.

GOAL 4) ENHANCE DIVERSITY BY ATTRACTING MORE STUDENTS, FACULTY, AND STAFF FROM UNDERREPRESENTED GROUPS, AND BY NURTURING INTERCULTURAL UNDERSTANDING INSIDE AND OUTSIDE THE CLASSROOM

We set a goal of 16 percent minority enrollment by the year 2015. In the fall of 2011, we reached that ambitious goal. The vision and leadership of Dr. Charles Robinson, at that time vice chancellor for diversity affairs, led to the arrival of the most diverse and academically accomplished freshman class in the institution's history. Dr. Robinson established new programs that helped Black students obtain a superb education at the University of Arkansas. They included the Razorback Bridge Scholarship Program, Summer ACT Academies, and the Delta Schools College Completion Consortium. We had significant increases in the number of African American students and Asian and Hispanic students. Dr. Robinson would go on to be provost and vice chancellor for academic affairs and then serve as interim chancellor at the time of this writing. Dr. Robinson was the catalyst for a number of new diversity and inclusion initiatives, and he deserves much of the credit for the substantial progress we made in diversifying both our faculty and our student body. Because of his efforts we revised our diversity goals to be at 20 percent by 2021. We are very proud of the fact that minority enrollment increased 54 percent during our time.

University campuses are the testing ground for new ideas and theories, and the places best equipped for conservatives and liberals, Muslims and Christians, Jews and Gentiles to educate each other about their differences and their similarities. All students should be welcome at the University of Arkansas. Whether they come from low or high socioeconomic backgrounds or high- or low-income families, whether they are religious or agnostic, gay or straight, young or old, Alaskan or Arkansan, redneck or Texan. Diversity makes the unusual familiar and the intolerable understandable. It turns strangers into friends and humanizes behaviors and practices that otherwise seem foreign or upsetting.

Diversity increases the measure of understanding in this world, the quality of compassion, and the level of tolerance and respect. Diversity illuminates the darkness of ignorance and diminishes the unsettling threats of the unknown.

GOAL 5) IMPROVE GRADUATION RATES AND DEGREE-COMPLETION TIMES

To fulfill our role in advancing the state of Arkansas, we had an important task before us to not only increase our enrollment in undergraduate and graduate programs but also increase the number of students who succeed at the university by earning degrees. Since the 2000–2001 academic year, the six-year graduation rate for the University of Arkansas increased dramatically from 45 percent to 59 percent for first time, full-time degree seeking freshmen. Given the academic quality of entering University of Arkansas freshmen, we set a goal of 70 percent of our first-time, full-time degree seeking freshmen graduating within a six-year timeframe by 2021.

GOAL 6) PROVIDE HIGHLY COMPETITIVE COMPENSATION PACKAGES FOR THE PURPOSE OF RECRUITING AND RETAINING THE VERY BEST FACULTY, STAFF, AND GRADUATE STUDENTS

Unfortunately, throughout its entire history, the University of Arkansas has built its programs on the backs of our faculty. To put it bluntly, for many years the university was simply not paying its faculty what they deserved. As an example, in fiscal year 2010 the salaries for University of Arkansas associate and full professors were lower than those for benchmark schools in the SEC and in the midwestern states. The salaries of associate professors were 5 to 7 percentage points below benchmark institutions. As an initial step to address this gap, we increased the amount a faculty member receives when they are promoted to another level, such as associate professor to full professor. This went a long way in boosting the salaries of our faculty, but it is a continuing, slow and difficult task to make much progress. Small annual merit increases simply do not keep up with the increases other institutions are providing in the market, and if the increase is virtually the same as inflation, we are making no progress at all. This disparity factored into a wide salary gap between the University of Arkansas and our peers.

We also needed to make progress in the compensation of our staff. As a public university we were governed by the state compensation plan for the more than 2,300 classified staff members who were paid through the regular operating budget, which came from the following: state-appropriated dollars; tuition and fee revenue; and the auxiliary funding from sources such as housing, dining, and athletics. Despite recent attempts to address low entry-level salaries, the state compensation plan did not keep pace with the market for qualified staff in Northwest Arkansas.

I was sitting at my desk late one evening when Dottie, our university assigned cleaning person, entered my office to perform her routine of cleaning, dusting and emptying the trash. She told me proudly that her daughter just got her degree from the University of Arkansas, and she herself would be quitting her job to take a similar one at the Farmington High School. I congratulated her on her daughter's accomplishment, and then asked why she was leaving the UA to work for the Farmington Public Schools. She informed me that the pay at Farmington was considerably more than what we could pay her by law. Now that her daughter had obtained her degree, she no longer needed the tuition discount and wanted to make more money. Come to find out, many of our employees were in the same boat. After their kids earned their degrees they would leave for greener pastures.

We worked very hard with state officials to try to get compensation levels to a higher rate. At the time of this writing there is still much, much more work to be done.

We also knew that we had to improve our benefit packages, such as health insurance plans, life insurance and long-term disability insurance, and retirement plan options. These were controlled by the University of Arkansas System and we did not make very much progress during my administration. Part of the reason is that we were tied into all of the other campuses in the system, and did not have the ability to make changes in our benefit packages.

Many of us on the Fayetteville campus believe this was detrimental to serving our faculty and staff, and providing the best benefit package possible. System officials would always tell us that being in a package with other system campuses saved us money, but we were very skeptical of such statements being reality. Due to very large expenses by the UA medical campus in Little Rock—in particular the high cost of malpractice settlements—we were convinced it drove up our campus costs measurably.

GOAL 7) INCREASE FUNDING IN BOTH RESEARCH AWARDS AND FEDERAL RESEARCH EXPENDITURES

A truly great university must increase funding in both research awards and federal research expenditures. In 2011 the Carnegie Foundation for the Advancement of Teaching moved the University of Arkansas to the highest classification of colleges and universities —level one, with very high research activity, placing the University of Arkansas among the top 108 universities in the country. We were proud of this accomplishment. The classification speaks volumes to faculty and students across the country and the world about the quantity and quality of research efforts and graduate production. The classification is based on the investment by the university in research efforts and doctoral degree productivity.

GOAL 8) MARSHAL THE UNIVERSITY'S EXPERTISE, PROGRAMS, FACULTY, STAFF AND STUDENTS TO GROW THE STATE'S KNOWLEDGE-BASED ECONOMY AND TO ADDRESS MAJOR ISSUES CONFRONTING ARKANSAS AND THE WORLD

As Arkansas' flagship land grant institution, the university needed to play an important role in positioning the state economy for the 21st century, as well as building the leadership core to address major issues confronting Arkansas and the world. Under John White's leadership and continuing into my administration, we identified five interdisciplinary research strengths:

1. Nano science and engineering
2. Health, including chronic disease research, health and wellness, healthcare delivery, and health policy
3. Energy and the environment, including traditional and renewable energy sources and smart grid
4. Supply chain management, transportation and logistics
5. Food safety and food protection

Each of these research areas boast talented scholars and researchers from multiple colleges within the university.

One program inaugurated in 2009 was the Johnson Fellows initiative. It would promote goal number 8 by bringing high-level alumni to campus to meet students and faculty, and to give lectures on important topics of interest and concern. The idea actually came from Penn State, which had sponsored such a program for many years. I mentioned the idea to Jeff and Marcia Johnson. Jeff was serving as president of the Arkansas Alumni Association, and liked the idea so much he provided a generous endowment to make it a reality. Jeff was a prominent physician in Springfield, Missouri, and a loyal and supportive alumnus. Marcia was a Drury University alumna, but had adopted Arkansas and was very engaged in our activities. Since they endowed the Johnson Fellows program, the UA has benefitted from a stream of prominent alumni coming to campus and sharing their remarkable expertise.

They have included:

T.J. Holmes, a native of West Memphis who now resides in New York, is a news anchor and correspondent. During his 20-year journalism career, Holmes has reported around the country and the world on major news events, from presidential elections and the Olympics in Athens and Rio to natural and man-made disasters.

Mack McLarty, chairman of McLarty Associates, an international strategic advisory firm he co-founded in 1998 following a distinguished record of business leadership and public service, including various roles advising three U.S. Presidents, including serving as the White House Chief of Staff for President Bill Clinton. He is also chairman and president of the McLarty Companies, a fourth-generation family transportation business.

Cordia Harrington, founder and CEO of The Bakery Company in Nashville, Tennessee.

Lt. Gen. Marty Steele, president and CEO of Uncommon Leadership, LLC, in Tampa, Florida. He enlisted in the Marine Corps in January 1965, and culminated his military career as the deputy chief of staff for plans, policies and operations at the headquarters of the U.S. Marine Corps in Washington, D.C.

GOAL 9) PROVIDE A SUPERIOR CAMPUS LANDSCAPE AND CARRY OUT THE RENEWAL AND RENOVATION OF EXISTING FACILITIES, AND THE DESIGNING AND BUILDING OF NEW WORLD-CLASS FACILITIES

In the first year of our administration we identified critical new space and facility upgrade goals, as well as a number of buildings with urgent deferred maintenance needs. Since those early days the burgeoning enrollment created the need for additional classrooms, laboratories, athletics venues, and on-campus housing, as well as expanded food services.

We were able to make progress because of a facilities fee which was approved by the board of trustees in 2008, and supported by system president Alan Sugg, to address the university's need for additional space and the crucial maintenance needs that could no longer be avoided or allowed to go unresolved in the campus physical plant. Some of the projects we undertook were:

- The Epley Center for Health Professions, which would house the School of Nursing and other health profession programs.
- The Jean Tyson Child Development Study Center, which provided educational and research opportunities for students, faculty and children.
- The completion of the Nanoscale Materials Science and Engineering Building.
- The renovation and addition to Vol Walker Hall.
- The renovation of Ozark Hall (Gearhart Hall).
- A new multi-million-dollar Football Center.
- The renovation of the Science Building.
- The renovation of Kimpel Hall, a general teaching classroom.
- The renovation of Davis Hall.
- The renovation of University House.
- The renovation of the Army ROTC building.

- The building of a new auditorium and classroom building: Hillside Auditorium.
- A new College of Engineering facility at the Research Center campus.
- Remodeled classrooms in the Bell Engineering Center, Engineering Hall, and the Chemical Engineering Building.
- A major renovation of the Engineering Research Center, including teaching laboratories for the new department of Biomedical Engineering.
- A general reconfiguration of Mullins Library. We reconfigured the space in the library to accommodate computer stations, a tutoring center, and a writing center, as well as an enhanced learning center. We created several casual reading areas for group study, plus wireless computer access and larger, quiet computer and study areas in the periodicals room.
- A renovation of the Arkansas Union providing 6,000 square feet of modern fitness floor space equipped with the latest cardio and weight machines.
- A renovation of the HPER building providing additional space for fitness facilities named after Miss America 1964, Donna Axum.
- The building of a gaming studio and digital media lab in the Arkansas Union, as well as a technology lounge and recording studios.
- The purchase of buildings that formerly housed the offices of Southwestern Energy in north Fayetteville near the Northwest Arkansas Mall. The 26,000 square-foot building, as well as the adjacent 31,000 square-foot building, were extensively renovated, and the two buildings enabled the university to relocate administrative offices that had previously been in Hotz Hall. It also became the new home of the Spring International Program as well as space for classrooms and offices. We called the complex Uptown Campus.
- The complete renovation of Hotz Hall for much-needed

student housing. Hotz Hall had been taken offline many years previously and converted into an administration building housing various offices. We decided to retrofit the building and restore it to its original purpose of student housing. We needed a facility to house Honors College student freshmen, and Hotz Hall became the residence for our first-year honors students. The building, when renovated, exceeded all of our expectations and became a treasured dormitory for our top academic freshmen.

Educators David and Sharon Hunt, parents of son-in-law Justin; David and Jane Gearhart; Donna Axum Whitworth, Miss America 1964; Bryan Whitworth

- An addition to Vol Walker Hall, named for alumnus Stephen L. Anderson who was the president of the Donald W. Reynolds Foundation.
- The success and promise of athletics programs led intercollegiate athletics to develop a wide-ranging athletics facilities master plan to provide a vision for the next 30 years. The plan was developed with facilities

management to maintain the overall mission and goals of the university campus growth plan, as well as to meet the needs of student-athletes competing in the Southeastern Conference and across the nation. The total plan would cost $325 million, but when finished would boast some of the SEC's most impressive football facilities, adding to the outstanding baseball, softball and track facilities. The master plan covered all sports teams and included upgrades to existing facilities, construction of new practice and administration facilities, and facilities for academic support for student-athletes.

- In the fall of 2011, the restoration and renovation of Peabody Hall, which houses the Department of Curriculum and Instruction in the College of Education and Health Professions was completed. Many features of the historic building were restored to its original condition, including the red brick exterior.
- In the fall of 2011, the College of Engineering acquired a LEED-certified building which we named the Cato Springs Research Center. It included 4,000 feet of laboratory space, as well as office space for faculty and 50 graduate students.
- The Garland Center project opened in 2010. It added 1,500 parking spaces for students, faculty, staff, and campus visitors, and featured a 30,000 square-foot bookstore and 20,000 feet of private retail shops. That project won numerous awards for excellence in architecture and construction, and garnered national attention from the American Institute of Architecture and the National Association of College Stores.
- With its rapid growth in enrollment, the university needed a new general classroom building. We named the facility at the top of Dickson Street Champions Hall, and it provided much-needed space for instruction and learning. The athletics department paid for the building with revenue from SEC TV contracts.

- To accommodate record freshman enrollment, the university renovated unused campus residential facilities, including Bud Walton Hall, Buchanan-Droke Hall, Wilson Sharp-Darby Hall and Gladson-Ripley Hall.
- A new residence facility, Founders Hall.
- We also undertook a total replacement of our signage and wayfinding system, from outside the primary entrances of campus to the entrances of individual buildings, and everything in between.
- To celebrate their one hundredth-year anniversary on campus, the Arkansas Alpha chapter of Pi Beta Phi dedicated funds toward the construction and implementation of the Pi Beta Phi Centennial Gate.
- The iconic Greek Theater, a gift many years ago in commemoration of the founding of Chi Omega on campus, was totally renovated, with partial financial support from the sorority.

GOAL 10) PURSUE A CONSISTENT AND AGGRESSIVE PROGRAM FOR THE MAINTENANCE AND IMPROVEMENT OF THE INSTITUTION'S LIBRARIES AND TECHNOLOGY RESOURCES

While we made major renovations to Mullins Library, we still were lagging behind many of our peer institutions in terms of library facilities. We undertook a number of projects that would strengthen the university's libraries, including a mobile version of the library catalog, a website to collect free online access to scholarly materials, as well as other important projects to try to keep our libraries in top condition.

GOAL 11) PROMOTE ENVIRONMENTAL SUSTAINABILITY

We believed sustainability was not a fad at the University of Arkansas and should become a way of thinking, acting and living. We wanted to strengthen the university community's commitment to sustainability. In 2009 I approved the University of Arkansas Climate Action Plan putting the University of Arkansas community on the path to address complex sustainability issues in a comprehensive systematic and consultative approach. Every college at the university became directly engaged in sustainability. We began a Sustainability Consortium in partnership with Arizona State University in 2009. Particularly important to us was the decrease in net greenhouse gas emissions.

I wish I had done more for the very, very serious issue facing the world: climate change. Scientists are telling us that, if carbon emissions are not controlled and dissipated, our world will be facing apocalyptic issues in only a few short years. The prospects are scary, and we have an obligation to do all that we can to alleviate the issues facing humanity. I worry about the world our grandchildren will be facing.

GOAL 12) ESTABLISH AND MARKET A QUALITY BRAND REPUTATION FOR THE UNIVERSITY STATEWIDE, NATIONALLY, AND INTERNATIONALLY

We realized a quality brand reputation for the university was very important to our efforts to become a top 50 public research university. We added resources and personnel to properly position the university in brand management. We created several objectives: making the University of Arkansas the post-secondary school of first choice for Arkansans; demonstrating the university's role and function as a valuable partner, resource and catalyst for Arkansas and her people; establishing broader and deeper affinity and commitment to the university among its base of current and potential supporters; increasing the university's state, national, and international reputation as one of the nation's premier public universities; helping encourage public and private investment in ways that sustain excellence and affordability.

It was at this time we adopted a research-based brand management and marketing phrase that was most popular across campus and beyond: "The You of A." We had hired a branding company in Texas to help position the university in new and exciting ways. They came up with the phrase, "The You of A." It resonated with alumni and parents across the nation, and I received many letters and emails from our constituents congratulating the university for inspirational branding.

GOAL 13) FOSTER THE ARTS ON CAMPUS AND THROUGHOUT THE REGION

In 2012 the university became an all-Steinway school, providing students and faculty with the highest quality pianos for instruction and performance. Only 113 colleges and universities in the world can claim that status.

In the summer of 2013, we began the conversion of the historic field house into a performance hall, which dramatically increased the number of performances the department of music could host in an academic year. We received extraordinary support from Jim and Joyce Faulkner of Little Rock to complete the conversion. For the first time the department of music was able to accommodate large ensemble groups and sponsor clinics and other outreach initiatives. The Faulkners were special people, most generous, and supporters of the arts across Arkansas. Jane and I had become close friends with the Faulkners, and even traveled with them to Abaco in the Bahamas. The new concert hall would never have happened without their philanthropy.

We also completely renovated the Stella Boyle Smith Concert Hall as a venue for solo and small chamber ensemble performances. The 238-seat hall is home to more than 300 concerts annually. The Stella Boyle Smith Foundation of Little Rock made a generous grant, which enabled us to accomplish the renovation. The officers of the foundation are Cathy and Mike Mayton, who have been most generous towards the university with a number of projects, including artwork in Fowler House. Mike is a prominent lawyer in Little Rock with offices in West Memphis, and Cathy had an amazing career in fundraising and development.

Mike and Cathy Mayton, UA benefactors, presenting a Carroll Cloar painting to hang in Fowler House, the chancellor's residence.

The Stella Boyle Smith Foundation has given away millions of dollars to many worthy programs across the country. The late Stella Boyle Smith, who died in 1994 at the age of 100, was well known for her love of music and philanthropy. Smith was a Little Rock philanthropist and founder of the Arkansas Symphony Orchestra. She was born in Farmington, Missouri, into a large, musically-inclined family. The family moved to Arkansas when she was two years old. She began singing at the age of three and graduated from high school at 14. Smith enabled many students around the state to attend college through the more than 200 scholarships she financed.

We created a public arts oversight committee made up of university faculty, staff, students, and community leaders, and created a public art master plan to actively move forward with adding public art to the campus. The first work of art commissioned was a sculpture created by Bryan Massey. The work honored the legacy of Silas Hunt and was dedicated in the fall of 2012.

We also created other prominent works of art in various buildings across the campus. We started collecting art for Fowler House through the generosity of alumni and friends. Fowler House now features a collection of more than 25 works of art by Arkansas artists. These works contribute to the elegance and beauty of the chancellor's residence and spotlight some of our most talented Arkansas artists.

GOAL 14) EXPAND OUTREACH THROUGH DISTANCE EDUCATION AND PARTNERSHIPS WITH OTHER INSTITUTIONS

We were determined to be a leader in developing quality courses for online delivery to undergraduate and graduate students. In 2012 Provost Sharon Gaber announced the realignment of global campus administrative units to focus on distance and continuing education, and appointed Dr. Javier Reyes to the newly created role of vice provost for distance education. Dr. Reyes did an extraordinary job in building our distance education programs. We quickly tripled the number of online course offerings to more than 500 courses in 26 degree programs. We became the largest online degree program in the state by far, and a leading program in the SEC. Most of the campuses in Arkansas, and certainly within the UA System, had a plethora of courses online for students. However, UA System president Don Bobbitt created eVersity to further expand online course offerings and degree completion. Many of us could not understand why. More on that later.

GOAL 15) GROW PUBLIC SUPPORT AND THE ENDOWMENT THROUGH ENHANCED RELATIONSHIPS WITH CONSTITUENTS AND SOUND INVESTMENT STRATEGIES

By 2015 we were fast approaching an endowment with a value of $1 billion. This incredible progress was made possible through the Campaign for the Twenty-First Century which added measurably to our endowment. For many years the university lagged behind other institutions in the SEC in the size of our endowment. New endowments for chairs and professorships, as well as scholarships, enabled the university to attract and retain top faculty and students. Unfortunately, legislative support continued to wane. We estimated we were underfunded on an annual basis by $45 million in state legislative support.

We knew that soon the university would need to launch another major capital campaign, as fundraising had taken on a huge role in our future. We could never accomplish all the things we wanted to without private gift support. The first item of business was to find a new vice chancellor of University Advancement. I launched a nationwide search to find a topflight executive who could continue our upward trajectory. The person needed to have major university experience and major gift fundraising experience. Those people are not easy to find.

I had worked at Penn State with an associate vice president by the name of Brad Choate. I called him and he applied. The search committee selected him as their top choice and after interviewing a number of candidates I offered Choate the job. He was vice president at the University of South Carolina, and had previously been at the Minnesota Medical Foundation as chief fundraiser.

We set about to form a nucleus of volunteers to get us started with the quiet phase of the campaign. We invited many of our strongest benefactors to assist once again with a major effort. Boyce Billingsley, Marilyn Bogle, Johnelle Hunt, Bob and Sandra Conner, Reynie Rutledge, Doug and Shelley McMillion, Bill Dillard and Lee and Beverly Bodenhamer all readily agreed to be campaign committee officers. It was a blue-ribbon executive committee, and we were once again in a major fundraising effort.

We would publish a TAP report each year giving updates on the progress we were making.

CHAPTER 47
UNIVERSITY SYSTEMS AND THE FLAGSHIP CAMPUS

> *Indeed, it may be that university systems are inimical to the health of public flagship universities and to the states and regions they serve.*
>
> — ROBERT BERDAHL, STEVEN SAMPLE AND RAQUEL M. RALL

I knew I was on to something when, in 2009, I casually mentioned to the assembled group some of the difficulties I had experienced with the system administration. As chancellor of the University of Arkansas I was in a meeting with the Southeastern Conference presidents and chancellors.

From the beginning I felt intimidated by the other presidents and chancellors in the SEC. After all, I was not a true academic and wasn't sure I had earned my stripes to be sitting with the academic talent in the room. The SEC Commissioner, Mike Slive, was welcoming and supportive in helping me become acquainted with the other CEOs, and I will always remember his incredible kindness to me during the first few meetings as the new kid on the block. My trepidation quickly dissipated after one of the presidents said to me before one of our meetings, "You will spend the first year wondering how you got here. Then you will spend the remaining time wondering how the other presidents got here." I suppose that quote was spot on. All of us had our idiosyncrasies, and none of us ever shied away from a verbal fight about any issue we perceived impacted our campus. But generally we got along fine, and I became close friends with many of the presidents from SEC schools and still maintain those friendships today.

What followed from practically all of my colleagues, after mentioning issues with university systems, was a rant and wholehearted "Amen" that was frankly unexpected by me. Naively, I had no idea my frustration was shared by so many flagship campus CEOs.

In fact, one campus CEO said to the assembled group of prestigious SEC administrators that he "would never again work for a university with a system."

Frustration with this organizational structure has reached a peak in recent times.

Systems are bad for flagships. That is one of many observations reached by Robert Berdahl, chancellor emeritus of the University of California, Berkeley; Steven Sample, president emeritus of the University of Southern California; and Raquel M. Bell, a Ph.D. candidate at USC. In a 2014 article titled "Are Systems Bad for Flagships?" which appeared in *Inside Higher Ed*, the authors asserted: "Yet despite the prevalence and best intentions of systems, it's not clear any longer that good state systems lead to good university governance. Indeed, it may be that university systems are inimical to the health of public flagship universities and to states and regions they serve."

Historically, most systems were established in the last 50 years, and were created for better efficiency and optimal operating principles. Legislators, governors, and governing boards saw it as a way to have more synergy among multiple campuses with a by-product of saving scarce resources through procedures like joint purchasing. Curriculum decisions would be made to keep campuses in line, and avoid the proverbial "mission creep" and the creation of multiple degree programs that might already be operating at another system campus. Many thought state legislatures would respond with generous appropriations. From my vantage point, after watching this for 45 years, none of these hoped for advantages have come to fruition.

What did happen was the dumbing down of the flagship campus while at the same time placing it at the equivalent level of other much smaller campuses in the system with no research agenda and lower academic standards. Along the way, systems became bad deals for campus flagships.

An inherent weakness of systems is the natural separation of the campus CEO from the governing board. Oftentimes, statements by the flagship CEO to the system CEO are misinterpreted or even worse not reported to board members at all. Yet direct communication with a board member, say, to clear up a matter, is often discouraged or even prohibited. Many system officials become jealous of the campus executive, who is usually in the spotlight, more so than the system head.

At the University of Arkansas, for many years, the head of the system was also the CEO of the main campus in Fayetteville and continued to be housed on that campus. This model was in operation until the inherent jealousies of Central Arkansas and Northwest Arkansas caused the legislature to create a chancellor for the Fayetteville campus. Or, to put it perhaps more succinctly, the University of Arkansas at Little Rock didn't particularly like reporting to the head of the flagship Fayetteville campus, so a separate chancellorship was born.

The only problem was that nobody seemed to know who should crown the homecoming queen, the system president or campus chancellor. Their offices were housed down the hall from each other and administrative confusion was rampant.

Thankfully, after much administrative turnover, the board hired a new system president who moved the system offices to Little Rock. That president, Alan Sugg, who served for 21 years until 2011, understood the differences between systems and campus administration and things tended to operate relatively smoothly during his long tenure. He gave his chancellors space to make critical decisions, and when the going got rough he backed them up, unless he determined their decision was clearly wrong. He also encouraged his chancellors to have relationships with the board of trustees and often would ask a chancellor to call a trustee and explain a policy to that board member. He expressed no jealousy whatsoever and kept the system from interfering with the campuses. Under Sugg's leadership, the campuses were the most important part of the University of Arkansas, not the amorphous system.

Alan Sugg, President of the University of Arkansas System, congratulating David Gearhart after being named chancellor by the board of trustees.

Sugg also was a great communicator. During my time I spoke with him almost daily. Our communication was mutually beneficial and satisfying. He kept me informed and I did the same about critical campus matters. The best way to describe his operating principle was a partnership with the people who reported to him.

Other institutions have experienced similar issues. For many years, at the University of Tennessee, Knoxville, the department of intercollegiate athletics reported to the system president, which must have caused a little more angst than the problem of who crowned the homecoming queen. (Fortunately, that model did change, and athletics now reports to the chancellor of the campus).

In recent times, many universities have exhibited outright battles between the head of the system, system board and the CEO of the campus, particularly the flagship.

In 2015, at the University of Missouri, the system head and the campus chancellor were at odds over racial tensions on campus, each blaming the other for what was ultimately their joint demise, as reported in *The Washington Post*. It just didn't appear that the president and chancellor could get on the same page about the issues and what to do about them.

At the University of Wisconsin in 2016, the faculty of the Madison campus voted no confidence in the university system president and its board of regents. The vote was a culmination of issues concerning tenure and shared governance. As reported in the *Wisconsin State Journal*, faculty claimed the system board and president were damaging the flagship's reputation and ignoring academic freedom and due process. Faculty were also extremely upset that the system did not do a better job in negotiations with the governor, who made huge cuts in the campus budget. This all culminated in a serious move to secede from the system altogether.

In 2011, at the University of Oregon, the state system board of higher education fired a popular president at the behest of the governor over public disagreements on budget, faculty raises and autonomy, which demoralized the state's flagship campus. According to *The New York Times*, the president was widely viewed as having done a superb job, with record enrollment, record fundraising, and high board scores of entering freshman students. Many felt the university had been on a roll under the president's leadership.

As reported in *The Austin Chronicle*, what became a major public clash in 2014 between the system chancellor and governing board and The University of Texas at Austin campus president, led to the campus president's orchestrated resignation, much to the chagrin of campus faculty and students.

And at Texas A&M University in 2015, according to *The Texas Tribune*, the system chancellor asked top officials at the flagship campus to submit letters of resignation before a new campus president started his tenure. He rationalized his directive as a way to help the new president, but it created a national discussion and campus controversy and insecurity.

The Chronicle of Higher Education reported in 2018 that, at The University of Maine System, the presidents of the various campuses would have their speeches color coded red, yellow or green depending on the level of political sensitivity. Red would be prohibited speech, yellow borderline and green apparently acceptable, all to be adjudicated by a system committee. Good luck to the system board of trustees and chancellor in administering that new policy!

In 2021 the American Association of University Professors launched an investigation of The University of North Carolina system, claiming it had violated principles of academic governance and for "persistent racism" over the tenure denial of Nikole Hannah Jones. According to *Inside Higher Ed*, the AAUP claimed the system had been responsible for the use of political pressure, which "obstructed meaningful faculty participation in the UNC system."

For sure, systems are inherently bad for flagships and are organized to the benefit of the system, not the campuses. They dumb down the campus CEO and relegate the position to one of subservience to a system official who is more bureaucrat than academic leader. It separates the main campus leadership from the governing board, and adds another layer of administration between the two, hampering communication and strategic direction.

Systems are bad for flagship campuses!

CHAPTER 48
INTO THE FRAY

> *In the concrete jungle it's sink or swim: you can't be timid or tentative; you have to forge through, make your mark, enter the fray.*
>
> — BELINDA JONES

NWACC

As I hit the ground running financial concerns were not the only issue confronting the university. It was certainly true that we were virtually broke, but several other matters needed close attention.

One of the first problems I experienced was with Northwest Arkansas Community College. As mentioned previously, I was never a big proponent of building a community college so close to our campus. I always felt the University of Arkansas should have provided the impetus to start such a campus and run it from the flagship. We clearly could have been the progenitors of NWACC and eliminated much of the duplication that the state could not afford. But that horse was out of the barn and we needed to be as supportive as possible and partner with them on academic programs.

NWACC, like most community colleges, experienced many challenges. Most folks don't realize the myriad of issues that have faced community colleges from their earliest days. While it is certainly true that they do have a place in our educational sphere, they have very low graduation completion rates. In fact, less than half of students who attend a community college get a degree, and fewer transfer to a four-year institution to obtain a baccalaureate degree. A student is many times more likely to get a four-year college degree if they start at a four-year college. Many community college enrollees are simply not prepared for the rigors of college life and do poorly in their first semester. While most two-year schools brag about preparing students for a job and the workforce, a large number don't really fulfill that mission. In recent years, enrollment at community colleges has dropped dramatically as the number of 18 year olds has declined precipitously. At the time of this writing the Biden administration has proposed free community college tuition for students, which could greatly assist in beefing up the enrollment patterns, but most likely won't fix the other inherent problems. Unfortunately for community colleges, it looks like that particular Biden promise will not come to fruition.

Dr. Becky Paneitz was the president of NWACC. She was a passionate advocate for her college and a hard charger. We had a few mutual programs with NWACC when I became chancellor, but was told by a few staff members that she could be difficult to deal with and was always looking for a partnership that benefitted NWACC more than the UA. I couldn't really blame her for advocating for her campus, after all, that was her job.

One bright sunny morning I received a call from the chancellor of Arkansas State University, Jonesboro, informing me that his dean of business had told him the ASU College of Business was going to begin offering a four-year degree on the campus of Northwest Arkansas Community College. He said that he would want to get a call like that from me if UA Fayetteville was about to offer a degree in his stomping grounds and he was just giving me a courtesy call. I greatly appreciated his candor. I immediately called Alan Sugg to see if he knew anything about it. He did not and was not happy, and suggested I call Jim Purcell, the director of the coordinating board of higher education.

Purcell was less than helpful and dodged the question. He responded by saying colleges were free to develop partnerships with other colleges. I suspected he very well knew about this action, but never leveled with me. I told him we were opposed to it, and could not imagine he would be in favor of it. After all, this would be a duplication of effort and something the state could not afford. I told Purcell this action was pure mission creep and that I had heard for some time that Paneitz wanted to turn their campus into a four-year degree-granting institution, and this must be their first incursion into making that a reality. Purcell said nothing. He obviously was supporting NWACC and Paneitz, and had no intentions of helping us with the issue.

I called a meeting of my executive committee (cabinet) to discuss the matter and develop a game plan in opposition. We were not about to allow ASU to begin offering baccalaureate degrees at NWACC and we were quite angry that Paneitz would even entertain such a concept. We were 20 minutes from her campus and offered an array of baccalaureate programs already. If she wanted some type of partnership, we could easily discuss it with her.

So I set up a telephone call with Paneitz to inform her that I had discovered her plans, which she seemed to be doing clandestinely. The phone call didn't go well. We were polite with each other but direct. I accused her of being secretive and keeping such a move confidential and she denied it. She asked if we could meet in person and I agreed.

I then began calling several corporate executives in the area who supported both the UA and NWACC. I also called a member of the NWACC board of trustees who I knew well. I basically told them we could not sit still and allow ASU to offer a baccalaureate program so close to our campus, nor could we allow NWACC to become a four-year institution. Every person I called agreed with me, even the NWACC board member. One executive, Kirk Thompson, president of J.B. Hunt said he was going to call Paneitz and complain and inform her that his company's support would dry up if she proceeded. I knew I had the philanthropic community behind me. I next let Sugg know that I was meeting with NWACC and planned to tell them we would not allow them to start a four-year program with ASU. Sugg wholeheartedly agreed.

The meeting with NWACC officials was just shy of a shouting match. They brought three officers with them and I had with me the provost and vice chancellor for government at the meeting. I made it crystal clear we were opposed to their plans and would fight them if they proceeded. I also made it very clear that I did not appreciate the clandestine nature of their operations.

NWACC abandoned the plan to have ASU offer a baccalaureate degree on their campus. The decision certainly didn't help my relationship with Becky Paneitz, who would remain at NWACC until 2013. To this day I cannot comprehend what she was thinking by asking ASU to offer a degree on her campus while we were 20 minutes away.

ICE STORM

On January 26, 2009, Northwest Arkansas experienced one of the worst ice storms in history. I had been chancellor for a little over six months, and it was a major catastrophe for the campus. Luckily there were few campus accidents as we closed the campus immediately and kept it closed for over a week. Some physical plant workers were injured but not seriously. One worker may have suffered a heart attack during clean-up, but fortunately recovered.

The region saw over two inches of ice accumulation followed by a snowfall a few days later. The temperature was well below freezing, so the ice just hung on the trees and buildings for days. It was reported that over 100,000 people lost power, some for over two weeks, as did the bulk of our campus.

Jane and I hunkered down at Fowler House with no electricity or water. We built a fire in the fireplaces, but that really didn't help much. We were without power for ten days. We finally went to stay at Jane's sister's home, which got power back after a week. Seven days at Fowler without electricity was brutal. Mike Johnson called me on my cell phone to tell me the status of the campus, but said I really should not go onto the campus as it wasn't safe. After being cooped up for a few days I did not take his advice and ventured out from Fowler to inspect the campus.

The only way to describe it is a winter wonderland but heartbreaking at the same time. Ice was everywhere and the pine trees were bent over and many broken. The campus was a mess with downed trees and broken and damaged shrubbery everywhere. The amazing physical plant workers were out in full force, and a few of them lightly scolded me for walking about the campus, worried that a limb or ice might fall on me. As chancellor I just felt I needed to inspect the damage firsthand. Some of our buildings had pipes burst and caused terrible water damage. Later I learned the ice storm had done almost $100 million worth of damage in the area. It was estimated that 3,000 trees had to be removed and as many as 20,000 pruned because they were deemed hazardous.

On our campus alone it cost us about $2 million in damage, and we lost numerous trees, a few over one hundred years old. It would be several months before campus would be cleaned up. ROTC students spearheaded a drive to help clean up the campus and I spent two days among them raking limbs and picking up debris.

INAUGURAL

Soon after I was named chancellor, a few members of my administration asked when I would like to have a formal inaugural celebration and investiture of office. I suppose those types of ceremonies have their place at colleges and universities, but for me it seemed a waste of money. The main purpose seemed to me to be self-aggrandizement and more of an ego trip than anything else.

Don't misunderstand me, I certainly have an ego, but spending $50,000 to $100,000 for an inaugural program seemed absurd during tough financial times. I was told the funding for the inauguration had already been appropriated. I decided to forgo a formal investiture and instead used the funds to create new scholarships for deserving undergraduate students who were entering the university in the fall. After all, I had been driving home the message of putting students first, and this seemed to be a good time to practice what we were preaching.

We created what we called the Inaugural Scholars Program and provided 50 one-time scholarship grants valued at $1,000 each. The inaugural scholars were to be selected from the new freshman applicant pool, which required students to submit high school grades, test scores, an essay, and a résumé and, most importantly, have financial need. A semifinalist pool of the top students, both academically and with respect to need, would be selected and forwarded to an appointed selection committee. The committee would be responsible for selecting the most suitable 50 students to receive the scholarship.

I received multiple emails and messages from people across the country thanking the university for spending the funds in this manner.

ACADEMIC AFFAIRS COMPETING WITH STUDENT AFFAIRS

Throughout my career I have experienced a tug-of-war between academic affairs and student affairs. At a number of institutions, the vice chancellor for academic affairs and the vice chancellor for student affairs both report to the CEO. I witnessed firsthand a number of chancellors and presidents needing to referee issues between two senior officers. I certainly witnessed this when I was vice chancellor at the University of Arkansas. It seemed the two officers were in constant conflict over important issues, which required precious time from the chancellor to negotiate the disputes.

At most institutions the chief academic officer is considered the number two person on campus. I would venture to say that is the way it is at 95 percent of colleges and universities throughout the United States. After the chancellor, the provost is next in line of authority. The individual's title might be "executive vice president" or "executive vice chancellor," or may even have the word "provost" attached to the title. A few institutions place the chief business officer at the same level as the provost, but this is an exception to the rule.

Academic affairs and student affairs need to be closely aligned and in sync. They must work in tandem and seamlessly and not appear to be in conflict. That is hard to accomplish when both officers report directly to the chancellor. The chancellor becomes the individual who must referee any conflict, and that can happen many times.

When John White decided to step down as chancellor, his vice chancellor for student affairs also decided to retire. This gave me an opportunity to change the reporting lines and put student affairs under the provost. Thereafter I would not be in the middle of disputes between the two offices. I appointed an internal committee to study this option and they came back to me with a recommendation to have student affairs report to the provost and not the chancellor. Early in my administration I made this change. Not everyone was happy. Many of the student affairs personnel felt their positions were diminished, since their division no longer reported directly to the chancellor. It was controversial on campus. I did invite the person who headed up student affairs to be on the chancellor's executive committee so he would be involved in all decision making.

I do think this model works best for an academic institution. After I retired the new chancellor changed the reporting lines and had the chief student affairs officer report to him. He changed the reporting lines back to the provost before he left the university abruptly.

NEW LOGO

In early 2009 Tysen Kendig, our associate vice chancellor for university relations, approached me about the need for a new graphic identity or mark for the University of Arkansas. The logo we were using was well over 30 years old and did not duplicate well. Tysen believed it was time we had a new mark for the university. We encouraged all university-wide units to use up existing materials, but not to order any new materials with the old logo. We wanted to encourage the various units to exhaust existing supplies and not be wasteful.

Instead of hiring an outside agency to do the creation of a new logo, we decided to use our internal creative staff for the job. Roy Cordell in university relations created the new logo and it was almost universally accepted.

Logo design by Roy Cordell

ALPHA GAMMA RHO

Shortly after I assumed office, I was told by Danny Pugh, head of student services, that the Alpha Gamma Rho fraternity house on Razorback Road had very serious issues, which needed immediate attention. The university had been in discussions for many years with the AGR house corporation about their debt to the university, the condition of the house, safety issues, and chapter viability. AGR owed the university over $500,000 for repairs to the physical plant, life safety measures, and net operating losses. No action came forward to attempt to clear out the debt. In addition to that substantial debt, the estimated deferred maintenance on the house was well over $650,000, and we had been dealing with that level of maintenance neglect for multiple years. Over the past five years the house had been operating at less than 50 percent capacity, and diminished to less than 39 percent occupancy in 2009. The chapter ranked at the bottom in membership among the 13 houses, and the most recent recruiting showed abysmal numbers. On top of that, the cumulative grade point average of members was the lowest on campus with a GPA of 2.75.

For several years, student services had tried to get the AGR house corporation to take these and many other issues seriously. While some members of the house corporation pledged to solve the issues, nothing happened.

AGR had a proud heritage on campus for many years. The last thing we wanted to do was close the house. We offered the fraternity an option to move into a residence hall and occupy a reserved space for the house members so they could be together, in hopes of resolving the issues amicably. We also assigned one of our very best development officers, John Tolleson, to help the fraternity raise funds for the house. Tolleson worked diligently to launch a campaign to raise funds from AGR alumni. He personally called on several alumni for major gifts to help solve the problems facing the chapter. He invited me to make calls with him and place proposals before some of the wealthier alumni. The final amount raised was less than $15,000. Alumni just didn't seem to have any financial interest in helping the chapter. Many of the fraternities and sororities on campus had raised several million dollars to rebuild their houses. The Pi Beta Phi sorority even raised over $1 million for the Centennial Gate heralding their 100th year on campus. Sigma Nu, Sigma Alpha Epsilon, and Phi Delta Theta were all in drives to renovate their houses. Later a number of the sororities would also launch successful drives to better their houses and add additional space. But, despite repeated attempts, AGR just couldn't raise any funds of substance for the house.

Word started spreading that the house was going to close, and it was the university's fault. The administration should forgive the loan and fix up the house at its cost, was the battle cry. I received a letter from a prominent faculty member and AGR alumnus, who excoriated me for not being willing to help his fraternity house. He had virtually no correct information, and admitted he had spoken to a few alumni who told him we had not been cooperative. I quickly disabused him of the inaccurate information.

Remember, this was a time when the university had virtually no reserves and had just experienced a terrible ice storm that cost us dearly. We came close to not being able to make payroll. We simply did not have any funds to spare for fraternity renovations. Besides, we were concerned about setting a precedent for bailing out other Greek houses in the future by using state money for a private concern.

We finally had to close the house because of fire safety issues. The fire marshal made it clear that, without the basic repairs, the house simply was not safe for occupancy. We notified all of the house occupants that the house would be closed on a specific date and posted flyers in the house. A couple student members didn't get the memo or decided to ignore the notification. One evening they broke a window and climbed into the house. Apparently, they were trying to retrieve something they had left behind when the house closed. The police just happened to be driving by when it happened and arrested the students. Their families were not happy with us or their sons. Luckily, we were able to have their records expunged with little or no harm done. One dad wrote me a note saying if we caught his son anywhere close to the AGR house he would send his son to a college in Memphis!

We were tired of being ignored and carrying debt for several years. We were finally able to meet with some AGR alumni who took our pleas seriously. As it turned out the leasehold was sold to the Arkansas Alumni Association for future expansion and the house was demolished. In 2013, AGR launched a campaign to raise funds for a new house but nothing materialized. Rumor is, they do still want to build a new house, but it will take generous alumni support to make it happen.

One rather humorous aside: I was attending an alumni council meeting at the alumni center. The room where the meeting was taking place had a bird's eye view of the AGR house. All of a sudden, in view of all attendees, we could see members at the house coming out of the bathroom buck naked. It got a laugh and a staff member quickly pulled the window blinds, but it was too late to spare the students some embarrassment for their shortcomings.

BENCHMARKING

John White believed passionately in comparing our campus to other universities in an effort to keep striving to be better and reach the goal of becoming a top-50 public research university. I wanted the same thing, and continued our benchmarking efforts under the very capable guidance of Kathy Van Laningham, vice provost in charge of planning and institutional research. White appointed Kathy to the position in 2000 and I benefited from her considerable expertise. She was smart, quick, and fun to work with and had an infectious laugh. She worked well with all groups and contributed much to our overall success.

Through Kathy's efforts we compiled a list of information, which we disseminated to stakeholders across Arkansas and beyond. We found most people who read the information had little or no idea about what Arkansas faced in moving our state forward. The most debilitating discovery was that the legislature was mostly uninformed.

- Arkansas has a population of approximately 3 million people, but has over 40 institutions of higher education. If you add colleges that only offer certificates, the number is over 50.
- The average distance an Arkansan had to travel to reach the nearest 2- or 4-year public institution was 9.5 miles.
- Within a 75-mile radius of Little Rock, there are 7 four-year public universities.
- Many legislators view the role of higher education in economic development to be employment of faculty and staff, rather than improving the economy by educating more Arkansans.
- Arkansas ranked 49th in the United States in the percent of adult population with at least a bachelor's degree, and 48th in per capita income.
- Arkansas does not have a capital budget for bricks and mortar and renovation projects to support higher

education. Institutions are totally on their own. Capital needs on our public university campuses exceeded more than a billion dollars.
- According to the Arkansas Department of Higher Education, the Fayetteville campus alone is underfunded by more than $40 million on an annual basis.
- In the SEC, only Ole Miss and Mississippi State have lower average salaries for professors and staff than the UA.
- Arkansas public institutions have one of the lowest ratios of faculty to student in the nation.
- The state provides less than 15 percent of the revenue needed to operate the University of Arkansas flagship campus.

This information should worry all citizens of our state.

PRYOR CENTER

In 1999 Senator David Pryor and his wife Barbara established the Pryor Center for Arkansas Oral and Visual History with a gift of unexpended campaign funds of $220,000. The Pryors idea was to capture recorded interviews of significance to the history of the state. I thought it was a marvelous idea, as did John White. We both knew, however, that as generous as the gift was, it would in no way finance such a sizable undertaking. Much more revenue would be necessary to achieve what the Pryors had in mind. Pryor was a 1957 graduate of the university, and then received a law degree in 1964. He went on to become a congressman, governor, and United States Senator. Barbara was a Fayetteville native. Barbara's brother, Scott Lunsford, was a high school friend of mine and worked for the dean of Continuing Education.

Late one evening I received a call from Senator Pryor telling me his brother-in-law, Scott Lunsford, was having trouble dealing with his boss in continuing ed. He thought Scott's job might be in jeopardy and wanted advice. He then told me that if Scott was terminated, he would serve as his lawyer. Pryor was one of the most well-known politicians in the state and knew everyone of consequence. I had not known him to be one to throw his weight around, and concluded this was a serious matter that needed some immediate attention. The next day I spoke with John White and told him I thought we needed to intercede in the matter. Next, I went to see the dean of Continuing Education to see if Scott's job could be salvaged. From what I could deduce, there was a serious personality conflict between the two men that was past being able to rectify. The only way out of this mess was to relocate Lunsford to another department.

I had a real need for someone to do videos for my division, particularly for our billion-dollar campaign. I knew Lunsford to be a talented videographer and felt he might work out in university relations. I went back to see the dean and made him an offer. If he would pick up Lunsford's salary for six months, I would take it over then and move Lunsford to my division. Of course, I had no idea where I would get the funding after the six months expired.

Scott came to the division and worked out well. He was a real talent and created a number of videos we used for the campaign.

As for the Pryor Center, it became a money pit. We tried to raise private funds and were somewhat successful, but the level of support needed far outpaced the private giving. Then, in 2005 Don Tyson made a $2 million gift to the Center. Finally, the program was no longer struggling and had revenue to start making things happen.

Scott Lunsford started making noise that he wanted to work at the Pryor Center named for his sister and brother-in-law. The Pryors wanted that to happen as well and he transferred to the center and eventually became an assistant director. It wasn't always smooth sailing by any means, as Lunsford most likely saw himself as the number one rather than number two at the center. The taping of interviews got off to a very slow start and I could tell the Pryors were frustrated that very few interviews were being conducted.

When I assumed office in 2008, the center was still in its infant stages. Still, little progress had been made interviewing people, and a number of administrative issues and conflicts were beginning to be raised by the Pryors. The center at the time reported to the university libraries, but that was not a match made in heaven. Constant conflicts arose, and it seemed I was being called on with frequency to referee the issues. Finally, the Pryors came to see me and wanted to be moved out from under the library. They really didn't have much cause for wanting the change, but were very definite that a change needed to be made and soon. Then I started hearing from members of the volunteer board, who were also asking for a change.

I decided to put the Pryor Center directly under the office of the chancellor and asked Judy Schwab to manage it. The director would report to her. Judy did yeoman's work, but I felt badly I had dumped it on her. I was just trying to keep the Pryors happy and not cause continuing conflict. Judy with her calm demeanor was able to keep the pot from boiling over. However, the Pryors did express displeasure in the director of the center and we finally had to make a change.

The center had outgrown the library, and due to the administrative reporting change didn't really belong there. I knew we needed to find suitable space, and soon. The former First National Bank Building on the east side of the Fayetteville Square was up for sale and the price was right. We were growing rapidly and needed more space for a variety of programs and projects. We decided to purchase the bank building and put the Pryor Center there. We had actually looked at the Old Post Office in the middle of the square, but the seller wanted too much money, and we could never come to a deal.

We put the Pryor Center name prominently on the former bank building, and did renovations to the facility. We spent considerable funds on the total project, but believed the Pryor Center was something the state needed, and would be appreciated by historians for decades to come. I personally felt the Pryors were pleased with their new quarters. The center continued to have leadership issues after I retired, and Professor and former Dean Bill Schwab was appointed director, and the center was administratively placed back under the Fulbright College.

But my story about the Pryors, or at least the senator, doesn't end there. More later.

ROME CENTER

The University of Arkansas is a leading institution for international programs. Our students study abroad across the globe in nearly fifty different countries each year. A major component of the Honors College is numerous study-abroad programs, including community development projects, research opportunities, internships, service learning, and study tours. I was a huge proponent of such programs, having seen firsthand the impact they can make on students who benefit their entire lives from such experiences. Besides, we had funds for study abroad as it was a component of the Walton $300 million gift.

One of the longest-running international programs is the Rome Center. It began as a program in the school of architecture, but has expanded to include many other academic areas and is open to students from other institutions. The University of Arkansas Rome Center is housed in the historic palace, Palazzo Taverna, just minutes from the Vatican. Piazza Navona and the Pantheon are some of the most important architectural and cultural sites in the Western world. Students live close to the school in a secure and safe neighborhood with 24/7 on-site support, tracing the paths of ancient Romans and centuries of Christian pilgrims as they make their way to classes each day. The palace was referred to by Dante in his literary masterpiece, *The Divine Comedy*.

Jane and I were invited to visit the center early in my administration. We put it off for a couple years given all of the priorities at the main campus, but finally made the trip to Rome and spent several days interacting with faculty and students. At the time the center was being housed in an overcrowded facility, which inhibited program growth and the ability to admit students from other institutions and disciplines. After seeing the operation, I decided that we needed better space, and budgeted increased funds so the Rome Center could move to the Palazzo Taverna. The new facility is spectacular, and offers our students an unparalleled opportunity to explore ancient Rome and historic cultures throughout Italy. When in Rome I highly recommend a visit to the new quarters.

CHAPTER 49
THE RAZORBACK FOUNDATION

> *You miss 100 percent of the shots you don't take.*
>
> — *WAYNE GRETZKY*

In early 2008 our athletics director, Jeff Long, made me aware of some issues he was having with the president of the Razorback Foundation, Chuck Dicus. He had headed up the foundation for 17 years, and had been hired by Frank Broyles. He was a former Razorback football star during some of the glory days of Razorback athletics. I liked Chuck personally and Jane had a close relationship with his wife. We didn't socialize together, but knew them and respected them very much. We had gotten along pretty well when I was vice chancellor. I remember when I became chancellor Chuck took me to lunch and presented me with a box of cigars.

But I also knew he could be difficult at times and had a stubborn streak. That didn't really bother me as I had dealt with stubborn folks all my life. In fact, stubbornness was one of my qualities!

Long told me he was having trouble dealing with Chuck. He felt that Chuck was wanting to make decisions that normally the athletics director should make, by using Razorback Foundation funding to hold up decision making. Long's feeling was that it should be his decision to decide how to spend Razorback Foundation funds and Chuck's job to raise, invest and disperse them. After all, Long reasoned, the funds were given for the express purpose of supporting the athletics program. During Frank Broyles' time as AD, he would use Razorback funds as he saw fit, and the foundation board always went along with the AD's express wishes and needs. Now we had a new AD, and he didn't seem to be getting the same courtesy.

Besides that, Long felt the Razorback Foundation had become stale, and we should be raising much more from athletics constituents. His staff shared with me benchmark data showing we were much lower than other institutions of similar scope and size. Having been on the development side for ten years, I also knew firsthand that we could do better. It appeared to a number of our development professionals that our athletics fundraising could be much more robust.

I suppose technically, and even legally, the foundation board has the authority to hold up any funds they deem necessary, but the likelihood of that happening during Broyles' time was remote. Of course, if there was a question of using the funds illegally then the foundation board would have a fiduciary duty to intervene. But that was not what the issue involved. Long claimed that Chuck actually wanted to be at the table when athletics department issues were discussed, and he wanted to be involved in the decision making. The last thing Long wanted to do was have another layer of approvals for his agenda as AD. Most donors to the Razorback Foundation give unrestricted, except for those capital gifts designated for a building project. At that time the foundation was not raising any funds to speak of for endowment. Broyles didn't like raising funds for endowment as he needed the money immediately and didn't see building an endowment as important. Long believed building a strong endowment could provide yearly income for a variety of projects and I certainly agreed.

So, I was confronted with a real dilemma early on in my tenure. I decided to meet with Chuck to see if I could ameliorate things with Long. From the outset I could tell Chuck was not in a mood for compromise nor my direction. I asked him to meet with Jeff Long and try to form a relationship that would work. He told me that he had been at the university for many years and was a former athlete and alumnus, and Long should come to him first. I admonished him that he was going to have to get along with the new AD and not the other way around. The AD had been approved by the administration, the board of trustees was very happy with the selection, and he needed to get on board. He wasn't hearing me. I was very upset about the situation and knew we were headed for a colossal blow up.

A few months later Long came to me and said things were not getting any better. I reached out to president Sugg who had been on the selection committee for Long and asked his advice. Sugg said he would talk with a few trustees, but his initial thinking was that Chuck had to get on board, or he would have to find another job.

Chuck Dicus did not work for the university, me, Sugg or the athletics director. He worked for the Razorback Foundation board. He was not a university employee. The board set his salary and had the exclusive authority to make a change in leadership. Sugg and I made an appointment to see the chairman of the Razorback Foundation to inform him of the problem. We didn't hear anything for some time. Then, all of a sudden, I received a phone call from Frank Broyles. He told me members of the foundation board had contacted him to discuss the Dicus issue—one in particular who called him was Jim Lindsey. Broyles had told the board members that, in his opinion, Dicus had to get in line or leave. Jim Lindsey called me, and apparently Frank's voice was all he needed to be supportive.

Chuck met with the Razorback Foundation board and resigned his position soon thereafter. I know the board treated him very well financially in making the transition. I was sad about the entire episode, but felt secure in that we did all we possibly could to work through it.

Unfortunately, the ordeal ruined Jane and my relationship with the Dicus family. I regretted that very much. I liked both Chuck and Cathy, and Jane had done some work with Cathy and they had a good friendship.

In 2012 the contract between the university and the Razorback

Foundation was set to expire. Even though the foundation was a legally independent organization, it only works if the athletics director and the Razorback Foundation are in sync. There were several issues I believed had not yet been adequately reconciled, and felt they must be resolved before entering into a new agreement with the Razorback Foundation. I believed the original foundation bylaws had served the university, foundation board, the athletics department, and the athletics director well through the years.

The Razorback Foundation had helped form the basis of a self-sustaining financial model, which we continued to build on; however, just as the demands of maintaining a nationally-competitive athletics program had evolved, it had become imperative that we move forward in the modernization of the Razorback Foundation and its bylaws to assist the athletics department in managing a budget that would surpass $100 million in the foreseeable future. I felt it was vital that we acted to update the Razorback Foundation to meet the needs of our program and our more than 460 student-athletes in 19 sports. While our best intentions were to work together to address these issues prior to the expiration of the current contract, very busy schedules and unforeseen circumstances, as well as perhaps some convenient delays, had not allowed adequate time for a thorough vetting and ultimate resolution on an extension. There were several very important goals Long and I felt strongly about as we moved forward. We needed a full financial audit and tax compliance review by an independent firm. We desperately needed to update and modernize the bylaws and constitution. We needed to improve the foundation's financial reporting processes, and, finally, we needed to develop a Razorback Foundation marketing strategy in response to the customer service survey conducted by an independent agency and presented to the board in the fall. It was vital that we updated the foundation for the modern era.

CHAPTER 50
FRIENDS

> *What draws people to be friends is that they see the same truth. They share it.*
>
> — C.S. LEWIS

Jane and I had many university friends and associates, and became very close to a number of benefactors, especially those who served on the campaign executive committee and later the board of advisors, as well as the board of trustees. But we always had a small set of non-university friends who we socialized with on a regular basis. They were benefactors as well, but our relationship with them was not based on that. They were our special circle of friends who we spent many evenings with, and it gave us a good release from university matters. Included in that circle were Nancy and Larry Bittle. Larry was a State Farm Insurance executive who had built a phenomenal business in Fayetteville. I called him Mr. Fayetteville as he literally knew just about everyone in Northwest Arkansas.

Greg and Hannah Lee were another couple we enjoyed and saw regularly. Greg was retired from Tyson Foods where he had run their international division, and had traveled all over the world in that capacity.

Spencer and Bicky Higginbotham and Kay and C.R. Magness rounded out our close immediate friends. Both Bicky and C.R. were local physicians.

Jeanie Fox and Cathy Oxford Bozynski were two high school friends of ours and we have stayed close through the years.

Jane had so many friendships with a score of people too numerous to mention. We were blessed with a number of friends all across the country who filled our lives for the better, especially in times of stress. We also socialized a great deal with Jane's sister and brother-in-law, Beth and Larry Wilkins. Both of them were physical therapists which I would regularly put to good use when my back would fail me.

Dear friends and UA benefactors, Larry and Nancy Bittle, with the Gearharts.

HEARTFELT GENEROSITY

During my time as chancellor and vice chancellor at the university we had many extraordinarily generous benefactors. In so many ways we built the institution because of the philanthropy of hundreds, if not thousands, of alumni, friends, parents, foundations and corporations giving generously to help the university achieve excellence. We had to rely on this astounding generosity because we were not getting any new funds from the legislature, and, in point of fact, had lost funds in our state appropriation.

It is, of course, impossible to mention everyone who contributed to the university. I can only say how absolutely grateful I am to them for answering the call to support the University of Arkansas.

There is one person, however, who deserves mention because of his unbelievable and thoughtful support of his alma mater. His name was Charles Baughn. Charles was born in 1912 and graduated from the University of Arkansas with a degree in civil engineering in 1935. Charles graduated from Gravette High School and enrolled initially at the University of Tulsa but then transferred to the University of Arkansas where he earned his degree. He lived to be 97 years old.

Because he and his wife Alice had no children, they wanted to help future generations achieve success through education. They decided to create a scholarship fund at the University in the College of Engineering. Because of their generosity, countless students have been the recipients of their scholarship funds. The impact of their generosity can be seen, not only in the students and their families whose financial burdens were eased, but also through the work their degrees allowed them to do in various engineering fields. Charles was a fabulous example for students about the meaning of giving back.

Charles had a loving and generous spirit that will long be remembered by the university. For generations to come, he will be helping students achieve success, and most of them will have never known him or had the opportunity to meet him. For several years he would come to the university to meet the scholars who he helped. He lived in Thousand Oaks, California, and making the trip would become a burden for him in his later years. I had the opportunity to see him when he came on his trips to the university as well as when I visited him at a retirement home in California.

Charles and Alice begin accumulating antique pewter early in their marriage. Some of the pewter he collected dated to the 1600s. They loved their collection very much, but loved students even more. They decided to sell the collection and obtained a very nice price from another collector. They took those profits and created a scholarship fund for the benefit of engineering students.

Charles was a wonderful person—warm, inviting and with absolutely no ego whatsoever. His only desire later in his life was to benefit his students. Charles continued to make annual contributions to his scholarship fund right up until his death in 2011. On my last visit to see him in California he was suffering from dementia, and it was hard to communicate with him. I had previously given him a Razorback blanket, which he proudly displayed in his room at the retirement home. When he died, his niece told me that he gave her strict instructions to return the Razorback blanket to me as a remembrance of his love for his alma mater.

Future generations of students will be remembering Charles for decades to come.

Another story of selfless generosity is a major multi-million-dollar gift by Joe and Judi Schenke. The Schenkes were from Chicago where Joe was a pilot for United Airlines. Judi was a real estate broker. They decided to make their home in Fayetteville when they retired, and have been dedicated supporters of the University of Arkansas. Their amazing generosity will benefit many students with scholarships.

TIME WITH STUDENTS

From the very first day of my new job, I wanted to find time to spend with students. Special time—not just an occasional brush by—but quality time getting to know as many as I could. I would regularly meet with the student body officers (ASG, Associated Student Government) and get to know many of them, especially the presidents. I'm still in contact with many of them today, and officiated the wedding of one of them after I retired. We did not always agree on every issue by any means, but we developed a mutual respect for each other and never had any serious problems. When I retired most of them came back to a meeting of our board of advisors and spoke, which was most thoughtful and greatly appreciated. I was very blessed with marvelous student government presidents the entire time I was chancellor. They were smart, cooperative, supportive of university initiatives and great students. I greatly enjoyed spending quality time with them. I would have a standing meeting every month and called meetings whenever needed. Many of them became great friends who I'm still in contact with today.

Although not technically president during my official time, Nate Looney was president the year I was appointed, 2007–2008. Nate went on to the Clinton School of Public Service and the Hillary Rodham Clinton School of Law, earning both degrees simultaneously. He practiced law for a few years and ran for the General Assembly. Jane and I sponsored an event for him, raising funds for his campaign. Unfortunately, he lost the election because of the conservative Republican wave in Arkansas. He would have made a marvelous state representative. He founded Naturally Blue, an Arkansas PAC, and even got a mention in the *New York Times* about his efforts. He would later leave law practice and go to work for Arkansas Children's Hospital as a fundraiser. Nate is a remarkable person, and we remain close friends.

Carter Ford was president my first official year 2008–2009. We got along extremely well and have stayed in touch off and on. He is a very successful State Farm agent in Batesville, Arkansas.

Following Carter was Mattie Bookhout 2009–2010. Unfortunately, I have not kept up with Mattie, but I believe she lives in Arizona. She did a superb job as ASG president.

Billy Fleming was next, 2010–2011. He is the Wilks Family Director of the Ian L. McHarg Center in the Stuart Weitzman School of Design at the University of Pennsylvania. Billy is co-editor of the book *A Blueprint for Coastal Adaptation: Uniting Design, Economics, and Policy* and author of the forthcoming *Drowning America: The Nature and Politics of Adaptation*. It was my distinct privilege to perform the wedding ceremony of Billy and Stephanie Grise in June 2017. They are dear friends.

Michael Dodd served in 2011–2012 and is now an executive for Walmart in Bentonville, Arkansas. I get to see Michael quite often at Northwest Arkansas events. He had a good political mind and I always thought he might go into politics.

Tori Pohlner (Bogner) works for Signature Bank in Fayetteville and was president 2012–2013. We have stayed in touch and she too was a fabulous president.

James "Bo" Renner served next, 2013–2014. He practices law in Fayetteville with a prestigious law firm where he is a partner, and is doing very well. Bo is an outstanding lawyer, and his politics are very, very conservative. Despite being on opposite sides politically we got along extremely well.

The last president of ASG during my time was Daniel McFarland, 2014–2015. Daniel is one of the brightest people I have ever met and just an outstanding gentleman. We have stayed in close touch and we are good friends. He currently serves as assistant administrator at the Johns Hopkins Children's Center, Johns Hopkins Hospital in Baltimore, Maryland.

I read in *The Chronicle of Higher Education* about a college president who helped freshmen students move into their residence halls, and even spent the night in one of the halls with students. I thought that was a grand idea and decided to do the same thing. Come move-in day I put on my t-shirt and shorts and reported to the residence halls. I spent most of the day moving in hundreds of freshmen and meeting their parents. Other than the refrigerators and couches and huge, heavy boxes, it was a most enjoyable day for me. Since it was in August it was beastly hot, and I always left the activity totally wet from sweat. But the look on the faces of students and parents when they saw my chancellor name tag was priceless. I continued to participate in move-in every year of my time as chancellor. I still get comments today from folks I run into, thanking me for helping carry their belongings up multiple flights of stairs.

I then thought it would be a neat idea to spend the night in a residence hall with students. Student affairs assigned me to a hall filled with international students from across the world. I stayed up until 1 a.m. playing card games with the students and enjoyed myself immensely. You learn a great deal about students when you participate with them in that type of activity. About 4 in the morning, I awoke literally freezing as the residence hall had the air conditioning on full blast. My tiny blanket did little good. I lay in bed for about 30 minutes shivering and then decided to get up and face the cold room. I headed back to Fowler House for a very hot shower and got back to the students in time for breakfast.

Another activity I did on a regular basis was to buy coffee for anyone who entered at a chosen on-campus coffee shop. I just stationed myself at a table and told the waiter I would pay for anyone who entered the shop and wanted some coffee. Several of the students would stop by my table for a brief chat and thank you. When huge crowds started forming at the shop it became almost unmanageable. They had to bring in more waiters to handle the crowd. I was then told by one of the students that they saw "Free coffee," on social media, which caused the flood of students and even a few faculty. They were not there to see their chancellor but to get free coffee! I couldn't excuse myself because of the line of students, even though I was getting late for my morning appointments. The final bill was $1,800! I learned my lesson and next time had debit cards printed up, which gave $5 so students could get a free cup of coffee. I started handing those out until Don Pederson told me that it could be in violation of a student's financial aid package. I didn't tell Don but continued handing out the cards until all had been used. So much for Students First. It was the thought that counted I suppose!

I tried to send out a message as loud and as clear as possible about helping students and breaking down barriers. I told the staff to do everything possible to solve a student's problem without sending them packing to someone else. Try to reply via email or phone call the very same day it comes to you. Don't keep students waiting. If you tell a student no, tell them why. We should live in a "yes" world, not a "no" world.

Also, in those early years of my time as chancellor, I enjoyed very much visiting high schools and two-year community colleges. Suzanne McCray initiated the visits as a recruitment program, and we visited mostly high schools in south and eastern Arkansas in some of the poorest rural communities. A few times we even held a book drive and delivered the books to the schools.

CHAPTER 51
PRESIDENT OF PANAMA

> We should keep the Panama Canal. After all, we stole it fair and square.
>
> — SENATOR S.I. HAYAKAWA

In 2009, a 1973 alumnus of the University of Arkansas, Ricardo Martinelli, was elected president of the Republic of Panama. To our knowledge, it was the first and still is the only time the university had a head of state as an alumnus. His father was of Italian descent, hence his Italian surname, but he was born and grew up in Panama. He never thought about going into politics until the mid-1990's, when he formed a new political party in 1998. In 2004 he ran for president, but was soundly defeated. In 2009 he ran again and was elected by over 60 percent of the vote. He ran on a pro-business platform and united several coalitions. In Panama presidents are limited to one term. In my naiveté I asked him why that was, and he kindly responded, Panamanians don't like people to serve lengthy terms like a few former presidents of our country. Message delivered.

Martinelli became a member of our advisory board and made a

generous scholarship endowment gift to the university for Panamanian students attending the UA. He made several trips to the campus during his time as president. Martinelli loved people and loved a good party. One of his favorite things to do was go to Maxine's, a local bar in Fayetteville when he was a student. He had been very friendly with the Sigma Nu fraternity while he was a student, but never initiated because of the discriminatory practices of the time. The Sigma Nus decided it was long overdue and initiated him during one of his trips back to campus.

During his time as president of Panama, the university initiated several trips to visit him at the presidential palace. I was privileged to be on one of those trips to Panama City. Martinelli rolled out the red carpet for our visit. He held a spectacular and elegant luncheon at the presidential palace for our group. We also met with several higher-education dignitaries, and established an exchange program for students and faculty. The trip was highly successful.

Accompanying me on the trip was Dr. and Mrs. Paul Noland. Paul was a former professor of animal science and had spent two years, 1955 to 1957, in Panama on an animal research project there. Noland's work was recognized by Panama in 2009 when President Martinelli presented him with the Order of Vasco Núñez de Balboa, the nation's highest civilian honor. Martinelli credited the Arkansas program Noland developed with stimulating Panama's agricultural growth and enhancing academic ties with the university. After our trip scores of Panama students flooded to the university for their education.

In May 2013 we gave Martinelli an honorary degree.

When Martinelli left office in 2014 his approval rating was 65 percent. During his administration his approval ratings had hit an historic 90 percent.

When he was no longer in power, his adversaries launched an investigation of him for alleged crimes against the public. Martinelli claimed the allegations were totally bogus and based solely on politics. He fled the country and ended up in Miami. I was very worried the board of trustees might rescind the honorary degree, but they held off pending a trial. Martinelli was arrested in the Miami area in June 2017. He applied for political asylum but was extradited to Panama in 2018. Fortunately, in August 2019 a three-judge panel declared him not guilty and ordered him released from incarceration. He was totally exonerated. His arrest had been motivated by politics.

CHAPTER 52
PRESSURE TO MOVE OUR NURSING PROGRAM

> *He pulls a knife, you pull a gun, he sends one of yours to the hospital, you send one of his to the morgue.*
>
> — AL CAPONE

I received a call from Alan Sugg early in my administration to meet with the University of Arkansas for Medical Sciences (UAMS) administrators Dan Rahn and Peter Kohler, to discuss the possibility of physically placing our nursing program at UAMS Northwest Arkansas. UAMS Northwest Regional Campus was looking for occupants to fill up the old Washington Regional Hospital where they were located. Our dean of the College of Education and Health Professions, Reed Greenwood, had alerted me to the issue, and was a huge proponent of relocating the program to their campus. Naturally, I accepted the invitation to meet and tour the facility.

I was less than impressed. It was true that we did need new facilities, as we had outgrown the building we were located in, the old infirmary on our campus, and we wanted to expand the nursing program due to the serious shortage of nurses in Arkansas and across the nation. But the old hospital building was just that, an old hospital.

Peter was his usual gracious self and gave me a tour of the entire facility. He then took me downstairs and we wound around the corridors and finally came to a set of double doors. A plaque was on the wall reading: "Morgue." That was where our nursing program was to be located. In the windowless basement in the former morgue. At first, I figured Peter was teasing me and expected any minute to be led back upstairs to more inviting quarters. Peter was not kidding. The former morgue was to be our new headquarters for our nursing program. On top of that, they had no funds for renovation, and we would be responsible for finding those considerable dollars in an already tight budget.

I calmly expressed my concern about the dingy quarters and asked if they had anything above ground! The answer was a polite no. All of the rest of the facility was already designated for other "future uses." I told Peter and his colleagues that I needed some time to consider the space and would get back to them. I certainly didn't show it at the time, but I was flabbergasted that they would try to pawn off on me such a terrible location for our prestigious nursing program.

I immediately called a meeting of the head of nursing and my senior staff. All were negative toward the offer. Some expressed the opinion that this would be the first shoe to drop in relocating our nursing program to be under the control of UAMS after the physical move was made. I then called Alan Sugg to get his read on things. Alan told me it would be nice to share system facilities, but if it didn't work with our plans he would not interfere. We turned Peter Kohler down, much to his surprise and regret. We would go on to build a new nursing building because of a very generous gift from Lewis and Donna Epley.

Years later I was relating the story to a member of the board of trustees. The trustee told me that UAMS had expected Alan Sugg to require me to move the nursing program, and they were shocked when he didn't.

CHAPTER 53
NO TUITION INCREASE

> *We have got to make sure that every qualified American in this country who wants to go to college can go to college—regardless of income.*
>
> — *BERNIE SANDERS*

A few trustees had become concerned about recent tuition increases and the possibility of pricing students out of the market, and rightly so. Because of the dwindling amount we received from the state budget each year, we had to raise tuition in order to pay the bills and have modest salary increases for faculty and staff. In an attempt to show the board good faith, we limited salary increases to people making under $100,000. We then held the line for any increases for vice chancellors and deans. That can have an unintended consequence, however, as some of your top people start looking for better paying jobs.

One trustee in particular began beating on me to hold the line on tuition increases. Sam Hilburn was an attorney from North Little Rock, and his term on the board was ending soon. He told me that he wanted at least one year of his ten-year term on the board to refrain from raising tuition. The year 2008 had been a horrible one financially for the nation and it seemed to me, if there was ever a time to hold the line on tuition, 2009 should be the year. I talked with Dr. Sugg, and we agreed we would not seek tuition or fee increases. It would be the first time in 35 years. Of course, the decision also meant no salary increases that year. I was very proud of the faculty and staff who reacted well in the face of no compensation increase. I don't remember getting any emails or letters upset about the move.

Looking back on it with the advantage of hindsight, I do not believe it got us any points from the legislature. Nor did we get any kudos from the media with the exception of a very tiny mention in the *Arkansas Democrat Gazette*. The other campus chancellors were upset with me, as it put a strain on what they could do as well. I received a few disappointed phone calls from the other chancellors telling me that our decision would greatly hurt their campus. However, Sugg did allow the other campuses to propose increases even though we did not. In those days, Sugg recognized each campus has a different set of circumstances and is unique. What one campus does in terms of tuition doesn't always apply to a different campus. He did not require unanimity of thought for the campuses.

Later, under Bobbitt as president of the system, I had to battle mightily to get even modest tuition increases. It seemed to me that some of the two-year campuses were getting much larger increases than the flagship campus. UALR got higher increases than the Fayetteville campus on several occasions. Our campus had very high enrollment and we were fiscally responsible, while UALR was hemorrhaging money. But we got penalized for doing a good job while campuses not so fortunate were getting higher tuition increases. Seemed antithetical to me.

CHAPTER 54
OUT OF STATE STUDENTS

> *We appreciate out-of-state students and how they bring different perspectives.*
>
> — DEREK HALL

Under John White's administration we had been giving scholarships to high-level students from contiguous states. We wanted to grow our student body, and felt it was imperative we do so at the earliest possible time frame. The University of Arkansas needed to be right-sized. We had far too many degree programs for a relatively small student body. Most of the SEC institutions were much larger than our campus, and we believed growth would help solve some of our critical financial problems. Even though we knew we would have to build more residence facilities, classrooms and labs, and add more faculty, we did believe the growth in our student body would give us some much-needed program dollars. The only place we felt we could make some traction in additional funding was growing the student enrollment.

Richard Hudson told me several of the state legislators were concerned about so many students coming from Texas. He identified a few Republican legislators who he thought could be helpful to us, and suggested I contact them. One was Davy Carter, who would later become the Speaker of the House of the Arkansas General Assembly. Richard said he was a reasonable person and would listen to our objectives. I reached out to Carter and provided him with information about our nonresident scholarship program.

At that time we had labeled the program the "New Arkansan Scholarship Award." I told Carter we wanted to be good stewards of state resources and maximize every dollar we receive from the state for the benefit of Arkansas taxpayers. In fact, scholarships in the form of academic out-of-state awards provided a way of doing just that. Losing the revenue stream provided by out-of-state students would be a catastrophic blow to the quality of academic programs and facilities we were currently offering Arkansas residents. Our long-term plan was to increase university enrollment to as many as 25,000 to 30,000 students, a student population we felt our existing physical plant could accommodate, with a few additions such as classrooms. I told Carter we would operate more responsibly with a fuller enrollment. Non-resident students were essential in reaching this goal, due to the relatively flat pool of high school graduates in Arkansas projected for the next decade.

I went on to say that I wanted him to be aware that we would always accept qualified Arkansas students over out-of-state students. No Arkansas student would be denied admission because of an out-of-state student. We had plenty of room to grow and we would always continue to accommodate Arkansans first and foremost.

Contrary to what some believed, the university did not lose money by giving scholarship support to highly qualified non-resident students. In administering the program, financial data were closely analyzed to make certain non-resident students would bring income to the university, and thereby to the state, and not drain resources. The New Arkansan Scholarship Award program had actually been in place for 13 years, attracting students from states neighboring Arkansas. The university realized net revenue from the program that was one and a half times greater than we realized before the policy was put into effect. In fiscal year 2009 the university awarded $15 million in non-resident scholarship support, but attracted $25 million in revenue by doing so. This $8 million gain over the cost of administering the program was vital dollars to our university. What's more, non-resident enrollment patterns indicated this revenue would have been lost to the university were the scholarship program not in place. If participating students had to pay out-of-state tuition, which is more than double in-state, most of these non-resident students simply would not have come to the University of Arkansas.

The question of course was the cost of educating these additional out-of-state students. From what we had seen, the cost was marginal. By way of example, while a homeowner sees only a slight increase in utility costs by renting out a room, he or she sees a much larger savings on his/her mortgage by adding the renters payment to his/her own. By operating on economies of scale, non-resident students add marginally to our fixed costs. The additional revenue enabled us to budget items that would not have been possible otherwise. One of those items was the urgent need for a greater number of permanent faculty. This need has existed for well over 25 years, and could only be addressed with the additional income from increased enrollment. The additional revenue also helped us keep our tuition increases among the lowest in the country.

I went on to tell Carter that, according to the Arkansas Department of Higher Education's funding formula, which the Arkansas General Assembly adopted in 2005, the university was underfunded by the state by approximately $40 million on an annual basis. Since 1998–1999, the percentage of state appropriations to unrestricted educational and general revenue for each full-time enrolled student at the university had declined from 58 percent to 46 percent. Furthermore, when adjusted for inflation, there is less educational and general revenue funding per student than a decade earlier. Most people didn't realize we were only receiving $120 million from state appropriations, with a total budget at the time of almost $800 million.

There were also other important factors to consider beyond increased revenue. The students brought in through the program were absolutely outstanding. Freshmen who came to the university from out of state under the program had an average ACT of 28 and a 3.8 average grade point. They were incredibly bright students. Most of the students came to the University of Arkansas because of the Texas top-10-percent rule—the law that guaranteed students who graduated in the top 10 percent of their Texas high school class automatic admission to state universities, the most popular being The University of Texas and Texas A&M University. This left a lot of very high caliber students who were not in the top 10 percent looking for alternatives. We were fortunate they wanted to come to the University of Arkansas instead of attending historically regional universities in Texas.

Also, attracting out-of-state students increased opportunities for native students to network outside the state. When they graduate, Arkansas students would be in competition for jobs with students from across the United States and all over the world. We wanted our students to have colleagues everywhere they go. We wanted our state to have supporters in every community across the country.

Many out-of-state students also became Arkansans and contributed directly to the tax base. A study conducted by the University of Arkansas Economic Development Institute in 2005 showed nearly 85 percent of all responding graduates—no matter where they were from—wanted to return to Arkansas at some point. Out-of-state students were a counter to the brain drain that had plagued Arkansas for years, as too many of the state's best and brightest students left the state. In fact, students who matriculated at the University of Arkansas were seven times more likely to stay in the state after graduation, thereby growing the knowledge base of the state's economy. These imported college graduates, these new Arkansans, were likely to be happier and wealthier, participate in their community and government, and ultimately live longer—just the type of individuals needed to enhance the economic vitality of Arkansas.

I explained to Carter and other legislators that the University of Arkansas was by no means the only university that offered programs of this type. In fact, many institutions across America offered in-state tuition to residents from neighboring states, and had done so for many years. Such programs had been shown to build revenue, as well as keeping in-state tuition lower for resident students. Such programs also built diversity and gave citizens from neighboring states the opportunity to get a quality education that may have been closer to their home than their own in-state college or university.

I further indicated many citizens of Northeast Oklahoma and Southwest Missouri had a geographical affinity for the University of Arkansas a short drive away; they felt connected to this institution and wanted to come here, which is what drove the New Arkansan Scholarship Award program for students living in states neighboring Arkansas.

The competition for these students in our region became intense. Our policy was keeping us competitive with several major universities. As a point of comparison, The University of Alabama had 24 recruiters who lived full time outside Alabama in order to be more effective when recruiting out-of-state students. Alabama provided lucrative scholarships for high-quality, out-of-state students, which exceeded out-of-state tuition benefits, allowing them to become a top recruiter for National Merit Scholars. The University of Oklahoma was famous for a similar program, which had transformed them into the leading public university recruiter of National Merit Scholarship recipients, draining many from Arkansas.

I was hoping state legislators would agree the scholarship award program represented a sound financial strategy that benefits both in-state and out-of-state students, as well as the state of Arkansas as a whole. It provided a means of making up shortfalls in state appropriations, as well as keeping tuition increases modest.

Unfortunately, we continued to be criticized for taking too many Texas students. For many legislators, it was all about Texas. My rhetoric didn't seem to make a difference. Almost immediately we got objections from members of the General Assembly, who said we were bringing too many Texas students to Arkansas.

For the life of me I did not understand their reasoning. Students were students and what difference did it make where they came from? These were excellent students with high board scores and grade point averages, and we were bringing them to our university because we had room and we wanted to grow. I suppose the objection from legislators was the simple fact that they were from Texas. Arkansas has always had a rivalry with Texas on so many levels, and I guess legislators did not want their flagship university populated with too many Texas students. I guess we were not supposed to like Texas, even if it benefitted us economically. That is xenophobia on steroids.

The objections were unfathomable to me and just didn't make sense. The legislature was not giving us the funds we needed to operate—and, in fact, we had lost a sizable amount of our legislative appropriation the last few years. We had to find a way to make up lost revenue, and growing the student body by accepting highly qualified, out-of-state, and, yes, Texas students made complete sense. We put together a pamphlet which heralded the many advantages of out-of-state students and sent it to all legislators. The complaints continued from some legislators that we were bringing too many Texans to Arkansas.

Other universities that had similar programs besides the The University of Alabama and The University of Oklahoma included: Arizona State University, Clemson University, Georgia Tech, Indiana University, Louisiana State University, The Ohio State University, Penn State University, Purdue University, The University of Iowa, The University of Kansas, the University of Kentucky, and The University of Mississippi to name only a few. Our program was very similar to some of the best public institutions in the nation. Without our New Arkansan Scholarship Award program, many students would end up at other prestigious schools and we would lose enormous revenue.

Years later, after I had retired as chancellor, the university started giving the out-of-state student discount to students from any state. I guess the objections by members of the General Assembly had quieted and the university was able to continue to grow the student population. But during my time I thought the objections were insane.

CHAPTER 55
SEVERE BUDGET CUTBACKS

> Due to budget cuts the light at the end of the tunnel has been turned off.
>
> — AARON PAUL

In January 2010 the university was notified that it would have major cuts to the 2009–2010 state appropriation. The combined total of state cuts in that fiscal year would be $5,100,000. When combined with a $5 million cut in fiscal 2009 the university's state funding line had been reduced by $10 million over the last 18 months.

This was devastating to our financial position. We certainly understood the difficult fiscal dilemma faced by the state, and I knew that Governor Beebe was doing everything possible to lessen the impact of the cuts. We had been able to weather the economic storm much better than many of our peers nationally, but these cuts had dire consequences that directly threatened our mission as a major academic and economic engine for the state.

We immediately implemented a hiring freeze for all positions. In addition, departments throughout the university were asked to further tighten their belts and strive for additional efficiencies, as well as cuts to academic and outreach programs. Of course all units of the university were already participating in a comprehensive cost saving initiative that had resulted in a high level of economizing over the past year. We were also trying to be sensitive to students and their families during the economic crisis. Fee increases were kept to their lowest level in nearly a half a century. Unfortunately, we expected that the university would have a very limited budget in the foreseeable future, and we were trying to prepare for fiscal challenges. It was a tough time to be chancellor.

CHAPTER 56
ALCOHOL

> First you take a drink, then the drink takes a drink, then the drink takes you.
>
> — *F. SCOTT FITZGERALD*, THE GREAT GATSBY

Like most institutions of higher education on a national level—and for that matter high schools—at the University of Arkansas the consumption of alcohol had become a serious problem. We had experienced several close calls after a few students had consumed dangerous levels of alcohol and almost died. In the Phi Delta Theta fraternity house, one student came very close to expiring after a hazing incident where he drank way too much. The pledges of the fraternity were required to drink an entire bottle of whiskey followed by two six packs of beer. One pledge developed alcohol poisoning and was left unattended for several hours. When discovered in the early morning hours he was rushed to the hospital where he barely survived. We immediately closed the fraternity and disciplined all of the fraternity members. In fact, the national fraternity authority wanted to close the house permanently, but we were able to intervene and instead proposed severe penalties that allowed the fraternity house to remain on campus and recolonize, but required all current members to resign.

In another incident, a member of the Sigma Chi fraternity had too much to drink on Dickson Street, and on his way back to the house took a shortcut across railroad tracks. He either passed out or fell asleep and a train rolled over his arm. For many hours we felt certain the student would die from the accident. Fortunately, he survived, but with the loss of his arm. I remember distinctly going to the hospital to see the student's parents while he was in intensive care. His fraternity brothers told me that he was a tough young man and if anyone could survive such an ordeal it would be him.

Across the nation a number of colleges and universities had lost students to alcohol poisoning. By any measure it was tragic and completely avoidable, but continued to happen with great frequency. Many of the incidents were tied to fraternities that displayed irresponsible and totally unacceptable behavior.

We held numerous clinics on campus trumpeting the serious problems with alcohol abuse. We even required our students to watch an instructional video about the problem, but found that few students logged on to watch the video. We started monitoring fraternity parties and requiring police to be present in hopes of curtailing the problem. It seemed as though everything we tried was too little or had no real impact. We were extremely frustrated and worried every day that we would have a death on campus because of alcohol abuse. I posted a number of videos that were sent to our campus constituencies talking about the problem, and hoped the videos would be viewed.

I also sent a strongly-worded letter to all parents of students. I wasn't really certain it would have much of an effect, but felt the need to state our case. The contents of the letter follows:

> With the fall 2010 semester at the University of Arkansas upon us, we are pleased to have welcomed another exceptional first-year class to campus. This preparation includes addressing a subject that relates to a person who is very dear to you, your son or daughter. Like you, my wife Jane and I

also are parents. While we were delighted to see our son and daughter go off to college, we were nervous, as well. Students face many decisions, and we parents can't be there to ensure they make the safest ones. That's a part of what makes the college experience so unique. However, we still can encourage them to make informed, healthy choices, especially when it comes to the use of alcohol.

It's no secret that underage drinking is a common activity for college students across the country. This is partly because parents aren't there to impose limits and rules. I don't want to exaggerate the problem or demonize alcohol, but I do want to show the issue proper concern. The reality is, despite our best efforts to discourage underage drinking and encourage moderation for those of legal drinking age, there are those who continue to abuse alcohol.

At the University of Arkansas, we take a proactive approach to this issue. We educate students in the classroom, fraternity and sorority houses, and residence halls regarding alcohol. We remind them that alcohol is not a required part of the college experience. With alcohol-free functions like Friday Night Live and extended late-night hours at the HPER Exercise and Wellness Center, students have available to them numerous healthy social activities. This year, under the leadership of our vice provost for student affairs, we will be asking all new students to participate in an online alcohol education course. While these online programs are not a magic solution, they have been shown to reduce the incidence of high-risk conduct on other campuses.

In the event alcohol abuse becomes an issue, the Pat Walker Health Center offers early intervention and guidance through the Student Assistance Program. Counseling and psychological services offer one-on-one consultations and treatment.

Unfortunately, even with our comprehensive alcohol education program in place, some students will abuse alcohol. Fortunately, you can help. Research has shown that when you talk with your children about alcohol, they use alcohol less often and will be more responsible in their consumption. It's likely they already know the dangers of alcohol, but your genuine concern can make a big difference to them.

With this in mind, parents of students for whom we have electronic addresses will also receive an invitation and instructions to participate in the video program designed to assist you in communicating with your student about alcohol.

When students enroll at the University of Arkansas they are welcomed into an involved, inclusive community—a family. Each and every one of us wants to see your son or daughter succeed and graduate, and will be there to provide support through graduation and beyond. If you have any questions or concerns regarding alcohol, our staff members at the Pat Walker Health Center will be happy to talk with you.

On behalf of the University of Arkansas family, I wish you a joyful end of summer and fall and wish that your son or daughter has a successful, productive and enjoyable first year at the University of Arkansas. We will do all we can to make these the best years of his or her life.

CHAPTER 57
EXPANSION OF THE SEC

> *Hell, no! A tie is like kissing your sister!*
>
> — BEAR BRYANT

In 2010 both the Big Ten Conference and Pacific-10 Conference announced plans to expand to 12 members. Several presidents and chancellors in the SEC were worried that our conference might be left behind, and put pressure on the commissioner, Mike Slive, to investigate the possibility of the SEC expanding. Slive was an extraordinary leader and always on the cutting edge of almost anything related to college sports.

Several of us detected a slight reluctance on Slive's part to implement an expansion. After all, our revenues were healthy, and an expansion would mean sharing the pie with more institutions or greatly increasing revenues to keep everyone whole. Mike informed us that he really wasn't looking to expand, but most assuredly would explore our options under the presidents' and chancellors' direction.

Rumors were flying about which schools might want to join the SEC. There was no shortage of candidates as several institutions made us aware of their interest. The one school that pushed the hardest was Texas A&M, which wanted to leave the Big 12 and come over to the SEC. Other schools we discussed were The University of Texas, The University of Oklahoma, and Oklahoma State University. West Virginia University, Virginia Tech and the University of Pittsburgh were in the mix as well, although those three teams were pretty far east, and it would be expensive for teams to travel to those venues. Slive told us several conferences were implementing what was called "exit fees" to try and keep schools from abandoning their conference and coming to ours. The stakes were high, and the national media was relentless in tracking the smallest move or slightest rumor.

In August 2011 Texas A&M announced it wanted to join the SEC. In September the SEC formally invited Texas A&M to join. It was a unanimous decision by the presidents and chancellors who welcomed Texas A&M with open arms. The notorious Ken Starr, at the time president of Baylor University, threatened legal action if the move came about.

The next question was which school would be invited to round out the SEC to 14.

A number of the SEC presidents and chancellors, including me, wanted the University of Missouri. It was a member of the prestigious Association of American Universities, which was made up of the 66 leading research institutions in the nation, public and private. The campus, located in Columbia in central Missouri, was within easy reach of most of the SEC schools, and many of the presidents and chancellors knew faculty and administrators at Missouri.

I informed Mike Slive that I had a personal relationship with the chairman of the board of curators at the University of Missouri, Warren Erdman. Warren was a Westminster College alumnus and a vice president of Kansas City Southern Railroad. Slive asked me to call Erdman and tell him we were very interested in Missouri joining the SEC and gauge his interest and that of the board of curators.

After following orders, I determined that the curators were ready to accept an offer at any time. I called Slive back and informed him that I had accomplished his requested task. I could tell immediately that Slive was struggling with the information I gave him. He said

EXPANSION OF THE SEC

things had changed, and we were now looking at other potential universities to be the 14th school. He mentioned Pittsburgh and Virginia Tech as possibilities. I was not happy and made my displeasure known to Slive. I learned later that Slive was simply trying to maximize TV revenue, and had been told we needed to invite a school in the east to capture the eastern and Atlantic seaboard TV market.

I was very concerned that I had contacted a friend at the instructions of the commissioner and now the rug was being pulled out from under me. I immediately contacted several of my SEC colleague presidents and chancellors, all of whom assured me that they wanted Missouri. Later, Slive was a perfect gentleman and apologized for putting me in a precarious position.

In November 2011, the SEC officially announced that it had added Missouri as its 14th member. In 2025 The University of Oklahoma and The University of Texas will join the SEC.

CHAPTER 58
WALTON ARTS CENTER

> *Art is the only way to run away without leaving home.*
>
> — TWYLA THARP

When I was director of development for the University of Arkansas in the early 1980's, I accompanied Chancellor Nugent to see Sam Walton. The purpose of the meeting was to explore the possibility of a gift that would establish a performing arts center on the Fayetteville campus. The meeting was actually arranged by Mr. Walton, and we met for breakfast at a small hotel in Bentonville. Walton told us he needed a place to hold stockholder meetings and had an idea that would benefit him and the University of Arkansas. He said he would give $5 million to build such a facility, if we could raise the remaining funds. In those days that was a colossal gift, and we came away very excited about the possibility.

Originally the building was to be built on the University of Arkansas campus. A site location had been identified across from the current Fowler House on Razorback Road. This had the advantage of being able to utilize parking in the Razorback lot everyone called the "Pit." Unfortunately, politics entered the equation, and the

Walton Arts Center was eventually placed on Dickson Street and became a joint project with the city and the university.

In 2010 we started hearing a lot of noise that The Walton Family was giving serious consideration to building a new arts center in Bentonville. The mayor of Fayetteville and the president of the Fayetteville Chamber of Commerce panicked and were extremely concerned hearing of these plans.

The rumor was that the family wanted to build a much larger facility, and that it would no doubt be located in Bentonville close to the Walmart headquarters. The fear expressed by many Fayetteville citizens was that such a move would detract from the Walton Arts Center in Fayetteville. The Fayetteville facility had been stewarded by Helen Walton and was considered to be a real plum for Fayetteville. The movers and shakers of Fayetteville wanted the Walton Arts Center to remain in Fayetteville and did not want to have competition from a Bentonville venue.

The feeling was that such a new facility would greatly overshadow the center in Fayetteville and would be deleterious to our efforts in booking events in the future. As the mayor described to me, a new and larger arts center in Bentonville would have a major economic impact on Fayetteville and Dickson Street. Fayetteville would end up getting all of the minor performances.

I was certainly in a difficult position. I did not want to come out opposed to what the Walton family was planning, and certainly didn't want to ignite a war between Fayetteville and Bentonville. Folks from Springdale got into the act and proposed that a new Walton Arts Center be built on land available in Springdale. This further complicated a delicate issue.

The principal problem was that the facility in Fayetteville was woefully inadequate to bring in top performers. The building simply wasn't large enough and we were having trouble booking big-name events. For many years the Walton Foundation was subsidizing the programming to land big name events, but that all depended on the family's continued generosity in the future. I tried very hard to walk a delicate line so as not to upset either constituents in Fayetteville or the Walton family. I did not like being in that position.

The original concept of the Walton Arts Center was that it would be jointly governed by a board appointed by the university and the City of Fayetteville. What actually happened was that it became extremely difficult to book any university events at the Walton Arts Center. Time and time again the university would be turned away from holding some of its events at the center because of too many conflicts. I was getting barraged with complaints from faculty saying they were unable to use the Walton Arts Center for some of their concerts and other programs. It certainly didn't make any sense to me that the university was supposed to be governing the facility along with the city—actually the owner of the building—and we could not get our events scheduled. Evidence showed that too many times, when we tried to schedule an event, the university would be turned away with a simple explanation that it was due to scheduling conflicts.

The original idea for the center was that it would be a place where the university could hold its numerous educational and academic arts events. After all, that is what Sam Walton told us many years ago. He wanted the facility on our campus. Now we could not even get time for our performances. That just wasn't happening. I had lengthy conversations with Walton Foundation staff about our difficulties in scheduling our events, and while they were sympathetic nothing really changed. We started thinking we needed to have our own concert hall on campus, and decided we could convert the old men's gym into a concert hall. We just needed to find the funding, which no doubt would have to come from philanthropic sources. We set out to find benefactors who would enable us to reconfigure the gym and have our own first-class concert facility on the campus. Fortunately, Jim and Joyce Faulkner came to the rescue with a very generous gift, which enabled us to renovate the gym and turn it into a first-class concert and performing arts venue.

I was hoping The Walton Family Foundation would help us financially with the project, but they decided against making a grant. That was most disappointing to me personally. Since we were unable to use the Walton Arts Center as much as we needed, it seemed to make complete sense that they might be in favor of helping us build a new facility for our needs. It was not to be, but we fortunately were able to convince others to join in the effort.

All of a sudden, seemingly out of nowhere, the Walton Family reversed their thinking about a larger venue in Bentonville. They decided they would not build a new arts center and instead, would continue to subsidize the existing facility. To this day I'm not really certain what changed their minds, but I would suggest it may have been the third generation of the Walton Family who decided it was not a priority. The Fayetteville community was elated but I had mixed feelings, as I thought a new, much larger facility, most likely situated in Bentonville, would be a great addition to the arts scene in Northwest Arkansas.

Dear friends and UA benefactors, Greg and Hannah Lee, with the Gearharts.

Shortly after the decision was made to not pursue a new facility, members of the Walton Arts Center board came to see me. My brother Jeff was a member of the board and the chairman was my dear friend Greg Lee. They told me that they believed we really needed to make some serious changes to the governance model of the Walton Arts Center. They felt the governance model needed to be less restrictive and not under the thumb of the city and the university. They made some very good arguments and I agreed that I would assist them and be supportive of their plan.

The mayor and the president of the Chamber of Commerce were not happy. They wanted to maintain ultimate control over the operation of the Walton Arts Center. Since we had not been able to use the facility to the extent required, I had no problem with turning over control to a private board. Besides, we were building our own facility that would greatly enhance our campus performances. After much discussion a new governance model was adopted.

CHAPTER 59
GOOD NATIONAL PR

> *Fundraisers who rise to the top position at a college are considered thought leaders who have an understanding of the academic enterprise and a talent for managing both finances and people. They get there because they can deliver, in a broad way, the kind of leadership it takes to manage an academic institution*
>
> — *JOHN GLIER*

The Chronicle of Higher Education is the international trade journal for all of higher education. It is widely read by staff and faculty in education circles. In the summer of 2010, *The Chronicle* sent a reporter to Fayetteville to interview me about an article they were considering, investigating the number of presidents or chancellors who had emerged from fundraising and development positions. In recent years a handful of institutions had chosen leaders who had spent much of their careers in fundraising or alumni affairs, which had previously been unprecedented. Things were changing nation-wide and more advancement professionals were assuming presidential roles. The article was published in *The Chronicle* on July 4, 2010, and was titled "From Fund Raiser to President: An Uncommon Path Pays Off," by reporter and writer Kathryn Masterson. The article made the point that fundraising had become a huge part of a president's overall responsibilities. The article posited that presidents and chancellors should be recruited to some extent on their fundraising prowess. Masterson stated, "As government financial support declines and costs continue to rise, colleges have grown more dependent on generous donors to build new facilities, attract star faculty members and students, and start programs. Many new presidents have little fund-raising experience and feel insufficiently prepared for the task. But if campus leaders are expected to be their colleges' chief fundraisers, should boards of trustees look more often to those with backgrounds in raising money?"

The Chronicle reported in the article that The American Council on Education's 2006 American College President Study survey shows how crucial fundraising is to top executives' jobs. Fundraising was the activity that presidents said occupied the largest share of their time (37.7 percent), and the area they felt least prepared for. The reporter from *The Chronicle* also interviewed university benefactors. Boyce Billingsley, a major donor along with her late husband, says she made some calls as soon as she heard the previous chancellor was retiring. She admitted she called several trustees and put her two cents in saying, "We already have a chancellor here in training."

HONORARY DEGREES

> *I have two college degrees, four honorary doctorate degrees, and am in three halls of fame, and the only thing I know how to do is teach tall people how to put a ball in the hole.*
>
> — *COACH RED AUERBACH*

I have always thought the awarding of honorary degrees was an important undertaking for a major university. Not everyone does. Not until fairly recently did Penn State award honorary degrees. Such degrees are conferred as a way of honoring a distinguished citizen of the world whose contributions to a specific field or to society stand out. Such contributions can be in business, government service, science, education, world affairs, community service, and certainly philanthropy. During my time I asked the board of trustees to confer honorary degrees on a number of highly qualified persons, including Johnelle Hunt, founder of J.B. Hunt Transport Services, Inc.; Don Tyson, chairman of the board of Tyson Foods, Inc.; His Holiness, the Dalai Lama; philanthropist, Alice Walton; the president of Panama, Ricardo Martinelli; the governor of Arkansas, Mike Beebe; the president of Walmart, Mike Duke; and the vice chancellor of Oxford University and current president of New York University, Andrew Hamilton.

CHAPTER 60
PENN STATE, PATERNO, SANDUSKY, SPANIER

> *Our most saddening and sobering finding is the total disregard for the safety and welfare of Sandusky's child victims by the most senior leaders at Penn State. The most powerful men at Penn State failed to take any steps for 14 years to protect the children who Sandusky victimized.*
>
> — *FORMER FBI DIRECTOR LOUIS FREEH.*

As previously mentioned, we spent 13 years in State College, Pennsylvania, when I worked for Penn State University. We knew Jerry Sandusky and his wife, Dottie, very well, and I worked closely with Joe Paterno raising funds for the university. Jerry had served as an assistant football coach for over 30 years at Penn State, and at one time was slated to take over as head coach when Paterno retired. We left Penn State before Graham Spanier became president but had met him on several occasions. We also knew well the athletics director, Tim Curley, and the senior vice president for finance, Gary Schultz.

When the story broke in March 2011 regarding child molestation by Sandusky, we were shocked beyond words. With the benefit of hindsight, we would remember often seeing Sandusky in horseplay with young kids, but didn't really think too much about it as Sandusky just seemed like a big kid who liked children. We now know he was a child predator of the worst magnitude.

I was sitting on the screened-in porch at Fowler House watching the news unfold when Paterno and the Penn State president, Graham Spanier were fired by the board of trustees. Our son Brock was with us and commented before the announcement was made that Paterno and the university president would lose their jobs. I told Brock they were too powerful to be fired. I was dead wrong, and Brock was prescient.

Paterno, Spanier, Schultz and Curley all lost their jobs that evening. After the announcement student groups formed and trashed State College. Several police cars were overturned, and it was a virtual riot.

Spanier, Schultz and Curley were charged with perjury, obstruction of justice, failure to report suspected child abuse, and other charges. The Penn State board of trustees hired former FBI Director Louis Freeh to conduct an investigation. His report was extremely damaging to all involved. The report stated that Penn State's longtime head football coach Joe Paterno, along with Spanier, Curley and Schultz, had known about allegations of child abuse by Sandusky as early as 1998, had shown "... total disregard for the safety and welfare of Sandusky's child victims ..." and had "empowered" Sandusky to continue his acts of abuse by failing to disclose them. Spanier, Schultz and Curley would serve short jail sentences, even though Spanier would fight the sentence in an attempt to stay out of jail for almost ten years.

Sandusky would be convicted of 45 counts of child molestation and was sentenced to a minimum of 30 years and a maximum of 60 years in prison, effectively a life sentence.

The NCAA would impose an unprecedented fine on Penn State of $60 million, plus a slew of sanctions, probation and loss of scholarships. Penn State would pay victims of Sandusky's abuse over $100 million.

There were many good people who believed the Penn State

board of trustees had rushed to judgment, especially as regards Paterno. No one had done more for Penn State than Joe Paterno and it was unfathomable he would be fired. Personally, I believe Paterno didn't completely understand what Sandusky was doing to young boys or possibly chose not to "go there." As far as the culture of Penn State contributing to the problem, I have no doubt that it did. Penn State was a closed society unto itself. Decision making was in the hands of a very small number of senior people. Decisions were typically not shared until announced and little to no input was requested from parties affected. I experienced that process when I was there, and it continued under Spanier.

During the Sandusky ordeal I was contacted by the Penn State Alumni Association and asked to comment about how the Sandusky affair might affect Penn State's ability to hire their next president. My comments would appear in the alumni magazine. I had avoided commenting on anything having to do with the Sandusky issue since I knew so many of the parties to the crisis. I felt my comments would be misconstrued as piling on. I had been contacted by numerous national publications but decided my personal comments would do nothing to help heal the situation and declined to be interviewed by all of them.

Our daughter has two degrees from Penn State. The whole ordeal was tragic on so many levels. But Penn State is an amazing institution and has bounced back from the tragedy, and is now stronger than ever. The Penn State board just hired the first female as president. The university has a bright future.

CHAPTER 61
A COMPACT WITH THE PEOPLE OF ARKANSAS

> *The great object of the institution of civil government is the improvement of those who are parties to the social compact.*
>
> — *JOHN QUINCY ADAMS*

In early 2011 the presidents and chancellors of the state's higher education institutions decided it was necessary to create a compact demonstrating to the leadership of the state our commitment to the ideals of higher education. At that time, we had not received any increases in our state appropriation, and a series of editorials in the statewide newspaper, as well as other articles in a number of publications, had been deleterious to our efforts. Our institutions were being hammered as bloated and wasteful and only interested in more money from the legislature. Many Republican legislators were criticizing higher education, claiming we were not getting the job done in educating students and moving them into the workforce. We believed the criticisms were unfounded, but nonetheless caused some segments of the population to be negative toward our colleges and universities in Arkansas.

At a meeting of the presidents and chancellors, I was asked to draft a compact that would set the record straight about our deep commitment to higher education in the state. I wasn't at all certain I was the best person to draft the compact but agreed to do so in spite of my reservations. On top of that, I wasn't really certain a compact would make a difference to the General Assembly.

We had just witnessed a huge snowstorm in early February 2011, and I took the opportunity while we were closed down to draft the compact. I called it a "Compact with the People of Arkansas." It was designed to show our citizens we understood the criticisms and took them seriously. The following is the compact agreed upon by the presidents and chancellors after many contributions and several iterations:

> The presidents and chancellors of the state's baccalaureate, masters and doctoral degree-granting institutions hereby pledge the following 15 points to the people of Arkansas, our independent boards of trustees, the General Assembly, the governor and other Constitutional officers:
>
> 1. To be fully transparent and accountable in all decision making. As college costs continue to rise, the importance of full disclosure of information about programs, finances, and performance to the citizenry becomes an increasingly important factor for the public.
> 2. To spend the state's resources, as appropriated by the General Assembly, carefully, prudently and appropriately with a strong commitment to cost savings and cost containment.
> 3. To hold ourselves to public accountability on performance measures and key indicators that demonstrate to all citizens progress is being made continuously toward the quality of our programs and efforts.
> 4. To protect the environment and invest in energy efficiencies and sustainable business practices.
> 5. To work collectively with primary and secondary schools to lower remediation rates and help better prepare

students for the rigors of college life and work so they are able to access the American opportunity system through a baccalaureate degree and beyond.
6. To work collectively on academic collaboration and unique partnerships between and among two-year and four-year institutions to make student transfer as seamless and efficient as possible.
7. To meet the governor's challenge of doubling the number of degrees produced by our institutions of higher learning by 2025.
8. To dramatically increase the number of our citizens with a baccalaureate degree.
9. To keep tuition and fee costs for students as low as possible, while recognizing the need for increased state support and the importance of maintaining academic quality and upkeep of our sizable physical facilities.
10. To continue our collective commitment to expand the diversity of our student bodies and significantly increase the number of faculty and staff with persons of color and underrepresented groups.
11. To reach out to current and future student veterans, helping them to navigate the processes of enrollment, coordinate access to services, and reduce barriers to their full participation in campus life.
12. To work with all students to help them realize their goals and aspirations and to succeed in producing graduates with the ability to think globally, act locally, and value learning for a lifetime.
13. To assist students with financial aid and scholarship support so no student in Arkansas is denied a four-year degree because of his or her inability to pay.
14. To bolster our efforts to accommodate nontraditional and transfer students who are equally important to the goals of increasing the percentage of the Arkansas population holding a bachelor's degree or higher, and helping to bring higher wage jobs to the state.

15. To be entrepreneurial in seeking additional sources of revenue for key initiatives and student support. While public funding will continue to compose the crucial backbone of our operating budgets, we pledge to seek other revenue sources including private gifts, external grants and contracts. Spillovers of knowledge from research often translate into new products and services and new jobs for Arkansas. Our institutions are enhancing the success and competitiveness of a growing number of emerging technology companies that can sustain economic prosperity in Arkansas.

We concluded the compact with the following statement:

Our baccalaureate, masters and doctoral degree-granting colleges and universities in Arkansas cannot achieve the ambitious compact outlined above without the concerted efforts and support of the legislative and executive branches of state government. We pledge to do our part in growing the economic base of Arkansas and improving the lives of our citizens. The prosperity of our state and nation, not to mention individual citizens, depends on the acquisition of higher education. Our ability to move forward productively in all areas of society depends on an educated workforce and informed citizenry. We pledge collectively and cooperatively, as the presidents and chancellors of our state colleges and universities, to work as hard as humanly possible toward the achievement of the 15 points above.

We scheduled a time to present the compact to the public with a media conference at the state capitol. Most of the presidents and chancellors attended the conference. We had large placards created that delineated the 15 points, and placed them in key locations in the capitol building. We were excited about the compact, and thought it touched on just about every issue that legislators should be concerned with regarding higher education.

We received feedback from the governor's office that they liked our efforts and appreciated what we were doing. But that was about the extent of it. We had a little comment from legislators and even some criticism. There were a few favorable and unfavorable editorials regarding our work. We decided to send the compact to all public university chancellors and presidents across the country and received numerous responses and congratulations. A few institutions asked if they could borrow from our prose for their own purposes and we readily agreed.

Looking back with the benefit of hindsight, I don't think the compact made much of a difference. Our institutions were stretched very thin from a financial standpoint, and it would be several more years before any additional state funding would flow to our public colleges and universities. It all seemed to be a process that paid few dividends and became a disappointment to all of us. Perhaps we were naïve to think that "words" would make a difference. It became obvious to us that the compact did practically nothing to rally support for our institutions. Despite little reaction from legislators, it was still important to publish the 15 points.

CHAPTER 62
FOOD PANTRY

> *One of the most compelling stories I heard was that faculty and staff all over campus were installing microwaves and then buying macaroni and ramen noodles, and other foods, with their own money, to discreetly feed students who did not have money for something to eat.*
>
> — *JANE BROCKMANN GEARHART*

Jane has always had a special place in her heart for people who go hungry. Just the thought of a child not having enough to eat brings tears to her eyes. I'm not too sure where that comes from, except to say that Jane has a big heart of gold. Food insecurity became one of her many special causes where she gave time and resources. She was well schooled in the international issue of food insecurity. She kept up to date on the latest trends and issues.

In 2011 she became aware that some students wanted to start a food pantry on campus. She learned many students and staff have very serious food insecurity issues and believed a food pantry would alleviate some of the acute need.

Founded in February 2011, the Full Circle Campus Food Pantry was established as an emergency food assistance program to distribute food and personal products to all members of the U of A community. According to a campus survey, 38 percent of students at the university experience food insecurity during their time on campus, a number I found astonishing. According to the *Journal of College & Character*:

> "Food insecurity is a threat to student success on college campuses in the United States. It has the potential to impact academics, wellness, and behavior—all factors that have bearing on student retention and graduation rates. There exists an invisible student population on college campuses—those who are experiencing food insecurity. The issue is hard to see because of its cross-cutting nature and the fact that most people who are experiencing poverty want to keep it hidden due to stigma and shame. Regardless of its lack of visibility, the negative impacts of food insecurity on student success are real."

Jane started discussing the issue with staff members in the student services area in 2010. The main stumbling block was finding appropriate space for the operation. Space was at a premium. Plus a few folks were downright opposed to what they called "giveaways." In fact, the spouse of a very senior development officer told Jane that she was opposed to the pantry, because you would never know if people using it really had a hunger issue! When I heard that I was appalled. How many folks would show up at a food pantry unless they had real need? And, if they did show up and didn't have real need, so what? The percentage of people who would do that had to be miniscule.

I spoke to my space go-to guy, Admiral Mike Johnson and he immediately located prime space for the pantry.

In 2015 the pantry would be named the Jane B. Gearhart Full Circle Campus Food Pantry in honor of Jane's extraordinary commitment to the university in general, and food insecurity in particular. At the dedication of the naming, Jane gave a marvelous talk on hunger issues to a packed crowd in the rotunda of the administration building. She told the assembled group that when she informed me of the naming in her honor, I said, "Oh wonderful, the Mrs. G. David Gearhart Food Pantry." It got a thunderous laugh at my expense, but I loved it.

When we launched our pantry, we were one of the first 20 pantries in the country—we were about number 15. We were the first in Arkansas and the SEC.

So many universities visited our pantry in its early founding, and they still come today. The University of Missouri, Texas A&M University, Pittsburg State University, Northeastern Oklahoma University, Arkansas State University, Arkansas Tech University, University of Central Arkansas, Southern Arkansas University, University of Arkansas Little Rock, University of Arkansas Fort Smith to name but a few.

According to the College and University Food Bank Alliance, over 800 campus pantries exist across the country. We were one of 15 campus programs nominated for the Obama administration's initiative, College Champions for Change, in the spring of 2012. We were one of five campuses invited to the White House to dialogue about our work. We came in second behind the University of Massachusetts in national voting for Champions for Change.

CHAPTER 63
RIGHTING A WRONG

> *Against racial integration of all schools within the Little Rock School District.*
>
> — ORVAL FAUBUS, GOVERNOR OF ARKANSAS FROM 1955 TO 1967

Lothaire Scott Green taught in the Little Rock public schools for 43 years. She was the mother of three—including Ernest Green, one of the Little Rock Nine and the first Black graduate of Central High School. The Little Rock Nine were a group of African American high-school students who challenged racial segregation in the public schools of Little Rock in 1957.

Lothaire Scott Green sued the Little Rock School District in the 1940's demanding equal pay for Black teachers. She was assisted by an NAACP legal defense fund lawyer, Thurgood Marshall, later a Supreme Court justice.

In 2011 I received an email from Treopia Washington, Ernest Green's sister and daughter of Lothaire Scott Green, telling me that her mother had never been given her degree at commencement in 1951. At that time Mrs. Green was not allowed to attend graduation ceremonies to receive her diploma. She took many of her classes off campus in a trailer.

Treopia wanted her mother to be given the opportunity to posthumously receive her master's degree in education during a public graduation ceremony. Her mother passed away in 1976, and Treopia had carried the hope that perhaps, one day, she might get to see her mother honored with a diploma at a graduation ceremony. Treopia, who was a teenager at the time, recalls the day her mother received the package in the mail containing her graduation diploma and a letter from the university that basically said, here's the degree but you are not welcome at the ceremony.

What happened to Mrs. Green was simply wrong, we all know that today. When I received the email from Treopia, I was heartbroken. While it is hard to right the wrongs of the past—it was 60 years ago—it doesn't mean we shouldn't take this opportunity to make things right by acknowledging and addressing what happened. We decided we would posthumously award the degree at the May commencement ceremonies and Treopia would accept the degree on behalf of her late mother. Walton Arena was packed full of parents, graduates and families as I called Treopia Washington to come forward to receive her mother's diploma. Many were openly weeping after hearing the story of 60 years ago. Treopia received a standing ovation, which seemed to go on for several minutes.

Charles Robinson told me later it seemed ironic that we boasted of being the first higher education institution in the South to admit Black students but would not allow them to receive their diploma at the ceremony.

CHAPTER 64
VETERANS

> *There is nothing stronger than the heart of a volunteer.*
> — GENERAL JAMES H. DOOLITTLE

I never served in the armed forces. My draft lottery number was high, and the nation went to an all-volunteer force soon after I graduated from college and I was never called to service. In some ways I regret that, as I have always had a very special place in my heart for those who have served. Perhaps my feelings came from the loss of an uncle in World War II and the stories as told by my grandmother Gearhart. I suppose I could have entered the service voluntarily, but I didn't.

I wanted to do more for our veterans at the university to show them our appreciation for their unselfish service. We put our heads together and decided to create the Veterans Resource and Information Center. Dr. Danny Pugh (who would go on to be vice president for student affairs at Texas A&M University) was instrumental in moving our project forward. Erika Gamboa was also indispensable in leading the opening of the center and serving as the director. As a veteran herself, she understood the very special needs of the students who had, or currently were, serving their country in the armed forces.

The center serves as the central point of contact for prospective or current University of Arkansas military-affiliated students needing assistance with the admissions process, applying for military educational benefits and scholarships, and referrals to various academic departments around campus. Shortly after the establishment of the office the university became a "Military-Friendly Institution."

CHAPTER 65
ARKANSAS DEPARTMENT OF HIGHER EDUCATION (ADHE)

The vice presidency is not worth a bucket of warm spit.

— *JOHN NANCE GARNER*

The ADHE was originally established as the Commission on Coordinating Higher Education Finance in 1961. It was renamed and reorganized as the Department of Higher Education in 1971. Later it would change its name to the Division of Higher Education. I suppose that sounded more important than department.

My general feeling was that it was a bureaucratic agency with very little real power and influence. It consisted of 12 board members appointed by the governor, who served six-year terms. Its main purpose was to review and approve academic programs in an attempt to keep mission creep and duplication of programs at a minimum. During my seven years as chancellor, I don't remember a single time the division failed to approve an academic program that a university wanted. Mission creep and duplication was rampant throughout Arkansas institutions of higher education. The division seemed like a rubber stamp to most of my colleagues, and too much politics entered the discussion. If a university wanted a program, they would lobby their state representatives and apply enormous pressure to ensure the program was approved, usually unanimously.

James Purcell became the new director in 2008. From the very beginning he seemed determined to shake up higher education in Arkansas, but not necessarily in a good way. I found him lacking in communication skills. My first meeting with him was a get-acquainted session, which left me void of any clue as to his agenda. I would soon discover that agenda included the University of Arkansas.

In 2010 Purcell hired the National Center for Higher Education Management Systems (NCHEMS) to review policies related to graduation rates. I was aware of NCHEMS, but had not done any business with them. It is a non-profit organization that claims its mission is to improve decision making in higher education. Purcell and NCHEMS sent Dr. Aims McGuinness to our campus to review policies related to graduation. McGuinness was a senior policy consultant for NCHEMS, and had worked with Purcell previously. From the very beginning I had a bad feeling about the visit.

I invited a host of campus officials to a meeting with McGuinness to discuss retention and graduation rates. We were hoping it would be a productive meeting about his experience with successful strategies, and to share issues of specific concern to our campus.

Dr. McGuinness began the conversation by thanking us for having him to the University of *Northwest* Arkansas. Everyone in the room was shocked by his referring to us as the University of *Northwest* Arkansas and there was an audible rumble through the room. As the land grant, flagship institution of the state this was demeaning and in poor taste. After observing our audible reaction, he admitted to the assembled group that it might have been a poor joke. No one at the meeting but him laughed. It was a bad joke, and it was in keeping with his tone and attitude for the rest of the meeting.

Much of the data he provided to the assembled group was completely inaccurate:

- Based his conclusions on inaccurate data he explained that the graphic entitled

- "Public Research Institutions—Bachelor's Degrees Awarded per 100 FTE
- Undergraduates, 2006–07" was based on data only from our campus and UAMS.
- This was not accurate. Instead it included UALR rather than UAMS.
- Not only was his data flawed, but his attitude was one of condescension and arrogance.
- Had the data been accurate and included UAMS instead of UALR, we would have been listed as 19.1 bachelor's degrees awarded per 100 FTE graduates. This is a dramatic difference from the 16.7 per 100 that he presented to us. With the correct data, we would have moved ahead of more than ten other states.
- He had touted that the U of A had a 17 percent graduation rate. The UA graduation rate for federal reporting was 59 percent.
- The NCHEMS report stated that Arkansas exports more people with bachelor's degrees than it imports. Data on its own website indicated that was not correct. One state report on the NCHEMS site showed a deficit in young people with bachelor's degrees and showed Arkansas as a net importer of people with bachelor's degrees.

He had dramatically skewed the data. When we challenged him, he aggressively argued with us. The lack of veracity with which he defended the data made us question his research. McGuinness was condescending and his approach was accusatory on the basis of erroneous data. I wrote the president of NCHEMS and lodged a complaint. I copied the governor, Alan Sugg and Purcell. I have no record of a reply.

The NCHEMS final report was full of mistakes and inaccuracies. It also questioned our program giving tuition breaks to out-of-state students with high board scores, the New Arkansan Scholarship Award program, which had been so successful. I requested time on the Higher Education Coordinating Board to challenge the findings.

Dr. Charles Allen was the chairman of the board and a good friend, and I appealed to him for time at a future meeting. He wrote Purcell asking him to accommodate my request. Purcell refused. Other presidents and chancellors had presented issues before the full board, but Purcell would not allow me to have my day in court. He simply told his chairman that it wasn't appropriate.

Nothing of any consequence came of the report and I have to assume that it was deep-sixed.

Then in January 2011 Purcell criticized our New Arkansan Scholarship Award program in the statewide newspaper. Purcell said that our financial woes, including a tuition increase, were related to our 13-year waiver policy for high-end, out-of-state students from contiguous states. It was totally bogus and unsupported by any facts. He was quoted as saying, "They are giving away their product, which is quality education."

I was livid. His comments were unconscionable on any level. He was supposed to be promoting higher education, not diminishing it. On top of that, his comments were completely erroneous and supported by no factual data. We had shown accurate data that verified that the program brought several million dollars to the university that otherwise would have been lost. This was critical revenue for the university. I assumed that Purcell was paying me back for questioning the NCHEMS report.

I asked former chancellor John White to contact Governor Beebe and make him aware of the fallacies that were being claimed by Purcell. White was highly respected by Beebe and I thought a favorable word would help the cause. White too was incensed by Purcell's comments and agreed to my request.

Alan Sugg was incensed by Purcell's comments as well, and sent a memo to the board of trustees that completely supported my position regarding the partial waiver for academically qualified out-of-state students. He stated that Purcell was unenlightened and just plain wrong. His comments found their way to the governor. I appreciated Sugg backing me up with our trustees and elected officials.

Purcell didn't stay long after his comments about the flagship, which ignited a firestorm. He resigned and accepted a similar job in

Louisiana. He would then go to Rhode Island for basically the same job. In 2017 he became the executive director of the Alabama Commission on Higher Education.

On September 12, 2019, an article was published in the *Alabama Political Reporter* by Bill and Susan Britt that claimed, "a new methodology adopted by the Alabama Commission on Higher Education (ACHE) led to Auburn University being short-changed in the budgeting process."

The article goes on to state:

> ACHE Executive Director Dr. Jim Purcell who holds a doctorate from The University of Alabama tried to explain away why Auburn University received a significantly reduced percentage of state funding, but what he did not reveal were his close ties to the company who had recommended the cuts or allegations of misdeeds against the organization.
>
> What is also seemingly apparent is the use of questionable data comparisons between nationwide institutions and Alabama's schools of higher learning to determine funding allocations for the state's colleges and universities in fiscal year 2020.
>
> Colorado-based vendor, the National Center for Higher Education Management Systems (NCHEMS) was hired by Purcell to conduct statistical peer equity adjustments for each public institution, which dramatically lowered Auburn's percentage of state funding for fiscal year 2020.
>
> While the budget issue was eventually resolved, lingering questions about the process remain.
>
> Records going back to 2003, suggest this was the first time ACHE had used this type of peer review formulation to determine funding recommendations for state colleges and universities.

Purcell was named Alabama's State Higher Education Executive Officer in April 2017, previously having served in similar capacities in Rhode Island, Louisiana and Arkansas.

During his tenure at these agencies, Purcell contracted NCHEMS, the same group who performed Alabama's peer equity review for various projects.

NCHEMS is a vendor Purcell repeatedly hired as he moved from state to state holding jobs in higher education.

Public records show Purcell accepted money from groups with close ties to NCHEMS. These financial ties can be seen in Purcell's state disclosure forms.

While serving in higher education roles in the states of Arkansas and Louisiana, Purcell received money from NCHEMS' associates.

In 2016, it was revealed that NCHEMS conspired with the Nevada System of Higher Education (NSHE) and its Chancellor, Dan Klaich, to prepare a fake document designed to mislead members of the Nevada Legislature.

I leave it to my readers to form your own opinion of Jim Purcell.

CHAPTER 66
AMENDMENT 33

> *When you combine religion and politics, the result is politics.*
>
> — PASTOR W.B. MOORER

Criticism of higher education from members of the General Assembly had escalated into an issue of concern for all of us. Alan Sugg was particularly concerned about what he was hearing In Little Rock. State Senator Jimmy Jeffress wrote an op-ed in which he argued for the repeal of the 68-year-old amendment to the Arkansas Constitution, Amendment 33.

In response to the abrupt firing of the University of Arkansas President Bill Fulbright for political reasons in 1941, the people of Arkansas passed amendment 33 to protect colleges and universities from external politics. Governor Homer Adkins, a member of the Ku Klux Klan and avowed segregationist, was a political opponent of Fulbright's mother, Roberta, who had backed someone else for governor, and he lashed out at her by packing the university's board of trustees, which proceeded to fire the young future congressman and senator. It was a callous exercise of political gamesmanship, and caused a monumental uproar of public opinion. Fulbright would later defeat Adkins for the U.S. Senate.

Amendment 33 was designed to give more power to boards of trustees of higher education institutions. Following severe public outrage over Adkins's actions, Robert A. Leflar, dean of the university's law school, wrote Amendment 33. The proposal made it to the general election ballot of 1942. Voters narrowly approved it, 39,756 to 38,167. The amendment curtailed the power of the governor from removing without cause any member of a board of an institution of higher learning. It also prohibited the legislature from increasing or reducing the membership of an institution's board. Amendment 33 was designed to give higher education in the state some level of independence and freedom from the political grip of governors and legislators.

While higher education had never used Amendment 33, with the exception of a lawsuit that was settled in 1995 concerning the University of Central Arkansas, presidents and chancellors believed that it offered some protection to higher education in the state. State Senator Jeffress wanted to remove tuition-setting authority from college and university boards and give that authority to the Arkansas legislature. Of course the legislature had ultimate say over the state appropriations for higher education, which was the ultimate control lever over public colleges and universities in the state. Many felt that Amendment 33 had little real power, due to the purse strings being ultimately held by the legislature.

Every so often a public college president would ceremoniously waive the Amendment 33 flag in hopes of scaring off some legislative enactment that would damage higher education.

I was always in favor of testing Amendment 33 to see if it did have any clout and if it did, in fact, give any independence to our colleges and universities. However, the university's lawyers didn't want to establish any precedent, and were worried that it would aggravate legislators and cause a repeal of the amendment or even lower state appropriations. I always believed that it had no impact if we were not willing to use it at the proper time. Still to this day there has never been a test case to determine if Amendment 33 carries any real weight, and it remains unsettled law in Arkansas.

CHAPTER 67
MILESTONE

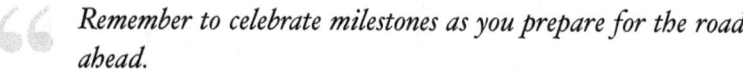

> *Remember to celebrate milestones as you prepare for the road ahead.*
>
> — *NELSON MANDELA*

In February 2011 the University of Arkansas achieved a milestone. We were elevated to the highest possible classification by the Carnegie Foundation for the Advancement of Teaching during its recent reclassification of the nation's 4,633 universities and colleges. The University of Arkansas became one of just 108 schools with this distinction. The new status reflected the kind of return on investment the University of Arkansas was producing for our state and nation. The Carnegie classification was widely accepted as the standard categorization of accredited United States universities and colleges. The classifications are based on a range of quantitative data related to the number and nature of doctoral degrees awarded annually, the amount of research grants occurring, and other measures of scholarly productivity.

The action was based on each institution's 2008–2010 performance numbers. The elevation to the highest classification was primarily a result of sustained increases in the number and diversity of doctoral degrees awarded and research grants and contracts received. It reflected the university's transformation as a truly world-class institution. It documented our advancement as a nationally and internationally influential research university. We reached this top status as a result of the innovation, productivity, and successful collaboration of our university's faculty, students and staff.

CHAPTER 68
FACULTY ATHLETIC REPRESENTATIVE

> *It's because of Dr. Hunt that I can sit in recruits' homes and honestly tell them the University of Arkansas and its people can prepare you for any challenge you will face.*
>
> — *COACH MIKE NEIGHBORS*

The Faculty Athletics Representative (FAR) is an important position at every university. All SEC and NCAA institutions have an FAR. They are always a member of the faculty, and are designated by the chancellor or president to serve as a liaison between the institution and the athletics department. The role is to ensure that the academic institution establishes and maintains the appropriate balance between academics and intercollegiate athletics. The FAR provides assurances for the academic integrity of the athletics program and for the maintenance of the welfare of the student athlete. They are called upon to review information relating to the academic well-being of the student athlete to ensure the athletes who attend can and do thrive academically. They are called upon to make sure that student-athletes meet the academic requirements of the institution before they can play in a particular sport. The FAR is encouraged to meet regularly with the president or chancellor, as well as the director of athletics.

Jeff Long thought that it was time to make a change in our FAR, and asked me to propose names for consideration. One name came immediately to my mind and that was Dr. Sharon Hunt. Dr. Hunt was a professor of kinesiology and had been a former interim dean of the College of Education and Health Professions. She had an esteemed career and was highly respected as a professor with a long-lasting positive impact on students. She also had been productive in her academic research related to physical education and recreation. I decided that she would be the perfect individual to serve as our FAR and proposed her name to Long, and he agreed she was a perfect choice.

Dr. Hunt was a devoted wife, mother and grandmother, a steadfast member of her church and a dedicated citizen of her beloved Fayetteville community. Not only was Dr. Hunt an exceptional member of the faculty, but she was an exceptional person. She was caring, giving and always supportive of others. In 2010 I appointed her to the position, and she became the first woman and first non-lawyer to be named to the post. I believed it was a trailblazing moment for the University of Arkansas and helped serve as an inspiration to other women, including Razorback student-athletes.

The only issue that concerned me was the fact that her son was married to our daughter. I didn't want the ugly head of nepotism to be raised, but thought she would do such a marvelous job I went ahead and appointed her. I expected I would receive some criticism for the fact that I had a family relationship with her. I never received a single question about her candidacy. She was universally accepted and everyone I spoke with was wholeheartedly supportive. Earlier we had appointed a women's commission on campus, and I heard from a number of the members of the commission congratulating me on Dr. Hunt's appointment, which spotlighted women's issues.

Dr. Hunt would serve in the capacity of the FAR for seven years. When she stepped down from that position, her colleague FARs held a celebration of her term during her last SEC meeting. The compliments flowing about her time in that job were immense, and she represented the university with incredible expertise and influence. She and her husband David, public school administrator, are active members of the Fayetteville community.

CHAPTER 69
ANOTHER ATHLETICS CHANGE

> *If you aren't fired with enthusiasm, you will be fired with enthusiasm.*
>
> — *VINCE LOMBARDI*

Our basketball program was in far worse condition than most understood when Coach John Pelphrey took over the program in 2007. The first sign of this was when Coach Dana Altman accepted the job, and then resigned shortly after finding out about the lack of academic performance by the then-current student-athletes and the lack of academic support programs to assist our athletes. Altman also found a large unaddressed drug problem among the student-athletes and this, coupled with a six-member senior class of which none were projected to graduate, proved to be more than Coach Altman was willing to take on.

Most people don't realize that Arkansas basketball problems were widely known in the basketball coaching world and resulted in a very limited pool of coaches who had an interest in our head coach job. Pelphrey was very eager and willing to take the job because of all the great things we know that exist here at the University of

Arkansas, and despite knowing the challenges he would face as our next coach. He knew it was not a quick fix and that it would take many years to turn the program around. Pelphrey had finished his third season with a winning percentage of .526. It is worth noting Coach Richardson had a .571 winning percentage after three years and Stan Heath had a .453 percentage. Stan Heath was given five years to lead the program.

Unfortunately, the board of trustees started making noise that they wanted a change in coaches after only three years with Pelphrey. They didn't think Pelphrey was getting it done. Jeff Long believed that to change coaches after only three years would hurt our ability to attract a quality coach, because we would have cut short our commitment to Pelphrey. Long also believed Pelphrey had reestablished discipline in our program and that he was recruiting better student-athletes and better character in the young men he was bringing forward. Jeff Long believed we needed to give Pelphrey more time. I had my doubts about Pelphrey's ability to move the program forward, but I believed that I had to listen to my athletics director and allow Pelphrey to stay longer. He was a good man who had a lovely, engaging spouse, and was committed to being successful.

But things got worse. Pelphrey just wasn't winning enough games and the fans were not excited. Even more important, the board of trustees was pounding on me to tell Long to fire him. I sat down with Long, and we counted trustee votes. Clearly, we were outnumbered, and the handwriting was on the wall. After four seasons Pelphrey was fired in 2011. Long wanted to give him a fifth year, but realized that would cause a rebellion among fans and the board. Pelphrey was 69–59 with the Razorbacks, including an 18–13 record that season. Arkansas lost to Tennessee in the opening round of the Southeastern Conference tournament, the third straight first-round exit for the program. Arkansas finished fourth in the SEC West and people were out for blood. Pelphrey had three years remaining on his contract and we negotiated a buyout. I was sad at the dismissal and the fact that Pelphrey could not make things happen. He inherited a mess, and we knew it could take years to turn things around. But winning was the name of the game in all sports. No longer was college athletics the social glue that was supposed to hold campuses together. College sports was an industrial complex and winning was king.

DODGED A BULLET

Immediately after Pelphrey was fired I received an email from one of our trustees. He said that he had multiple contacts from associates of former Indiana and Texas Tech basketball coach Bobby Knight. He told me that Knight wanted to be considered as our next basketball coach. He offered to send me and Jeff Long the coach's contact information including his cell phone. Apparently, Knight was chomping at the bit to get back into college coaching, and thought he could be an asset at the University of Arkansas. The trustee went on to say he thought Knight could be an immediate solution for enthusiasm and excitement at Bud Walton Arena. He urged me to meet with Knight, and further informed me that Knight was not looking to make a lot of money as he was financially secure, and we could probably get him cheap!

Bobby Knight was indeed a storied basketball coach who had won many games. He was known as one of the most successful coaches in the history of the game. He had also been praised for running clean programs, and a large percentage of his student-athletes graduated with a degree.

However, there was another side to Bobby Knight. He was an outspoken and controversial figure, and famously threw a chair across the court during a basketball game where he was ejected. He had also been arrested for having a physical confrontation with a police officer. He regularly displayed volatility and allegedly grabbed the neck of one of his players during an altercation. After multiple run-ins with his president, Myles Brand, he was fired in the fall of 2000. (Brand would go on to be the president of the NCAA.)

I replied to the trustee that I appreciated his recommendation, but hiring Bobby Knight would not work. I explained there was just too much baggage to consider him. The faculty would absolutely have a fit and the media would have a field day. When Knight was hired at Texas Tech, he was opposed by a faculty group that was quite vocal. The university would be subjected to absolute disdain and national criticism. I told the trustee that I would be very much opposed to even considering him. Knight had very little respect for university administration, and I thought hiring him as our basketball coach would be a blackeye for our institution. It could end in disaster.

I was, of course, very concerned the trustee might push the matter and it could become public and a huge problem. Knight still had quite a following in Indiana and Texas, and I suspected many Razorback fans would welcome him as our coach. I could see a groundswell of support for his candidacy. Jeff Long was also very much opposed to the idea and didn't want anything to do with hiring him.

Fortunately, the trustee dropped the matter, and it was not pursued. We dodged a bullet.

Ten days later on March 23, 2011, Mike Anderson was hired as the new basketball coach. Rumors had been spreading, even before the dismissal of coach Pelphrey, that Anderson would be tapped. Anderson had been the coach at the University of Missouri since 2006. But he spent 17 seasons as an assistant coach under the "40 minutes of hell" that fans had been desperately asking for since Nolan Richardson's departure in 2002. Anderson's overall record was 200–98 in nine seasons as a head coach at The University of Alabama-Birmingham and Missouri. He has made the NCAA tournament five times, reached the Sweet 16 twice, and the Elite Eight once. The fans were beating down the door to bring him back to Arkansas.

I attended a Razorback baseball game in Little Rock before we offered the job to Anderson where several trustees were present in a box next to mine. The lobbying was off the map. Every trustee present put heavy pressure on me to name Anderson as the next coach. They did not want a search, and had made up their minds that Anderson was the first and only choice. "Get it done," I was told. Of course, NCAA and SEC rules prohibit trustees from interfering with hiring and firing of coaches, but that didn't stop our board members. It was made clear to me that they had decided who they wanted and were not going to take no for an answer. Fortunately, Long was positive toward Anderson, but needed a few days to at least check out a few more potential candidates. I was pushing Anderson, but Long had a few lingering reservations early in the process. He asked me to give him a couple more days to come to closure.

I was getting a haircut when Jeff Long called my cell phone to tell me Anderson had accepted the job. I was elated and knew the fan base and the board of trustees would be as well. Ron Childers of The Headwaiter shop off the Fayetteville square had cut my hair for many years as well as Jane's. He also had Jeff Long as a client. We jokingly called him the "barber to the stars," since he had so many well-known customers. When I hung up the phone from Long, I decided to let Ron in on the secret of Anderson accepting our offer. Later the media asked me where I was when I got the news that he had accepted and told them I was at The Headwaiter getting my hair cut. A TV news crew promptly rolled up to Ron Childers' shop to interview him as the first Razorback fan to learn the news. Ron got his 15 minutes of fame that day!

Former basketball standout and future university trustee Tommy Boyer was putting pressure on Long to look at coaches who Long did not believe would ever come to Arkansas, but as a courtesy to Boyer, tried to contact a few of them. After the announcement of Anderson, Boyer would send me a note saying that Arkansas just hired a top 50 coach, apparently his way of expressing displeasure.

Jane and I invited dear friends Jodi and Mel Melhorn from Harrison, Arkansas, to accompany us to the announcement of Anderson as our new head coach. The announcement was held in Bud Walton Arena and was attended by over 5,000 fans. It was electrically charged, and the fans were on fire. It was obvious the fan base was ecstatic for Anderson and cheered and called the hogs as never before. After the announcement, which was carried live on most of the TV networks and many radio stations, we accompanied our friends to a local eating establishment, Hugo's, off the Fayetteville square. I let Jane and our friends out of the car and went to find a parking place. As I entered Hugo's, a packed lunch crowd gave me a spontaneous standing ovation. At first, I looked behind me to try to determine who they were clapping for, until it dawned on me that I was the subject of their glee. That was how happy and pleased the fan base was that Mike Anderson was returning to Fayetteville as our head basketball coach.

Of course, nothing is forever. Mike lasted eight years, but was fired in 2019 by a new athletics director, Hunter Yurachek. Anderson went 169–102 with the Razorbacks. The Razorbacks made five postseason tournaments on his watch—three trips to the NCAA and two to the NIT. Arkansas went 18–16 that season and reached the second round of the NIT. Anderson had a career record of 369–200. He went 111–57 in five seasons at Missouri, including NCAA appearances in each of his last three years. He went 89–41 at UAB from 2002–2005, and never posted a losing season in 17 years as a head coach.

But it wasn't enough. The fans and the board wanted more. That's the way big-time sports works, whether professional or collegiate. You have to win and win big. The explosion of coaching salaries over the last 20 years has produced an absolute necessity to win. If an institution is going to pay that kind of money, they must demand wins and lots of them.

Is it fair? Probably not! But I was part of the problem as I authorized the huge salaries during my time as chancellor. It has all gotten way out of hand, to the point of absurdity. But what is one to do? What is the solution? We keep feeding the alligator in hopes it will eat us last. It is against the law for SEC chancellors and presidents to try to curb the rise in salaries through collusion.

Mike would go on to become St. John's University head coach and be named Big East coach of the year in 2021. That same year he was given a six-year contract extension.

Jane and I were very sad to see Mike and Marcheita Anderson leave Arkansas.

Mike Anderson still has never had a losing season.

CHAPTER 70
OPEN DOOR

> *An open-door policy doesn't do much for a closed mind.*
>
> — AUTHOR BOB NELSON

When I became chancellor, I wanted to have an open-door policy. I wanted any faculty member, staff member or student to feel comfortable coming to see me about any issue. Because of my busy calendar it might take several days to schedule an appointment, but I wanted university constituents to feel comfortable visiting my office.

During my seven years as chancellor I had a steady flow of folks in and out of my office. I would always tell them that, if their issue involved another university official, then I would need to contact that individual after the meeting. While I wanted to be available to anyone, I also felt it important to be certain that those persons coming to see me knew I would not make a decision without involving the university officer in charge of the appropriate area.

I would regularly have disgruntled staff or faculty members, as well as students, come to see me about various issues, and it could be burdensome at times. My office staff wanted to screen people who wanted to see me, and send them to other staff members, but that was not my style. There were days I should have taken their advice. However, I felt strongly that anyone should avail themselves of the opportunity to meet with the chancellor. I have known many university presidents who disagreed with that position, but for me it just seemed like the right thing to do.

Early on in my administration an international student came to see me. His name was Qusay Alfaori. Qusay was originally from the Kingdom of Jordan and was an outstanding student. He had no agenda and told me that he just wanted to meet the chancellor of his university before he graduated. He would stop by the office multiple times while I was chancellor. Later we would become close friends.

He even brought his father and grandfather by to see me, and we had a delightful visit. At the time his father was an instructor in the Fulbright college. His grandfather lived in Jordan and spoke no English. He was a stately man from a prominent family in Jordan and arrived at my office in Jordanian garb. He brought me a beautiful Jordanian robe and other accoutrements as well as many other gifts from the old country.

Qusay knew what he wanted to do with his life from a very early age. He wanted to be a physician, and was hoping to go to medical school and study to be a brain surgeon. He was a straight A student at the University of Arkansas and was enrolled in biomedical engineering, a relatively new program at the university. He was articulate, very presentable, and many times would wear a coat and tie when he would come to see me. I was impressed with him.

In his senior year, Qusay began applying to medical schools. He was interested, at that time, in enrolling at the University of Arkansas Medical School, but applied to several other medical schools around the country. He had taken the MCAT test and did very well. He seemed to me to have all of the ingredients to make an excellent physician. He asked me to serve as a reference and I did so happily.

A number of students interested in medical and law school would ask me to assist them by being a reference. If I knew them reasonably well, I would always agree. If I did not know the student, I would spend an hour or so with them getting to know them and then would look at their transcript and talk with the head of student affairs. I just wanted to be certain the student was capable of meeting the rigors of law or medical school and didn't have any serious disciplinary issues. Many of the students who asked me to serve as a reference were international students.

Good friends Loy and Qusay Alfaori, former students at the UA, on the occasion of Qusay getting his white coat from Texas Tech Medical School.

I became aware international students were having a very difficult time accessing American medical schools. In fact, if they did not have a green card it was virtually impossible to get into a medical school in the United States. I suppose that made sense, but I regretted it very much as most of the students were quite qualified. But, even with a green card, I began to realize obtaining a spot in an American medical school was most difficult for international students. I learned that, if an international student with a green card was accepted to medical school, many times they had to pay for all four years of medical school up front. That was a clear deterrent to most of the international students and seemed unfair and discriminatory to me.

At the time Qusay did not have a green card, but had applied for one and was waiting for a decision. It seemed as if it was taking forever for him to obtain a green card from the federal government. I offered to assist him by contacting members of our congressional delegation. Our congressman, Steve Womack was particularly helpful and used his contacts to speed things along. Finally, after many months of doubt, Qusay received his green card.

The first time he applied for medical school at UAMS he was put on a waitlist. He was told that, if he would commit to working in a rural area in Arkansas for multiple years after graduation as a general practitioner, he could be admitted. He struggled with the decision, but felt strongly that he wanted to be a surgeon and turned down the offer. I wasn't sure he did the right thing. He would spend the next two years applying to medical schools across the country.

Some of his friends who had lower board scores and grade point averages, but were Caucasian and American citizens were able to get into medical school. It was very frustrating for Qusay and for me, as well as his professors, who knew he was an outstanding student.

While waiting on a decision on medical school, he decided to get his PhD. He was able to get his doctorate in two years, one of the shortest time frames for any graduate student in the history of the university. His PhD was in biomedical engineering and his major professor was the former provost of the university, Dr. Ashok Saxena. He invited me to attend the session where he would present his dissertation, and I was extraordinarily impressed. Unfortunately, one of the professors on his committee objected to the timeframe it took for him to get his degree, but the overall committee passed him with flying colors.

After applying to medical schools and being rejected several times he decided to retake the MCAT and improve his scores. By all measures he had excellent scores to begin with, but he wanted to do everything he could to access medical school. After a series of rejections, he decided to move to Texas and become a Texas resident so that he could apply to Texas medical schools, since there were so many in the state. Finally, he was accepted into medical school at Texas Tech University. At the time of this writing he is in his second year of medical school, and I'm told he has stellar grades. I'm confident he will make a superb surgeon.

Having participated in the application process for Qusay and many other students, I have become convinced that being accepted to medical school for international students is a crapshoot. There seems to be no rhyme or reason why these superb students are not given an opportunity to become a physician. Medical schools will tell you that one of the reasons so few students gain admission is because of the relatively small number of residencies available. However, I firmly believe there is discrimination against students from foreign countries, even if their credentials are superior to other students who are admitted. There is a great deal of evidence supporting this issue. Permanent U.S. residents, those who hold a green card, may apply to U.S. medical schools on the same basis and through the same mechanisms as any U.S. citizen. Foreign nationals on student visas who have been educated partly or fully in the United States have very limited options and an extremely difficult, if not impossible, hurdle to gain admission to medical school.

According to an article by Missouri State: "Generally, publicly-supported or publicly-assisted medical schools admit very few to no foreign nationals. Among private medical schools, the policies and numbers of students accepted vary. About 50 of the 126 U.S. medical schools state in their admissions policies that they will accept foreign nationals who otherwise meet admissions requirements.

When one examines the numbers of applicants, these represent a small percentage of the 38,000 medical school applicants and 22,000 medical school matriculants. Of these, most private medical schools will accept competitive applicants only if they pay for their schooling in advance."

Azan Zahir Virji, a Harvard-educated student from Tanzania, wrote an article for the Association of American Medical Colleges (AAMC) where he had this to say about international students accessing U.S. medical schools:

> "If your end goal is to be a physician, you should not go to the United States for college. This was the advice I received as a high school student in Tanzania while considering where to apply to college. My advisor made it clear that my chances of being accepted to a U.S. medical school were slim, predominantly because very few schools accepted international students. Moreover, as a low-income student, my advisor warned me that a medical degree in the United States was financially inaccessible. I decided to take my chances anyway." He would vow that "if I ever got into medical school, I would do my part to ensure that the next generation of immigrant doctors felt supported, received the guidance they needed to apply, and had people they could look up to."

And then there is this from Amherst College:

> "It is significantly more difficult for international students to be admitted to medical school in the U.S. to train as medical doctors, even if those students have graduated with good records from a U.S. college or university. A significantly smaller number of U.S. medical schools will consider applications from students who are not U.S. citizens or permanent residents. Among those medical schools that may consider international applicants, an even smaller number offer any scholarship aid. International students are not eligible for the government or non-government loans that

most U.S. citizens and permanent residents use to finance their medical educations. When a U.S. medical school does accept an international applicant, the school often demands payment of up to four years of tuition before the student is allowed to begin; the cost can exceed $200,000."

In 2022, Alice Walton announced she was going to partner with the renowned Cleveland Clinic and Washington Regional Medical Center in Fayetteville to create a regional health system to improve health outcomes across Northwest Arkansas and beyond. The announcement followed the news last year of a joint initiative through the Alice L. Walton Foundation and Cleveland Clinic to identify ways to provide access to Cleveland Clinic's renowned specialty care services in Northwest Arkansas. The initiative was formed after a study highlighted that area residents frequently leave the region in order to receive specialty care.

Through these two initiatives, the Alice L. Walton Foundation and Washington Regional Medical System intend to work with Cleveland Clinic to support the growth of health care services in the region.

In 2020, Walton announced the formation of the Whole Health Institute, and in 2021 she announced the formation of the Whole Health School of Medicine and Health Sciences. Both of these organizations, based in Bentonville, Arkansas, focus on redesigning the systems that impact health and well-being with the goal of making whole health accessible and affordable to all.

The one question many were asking was why the University of Arkansas for Medical Sciences campus in Northwest Arkansas was left out of the equation. Strong rumor has circulated that the Walton interests may have found it difficult to deal with UAMS and the University of Arkansas System, and this frustration led to partnering with other entities. If so, it is a huge disappointment for the University of Arkansas System.

CHAPTER 71
UNDOCUMENTED

> *Education is the gateway to the American Dream. But today our immigration laws make higher education—a virtual requirement for financial security—out of reach for more than one million undocumented students.*
>
> — WENDY KOPP

Jane and I had been invited to have dinner with a trustee at his home while I was chancellor. During dinner he asked me about undocumented students and wanted to know why they get in-state tuition. He didn't think that was right, and that only U.S. citizens should be allowed to get in-state tuition. He felt very strongly about the issue. I tried hard to explain our position, and that we give in-state tuition to anyone who graduated from an Arkansas high school. He said he planned to talk to Governor Beebe about the issue and thought it should be changed. I asked him not to do it and gave him and his wife all of the reasons why it would be a bad idea and hurt several young people who grew up in Arkansas and just wanted a higher education.

Soon after the dinner our campus was informed by the Arkansas

Department of Higher Education that, if we allowed undocumented students to pay in-state tuition, we were potentially at odds with federal law. I remembered the dinner with the UA trustee and wondered if that was what caused the governor to make the change. Before that, if undocumented students graduated from a bona fide Arkansas high school, and satisfied the necessary academic requirements, they were permitted to enter the university and pay in-state tuition. Now a student had to have a social security card and number in order to get in-state tuition. This was a huge change, which would be deleterious to many students.

An investigation determined we had a number of students enrolled who did not possess social security numbers and could be described as "unauthorized immigrants"—or what others might call illegal aliens.

But from our perspective, they were not aliens. They were from Arkansas—they had the high school degrees and transcripts to prove it. Now they were suddenly faced with having to pay out-of-state tuition, and there was a possibility—even probability—that most would have to drop out due to the increased expenses.

On the other hand, by choosing to support these students, and speak out for them, we risked immediately alienating a vocal segment of university stakeholders who felt unauthorized immigrants had no place in this country, not to mention our university. I also figured a number of legislators would be very much opposed to giving these students in-state tuition.

Ultimately, we decided to seek private funding to pay the substantial difference between in-state and out-of-state tuition for those students already enrolled at the University of Arkansas.

That the parents of these students broke the law was never in question. The justice of punishing their children was, in my mind. By and large, these students actually have lived in the state of Arkansas most of their lives, brought here from Mexico or Central and South America when they were very young. They have played on their Arkansas high school football and basketball teams, and they have been cheerleaders and band members.

Students like Jonathan Chavez, who graduated from Rogers high school with a 4.0 GPA and was a member of our Honors College—just a tremendous and hard-working young man who had earned his seat in the classroom. All he wanted was to be able to earn an education. He just wanted to be an educated man.

In January 2011 Jonathan took a Greyhound bus to Florida to visit his mother during winter break. When he stepped off the bus, he was immediately arrested by U.S. immigration and customs enforcement agents. We worked diligently to prevent his being deported and finally federal immigration authorities notified him that his case had been closed. Jonathan was a top scholar majoring in music. He had a phenomenal operatic voice and, strangely enough, while he was not a U.S. citizen, both of his parents were lawful permanent residents.

Many undocumented students are honors students, and all have become integrated into the social fabric of the community in which they grew up. For the most part, they speak English with an Arkansas accent. They think of themselves as Americans, not as citizens of their parents' country of origin. The fact that their parents entered the United States illegally many years ago is no fault of their own, though they live in constant fear of deportation. For all intents and purposes, they have been residents of this state, even if they have not been citizens of this country.

I also think it is important to note that we never suggested they get preferential treatment—just fair treatment. They are not taking another student's place—which is usually the concern in these kinds of situations—and they are not enrolled here at the expense of an American citizen. The University of Arkansas had the capacity to accept more qualified students, and we were working our hardest to do so, just like most other public universities in Arkansas. That's why we believed these students should be afforded the same opportunities as every other hard-working, academically eligible resident of Arkansas who has the right to attend state colleges and universities and pay the same price as their neighbor.

So here we see where diversity and social equity intersect. And we must ask ourselves: are we a mirror of our state, and if not, why not? According to the Pew Hispanic Center, there are approximately

144,000 Latinos in Arkansas, only half of whom were born abroad. They have created a rich and vibrant community in our midst. By and large, they are good neighbors. This population has a low crime rate and a high rate of home ownership. They have both a strong work ethic and strong family values. And they have a high regard for education. Quite simply, Northwest Arkansas would not be where it is today without them. Allowing these students equal access to a college education is also an issue of good public policy.

Latino youth represent an important part of the region's human capital. In a generation, a quarter of all Americans are expected to be Latino. We need to be integrating these students into our society as quickly and deeply as possible, not fighting to keep them out.

I also don't understand why we should have one standard for public schools, and another for higher education. Existing U.S. law is clear: Undocumented students have the same right to attend public elementary and secondary schools as do U.S. citizens and legal permanent residents. The Supreme Court made that case law many years ago. Why is there a different standard for higher education? Critics might argue that allowing these students to enroll will only encourage further illegal immigration—that it rewards their parents' crimes.

I certainly do not condone illegal immigration, and we should always obey the laws of the land. But the reality is, on a national level our immigration policy does not seem to be working, and much stronger prevention measures are needed to halt the flow of illegal immigrants. Punishing their children, a decade after the fact, is not going to fix the problem, but might, I think, do more damage than good to our community and our state. These are our friends and neighbors now. I think we should give them a hand up, rather than a push aside, which will only create more problems and resentment. Our university, and our society, will be stronger for it. Again, my point is that, in this instance, diversity follows social equity. If we are not as diverse as an institution as we are as a state or a society, then we may have a social imbalance.

Here is what is factual about undocumented people:

- They have created rich and vibrant communities in our midst.
- By and large they are extraordinarily good neighbors.
- This population has a very low crime rate and a high rate of home ownership.
- They have both a strong work ethic and strong family values.
- They have a high regard for education and religious values.
- Latino youth represent an important part of the nation's human capital.
- And, contrary to some opinions, they pay taxes, including income taxes.

Those are undisputed facts. We need to be integrating these young people into our society as quickly as possible, not fighting to keep them out.

It wasn't so long ago that many Black students didn't feel particularly welcome on our campus, and only a few decades earlier that Silas Hunt became the first African American in modern times to enroll in the university. I can clearly remember Black people being confined to the balconies of movie theaters, and not being able to use the same water fountains and bathrooms as white people. I remember the widespread use of racist slurs, malicious jokes, and the pervasive atmosphere of intimidation and intolerance.

This injustice has been addressed by courts of law, but the effects still linger, even years later. That also is something we worked very hard to address—not just allowing an underrepresented student a place, but letting them know they are welcomed and encouraged. I did not want to see a repetition of this with our Latino students, though obviously the illegal status of their parents makes the situation much grayer. Ultimately if we are to be a mirror of our society, then we must mirror its best face. We should mirror our society's virtues, and not its shortcomings—virtues such as: equality, justice, compassion, opportunity, respect and collaboration. When you look at the university, that's what you should see.

Diversity makes the unusual familiar and the intolerable understandable. It turns strangers into friends and humanizes behaviors and practices that otherwise seem foreign or upsetting. Diversity increases the measure of understanding in this world, the quality of compassion, and the level of tolerance and respect. Diversity illuminates the darkness of ignorance and diminishes the unsettling threats of the unknown.

The decision to disallow undocumented students to obtain in-state tuition came from Governor Beebe. His ruling surprised me greatly. I saw him as a humanist who respected everyone's right to an education. He believed in ideas of freedom and democracy and civil rights. It just didn't make sense to me that he would implement such a restrictive policy.

I then learned that, while he was attorney general of Arkansas before he was governor, he issued an attorney general's opinion that said if you gave in-state tuition to an undocumented student you would need to give it to any citizen of the United States under the equal protection clause of the constitution, regardless of the state they came from.

I immediately contacted faculty at the law school and asked them to do a brief for me about the governor's interpretation of the law. Professor Elizabeth Young was an immigration scholar and agreed to lay out her interpretation of the law. A few weeks later I received a lengthy brief from her indicating that Governor Beebe's interpretation of the law, in his AG's opinion, was not "good law." I sent it to the Governor through my vice chancellor for government relations, Richard Hudson, to be certain he received it. I didn't get a reply, so I called his office and asked for an appointment. I talked with Alan Sugg about the issue, and he told me that he suspected some of our trustees might not be happy with my opinion, which did not agree with the governor. However, Sugg did not call me off of the issue, and told me to do what I thought was right. I was grateful to Dr. Sugg for his support, although he never publicly made a statement about the issue. Chancellors and presidents don't like to speak publicly on issues that are controversial.

Recently I ran across an article in *The Chronicle of Higher Educa-*

tion, written by the president of Trinity Washington University, Patricia McGuire. Trinity is a Catholic-affiliated institution of approximately 1,800 students in Washington D.C. Her words resonated with me and I kept the article to share with my students. She said:

> "College presidents rarely speak out on issues that they consider too political for fear of alienating donors or governors or state legislators who might retaliate by withdrawing funding. This fear of making some powerful people angry—a fear of losing money—has debilitated not only the voice but also the real purpose of higher education, as the place where students should develop critical and moral reasoning habits that will serve them well in future positions of responsibility. If we presidents shrink from telling the truth out of fear of alienating people whose favor we crave, what are we teaching our students."

I was ushered into the governor's inner office for my appointment, and the governor was sitting there with seven staff members. It was intimidating. He listened to my briefing, asked a few questions—but it was obvious to me that he had not read the law school brief. He said I needed to convince his legal counsel, Tim Gauger, first, before he would consider making a policy change. The meeting was very short. I looked over to the governor's lawyer and said I would like to meet with him as soon as possible. I never heard from him. I tried several times to get an appointment, sent him letters and the legal brief again, but nothing. It was obvious to me that he was not going to advise the governor to make a change, and really didn't want to be bothered with my arguments.

On April 13, 2013, I sent Gauger one last letter to try to get him to come around on the issue. I had heard through the grapevine that he was not opposed to our arguments, and was encouraged to try one last time. I sent him a copy of Bill Schwab's book on the Dream Act, bipartisan legislation proposed in 2001 to address undocumented youth brought to the U.S. as children. I told Gauger the governor's policy essentially prevented these youth from obtaining a baccalaureate degree, and that every year hundreds of students were unable to fulfill dreams of attending college because they are required to pay out-of-state tuition and cannot afford it. I said this would be my final appeal for the governor to lift the decision requiring undocumented students to pay out-of-state tuition. I reminded Gauger the governor had said that, if I could convince his general counsel, he would act. I ended with a statement that the governor needed to be on the right side of history on this issue.

I never received the courtesy of a reply.

It was always uncanny to me that public officials did not feel they needed to answer questions from their citizenry, particularly when it was a prominent citizen like a public university chancellor. When you get to the top of the ivory tower, all folks below seem quite small. A good friend of mine who was the president of another SEC school told me that governors in particular don't like putting their thoughts in writing on controversial affairs. They don't want to be accused of anything controversial years down the road so they just ignore a reply. It is their modus operandi.

The issue did not go away, and literally hundreds of undocumented students in Arkansas, and thousands across the United States, were unable to go to college because they could not afford out-of-state tuition. It was a tragedy of Herculean proportions in my mind. We tried to help as many as we could with private gift support, but we simply could not support them all. I met with several of these students who just wanted a college degree. They cried in my office, and many felt their lives would not progress because of their inability to get a college education. They would not be able to access the American opportunity system.

In 2012 we decided to organize a program we called "Living in the Shadows in America." We held the event at the Town Center in Fayetteville on April 23, 2012, and opened it to the public. Over 1,000 people attended with standing room only.

Five young, undocumented immigrants addressed the crowd about their experiences as an undocumented person in the United States. It was a nationally relevant exchange about the experiences and challenges faced by illegal aliens who spent much, if not most, of their lives living in the United States. We received much national recognition in media outlets.

I began the session by saying that, regardless of one's feelings about immigration reform or the proposed Dream Act, we have a duty as citizens and as a university to learn more about the immigrant experience. More than two million young people were living illegally in the United States, nearly all of them brought to this country by their parents at a very early age. Most of them have attended, or are attending, elementary and secondary schools in this country. Over 65,000 of them graduate from American high schools each year. Many of them want to go to college in the United States, but because of personal factors and immigration status, most of them can't afford to do so.

The five panelists taking part in the discussion were brought by their parents to the U.S. at a young age and some of them did not have any connections or recollection of the country in which they were born. Two panelists were students who grew up in Arkansas; the other three panelists were recent college graduates who grew up in Massachusetts, New York, and Virginia, respectively. Their undocumented immigration status makes travel within the U.S. difficult and risky, and their ability to seek employment legally precarious.

The panelists were taking a significant risk by making themselves so publicly visible and we greatly appreciated their bravery and willingness to share their stories. They could have been arrested and ultimately deported. At that time the Fayetteville Police and UA Police were supportive of our work on the issues and provided safety for the persons who participated. If we had held the event in Springdale or Rogers, they very well might have been arrested.

We felt those who attended the event gained a much better insight into the experiences and challenges young undocumented immigrants deal with.

We had a significant police presence at the event. Fayetteville police had always been very helpful and cooperative on immigration issues, and some of our university police officers were of Hispanic heritage. Prior to the event we had a bomb squad do a sweep of the venue and restricted access for 24 hours preceding the event. We thought that we might have some protestors outside the building during the session, so we made arrangements to have designated protest areas cordoned off. The platform party was told to leave the venue as soon as the event was over for safety and security.

We debated whether we should have metal detectors at the event but decided that might be a cause of concern for attendees and decided against it.

Our police contacted national and statewide immigration authorities and none of them had any interest in detaining any of the panelists. They told our police that they were not at all concerned about the panelists, all of whom had been in the U.S. for many years and had no criminal activity. They said they had much bigger priorities.

We did receive a very threatening email from an LSU graduate who worked for an oil company in Little Rock. He had previously had a brush with the law for disorderly conduct and he had a concealed weapons permit. Our police tracked him down and determined him not to be a credible threat.

At the end of the event, a person in the audience rushed the stage and tried to grab the microphone. Fortunately he was intercepted by a UA police officer and kept from reaching the stage. Other than that episode we had no other problems at the event. However, after the event I began receiving a number of threats through the mail—and even by way of emails that were profane and insulting.

Over the course of seven years as chancellor I would receive a number of threats to my personal safety that required more than a brush off, so these latest threats were nothing new. It is, unfortunately, just part of the job.

A few of the emails and letters had to be taken seriously as they wished bodily harm on me, my family and others. Some in particular caused university police to post an armed officer outside my office and keep our office door locked. The campus police would also beef up patrols around Fowler House.

A student had been dismissed for making threats that he would "cause another Virginia Tech," and the police were very concerned he would show up at our office brandishing a weapon. They installed a security system under the desk of one of our assistants, which would notify police to come quickly to the chancellor's office. The police even asked me to notify my extended family about this particular person, and to just be generally cautious. We finally had to ban the former student from coming on campus. The student sued me and the university in federal court for discrimination, claiming he had a disability. The complaint was dismissed as well as the appeal.

I did receive a few letters and emails from conservative members of the General Assembly, all Republicans, expressing dissatisfaction with the event, and essentially telling me to keep my mouth shut about issues of immigration. I have no doubt they were stirred up by one legislator in particular: Jon Hubbard. Hubbard would write me multiple letters about the event and expressed his opinion that, by holding the event, we were in violation of the law by harboring criminals. I responded politely to Hubbard with explanations until his emails and letters became threatening and obnoxious.

Hubbard was a first-term Republican from the Jonesboro area at the time, and was well known to have some very peculiar thoughts on a number of issues. In his book, *Letters to the Editor: Confessions of a Frustrated Conservative*, Hubbard wrote:

> "... the institution of slavery that the black race has long believed to be an abomination upon its people may actually have been a blessing in disguise. The blacks who could endure those conditions and circumstances would someday be rewarded with citizenship in the greatest nation ever established upon the face of the Earth."

Talking about school integration, Hubbard described Black students as having "a lack of discipline and ambition," which he said "has hurt the entire educational system." He further stated that Black people don't "appreciate the value of a good education." Then he discussed immigration in his book, asserting that the Christians in America are likened to Germans in the era of Adolf Hitler, and saying, "the immigration issue, both legal and illegal ... will lead to planned wars or extermination. Although now this seems to be barbaric and uncivilized, it will at some point become as necessary as eating and breathing."

Hubbard began copying a large number of conservative legislators on his emails to me which sparked a flurry of emails bashing me and the university for holding the event. Some called on me to resign and asked the board of trustees to fire me. Hubbard also appealed to the attorney general to open an investigation about criminal activity that he alleged I committed by holding the forum. Shane Broadway, interim director of the Department of Higher Education, told me not to worry about the attorney general of Arkansas as he has no authority to investigate or have an opinion on any topic of federal law. Besides, Attorney General Dustin McDaniel was a good friend of mine and a Democrat.

In 2012 Hubbard won the Republican primary but was defeated in the general election by Democrat Harold Copenhaver.

We received so many letters from conservative legislators that Judy Schwab decided to develop a model of the response we were sending to all those who have written expressing their displeasure with the event. The letter follows:

> Dear:
> Thank you for your message. Please be assured that the April 23 event does not include, promote, or engage in illegal activity. The statute you referred to is not intended to address a person's participation in an educational activity such as our April 23 event. To be clear, the April 23 panel discussion provides our students and the general public a valuable learning experience. As you know, the issues surrounding undocumented immigrants are complex. For example, undocumented young people are legally entitled to attend public elementary and secondary schools in this country. The U.S. Supreme Court affirmed undocumented immigrants' right to a public education nearly three decades ago.

The courts have also affirmed First Amendment protections for undocumented immigrants, including the right to participate in an event such as the April 23 panel. At the same time, undocumented immigrants also have a number of obligations under U.S. and state laws. For example, the IRS requires undocumented immigrants to register for a taxpayer identification number, known as an ITIN, to enable the government to tax their income. Undocumented immigrants have to pay sales and property taxes as well. These are just a few examples of the legal expectations and recognitions our government has in place which recognize and address the presence of undocumented immigrants.

The public discourse in Arkansas and the U.S. about immigration laws and reform is being led primarily by newspaper commentators, talk show hosts, and TV pundits. However, relatively little attention has been paid to the unique situation facing young immigrants who, by no fault or action of their own, were brought to this country as children. Many of them have no recollection of life in the country of their birth. Many of them have no family connections there as well. Many of them are fluent only in English, a language that may not be spoken where they were born. They grew up in the United States, saying the Pledge of Allegiance each school day alongside classmates. Their sense of identity was shaped in this country, just as yours and mine were.

For these and other reasons, we believe our students and others would benefit from hearing first-hand about the experiences of young, undocumented immigrants. It will be educational, regardless of whether one agrees or disagrees with what they share or not. Exposure to their unique perspectives can help us all make better, more informed decisions as we exercise our civic responsibilities.

Thank you again for your message.

Sadly, the statewide paper, the *Arkansas Democrat Gazette* decided not to cover the event, even after numerous requests that they attend. We got word the decision came from senior leadership in Little Rock, and local ADG reporters were prohibited from attending, even though several expressed a desire to do so. One of their star reporters informed me directly that they were told not to attend and not to write about the event. It was a huge platform on a national topic of great importance, but the paper made a definitive decision to refrain from covering it. I suspected the paper decided it did not want to cover a forum that their publisher did not agree with.

I was very disappointed no one from the *Arkansas Democrat-Gazette* attended the session and covered it. This was a major event in Arkansas, with legislators, representatives from the governor's office, higher education officials, people watching on the web from around the nation and 1,000 concerned citizens in attendance from throughout Arkansas and beyond—and the ADG didn't even show up. I thought an editor's or reporter's personal positions about issues were not supposed to influence the actual coverage of news and events.

So much for fair and balanced reporting.

The "Statement of Core Values" espoused by *Arkansas Democrat Gazette* publisher, Walter Hussman, and appearing on page two of every issue of all of his newspapers, states, "Impartiality means reporting, editing, and delivering the news honestly, fairly and objectively and without personal opinion and bias. Credibility is the greatest asset of any news medium, and impartiality is the greatest source of credibility."

The journalism faculty at The University of North Carolina, Chapel Hill, Hussman's alma mater, have overwhelmingly objected to Hussman's core values being chiseled in granite at the entryway of Carroll Hall for students and faculty to see every day. It all stemmed from the unfortunate controversy surrounding Nikole Hannah-Jones, a prominent Pulitzer-prize-winning investigative journalist, who was denied tenure because of the objections of Hussman, who had given the School of Journalism $25 million to be named for him, most to be paid at his and his wife's death.

Hussman had criticized Hannah-Jones' opinions on the 1619 project, which focused on and re-examined slavery in the United States. After threatening a lawsuit, the trustees reversed their decision and offered her tenure, but she turned it down and accepted a position at Howard University. The campus exploded and journalism faculty signed a statement condemning the handling of her tenure position and hiring. In 2021 the National Association of Black Journalists gave UNC-Chapel Hill and Hussman its annual "Thumbs Down Award" for efforts that went against the mission of the organization.

Some of the criticism we received was that we did not give both sides of the debate at the forum. We never billed the event as a debate. We always maintained that it was for the purpose of hearing the unique perspectives of undocumented young people affected by our immigration laws.

One person was upset that we didn't include American citizens on the panel. Given that the event's theme was, "What's it like to grow up in America but not be an American?" you wouldn't expect to have American-born residents offering their perspectives. Similarly, you would not have wealthy individuals sharing their perspectives as part of a panel on living in poverty, or civilians participating with soldiers in a panel discussion of the trauma of battle. Not sure what that particular person meant.

The event was well publicized and open to anyone to attend. We did have folks from "Secure Arkansas" in attendance, a conservative organization on steroids. We gave all folks in attendance the opportunity to submit questions. We exhausted all the questions submitted by attendees, several were negative toward the Dream Act, and we did not discriminate as to the content of the questions asked. We contacted state and national organizations involved on both sides of the immigration debate (which is different from our panel's topic) and asked them to submit questions to the panel. With the exception of one rude and unenlightened question ("How fast can you pack your bags and leave?"), all questions were posed and responded to regardless of the affiliation of the person asking the question. Again, several questions came from people opposed to the Dream Act and negative toward undocumented students. We posed their questions exactly as they were given to us.

I stated early in the program that the University of Arkansas does not condone illegal immigration, but that immigration reform was a very complex issue facing our nation. I stated early in the program that I was personally in favor of the "Dream Act," which addresses—not condones—the presence of undocumented immigrants who were brought here as children.

I have personally met with hundreds of undocumented students who are not able to go to college because of their status. They may have played high school football, perhaps were a cheerleader, perhaps played in the band—but cannot continue on to fulfill their dreams of being college educated. It is a tragic, sad commentary for anyone in higher education. Our purpose was to focus on these young people and their problems and issues caused by living in the shadows.

We continued to plead our support for undocumented students, and others who came here as infants and wanted to live in the United States. One of the true heroes in our quest was Dr. William Schwab, former dean of Fulbright College and a distinguished professor at the university. Bill wrote two books on the plight of the undocumented. I wrote the foreword for his first book on the subject. We sent it to every member of Congress, and received many favorable responses. Bill continues to speak on the issues and write about the difficulties undocumented people are facing in our nation. American immigration laws still have not solved the problem at this writing.

I knew I had damaged my relationship with some Republican legislators, and possibly even upset some trustees by being so visible regarding the Dream Act. But silence can be the enemy to truth and justice. What will be a counterweight to wrong thinking and discriminatory practices if higher education chooses to remain silent?

I also knew, however, that college chancellors and presidents didn't always like to be vocal on controversial issues. Most would remain quiet, not wishing to rattle the conservative network that could include donors, legislators, and even trustees. Why should I stick my neck out to have it chopped off. But how can we provide a teachable moment to our students, or how can we live with our faculty if we don't at least attempt to speak truth to power. Maybe it wasn't the wisest course of action, but as I've already said, it was in my DNA.

Less than a year later John Diamond, head of university relations, sent me an email suggesting that I convene another panel to discuss the controversial issue of guns on campus. I had already spoken before a legislative hearing in opposition to guns, and we were able to stop the legislature from enacting a law that would allow students and faculty to bring guns on our campus, a victory that would be short lived. (In 2017 the Arkansas Legislature passed Act 562 allowing individuals—who generally must be 21 or over, with limited exceptions—with concealed handgun licenses and who have successfully completed up to eight hours of enhanced certification training, to carry concealed handguns on public college campuses with the following exclusions: athletics events with approved security plans, grievance and disciplinary meetings and public daycare or K–12 facilities, such as the Jean Tyson Child Development Study Center.)

Diamond said we could use the forum as a way to position the University of Arkansas as a national thought leader and play the role of "the great convener." He was supported by his boss, Brad Choate. I must say in retrospect, I wonder if they were trying to get me in trouble by sponsoring a touchy subject again.

I rejected the idea.

CHAPTER 72
DALAI LAMA

> *Once a year, go somewhere you've never been before.*
>
> — *DALAI LAMA*

His Holiness the Dalai Lama visited the University of Arkansas in May 2011. The Dalai Lama's visit was in response to invitations from Professor Sidney Burris, director of the honors program in the J. William Fulbright College of Arts and Sciences, and Geshe Dorjee, a Tibetan monk and instructor in Fulbright College. The two met with the Dalai Lama during their trip to India in the summer of 2009. The Dalai Lama's visit was being sponsored by the university's student-funded Distinguished Lecture Series, supplemented with private donations. University of Arkansas students and faculty would have first preference for seating in Bud Walton arena. This was a huge coup for the university and would be covered by media the world over.

The Dalai Lama is a spiritual leader respected around the world for his message of compassion, peace and non-violence, and he was awarded the Nobel Peace Prize in 1989 for his non-violent struggle on behalf of the people of Tibet. In 2007, the Dalai Lama was awarded the Congressional Gold Medal by the president of the United States, George W. Bush. Having him on our campus was an incredible opportunity for our students and faculty.

Burris led a committee to plan and organize a year-long series of events leading up to the Dalai Lama's visit. The events were intended to generate awareness, inform and enhance the issues related to the lecture, and to get the campus community engaged, involved and excited about the visit. Burris described the relationship that had developed in the past four years among University of Arkansas students, faculty and the international Tibetan community as warm and inviting. Burris credited that relationship with helping to convince the Dalai Lama to accept the invitation to visit Fayetteville.

His Holiness appeared in two forums on May 11. He took part in a morning panel discussion on "Turning Swords into Ploughshares: The Many Paths of Non-Violence." He delivered his keynote address, "Non-Violence in the New Century: The Way Forward" that afternoon. Both events were in Bud Walton Arena to over-packed crowds.

In addition to the Dalai Lama, Sister Helen Prejean and Vincent Harding participated in the morning panel discussion. Prejean is most well-known for *Dead Man Walking: An Eyewitness Account of the Death Penalty in the United States*, her 1993 non-fiction account of the execution of Patrick Sonnier and Robert Willie. The book, which spent 31 weeks on *The New York Times* best-seller list, was later developed into a film starring Sean Penn and Susan Sarandon, who ultimately won an Academy Award for her performance. In 2004, Sister Helen published *The Death of Innocents: An Eyewitness Account of Wrongful Executions*, a book inspired by her certainty that several of those whose executions she witnessed were, in fact, innocent.

Vincent Harding, one of the icons of America's civil rights movement, was born in Harlem and educated at City College of New York, where he received a bachelor's degree in history, and at Columbia, where he received a master's degree in journalism. In 1965, he received his doctorate in history from The University of Chicago. In 1958, as part of an interracial pastoral team, Harding traveled to Atlanta where he met Martin Luther King Jr. Impressed by Harding, King invited him to come to the South and join the African-American Freedom movement. Accordingly, Harding and his wife Rosemarie relocated to Atlanta, where they remained for several years, contributing to the efforts that would ultimately lead to the passage of the Civil Rights Act of 1964.

With His Holiness the Dalai Lama

The University of Arkansas board of trustees awarded the Dalai Lama an honorary degree, and board chairman Carl Johnson and University of Arkansas System President Alan Sugg joined me in the presentation.

I was asked to meet the Dalai Lama at the executive airport and welcome him to Fayetteville the day before his presentations. He was extremely gracious and immediately wrapped a prayer scarf around my neck, grabbed my hands and said a prayer. We wanted to have a dinner celebrating his arrival, but were told he retires for the day at 3 p.m., and seldom eats anything past that hour.

The event was a huge success for the University of Arkansas and for our students and faculty. It was one of the highlights of my time as chancellor.

CHAPTER 73
CHANCELLOR OR PRESIDENT

> *Gearhart can be president or chancellor, but he can't be both.*
>
> — GOVERNOR MIKE BEEBE

As early as 2009 Alan Sugg started making noise that he was thinking about retirement. He asked me if I had any interest in the system job. He said some trustees had mentioned my name to him, and he had promoted my candidacy as well. I had only been at the university as chancellor for a little over a year, and really felt I would be abandoning the faculty, students and alumni if I moved to Little Rock to accept the system presidency. Alan was not definitive about his timeframe, so we simply decided to postpone any further discussion until he had decided on a retirement date. But I knew a decision was coming very soon.

Fortunately for me, two more years expired before Alan decided to step down as president of the University of Arkansas System. He had served as president for over 20 years, and felt the time had come for a new person to take over. Alan called to inform me of his decision, and said he would be retiring at the end of the fiscal year on June 30, 2011.

Naturally, I tried to talk him out of it as I knew, selfishly, that a transition would have a very real impact on my future. Alan and I had gotten along extremely well, and I had tremendous admiration for him and his superb communication skills. In my opinion, he was a great president and left the chancellors to run the campuses as they saw fit. That's not to say he wasn't involved in campus matters. He could become very involved if there was a serious issue needing his attention. But what I admired about him was his candor, and his ability to make you feel as if you were part of the team. He didn't see it as the system versus the campuses, but rather the system supporting the campuses. He told me on many occasions that there was no way he could personally run the day-to-day operations of all of the campuses. He simply had to rely on his chancellors to run their campuses. He felt that he should not interfere with their administrative decisions unless he or the board of trustees deemed those decisions wrong minded. He further said that he saw his job as supporting the campuses and helping make them strong and successful. He didn't want a large system office. He was committed to keeping the system personnel to a minimum.

Sugg again asked me if I was interested in succeeding him as president. He said I had a lot of support on the board of trustees. He did tell me a couple of the board members, while supportive of my candidacy, thought there should be a national search and that I could apply for the position. Sugg wanted to know what I thought of that. I told him it could place me in a difficult position: If I did apply for the presidency and did not receive the nod from the board of trustees, that might make it difficult for me to remain as chancellor. I told Sugg that I most likely would not apply for the job and, furthermore, I loved what I was doing as head of the flagship campus. Sugg told me he understood completely, and couldn't blame me for not wanting to throw my hat in the ring if I wasn't the assumed choice. He then said I had the full support of the chairman of the board, John Ed Anthony, and that John Ed was going to push for inviting me to be president without a search. Sugg suggested I just let things take a natural course and see what kind of support I might have on the board.

On May 11, 2010, the announcement was made that Dr. B. Alan Sugg would retire effective June 30, 2011. It was a sad day for me. I had worked so closely with Sugg, and had great admiration for his skills as president of the system, that I hated to see him step down. I knew it was inevitable and that Sugg certainly deserved a long and fruitful retirement, but I hated to see him go and knew it would have a deep impact on me personally and professionally.

The immediate question for me was whether or not I wanted to entertain succeeding him. The chairman of the board, John Ed Anthony, had been quietly talking with board members. He called me before the Sugg announcement to let me know that he had all of the board members in favor of me being the next system president. He did confirm what I already knew, that a couple of the board members thought we needed a national search, but he did not see that as serious opposition. John Ed told me those trustees wanted me to become president and would not stand in the way by demanding a national search.

I reached out to several personal and professional friends to get their thoughts on whether or not I should accept the system job. I spoke with my brothers who encouraged me to remain as chancellor. I spoke with my dear friend Roy Shilling and he was more inclined for me to accept the system job. Then I spoke with former United States Senator and university trustee, David Pryor, and asked him for advice.

Pryor told me that I was a Fayetteville boy, and he thought I could do more good in Fayetteville rather than moving to the system. He said the system was more of a political job, and even though it was higher on the totem pole, he wasn't sure I would enjoy working with the legislature. Pryor told me his general feelings about the system job were that it was more administrative in nature. He reminded me that I would have no faculty, no students like I do on the campus, and that this might frustrate me. He saw me as a doer, not someone who liked bureaucracy, and he thought I should remain in the chancellor position.

On May 12, 2010, it was late in the day and I was working at my desk thinking about heading back to Fowler House. The phone rang and it was John Ed Anthony. He told me that he had all of the votes from members of the board, and he would like to announce me as president of the system the next day. I told him that I was honored to be asked to be the system president, but felt that I needed to remain at the University of Arkansas flagship campus for at least another year, or maybe two. I asked him if there might be any way I could serve in both positions for one year, and even perhaps two years. John Ed told me he would get back to me very quickly.

I had gotten to know John Ed well, and very much appreciated his candor and leadership. He was a very likable person, and you always knew where he stood on any issue. He was a good communicator and I felt very comfortable working with him. I admired his work ethic and liked him and his lovely wife, Isabel, very much. Jane and I had socialized with them and I considered them to be friends.

John Ed called me back that evening to let me know he had spoken with the governor, and the governor said to tell Gearhart that he could be the system president, or the chancellor, but not both. Then John Ed went on to tell me that the governor did agree that I could do both jobs for one year. After one year elapsed, I would have to move to Little Rock and give up the chancellor position. After much discussion with John Ed, I agreed to this plan even though I had mixed feelings.

As I said earlier, I believe strongly that a system administration hurts the flagship campus. The possibility of merging the president and chancellor positions into one held many advantages in my mind. The real advantage of one person to head both the system and the main campus would be the building of a true, integrated system, not a holding tank of disparate and disjointed institutions. I believed the time had come for this model, followed by several universities throughout the United States, to display to the citizens of Arkansas one university geographically distributed throughout the state, working in tandem to provide educational opportunities at low cost to the people.

The merged model would allow the university to build on the strengths of each particular institution, while eliminating redundancies and intra-system competition. I believed we could truly build a university that gives each campus the opportunity to stand out and promote its particular strengths. Combining the system job with the chancellor position would streamline administration and save costs, which would resonate in today's economy. I believed very strongly that no university system can function well without a very strong flagship campus leading the way. The Fayetteville campus could truly help lead all campuses toward common goals. I believed we needed the resources and intellectual capital of the flagship campus to benefit all of the campuses in the system. It would put the University of Arkansas clearly at the top of higher education with clout and control over the education agenda. The merger would allow for the ending of internecine battles, and create less competition and more cooperation, which would be best for the citizens of Arkansas. I was naïve. The horse was out of the barn and a merger was not going to happen.

I knew there were political machinations that would make it difficult to implement such a merger. I knew that there would be opposition in many quarters. Remember, not that many years ago the head of the Fayetteville campus was the president. We did not have a chancellor in Fayetteville until around 1984, and that was accomplished because of jealousy between Northwest Arkansas and Central Arkansas. It was just too late to try and reverse engines.

As is so often the case when dealing with boards of trustees, my acceptance of the presidency with John Ed got in the hands of the media; he was not happy, and neither was I. Several news articles started appearing in various publications, including the *Arkansas Democrat-Gazette* and the *Arkansas Times* indicating that I would serve in both capacities for one year and then move to Little Rock. Fortunately, the news articles were not mean-spirited, and even the *Arkansas Times* editor, Max Brantley, wrote a favorable article on the issue. Frankly, I was surprised that Max would write a nice article, given the lawsuit he filed against the university over the Walton gift. I just figured he was still smarting over the defeat, but he rose above that issue and made many favorable comments about my candidacy.

Soon after word got out about me becoming system president, I was visited by two members of the board of trustees. Milo Shult, vice president for agriculture, had announced his retirement, and they wanted me to commit to hiring a new vice president of their choice. They didn't want a search, but wanted me to simply confer the position on their candidate. I had not even been officially named and they were already telling me who I should hire. They were very unhappy when I told them that I would conduct an open search in an effort to find the best candidate possible. Their candidate could apply.

John Ed Anthony told me we needed to announce my decision to be the next system president, as well as the decision that I would remain chancellor for one year, now that the story was in the media. We agreed that we would make the announcement the next day. I had extremely mixed feelings. Fayetteville was my home, and neither Jane nor I really wanted to move to Little Rock. Of course, we were very familiar with Little Rock and had numerous very dear friends who live there, but Fayetteville was home.

We had experienced the Little Rock scene when we lived in Conway, and enjoyed the sophistication of the state's capital city. What troubled me the most was that I had only been at the Fayetteville campus for two years, and really felt that to leave would be abandoning my constituents, both on and off the campus.

Jane and I stayed up till 2 o'clock in the morning weighing the advantages and disadvantages of taking the system job. The bottom line was that we just weren't excited about the opportunity. I felt the system job was much, much different than being the chancellor of the flagship campus. I just wasn't certain I would enjoy what seemed to be a much more bureaucratic position. There were also family considerations. My brother Jeff lived in Northwest Arkansas as did our mother. Mother was aging rapidly and leaving Fayetteville and moving to Little Rock could be difficult on her.

After endless discussion, going back and forth, Jane and I decided at 2 o'clock in the morning that I would turn down the system job, and we would stay in Fayetteville as chancellor.

The next morning, I was at my desk early and the phone rang at 7:30 a.m. It was John Ed Anthony. He began the conversation by telling me we would announce to the media that I would be the next system president on that very day, and that he had system staff members working on the media release. He told me they would be in touch with me mid-morning. As John Ed was telling me how we would proceed, I interrupted him and said that Jane and I had talked it over to the early morning hours, and had decided to remain as chancellor of the Fayetteville campus. John Ed was not happy, but was a perfect gentleman. He said that he certainly understood our decision, but was disappointed. He tried to talk me into accepting the presidency, but I told him we were very certain and definitive in our decision. He accepted the decision and said that they would most likely start a national search.

The rest of the week I beat myself up as to whether or not I had made the right choice. I knew it was somewhat of a gamble, in that I did not know who the next president would be, and whether or not that person would like the way I parted my hair. If I didn't like the next president my life could become miserable. If I had decided to become the system president at least I might be able to carve out my own future. I got along well with all of the members of the board of trustees, and felt I had their respect and support. But of course, trustees change, and who knows who might become board members in the not-too-distant future. The chairman of the board, John Ed Anthony, was a good friend and I respected him greatly. But he would be leaving the board that very year. I just didn't know what the future might bring.

The board did launch a national search for a new president, and I was asked to interview each of the candidates. Unfortunately, some of the people who applied for the position ended up jumping out of the search even after they were interviewed. One was the then current chancellor of the University of Missouri, Columbia. I thought he would make an excellent choice as the system president, but he decided to stay put at Missouri. Another candidate was Dr. John Churchill. I knew Churchill very well, as he was at Hendrix College during my tenure there. He was an outstanding person and was currently serving as president of Phi Beta Kappa. I thought his interview went extremely well, but apparently the trustees were not enamored with him. Churchill was a very sophisticated, well-spoken person, and I suspected the board was a little intimidated by him.

Another candidate was my good friend Stanley Reed. I had known Stanley for many years. and Jane and I were very good friends of the Reeds. Stanley had been on the board previously, and was chairman of the board when I was selected to be the chancellor. I personally thought he would be an excellent choice as the system head, although he did not have an academic degree. He was a lawyer, so technically he had a doctorate (JD) but that really wasn't considered to be an academic degree, but rather a professional degree, and might not be accepted by faculty. Board politics prevented his candidacy from moving forward. I regretted that very much, because Stanley was an outstanding person.

Tragically Stanley died the day after his interview for president by the board of trustees. He was headed back home, and it is assumed that he had a massive heart attack and ran off the road. Jane and I were devastated by his passing. He was a good man.

Alan Sugg came back to me again and asked if I wanted to reconsider being the system president, since the search looked to be imploding. I told him that I was absolutely flattered, but we had made our decision and would remain in Fayetteville. Again, I had very mixed feelings.

Jane and I took a trip east with Greg and Hannah Lee, dear friends of ours. Greg had retired from Tyson Foods as the president of their international division, but part of his retirement package was use of the Tyson jet for a period of time after retirement. We had a wonderful trip through Massachusetts and Maine.

We were in Kennebunkport, Maine when I got a telephone call from Alan Sugg. He informed me they were now looking at Dr. Donald Bobbitt as a potential candidate for president. Bobbitt was currently serving as provost at The University of Texas, Arlington. He had previously been the dean of the Fulbright College at Fayetteville, and I knew him very well. In fact, I had invited Bobbitt to be my provost when I became chancellor. He said he very much would like to accept the job—but then suddenly decided to go to Texas.

Frankly, I was not happy that he told me he would remain at Fayetteville and then changed his mind.

Alan Sugg asked me what I thought about his candidacy for president of the system. I told Sugg that there may be some criticism that Bobbitt had never been a university president or chancellor, and that he was moving from a provost position to a system job. I had some reservations about his experience level for the system job. In my heart I didn't think he was ready to assume the position, and was hoping the board could find a sitting president to take the job.

Sugg asked me if I could live with Bobbitt as president and I told him that I could. Sugg said he could scuttle the choice if I had problems with the selection. I told him that I did not have a problem with Bobbitt, even though I wasn't certain he was prepared to take on the vast responsibility of the system presidency. I was on vacation and frankly, didn't really want to deal with the matter, so I told Sugg that I was OK with the selection. In truth, I did have some reservations but did not try to intervene. The system was having trouble finding a suitable president and needed to decide soon. I felt bad that I had accepted the job and then changed my mind, and did not feel I should be in a position to interfere with the selection process. Bobbitt was offered the job and accepted immediately. I had a new boss.

PART VIII
CHANCELLOR, THE LATER YEARS

2012–2015

In the end it's not the years in your life that count. It's the life in your years.

— ABRAHAM LINCOLN

CHAPTER 74
DIVISION OF AGRICULTURE

> *Let us in education dream of an aristocracy of achievement rising out of a democracy of opportunity.*
>
> — THOMAS JEFFERSON

Many folks outside of higher education have probably never heard of land-grant colleges, and most likely don't know the origins of the Land Grant Act. A land-grant university is an institution of higher education which was designated as such by state legislation, enabling that institution to receive funding from the congressional Morrill acts of 1862 and 1890.

Justin Smith Morrill was a congressman from Vermont. In 1857 he introduced a bill in Congress which was then vetoed by President James Buchanan. He resubmitted the bill in 1861 and it passed. President Abraham Lincoln signed it into law in 1862 at the height of the Civil War. It was one of the most important and significant pieces of legislation to impact higher education in the United States.

The act granted public land to states, which could then be sold to provide funding for the teaching of agriculture and engineering predominately. Every state in the union has a land-grant college. In

Arkansas, the 1862 land-grant institution is the University of Arkansas in Fayetteville. It was so designated by the state, and funding was provided so that agricultural and engineering programs could thrive. The act was really in response to the industrial revolution, and Congress believed they needed to be funding colleges and universities to support agricultural and engineering programs.

Later a second bill was passed by Congress in 1890, which created separate land-grant institutions for persons of color. The University of Arkansas, Pine Bluff is an 1890 land-grant institution. So from the earliest days after the federal legislation, the Fayetteville campus was clearly established as the exclusive land-grant institution in the state of Arkansas and later UA Pine Bluff became one after new legislation was passed.

I relate this history because it has an important bearing on the Fayetteville campus and its relationship to the system Division of Agriculture.

Before the Fayetteville campus had its own chancellor, the president of the University of Arkansas served as both the campus head and the head of the entire university and every campus across the state. In those days there wasn't anything called the University of Arkansas System and the president, headquartered in Fayetteville, was over all the other campuses of the University of Arkansas. Incidentally, this is the same format used at Penn State University, in that the president serves as the CEO of all of the campuses and many other institutions across the nation enjoy that arrangement as well.

When a chancellor was established in Fayetteville to serve the main campus some of the vice presidents under the president became system officers. One case in point is the general counsel of the university, who reports to the president in Little Rock. The other major unit that opted to report to the system president was the Division of Agriculture. Up to that point the person in charge of the division was on the Fayetteville campus and was in charge of the faculty and its agriculture curriculum and programs. All of a sudden, however, that person—the vice president for agriculture—became a system official. Almost overnight the agriculture programs and faculty in Fayetteville were being run by a system vice president who would eventually be headquartered in Little Rock. From the very beginning this administrative structure created a slew of problems. Suddenly, the Fayetteville agriculture campus faculty were being managed by a system official who did not report to the campus chancellor or provost.

This new operating procedure created numerous problems for the Fayetteville campus. To whom did the dean of the College of Agriculture report, the provost and chancellor in Fayetteville or the vice president for agriculture in Little Rock? Remember, the land-grant university established by Congress gave the authority for agricultural programs to the Fayetteville campus. It did not give that authority to an amorphous system Division of Agriculture. The land-grant legislation created funds for the Fayetteville campus.

From the very first day I was chancellor I experienced problems with the Division of Agriculture. They wanted to run the show. They wanted to make decisions about faculty and programs they deemed were under their authority rather than the campus chancellor. They would claim a faculty member as part of their domain if that faculty member was engaged in research and scholarship that brought in research funding to the university. Therefore we had a bifurcated system where some faculty on the Fayetteville campus reported to the system vice president, and some reported to the Fayetteville dean of agriculture.

Every chancellor of the Fayetteville campus had problems with the Division of Agriculture. Every single one, beginning with Bill Nugent. John White reminded me when I was first elected chancellor that I would also experience many issues with the division.

Since coming back to the university in 1998, we had five different deans of agriculture—all of whom left the university because of this bifurcated system. The dean was supposed to report jointly to the vice president for agriculture and the chancellor and provost of the Fayetteville campus. I've never felt a dual reporting mode made any sense whatsoever. These deans left the university because of the rancor that such an arrangement created. All of these deans were fine people with high-level credentials, but they simply could not operate under such a system.

The vice president for the Division of Agriculture in the system who had direct reporting lines to campus officials was the only system vice president with such an arrangement. It was the only position that had line authority to members of our faculty. Because of that, agriculture faculty and administration continued to be caught in the middle of an unnecessary and destructive internecine struggle over which organization had responsibility for agriculture programs on the flagship campus.

Reporting lines were confusing and counterproductive, and a serious detriment to the Fayetteville campus's ability to function as the intended land-grant university in the state of Arkansas. The original legislation made it very clear that agricultural experiment stations and research functions, both very important to a major land-grant institution, as well as the teaching and service missions established in conjunction with the land-grant mission, should be a part of the larger land-grant institution.

Higher education officials across the nation believe this is a critical and important relationship, which should be honored under the land-grant tradition. The Division of Agriculture robbed the Fayetteville campus of its land-grant mission, which was established under congressional legislation. The Division of Agriculture deliberately pulled away from the original land-grant concept of teaching, research, and public service by creating a separation of these three critically important attributes of the land-grant tradition. The separation is artificial and most detrimental to the Fayetteville campus mission as a flagship land-grant university.

Basically, the division wanted to separate the teaching and research mission of our campus, and that was anathema to the best traditions of the academy. I felt strongly that agriculture faculty who resided on the Fayetteville campus should be part of our administrative structure, not in an amorphous division at the system level. U of A, Fayetteville was the original, historically exclusive, and logical organization to carry out the land-grant agricultural responsibilities, rather than a bureaucratic system office. It would make more sense to have faculty in the Dale Bumpers College of Agricultural, Food and Life Sciences reporting to the dean of the College— saving the state the added expense of a centralized bureaucracy. The faculty expertise and the research facilities reside in Fayetteville, not in Little Rock.

During my time as chancellor, there were several Division of Agriculture directives that had a very negative impact on our faculty and staff residing in Fayetteville. The separation of teaching and research functions under two different administrators just didn't work. Many times the division wanted to change the offering of tenure-track positions to senior level faculty. They also wanted to create their own affirmative-action plans and reporting responsibilities. Probably the most difficult system issue was when they gave different salary increases to the faculty that they presumably controlled. Some faculty on our campus would get raises and some would not, depending on what faculty line they occupied. The division also wanted to separate the endowment funds given originally to the Fayetteville campus that they believed should be under their control. The entire mode of operation was a mess.

I was determined to resolve one issue between the campus and the Division of Agriculture over sharing costs to clean up a toxic waste site on the division's land. Don Pederson had advised me that the division owed the campus funds.

The sequence of events related to a hazardous waste site on Harmon Road, Division of Agriculture property operated from 1965 to 1984. Both the Fayetteville campus and the division used the site, with facilities management responsible for the collection and disposal of hazardous materials. In 1984 the Arkansas Department of Environmental Quality (ADEQ) notified the University of Arkansas that they considered the Harmon Road facility a hazardous waste disposal facility, which was unlawfully operating without a permit in violation of the federal Resource Conservation and Recovery Act (RCRA) and corresponding state legislation and regulations.

The university completed closure of the site, meeting all ADEQ requirements. Subsequent events brought the Arkansas Department of Health into the picture, with a different but conflicting set of requirements consistent with state and federal law and regulations. The university evaluated options that would comply with both state agencies. ADH approved our plan to remove the source of contamination, and the soil removal and disposal was accomplished by September 2007 with all payments completed by June 2008. Available records clearly indicate that probably more than half of the materials (estimated to be 55) came from the Division of Agriculture use.

The campus was willing to split the cost 50/50 with the division. The final cost was $4,366,685.32 with the division's share being $2,183,342.66. This cost covered only the final cleanup, and did not include approximately $715,000 spent on this site by the campus prior to 2004, for which reimbursement from the division was not sought. This request for funds from the Division of Agriculture by the campus had not been paid, or even booked as an obligation.

Division officers, Milo Shult and Mark Cochran believed they had no financial responsibility for the costs of cleanup, but never shared the basis for that belief of initial disposal. I could not imagine how the division thought there was any other rational and legal choice with regard to the subsequent removal and how it would be paid for.

Multiple years passed and the Division of Agriculture did not live up to their end of the bargain. After constant requests that were ignored, I finally went to Dr. Sugg with the issue. He studied the matter, and concluded that the division did indeed owe our campus reimbursement, and told them to transfer the funds to us. Had Sugg not ordered the payment we would have never received it. That's how the Division of Agriculture did business. Just ignore the campus and maybe they will go away!

In April 2010 Dr. Sugg sent me a copy of a letter written by the president of the Farm Bureau of Arkansas, Randy Veach. I knew Randy well, and had spent several days with him in Panama when we visited President Martinelli. Veach did not give me the benefit of copying me on his letter, which he sent to Sugg and the board of trustees. The letter accused me of wanting to destroy the Division of

Agriculture, and have all of the agricultural programs in the state report to the Fayetteville campus.

I never advocated or believed the Division of Agriculture should be under the Fayetteville campus. All I was interested in was having the faculty who resided on our campus under the aegis of our provost like all of the other academic units. I felt that I had a pretty good working relationship with Milo Shult, the vice president for the division. I certainly understood that Milo was trying to protect his turf at all costs. But it made no sense whatsoever to have our Fayetteville faculty report to a person in Little Rock. I can't help but compare the Division of Agriculture with the old empire of Great Britain, trying to hang on to their authority in faraway places when it made no sense whatsoever.

We had years and years of serious conflicts with the Division of Agriculture, and at one point the faculty came close to passing a resolution of no confidence in the division. There were constant problems with the administrative structure. One example, which may seem minor to some, was that a member of the agriculture faculty was told he should not wear a logo on his jacket from the Fayetteville campus. He should only wear items of clothing that had system logos. I thought that declaration was totally absurd.

I held a number of meetings with division staff in an attempt to find a solution to the problems of morale and system leadership. I did have serious problems with the issue of the dean having no relationship with the research component of agriculture, and how that was not in line with the land-grant traditions across the country. In meetings with department heads in agriculture, every one of them was very definitive about the need for systemic change to get all faculty and staff working on the same page.

Provost Sharon Gaber and I had been visited by a stream of senior faculty from Agriculture after Milo Shult announced his retirement. The central message was the same. The artificial separation by the Division of Agriculture of the land-grant tradition of teaching, research and service missions caused strife and concern, and defeated the inextricable link among the three missions that any faculty member of a land-grant institution needs to enjoy. The faculty and department heads were very upset about the division's decision to hold up tenure-track positions, and to do so without any conversations with campus officials. President Sugg actually reversed that decision, but it created a climate of fear and trepidation among faculty in all ranks and demoralized them. These problems stretched back 25 years.

Faculty expressed to me their fear of speaking out, believing their compensation would be affected by the division, and fearing repercussions if they were perceived to be more on the campus side rather than the division side. I also learned that staff from the Division of Agriculture were systematically telling our benefactors not to fund certain projects on our campus, but instead to give directly to division projects, and had copies of emails supporting this contention.

We implemented a faculty and staff maternity and paternity leave policy for our campus, but the Division of Agriculture decided that it did not apply to their folks, even though they were residing on our campus. No reason given. They denied their staff and faculty a very important benefit even though other ag faculty and staff got the benefit if they were on our budget more than 50 percent.

In February 2014 Provost Gaber asked three distinguished deans to compile an independent report on the relationship between the Fayetteville campus and the Division of Agriculture. The three deans were: Dr. Todd Shields of the Fulbright College, Dr. Bob McMath of the Honors College, and Dr. Tom Smith of the College of Education and Health Professions. Gaber asked for them to maintain strict transparency and give an unbiased review of issues needing resolution. They delivered a report on May 27, 2014. The three deans asked to interview individuals on the U of A campus who had knowledge of issues between the Bumpers College of Agricultural, Food and Life Sciences and the Division of Agriculture. A total of 19 faculty and staff from campus were interviewed between May 15 and May 20.

Each interview lasted from 20 to 60 minutes. After describing the purpose of the interview, individuals were simply asked, "Can you tell me some of the issues you are facing, or that you perceive exists, between the University of Arkansas and the Division of Agriculture," or "What is your perception of the relationship between the university and the division, and what do you think the causes are?" There were no additional set questions, individuals were allowed to respond to the open-ended question. Their answers often led to follow-up questions, but there was no standard set of questions.

Many of the people interviewed wanted to remain anonymous. Many indicated they felt caught between competing camps.

The report cited the following issues: (Not the entire list.)

Frequently, the structural relationship between our Bumpers College and the Division of Agriculture is reported to be modeled on Texas A & M or LSU. However, Texas A & M actually has combined the dean and vice chancellor (similar to our vice president) position. As such, the dean reports to both the provost of the university and the chancellor of the system. They have not segregated the responsibilities of the dean into teaching only and divided the college into two reporting lines. Similarly, LSU has restructured away from our model because of the inherent inefficiencies.

The current bifurcated structure contributes to conflicting directives and contradictory policies at all levels, from personnel and IT policies to the strategic direction of the overall enterprise.

A clash of professional cultures manifests itself in different interpretations of what it means to be a professor: USDA laboratory scientist vs. university professor with multiple duties.

Control of a high percentage of overall funding by the division, and the ways in which that control is exercised, unnecessarily limit the flexibility of units and individuals to carry out their missions. This shows up, for example, in rigid allocations of work time rather than accountability for successful completion of assignments.

Micromanagement created by the division reduces motivation for innovation and productivity, as does the creation of artificial boundaries among division, college, and university faculty. An example of the latter is lack of access to research space and equipment (the farm and elsewhere) for non-division agricultural research.

Mutual distrust on the part of division and university leadership leads to poor communications and conflict over how the work gets done. The division's branding effort goes to extremes and looks petty.

Concern over uncertain and declining federal, state, and county support to the division is well founded, but if the result is cautious management and little encouragement for bold innovation across the entire university and beyond, all parties will suffer at a time when a financial crisis looms for land-grant institutions nationwide.

The division reports to the president, and there is no reason for the chancellor and vice president to talk with each other. They have no reason to work things out. They have retreated to their corners and now don't trust each other.

The dean has a split appointment, and that is untenable. Serving two masters that don't trust each other is impossible.

Everything—all problems—stem from the dysfunctional administrative structure: Lack of communication, different people software (Basis vs Banner), duplicate accounting, incompatibility of web pages purposefully designed *not* to work with campus web pages. The administrative structure encourages duplication, inefficiencies, cross purposes, and things happen despite the bureaucratic nightmare created by this bizarre administrative structure.

Rather than trying to work out situations and problems, the division runs directly to the board of trustees and the president.

It is virtually impossible to make donors or prospects interested and happy because the left hand works against the right hand.

Three department heads have stepped down in the past year alone, because this structure is too difficult to work in and it is impossible to be successful.

Reporting lines are confusing and counterproductive, and a serious detriment to the Fayetteville campus's ability to function as the intended land-grant university in the state of Arkansas.

The original intent of the Hatch Act and later Grange Amendment made it very clear that agricultural experiment stations and research functions—as well as the teaching and service missions established in conjunction with colleges—be subordinate to the larger land-grant institution. Higher education officials, with very few exceptions, believe this is a critically important relationship, which must be honored under the land-grant tradition.

Agriculture faculty who reside on the Fayetteville campus, or reside elsewhere but work predominately with programs and functions of the Fayetteville campus, should be part of its administrative structure.

We have had a series of agriculture deans leave the university very unhappy and demoralized, and this has caused a crisis of leadership in the college. The primary reason for their decision to resign has been their working relationship with the Division of Agriculture. These deans were hired after national searches, and enjoyed the confidence of the search committee and faculty, and left to run other prestigious programs in other states.

Faculty have expressed their fear of speaking out, believing that their compensation would be affected. They have been led to fear repercussions if they are perceived to be more on the campus side rather than the division side. This has produced a climate of fear among agriculture faculty.

A longtime member of the faculty was asked by division administrators to refrain from wearing any article of clothing with a Razorback or U of A, Fayetteville emblem when out and around the state visiting members of the agriculture community. As you can imagine, in a community of scholars there's no place for managing by intimidation, fear, and retribution.

In my last year as chancellor, I was able to convince Bobbitt and the board of trustees to appoint a committee of the board to investigate the strife caused by the agriculture issues and arrive at some sort of solution or compromise. I made it very clear to all that my only interest was clearing up the reporting lines of the faculty and staff who were on our campus. If a faculty member resided on our campus, that faculty member should report to the campus.

Trustee Cliff Gibson, attorney from Monticello, was appointed chair of the committee. I found him to be extremely fair and judicious. He was an excellent listener and studied all of the materials we prepared for the first meeting. Provost Gaber and I came armed with a huge binder of evidence for our cause. Representatives of the system Division of Agriculture attended as did Bobbitt. It was a bloodbath. Soon into the meeting the system division officials became angry and hostile. They had no response to the numerous pieces of evidence we showed the committee, and simply denied everything. When we told the committee that we were the only university in the nation with this type of bifurcated agriculture system, they objected strenuously and said that was not true. When pushed they admitted there was one other. Only one other in the entire nation!

Trustees Gibson told me privately that he could understand our point of view and that we would need more meetings to work through the issues. But it was not to be. Provost Gaber accepted the position of president of The University of Toledo, and I announced my retirement before another meeting could be scheduled. One of my real regrets was that the committee would later be abandoned, and no changes ever made. Word on campus is that the same problems and serious issues still exist today.

CHAPTER 75
ATHLETICS TRANSFER TO ACADEMICS

> *I talk to student-athletes. I try to get them to remember that they're not just athletes, but student-athletes. You need to get an education, keep your hands clean and try to represent the university.*
>
> — EARL CAMPBELL

In 2012 Jeff Long and I began discussing the possibility of transferring some athletics revenue to the academic side of the university. The SEC institutions had recently signed a very lucrative TV package, which would bring in several million dollars in funds to the athletics department. On top of that, Long was raising several million more dollars per year in gift support.

Long readily agreed to help us pay for the new nanotechnology building, and also pay for a new classroom facility, Champions Hall. The total amount coming from athletics to help with these projects and others was $3 million. There were not very many athletics departments in the country supporting the academic needs of the university at this magnitude.

CHAPTER 76
GOVERNOR

> *When Woodrow Wilson, then president of Princeton University, was asked why he wanted to leave the life of an academic and run for governor of New Jersey he replied, "Well, that's simple, I want to get out of politics."*

In early 2012 someone created an anonymous Twitter account that wanted to draft me for governor. I still have no idea who created the account, but suspect it might have been a former student government officer.

The Twitter account featured my photograph and identified itself as "Arkansans hoping to draft our state's most accomplished leader into the 2014 gubernatorial race." It was a nice compliment, but was not going to happen. Even if I was interested, I knew no Democrat was going to be elected governor for a long time. I was contacted by the media, and told the reporter I was not running for governor or any other political office, ever. I went on to say that I still had a lot to accomplish at the university but might want to teach after leaving the post in a few years. I was asked, if I did run, would I be a Democrat or Republican? I said that I grew up around Democrats, but have always voted for the person rather than the party and wouldn't know whether to run as a Democrat or Republican. I guess that was stretching the truth.

CHAPTER 77
A NEW CONFERENCE CENTER THAT NEVER WAS

> *Nothing is more expensive than a missed opportunity."*
>
> — AUTHOR H. JACKSON BROWN, JR.

American business schools are known for providing continuing education programs for business leaders. The Walton College of Business would sponsor a number of these programs each year. The problem, however, was the inadequate facilities we had at the University of Arkansas to hold large conferences. The University of Texas built a massive college of business continuing education facility, and was one of the leading universities providing such programs. At Arkansas we were limited by the size and scope of our programs, because we simply did not have adequate facilities to engage business leaders.

When Doyle Williams was dean, he dreamed of having a facility in proximity to our business school. It would include meeting space and hotel and dining facilities, and would enable us to be a real player in the continuing education business. At that time we had to rely on an old facility on Fayetteville Square. Although it was attached to a hotel, the facility itself was woefully inadequate and dated. I thought Doyle's dream was worth pursuing. After all, Doyle was a highly effective dean with national and international fame.

I began discussions with the current dean, Matt Waller, about what I believed to be an important need for Walton College and the University of Arkansas. While Carnall Inn was a fine facility, it was much too small for our growing student body and alumni base. Dean Waller was enthusiastic and agreed it was a project worth exploring.

I appointed David Davies to investigate the possibility of building such a facility. As mentioned previously, Davies had been primarily responsible for building the facility on Petit Jean mountain, and was the best person possible to look into the matter. He worked diligently with Mike Johnson, head of facilities management, to see if it was even feasible. One of the problems we had at the university was no facility for large group dinners. We were leasing a facility off the Fayetteville Square or in Rogers, Arkansas, to hold banquets of any size over 75 people. This was a costly venture for our colleges, schools and alumni events.

What we hoped to do was find a hotel management company that would build the facility at their cost. It would be a turnkey project that would give us a continuing education building, as well as a larger hotel for the many programs, educational and athletics, we were holding on campus.

Davies delivered to me a very promising report, which he thought would work with minimal cost to the university. I started discussing the project with President Bobbitt and a few members of our board of trustees. There seemed to be widespread acceptance of the project. We had reserved a parcel of land right next to the business building where such a facility could be located. I was excited about the possibilities.

Unfortunately, after I retired as chancellor, the project was scrapped by a new chancellor who had different priorities. I still believe Doyle Williams' idea has considerable merit.

CHAPTER 78
LEGISLATORS

> *No man's life, liberty, or property are safe while the legislature is in session.*
>
> — *MARK TWAIN*

As chancellor I was expected to stay in touch with the leadership of the General Assembly. It was the part of the job I loathed the most. To be fair, there were a few legislators who were supportive and worked hard to help us achieve our quest to become a top-50 public research institution. But, unfortunately, they were in the minority. I always thought legislators viewed us in higher education as their employees. I guess we were technically public servant employees, so maybe they had it correctly. Some folks, however, see state representatives as employees of the public.

My feelings were that, as a tax-paying citizen of Arkansas, the legislature worked for us, not the other way around. That is anathema to our legislators.

Often, I would sit through a legislative hearing when some obscure legislator would ask a mean-spirited question in an attempt to embarrass or challenge a respected official in higher education. It happened regularly. At one particular budget hearing, which happened every year, a state representative began criticizing the University of Arkansas for spending academic funds on athletics. He went on for some time with his objections. I had no idea what he was talking about as all of our intercollegiate sports programs, men and women, were paid for by ticket revenue and private gifts, using no state funds. Finally another legislator spoke out and said his colleague was looking at the Arkansas State University line on the budget report, not ours!

Duly elected representatives should be revered in the community they serve. But some of the laws they pass are hard to understand.

Take the mask mandate. During the Covid pandemic, the Arkansas legislature passed a law declaring schools cannot decide if they want a mask mandate in their local jurisdictions. The governor signed the legislation. Then the governor had a change of heart, and asked the General Assembly to overturn the part of the law that prohibited mask mandates as Covid was surging. The governor called the Republican-led state legislature back into session to address the issue, but the majority stuck with the ban.

The Arkansas legislature approved a state law banning gender-confirming treatments for transgender youth, in spite of a national outcry from the scientific and medical community. One legislator called a transgender person an abomination in the eyes of God.

In 2021 the governor signed legislation allowing medical workers to refuse treatment to LGBTQ people. Earlier Hutchinson had signed a law prohibiting transgender women and girls from playing on sports teams consistent with their gender identity.

Later that same year two legislators went after Dr. Cam Patterson, the head of the University of Arkansas for Medical Sciences (UAMS), for following federal law in demanding vaccines for employees, saying it was contrary to state law. Representative Trent Garner wanted him fired and the other legislator, Bob Ballinger, wanted to withdraw state funding from UAMS. Unconscionable on so many levels.

Many of the legislators have no college education and absolutely no experience dealing with major organizations or institutions. In

2011 *The New York Times* published an article titled "Many State Legislators Lack College Degrees," which reported that, "Arkansas has the least formally educated Statehouse, with 25 percent of its 135 legislators not having any college experience at all, compared with 8.7 percent of lawmakers nationwide. It was followed by state legislatures in Montana (20 percent), Kansas (16 percent), South Dakota (16 percent) and Arizona (16 percent)."

The Chronicle of Higher Education conducted a study in 2011 indicating that only "60.4 percent of Arkansas legislators have a college degree." That ranks Arkansas 46th, ahead of New Mexico, Maine, Delaware and New Hampshire in collegiate attainment. Nationwide, the college degree rate among legislators is about 75 percent.

One can draw their own conclusions about exactly what this means for higher education in Arkansas, but it's probably not good.

In early 2012 I received an email from Jon Woods, a Republican member of the Arkansas House of Representatives. Woods was an alumnus, and I knew him fairly well. He would usually call me when he needed a favor like introducing his girlfriend to President Clinton when Clinton was on campus.

Apparently, he had watched a program on cable TV exploring the theories of the potential of "time travel." Woods was term-limited in the House and was running for the state senate and said, if he was elected, he wanted to sponsor an appropriations bill for the benefit of the University of Arkansas in the amount of $250,000 to build a time machine. Woods went on to say that Spike Lee was interested in a movie deal on the topic and would include the university name in the last few pages of the script. Woods would also be a character in the movie.

I politely called Woods and told him that we would pass on his project.

In 2017 Woods was found guilty of fifteen federal counts for his collusion in a kickback scheme involving Ecclesia College in Springdale, Arkansas. He is currently in federal prison.

SENATOR GILBERT BAKER

Another legislator who could be demanding was Senator Gilbert Baker of Conway. Perhaps because he worked for the University of Central Arkansas, he felt he had a license to demand the immediate attention of higher education on his whim. Baker was a powerful member of the state senate, and ranked third in seniority in his last term. He could not run again because he was term-limited by law. In 2009 he made a run for the United States Senate but lost to John Boozman.

In 2012 I received a call from State Senator Baker asking me to be in his office the next morning at 7:30 a.m. He told me to bring President Bobbitt with me. I had no idea what he might want from me, but Richard Hudson surmised he might be looking for a job! Arriving for a 7:30 a.m. appointment in Little Rock was not an easy proposition. I would have to either drive, requiring me to leave my house at 4:30 a.m., go the night before and stay in a hotel in Little Rock, or take the UA plane which was costly for one passenger. Besides, I had to completely rearrange my calendar. I would still need to leave by 6:00 a.m., but that didn't seem to be a concern for Senator Baker.

Bobbitt and I arrived at Baker's office promptly at 7:30. Baker had yet to make it into his office. We sat comfortably for 45 minutes until he arrived at his office at the capitol. He began the conversation by telling us we needed better people as our lobbyists. He was very critical of Richard Hudson and the system lobbyist, Melissa Rust. He said we needed to hire someone who had a great relationship with members of the General Assembly and could get their attention. He said It really needed to be a Republican since they were now controlling things in Little Rock. He then said that he wasn't really asking for a job. Almost immediately, he then said maybe he was asking for a job. He said that he thought he could get us a lot of money from the legislature, and his relationship with the governor was very good. Hiring him would be a huge financial benefit to the University of Arkansas. Oh, and by the way, he wanted to continue to live in Conway!

We both sat in complete silence and bewilderment. I finally spoke up and said that I didn't think Richard Hudson was retiring anytime soon. That didn't deter Baker; he thought a long transition period would be good for him. He then asked how old Richard was. Bobbitt made very few comments at all and kept virtually silent on the senator's proposition, except to say we would get back to him. On the way back to our cars I told Bobbitt that I thought the request was outrageous, and I had no intention of hiring him. Besides, I had an effective lobbyist in Richard. The only comment Bobbitt made was that he might have to hire him on a contract basis to keep everyone happy. On my return to campus I spoke to Richard Hudson who wasn't surprised at Baker's request for a job. He then told me what Baker did was patently illegal, since he was still a sitting legislator. Asking for a job was against state law. For one brief moment I thought about turning him into the ethics committee, but nothing would have come of it. I just bit my lip as I would do often when dealing with the legislature.

After Baker's term ended, he went to work for University of Central Arkansas president Tom Courtway as assistant to the president. I liked Courtway very much and we talked often about education matters. He was the real deal, and we could level with each other on tough issues we were facing. Courtway was also a very ethical person who always seemed to want to do the right thing. We had a great relationship. He was pulling UCA out of the doldrums following two failed presidencies. We talked about Baker and he told me that he really had no choice but to hire him, even though he had serious reservations. Baker's employment didn't last long. He was dismissed by Courtway in 2014. Later Baker was charged with federal bribery, wire fraud and conspiracy. He was accused of being the middleman in an alleged plot in 2013 to bribe former Faulkner County Circuit Judge Michael Maggio on behalf of Michael Morton, a wealthy nursing-home owner and campaign financier. Baker was found not guilty of conspiracy to commit bribery but deadlocked on remaining bribery and wire fraud charges. A retrial on the remaining charges is set for November 2022.

THE ANTI-ANTI-DISCRIMINATION BILL

In August 2014 the Fayetteville City Council passed an anti-discrimination law—known as Ordinance 5703. It was the first municipal law in the state to prohibit discrimination based on gender identification and sexual orientation. State and federal laws prohibit the hiring, firing and eviction of people on the basis of age, sex, national origin, race, religion or disability. Fayetteville's ordinance sought to add protections on the basis of gender identification and sexual orientation, which aren't covered in state and federal laws. The Human Rights Campaign, a Washington-based civil-rights group, helped to draft the ordinance to advocate for lesbian, gay, bisexual and transsexual equality. The Fayetteville law applied to the city, its employees, and contractors who do business with the city, and would include protection from discrimination based on ethnicity, familial status, marital status, socioeconomic background and veteran status. It also would exclude religious or denominational institutions, except to prohibit discrimination against employees who perform no religious duties.

For reasons not completely clear, the Fayetteville Chamber of Commerce announced its opposition to the ordinance. I contacted the chamber to seek an explanation and was told the chamber takes public positions on government policies when the policies are detrimental to the community because it is legally incomplete, vague or deficient in defining conduct to be regulated as legal or illegal. The chairman of the chamber, Bill Bradley, headed the Washington Regional Medical Center. I always believed Bill was a reasonable person. He said at a media conference, "While some may regrettably and erroneously choose to characterize our effort as something it is not, I can assure you that our membership abhors discrimination of every kind and support equal treatment for all. The exclusive focus of our informational campaign is that this law is seriously flawed." I didn't really know what that meant.

My feelings were that discrimination against anyone is bad public policy, and supported university regulations that had put in place a policy against discrimination based on sexual orientation. That policy had been in effect for decades, and was implemented during Chancellor Dan Ferritor's administration. I applaud Ferritor for a courageous move early on in the rancor over sexual orientation discrimination.

Then I was told the chamber voted unanimously to oppose the new regulation. I knew that could not be accurate because I was a member of the chamber board and was never notified of a meeting when the vote was to take place.

I immediately wrote a letter to Bill Bradley and Steve Clark, the chamber president. I told them that I would like to respectfully ask that the Chamber of Commerce board of directors rescind its recent action regarding the civil rights ordinance. While I served as an ex-officio member of the board, I was never invited to offer my opinion on the decision to issue a statement about the ordinance. Likewise, other ex-officio members were denied the opportunity to address the issue, including the mayor. I told them that the media release indicated the action was unanimously endorsed by the board members. Such a statement created the impression that I was in concurrence with their action. I felt strongly that the failure to include all ex-officio members in the discussion contributed to the perception that the board operated under a veil of secrecy and was opposed to any divergent views. Such a perception undermined the ability of the board to demonstrate that it consistently functions within the best traditions of our city, which embraces openness and fair play.

I knew many people favored allowing the citizens of Fayetteville to decide the issue at the ballot box in December, rather than having pressure exerted by the chamber. If, indeed, the law is vague and too broad, the court system of Arkansas will clarify the law in due course.

This became a flashpoint issue for our city. The chamber should be promoting harmony and prosperity, not creating crisis. Their weigh-in strained relations among town, gown, and individual citizens.

I did receive a polite reply from Steve Clark, whom I knew well, but he didn't give any real explanation for the chamber's action, except to repeat the chairman's point that the law was too vague.

Then on November 17 a letter came to me from 18 members of the General Assembly, all conservative Republicans, basically telling me I should mind my own business. The letter told me that I should not involve myself in a public dispute over the issue. I should stick to tending to the educational mission of the university and not a city council dispute. I responded to all 18 with a letter thanking them for their missive to me and explaining that the chamber asserted the vote was unanimous, and I had received numerous letters from faculty, staff, and students, as well as alumni, asking why I voted against an ordinance that opposed discrimination. I could not let that fallacy stand. I received no further reply from any of the legislators.

The letter was written on the stationary of Bob Ballinger, a member of the General Assembly. Senator Bart Hester signed the letter and had weighed in that there should be economic reprisals against the University of Arkansas because I had expressed my opinion on the issue. Other signatories to the letter were: Andy Davis, Jim Dotson, Charlene Fite, Justin Harris, Jack Ladyman, Mary Bentley, Jana Della Rosa, Laurie Rushing, Donnie Copeland, Robin Lunstrum, Rebecca Petty, Ron McNair, Karilyn Brown, Cecile Bledsoe, John Cooper and Jim Hendren, all Republicans.

Max Brantley, editor of the *Arkansas Times*, posted a piece on Friday, November 28, 2014, which made me smile and was much appreciated. In the article, titled "18 Legislators Object to Free Speech by UA Chancellor" he said:

1. This letter wouldn't have been written had Chancellor Gearhart written a public letter endorsing the resolution.
2. The Fayetteville chamber dishonestly suggested Gearhart supported the resolution. He was right to set the record straight.
3. The letter is a thinly veiled threat to take retribution against Gearhart and the university for his free speech.
4. Legislators have every right themselves to support or oppose the Fayetteville ordinance. They have every right to send a letter to someone with whom they disagree. But

they step over the line—and demonstrate a poor understanding of the First Amendment to the U.S. Constitution—when they use their legislative roles to suggest another public employee's ability to speak should be limited by his public employment.
5. The university *does* have an interest in this issue. It has an employment non-discrimination policy. The City of Fayetteville proposes merely to make that a matter of law.
6. The problem is not non-existent. The 18 legislators need only review the video of the marathon City Council meeting at which victims of discrimination testified. People also testified who openly expressed a desire to legally discriminate in housing, public accommodation, and employment.

In 2015 the anti-discrimination law was passed by the Fayetteville City Council. State Attorney General Leslie Rutledge, a Republican, appealed a lower court ruling upholding the Fayetteville ordinance, which prohibited discrimination against gay, lesbian, bisexual and transgender people in employment and hiring. Rutledge cited an Arkansas law forbidding cities and counties from extending nondiscrimination protections beyond those classes identified at the state level. The legislature passed that measure in 2015 after initial attempts by Fayetteville to enact an anti-discrimination ordinance failed.

Fayetteville and several other cities then passed ordinances in response to state law. In siding with Rutledge, the Arkansas Supreme Court held that the state civil rights law was the controlling statute. The court said Fayetteville's city ordinance was unconstitutional because it created a direct inconsistency between state and municipal law. The ACLU filed a brief in support of the Fayetteville ordinance.

In early 2015 the Arkansas General Assembly, the majority of whose members now belonged to the Republican Party, passed SB 202, widely seen as a response to Fayetteville's attempted ordinance, the law forbade municipalities from passing ordinances protecting groups not already protected under state law. The bill was clearly an act with discriminating intent against the gay community. Governor Hutchinson did not sign the legislation, but made comments to the effect that he harbored reservations about the bill so he let it become law without his signature. Walmart was courageous and came out against the bill. I sent the Walmart president, Doug McMillion, an email thanking him for his integrity and courage.

Then in June 2015, with a 5–4 ruling in the case of Obergefell v. Hodges, the United States Supreme Court announced that states cannot ban gay marriage, legalizing it nationwide. That seemed like progress. Then the Arkansas legislature passed a law that banned any medical "gender transition procedures" for individuals under eighteen years of age. Governor Hutchinson vetoed this bill, but the legislature voted to override the veto. Arkansas became the first state in the nation to implement such a ban.

In a landmark decision in 2020, the Supreme Court of the United States issued a decision in the case Bostock v. Clayton County, which held that the prohibition against sex discrimination in Title VII of the Civil Rights Act of 1964 includes employment discrimination against an individual on the basis of sexual orientation or transgender status. On January 21, 2021, President Joe Biden issued an executive order that implemented the U.S. Supreme Court's ruling in Bostock v. Clayton County. The Executive Order presumably has an impact on the lives LGBTQ adults and youth in the United States. The Biden administration issued the order to implement the Bostock decision after the Trump administration failed to properly enforce it across federal agencies, instead arguing LGBTQ people were not protected under federal civil rights laws.

Congressman Bruce Westerman of Arkansas issued a statement after the decision, "Setting aside the details of the case for a moment, I believe this decision sets a dangerous precedent of the justices legislating from the bench. Congress instituted Title VII—which prohibits employer discrimination on the basis of race, color, religion, sex or national origin—as part of the Civil Rights Act of 1975. In order to change a law, Congress must pass a law. Nine unelected justices should not overstep into Congress's jurisdiction."

The issue is far from over.

Arkansas had indeed become a red state, and it didn't look like things would change for some time. We all witnessed the horrific actions of a mob trying to take over Congress and reverse a legitimate presidential election through brute force. Donald Trump continues to claim that the election was bogus, and that he actually won the election—even a year after the siege on the nation's Capitol. I was home watching the NBC Nightly News on January 5, 2022 when I heard a commentator claim that 73 percent of Republicans still believe the election was stolen.

CHAPTER 79
APRIL FOOL'S DAY—SAY IT AIN'T SO BOBBY

> *Any 51-year-old white male likes to get a little on the side, and we should not fire him for doing what comes naturally.*
>
> — UNIVERSITY OF ARKANSAS TRUSTEE

April 1, 2012, began as a hopeful day. I boarded a bus along with colleagues from the University of Arkansas, and headed to Petit Jean mountain for a retreat. It was an annual excursion with the deans of the colleges and vice chancellors, as well as faculty, staff, and student representatives. The purpose of the retreat was to continue to expand and modify our strategic plan which we called the TAP Report, "Transparency and Accountability to the People of Arkansas." We used these retreats each year to make certain that, as an institution, our academic and administrative constituencies were, in effect, pulling together for the most important programs and projects, which we had all approved earlier. We had established multiple goals that affected every part of the institution, and we wanted to continue to make maximum progress in the years ahead.

We would spend the night at the Rockefeller Institute and attend multiple meetings outlining an ambitious agenda for the University of Arkansas. Folks on the bus seemed excited about our excursion, and we even used the ride to the mountain to listen to student government officers talk about their thoughts on our progress.

I was sitting in the front of the bus and Jeff Long was midway back. Suddenly he tapped me on the shoulder and said we needed to talk. He had just received a telephone call on his cell phone from his office informing him that Bobby Petrino had been in a motorcycle accident, and had been injured. Bobby was on his way to the hospital, but apparently the injuries, while serious, were not life-threatening. Petrino had been hired four years earlier by Long as our head football coach. He came to us from the Atlanta Falcons and brought renewed excitement to our football program.

Later, Long returned to my seat to inform me that there might be more to the crash than first reported. Apparently, Long had been told that Petrino was alone on the motorcycle—but now he had been given additional information. We would learn a couple of days later that Petrino had lied to Long, and indeed there was another person with him when his motorcycle crashed. Long said he would investigate the matter and be back in touch with me.

On April 2, the athletics department issued a media release saying that Petrino was by himself when he crashed his motorcycle. The statement said Petrino was expected to make a full recovery and that he was not wearing a helmet. Photographs were leaked to the media showing his extensive facial injuries. On April 3 Petrino attended football practice in a neck brace.

On April 5, Long was informed that Petrino was not alone when his motorcycle crashed but was with an unidentified woman who apparently was not seriously injured. Previously Long had questioned Petrino and was told numerous times by him that he was alone on the motorcycle.

On April 6, Long came to see me in my office, and said he believed we had a very serious problem with Coach Petrino. Long's investigation had revealed a number of problems concerning the coach. Over the next few days Long would discover a trail of deceit, which raised serious questions about Petrino's continuing service to the university.

On April 8, Long scheduled another meeting with me and related the conclusions he had reached after his investigation of the accident. Long told me Petrino was with a staff member by the name of Jessica Dorrell. Apparently, Dorrell had been hired by Petrino with no formal search process, which was clearly against university policy and Equal Employment Opportunity Commission (EEOC) guidelines. Petrino had told university officials he did not want to interview anyone else for the position, but wanted to hire Dorrell. Other candidates in the search would not be considered, obfuscating an open and fair search. Turns out the staff member was Petrino's mistress, and he had intentionally misled Long about their relationship and her presence on the motorcycle.

Petrino had ignored multiple times an effort by Long to get to the truth. He had lied about the staff member being with him, and tried to cover up his hiring of her without a proper search.

Long and I sat in my office and contemplated what action we should take. Petrino had won games and excited the fan base. Up to that point the future of our football program appeared to be in good hands, and the board of trustees was very pleased with the wins. We knew it was very likely we would get pushback from the board, and the fans in general, if we were to terminate Petrino. Long looked at me and said, "What do you think we should do?" I turned back to Long and said he was the athletics director, and what did he think we should do? Long immediately told me he no longer had trust in Coach Petrino, and didn't see how he could ever trust him again. Long went on to say that trust in this business is very important, and Petrino had broken the trust. No one was bigger than the program itself, and the fact that he had won games should not be a consideration. Long then turned to me and asked how I felt. I told Long that I agreed with him, and thought we needed to make a change.

It was a most difficult decision, but neither one of us knew how in the world we could stand tall with faculty and students if we allowed Petrino to remain as our coach. Integrity had to stand for something, and even though our football program was flourishing, it didn't seem to either one of us that success on the gridiron should enter into the equation. Petrino had lied to his boss. He had also given Jessica Dorrell money, which was a violation of NCAA rules. Even though we clearly knew there would be pushback, we decided at that moment Petrino had to go. Petrino was 51 years old, married, and the father of four children.

I called President Bobbitt and informed him of our decision. Bobbitt verbally agreed that parting ways with Petrino was the proper decision. I told Bobbitt that I thought we needed to call each member of the board of trustees individually and inform them of the decision. Bobbitt agreed. We set up phone calls that day with each member of the board. On the call was Bobbitt; our general counsel, Scott Varady; Jeff Long; and me.

Most of the calls went well. Some of the board members were extremely complimentary of the decision, including trustee Jane Rogers, the only female member of the board. She commended us for a very tough decision, and said we had her support 100 percent.

Unfortunately, two members of the board were very negative, and did not want us to dismiss Petrino. Their only argument was that he had won games and his personal life should not enter into a decision to fire him. One trustee in particular argued the point voraciously. I made a statement on the phone that I later regretted. I did not lose my temper, but I was very definitive in telling this trustee that I completely disagreed with his logic, and thought we needed to be people of integrity and not worry about how many football games we had won. At that moment I felt that I had lost that trustee's support after my perceived scolding of a trustee.

Another trustee made the statement: "Any 51-year-old white male likes to get a little on the side, and we should not fire him for doing what comes naturally," that is, having an affair with a young woman on staff. I was aghast. President Bobbitt made no comments whatsoever as we called the trustees. I wasn't sure if he would back us up in the final analysis even though he had told Long and me that he was supportive.

On April 9, a group of students held a rally in support of Petrino. They made it clear that they wanted him to remain as the head football coach. Even though the rally consisted of a relatively small number of students it put added pressure on our decision.

On April 10, Long called a press conference and laid out a laundry list of mistakes by Petrino. Earlier in the day our lawyers had advised Long to not be specific about the misdeeds by Petrino. I disagreed, and told Long he should be completely transparent and tell the public why Petrino was being fired. He agreed.

I could not attend the press conference, because our attorneys advised that I should stay away since Petrino would have the option to appeal the firing to me. I sat on the screened-in porch at Fowler House and watched Jeff Long make the announcement. During the evening press conference, Long laid out the case in detail. He said the following:

"Coach Petrino made the decision, a conscious decision to mislead the public, and in doing so negatively and adversely affected the reputation of the University of Arkansas and our football program. In short, Coach Petrino engaged in a pattern of misleading and manipulative behavior designed to deceive me and members of the athletics staff, both before and after the motorcycle accident."

Long fired Petrino with cause and told the media that he would not receive an $18 million buyout of his contract.

As I sat on the porch at Fowler House with Jane and our daughter, Katy, watching the media conference, I began to weep. Long was doing such a marvelous job explaining the whole affair that I just couldn't hold back the tears. When it was all over, I called Jeff on his cell phone and he answered. I told him that I was as proud of him as I had ever been of anyone and he began to weep as well. The pressure was enormous. Petrino would later tell the public he was very sorry for his actions, and that he let the fans down by making selfish decisions.

It was a painful decision any way you looked at it. I had always liked Petrino and gotten along well with him. The first few days of his tenure at the university he brought me a Razorback jersey with number "1" emblazoned on it. When I turned 60 years old, he gave me a jersey with the number 60. I also liked his wife, who was a very quiet person but most thoughtful. I hated that it had come to such an ignominious conclusion. I didn't feel sorry for Petrino—he brought it on himself—but I felt sorry for the fans, the university, Jeff Long and myself.

It was true that throughout Petrino's tenure I had received numerous complaints from fans who sat very close to the team benches at the games complaining about Petrino's profane language. I even wrote one back telling him that perhaps we could forgive football coaches when they used salty language. The person replied by email that you can never forgive someone who uses terribly profane language, and informed me that he had been in the army for over 30 years and never experienced that type of profanity, even in the army.

Petrino's attorneys advised him to appeal the firing, so he would be eligible for the buyout on his contract. I denied the appeal and so did President Bobbitt. As far as I was concerned the matter was closed. For weeks we received hundreds of emails and letters excoriating our decision. What helped to have a calming effect was that the students created T-shirts that said, "We are Long on integrity."

I knew that I had burned some bridges with a couple of board members. However, I felt in my heart that we had done the right thing, and that the dismissal of Petrino was completely necessary. To this day I have never changed my mind; even though it was a very difficult decision it was the right one. Later I would receive a telephone call from Mike Slive, commissioner of the SEC. He told me how proud he was of Jeff and me, and was most complimentary of our decision. Slive would later advocate for Long to be the first chairman of the College Football Playoff Selection Committee, a highly prestigious position.

The national media was very kind to the University of Arkansas and our decision and there were several national sports commentators who heralded the action.

But not all of the fans were happy. Long and I received hundreds of letters and emails on both sides of the decision. Many of them—even most—were extremely supportive of the action. However, a number were quite negative, and some were outright mean spirited, profane, nasty, and threatening.

One email that I saved was from my good friend and university benefactor, Gaston Gibson. I had developed a personal friendship with Gaston during the Campaign for the Twenty-First Century. He was a tremendous volunteer, and was primarily responsible for raising private funds to build a new Sigma Nu fraternity house on fraternity row. He sent me a beautiful email that summed up what a lot of alumni were feeling:

> "Dave, with the Tsunami of events created by Petrino's reckless actions and shameful behavior that had the potential of bringing our Razorback program to its knees for a long time, Jeff Long turned a smelly sow's ear into a silver purse. Jeff's handling of a possible no-win situation in front of local, state and national media—in my opinion—may have been one of our finest hours ever for our entire Razorback program, The University of Arkansas and the Razorback Nation that I have ever witnessed.
>
> "In a world where winning comes first most of the time and a world of media outlets that put much more emphasis on being FIRST with breaking news rather than FIRST making sure the news is accurate, you and Jeff Long took a different path. You put character, trust, honesty and integrity in your decision about Coach Petrino above everything else. You also took the time to get the information accurate. Jeff also—in my opinion—may have delivered one of the best recruiting talks for any parent that is considering the University of Arkansas for their child's athletic or academic future. His personal pain, sadness and concern for all that were and will be affected by the unfortunate events he had to deal with was present in his every word and expression. He and his family were in my thoughts and prayers while he was wading through this mess. I know that you were there for him.
>
> "Thank you both!!!!!!! Never have I been more proud to be an ALUMNI of the UNIVERSITY OF ARKANSAS. This should be a good lesson in life for us all that—good times and

bad times in our lives never come to stay but only to visit—how we deal with both defines us and the legacy we leave behind."

I was deeply grateful to Gaston.

Later Gaston contacted me about the color of the football team uniforms. This was around the time Phil Knight was purchasing new uniforms for every game for the University of Oregon football team. Some of them were off the charts in terms of color and style. Many of our student-athletes took notice and wanted to try different looks instead of the conservative red and white, our historic colors. Jeff Long agreed to allow them to explore something new and different. I was OK with it. Many were not.

Gaston sent me an email that read:

Dave,

There are a few things in my life I hold [as sacred] outside of my faith, family, freedom and country. They are absolutes that I can always count on, live with and give my unconditional support to no matter what. They are my compass, my beacon that holds steady when so many things in life become unsteady or cloudy. They reside in memories of my mind and have withstood the test of time. Here they are in no certain order:

The American Flag, Old Glory, The Red, White and Blue. The Pledge of Allegiance to the Flag, the Battle Hymn of the Republic, America The Beautiful, The Ten Commandments, two Very Close Friends for 50+ years and one's Character. Our most unique mascot, The Razorback, from the Cardinal long, long ago before colleges marketed themselves on TV with massive budgets and big fundraising in today's world through athletic exposure. The University Alma Mater with its beautiful words like none other. Our colors, Red and White under the Bright Blue Skies of Autumn in the Ozarks. So American, so beautiful. When I see the black uniforms as I did Saturday, I feel like someone died I knew well that had a big positive influence on me in my life and I missed the obituary and the funeral.

I look at other big-time athletics programs that sustain the test of time and realize they do not toy with their football, colors, namely The University of Alabama, Florida, Auburn, LSU, Texas, Oklahoma, Michigan, Southern California, Notre Dame, they may modify their fashion but not the colors. These universities treat their athletic uniforms like the USA treated The American Flag when Alaska and Hawaii were added as states my freshman year (1959) at the University of Arkansas. The design of the flag was changed not the colors. Did the Board of Trustees approve this color change when Nolan Richardson tried it in a small way in the 1990's? The baseball team in a small way? Or did the Board of Trustees recently approve the change of our school colors? If they did, I missed it along the way and apologize for this out of touch email. Otherwise, hope you and Jane are doing well.

I wrote a reply to Gaston:

Gaston:

Thanks for your email. Let me reassure you that the team colors have not changed and never will. The old red (cardinal) and white are indeed alive and well. What you saw Saturday was a special display of a predominantly gray or anthracite color developed by Nike in conjunction with the team. Many colleges and universities are doing this to allow input from team members and wear the latest gear from Nike. In fact, the Oregon Ducks sport different uniforms every game, compliments of Nike.

A recent poll of fans suggested that 37 percent liked the gray uniforms as a change and 23 percent did not. Reports from the team were very high, and the uniforms made them feel unique and emboldened, whatever that means. Don't worry, it is just meant as a little variety for the players, approved by the players to make them feel important and unique. The red and white will not be displaced, replaced or relinquished! Warm wishes.

I quickly learned many Razorback fans were upset by the uniform colors. I got tons of emails and letters across the country criticizing Jeff Long and me. I sent them all to Long and asked him if perhaps we should reconsider!

It was about this time that I was invited to be the master of ceremonies at the annual gridiron show. The Northwest Arkansas Gridiron was established 40 years ago in the tradition of the Washington Gridiron Club, producing performances that satirize the politics of the day. The NWA Gridiron is written, directed and performed by journalists in the area. I had my doubts about agreeing to be the MC, but after much thought and persuasion by some journalism faculty, I finally agreed to do it. They convinced me to wear a sweatshirt after intermission that said, "Damn it Bobby." I worked hard to make my part funny. Governor Beebe was in attendance and commented that he loved the evening.

CHAPTER 80
POST PETRINO

> *That's one thing you could never say about my college coach Bobby Petrino. He doesn't have a racist bone in his body. That mf hated everybody.*
>
> — *JAQUAY SAVAGE*

Sometime after the firing of Petrino, the board of trustees became very concerned about the leadership of our athletics program. Up until that time the board had been extremely pleased with the leadership of Jeff Long, but a couple members of the board of trustees did not want Petrino dismissed. These board members took out their displeasure on Long. Long's contract was up for renewal and those two board members were holding up the decision. The majority of the board was behind Long, but when you have at least two members concerned and expressing displeasure to the others it creates conflict. The board prefers that all decisions are unanimous. I reached out to President Bobbitt for his advice and support, but he was reluctant to sign off on a new contract without all of the board members in agreement.

When Petrino was dismissed it created a dilemma as to who

would be appointed as the head football coach in the interim. A search would take time and we needed to have someone who could manage the football program during the interim. The board of trustees was primarily interested in winning football games. The university had a history of dismissing football coaches even if they had winning seasons.

Houston Nutt was a good example showing how the board would become concerned if we did not compete in a bowl game. In 2006 the Razorbacks had a winning season, which excited the fans and the board of trustees. However, at the end of 2006 the Hogs would have three devastating losses to end the season—and on top of that, Darren McFadden did not win the Heisman trophy. Even though Coach Nutt showed he could win games, he was out as football coach and would pack his bags and head to The University of Mississippi, where he would coach the rebels for four seasons before being dismissed there as well.

Jeff Long made a colossal mistake in hiring John L. Smith after the Petrino dismissal. The former Michigan State and Louisville coach was hired away from Weber State to replace Petrino and signed a 10-month contract. Smith's tenure had a rocky start following a story in the Associated Press that he would have to file bankruptcy following land deals gone bad in Kentucky. Long claimed that Smith had not informed him of the bankruptcy.

Smith had also done a very poor job in front of the media, and had been criticized mercilessly for some of his comments that seemed pithy and off the mark. Smith had worked at Arkansas previously under Petrino, but left to return to his alma mater, Weber State. He reached out to Jeff Long to hire him back after Petrino quit, and Smith never coached a single game at Weber State.

In fairness to Long, he did have a very good reason for hiring Smith, even though it turned out to be a debacle. Long had tremendous confidence in the assistant coaches who Petrino had hired, and believed that under Coach Smith's leadership the team would continue to flourish with the same assistant coaches intact.

There were other reasons to hire Smith. He had a solid coaching record of 132 wins and 86 losses. He had previously been named the

Big 10 coach of the year when he was at Michigan State. He was a former Razorback assistant who knew the Razorbacks and the coaching staff. Bringing him on would provide a continuity of leadership that was sorely needed.

The media seemed very pleased with the hire and several commentators lauded Long for his decision. This meant the assistant coaches would survive the Petrino firing, and would not have to displace their families. Whenever a head coach is dismissed it generally means that most, if not all, of the assistant coaches also lose their jobs. Long was trying to keep that from happening, and believed in the staff who was in place and that they should continue in their jobs, even after the head coach had been dismissed.

It was an admirable position Long took, and he was only trying to keep the other coaches from having their lives completely in turmoil and seeking employment. I admired Long for his position, but probably should have interceded and demanded that we conduct a full search for a new head football coach. I would later be criticized in many quarters for allowing Long to run the athletics program without my intervention. I had faith in Long and didn't believe it was my place to interfere with his decision making. Unfortunately, hiring Smith was the wrong decision, and it ended up costing Long and me scrutiny by the board of trustees. As I look back on it, I should have told Long that he could not hire Smith, and spared Razorback nation a catastrophe.

The 2012 season was a disaster, and the Razorbacks had only four wins and eight losses. Long made the decision to dismiss Smith and start the whole search process over again for a new coach. The fans were not happy. The board of trustees was not happy. Throwing salt on the wound was the fact that Petrino had been a successful coach, but had been fired because of his personal and professional issues. Many of the fans and a couple of the board members did not really care about the reasons Petrino was dismissed, and held Long and myself responsible for the losing season. On top of that, Smith also had personal problems of a financial nature he was dealing with, and it further made Petrino look better in that, as a board member said to me, "Everyone has personal problems."

Long's contract was up for renewal. I talked with Bobbitt about the contract and felt strongly that it should be renewed, in spite of the fact that we had a losing season. Long was building a great athletics program across the board and raised millions of dollars for the program.

Then entered trustee John Tyson. Tyson started making noise that the board of trustees should undertake a vote of no confidence in Long. I called Tyson and tried to understand his thinking. He told me that he was not necessarily in favor of dismissing Long and might be convinced to award him a new contract, but he felt the board of trustees should enter into the discussion.

I had generally gotten along pretty well with Tyson. He and his father were major benefactors to the university, but his position on Long troubled me.

I tried to explain to Tyson that he really needed to allow the chancellor and the president to make the decision regarding a new contract, and that NCAA rules, as well as SEC rules, required that the board of trustees not become embroiled in these types of issues. That did not sit well with Tyson. I told him he would have to take up the matter with the system president if he wanted to pursue a vote of no confidence in Long. Looking back on it now, I probably handled the situation poorly and should have made an appointment to see Tyson and work to get him behind a new contract.

After the falling out, Bobbitt told me that he thought he could work with Tyson. John Tyson would resign from the board of trustees in February 2013. He was quoted as saying he was frustrated with the board's inability to make meaningful change in the structure and delivery of higher education in Arkansas.

My inability to bring closure to Long's contract because of some questions by members of the board upset Long very much. In recent months five major programs had come after him, including Stanford University, Penn State, Texas A&M, Nebraska and Clemson. I felt bad sending him a message of less than 100 percent full support, which caused him to question staying at the University of Arkansas. I believed in Long. I thought he had done an excellent job in a short time. His only major slip-up was hiring John L. Smith, but that was a big one. I knew our major benefactors, for the most part, liked Jeff Long. I suspected that the average fan base was not as enamored with Long, as I would get calls and emails from some fans saying he didn't return their phone calls. In my opinion, he had done so much to improve athletics we should not let him leave the university.

I felt strongly that the board of trustees should let the chancellor hire and fire the athletics director. If I failed the board then the solution would be to dismiss the chancellor and hire someone who the board had confidence in. I felt the whole ordeal had damaged my ability and authority to manage Long and our athletics program. I also knew that it had caused Long to second-guess his desire to be at the University of Arkansas. It was not a good scenario as we began a search for a new high-profile coach.

Long became very concerned that his contract had not been renegotiated and finalized. At one point he told me that he wanted to place a hold on the contract consideration while he looked at other opportunities. Long had accomplished some incredible things during his five years as athletics director. He had combined men's and women's athletic programs without a single complaint, grievance or lawsuit, and I felt that was a remarkable accomplishment. Other institutions like Iowa and Minnesota and, more recently, Tennessee had an extremely difficult time combining their programs.

The change in our academic culture in athletics during Long's tenure was remarkable. Students were now graduating. For many years none of our student-athletes in basketball left the university with a degree. Grade point averages had been abysmal, and Long had turned that around.

Long had also supported the academic programs of the university with athletic revenue, a first in university history. He had transferred $1 million annually to support university academic programs and another $1.5 million annually to build a new classroom building. His commitment to compliance had been unwavering and unquestioned. He ended an NCAA probation period as a repeat violator, which had plagued the program since 1997.

Long told me he questioned whether or not he should remain at the University of Arkansas, and that perhaps he should entertain offers from other institutions. He felt he had more to accomplish at Arkansas and wanted to stay, but only if the board of trustees was behind him.

In October 2012 I felt that I was in jeopardy of losing my athletics director. As chancellor, what I admired most was the improved graduation rates and grade point averages of our student-athletes. I was not naïve, and knew those very important accomplishments did not resonate with the fan base, nor did it resonate with some of our trustees.

Most student-athletes end their athletics careers after college, and only a handful go on to play professional sports. Getting a degree would allow them to access the work force and excel in life when their intercollegiate athletic years had ended. I knew only too well that we needed to work as hard as we could to get our athletes a college degree if they were going to make it in life. Long felt the same way. I had heard many coaches make comments suggesting that college athletes had no interest in academics and only wanted to play sports. I did not want that to be the case at the University of Arkansas, and Long was making excellent progress on our graduation rates. Long and I got along well during his tenure as athletics director. He was raising funds and graduating student-athletes.

He had proposed to me that we include a clause in his contract that said he could leave the university and suffer no financial damages if I was no longer chancellor. Ben Hyneman, one of our trustees, objected to this language and I convinced Jeff to remove it from the negotiation. He agreed to my request.

In the final analysis, and after a lengthy period of stalling, Bobbitt and the board of trustees agreed to offer Long a new contract. He would remain the athletics director for another five years before he was dismissed in 2017, again over the football program.

CHAPTER 81
BIELEMA

> *I promise you will never see me on a motorcycle with a blond.*
>
> — BRET BIELEMA

In 2012, we announced Bret Bielema was leaving Wisconsin to become the head coach of the Arkansas Razorbacks. Bielema had sent Jeff Long a note after Bobby Petrino was fired, complimenting Long on a most difficult but ultimately correct decision. Long remembered his kindness and reached out to Bielema to see if he might be interested in leaving the Big Ten to come to the SEC. Bielema was not happy with Wisconsin, because he felt that his assistant coaches were not being paid enough. He had also mentioned on previous occasions that he might like to coach in the SEC.

Long came to my office to sell me on Bielema. After an hour of discussion, I gave Long the go-ahead after I talked with Bobbitt and a few board members to gauge their support. Those I talked to didn't really know anything about Bielema, including how to pronounce his name! But they all were reasonably comfortable moving forward.

As I was doing my due diligence, I received a cavalcade of

support for Arkansas State University coach Gus Malzahn. Malzahn had worked for Houston Nutt's staff as offensive coordinator and wide receivers coach, and before that was a high school coach at Springdale High School where he had won a state championship. Malzahn and Nutt had not always gotten along, and Malzahn left Arkansas to be the offensive coordinator at the University of Tulsa. In 2011 he became the head coach at Arkansas State University. A couple of our trustees were pushing Malzahn hard. Some of our donors joined the chorus. Pressure mounted. Long did not believe Malzahn was ready for the head job at Arkansas but did agree to interview him.

John Tyson was pushing his friend and Arkansas graduate, Butch Davis, former head coach of The University of North Carolina at Chapel Hill.

I felt I needed to do my own due diligence on Bielema and started making a few confidential phone calls. I learned Bielema was the first head coach in Big Ten history to win ten games in his first season. Everyone I spoke with had rave reviews for Bielema. I didn't receive one single criticism from anyone who I confidentially spoke to, before or after we hired him. I suspected that trustees were also getting good reviews on him as they didn't try to interfere in the hire.

After we announced his hiring, we put together a hastily planned dinner at Fowler House to introduce Bielema and his lovely wife, Jen, to our board of trustees. It turned out to be a magical evening, and Bret gave a marvelous talk that was highly effective with the trustees.

I was sitting at my desk soon after we hired Bielema, and my assistant came in and said a person was on the phone representing James Patterson, the prolific writer. I could not imagine why he was contacting me, but quickly and politely took the call. Turns out that Patterson wanted to make a gift to the University of Arkansas for scholarships. I had read several of Patterson's novels. I knew he was quite prolific, but would discover later that he had sold more books in the past decade than any other writer in history, some 300 million copies of 130 novels worldwide. I couldn't for the life of me understand why he wanted to give a scholarship to the University of Arkansas.

I scheduled a phone conversation with Mr. Patterson and thanked his assistant profusely.

About a week later, the date arrived for my phone call with James Patterson. I found him to be absolutely delightful. We chatted for maybe ten minutes and he said he wanted to start a scholarship program at our institution. I got up the courage to ask him why he wanted to benefit our school just out of curiosity. The answer I received amazed me.

Ends up his wife is a graduate of the University of Wisconsin and an ardent football fan. When she heard Bielema was leaving to go to Arkansas she told her husband that Arkansas must be a pretty good place if they could lure away Bielema. Patterson decided that he would create scholarships for students at the University of Arkansas. Patterson established the James Patterson Teacher Education Scholarship in 2013 for eight incoming freshmen planning to major in elementary education. The very next year he doubled the number of scholarships. When I retired in 2015, Patterson was giving over $100,000 a year for scholarships at the UA. Patterson's gift to the University of Arkansas was similar to scholarships he has funded at Vanderbilt, Michigan State University, the University of Wisconsin, Howard University and Appalachian State University.

James Patterson is an amazing writer and a very generous man. Later I proposed his name to the board of trustees for an honorary degree.

We all thought Bielema was a good hire. I think he was a good coach, but after five seasons he would be fired through intervention of the board of trustees with Bobbitt's approval. He just couldn't win in the SEC and he lost the support of the fan base and the board of trustees. It would cost Jeff Long his job.

CHAPTER 82
CLOSING A STREET FOR CAMPUS SAFETY

> *Government's first duty and highest obligation is public safety.*
>
> — ARNOLD SCHWARZENEGGER

What seemed to me a very reasonable request turned into an unbelievable bureaucratic nightmare.

As you proceed up Dickson Street past the Kappa Sig fraternity house, property on both sides of Dickson Street is owned by the University of Arkansas. In the old days the street actually wrapped around and through the heart of the university on to Maple Street, but that access was closed many years ago, and only limited authorized access is allowed.

We had numerous pedestrian accidents at the top of Dickson Street after we built a number of classroom and lab buildings in that part of campus. We also opened a new residence hall with food service in that general area. The only way to access these facilities was to cross Dickson Street. We conducted a survey, which showed that over 7,000 students, faculty, and staff cross Dickson Street at all hours of the day, while traffic continues to flow past the top of Dickson Street. Much of the traffic was cars letting students out for classes and returning to pick them up. We contacted the city in July 2012 to inform them that we wanted to control vehicular access to the top of Dickson Street, for the safety of our students. We asked for the ability to control overall access in that two-block stretch on the very west end during the academic semesters (Monday–Friday from 7 a.m. to 6 p.m.). This amounted to 80–85 days each semester or a total of 160–170 days per year during those specific hourly time frames, which is less than half the actual day. Seemed a reasonable request to accommodate for the safety of our constituents. Little did we know it would be a minefield due to city attorney Kit Williams.

We had dealt with the city attorney on various other matters, such as ownership of the Continuing Education Building on the square, and the legality of the A&P Commission making a grant to the university for various purposes. The city attorney's office is a separate office, and does not report to the mayor as a direct report. He advises the mayor and the City Council on legality issues, and the mayor and council are apparently obligated to evaluate his opinion, but they do not have the force of law. Like an attorney general's opinion, they are just that: opinions.

All we were asking for was a solution to a very serious problem of students being hit by cars on the intersection of Dickson and McIlroy streets, surrounded on all sides by our campus. A number of our students and faculty had been injured and three seriously. We did not desire a transfer of property nor vacation of the street itself as we didn't feel that specific step was necessary to carry out our mutual focus on safety for our community.

What we got back from the city attorney was a diatribe of legal gibberish that said it was impossible to accomplish what we were requesting.

The city staff submitted the agenda request, but the city attorney's office pulled the council agenda, and provided a memo as to why the agenda item was pulled. Keep in mind, this was now December and our request was made in July. The city attorney gave a long and rambling explanation for his "no" opinion. His opinion was basically that law simply does not envision or permit the type of arrangement the university was suggesting in its request. The memo went on to say the city had the right to regulate traffic on its streets and could not contract that right away, citing court precedent. The city attorney further said the city has the ability to temporarily close a street to create "safety zones" during a construction project. This law permits these temporary actions, but not permanent closures. He went on to say that the city could consider our request Monday through Friday from 7:30 a.m. to 5:30 p.m., as a construction street closure and public safety request, and review the request under those terms, but this would only be during the construction process, and not a permanent arrangement.

I had always enjoyed a very good relationship with Mayor Jordan. I wrote him the following e-mail:

> Mr. Mayor: I must say that this whole issue is getting to the point of ridiculous. All we are trying to do is protect the lives of students, faculty, and staff. Yet it has become mired in a bureaucratic nightmare. Surely, we can all act reasonably and responsibly with that overriding objective in mind. Your administration is respected for getting things done. Let's get this done. It is getting sillier than feral cats!

(The city had a problem with feral cats, which had been reported in the media).

After a few weeks and threatening to use our police powers to accomplish our goal of safety, and Mike Johnson's patience, the city found a way to allow us to protect our students, faculty and staff and we placed signs closing access to vehicles at the top of Dickson Street. The mayor decided he would not follow the advice of the city attorney, or perhaps the attorney had a change of heart and didn't fight us. We had no more accidents at that intersection during my time.

No good deed goes unpunished!

CHAPTER 83
DISLOYALTY

> *The saddest thing about betrayal is that it never comes from your enemies.*
>
> — ANONYMOUS

> *Do not have evil-doers for friends, do not have low people for friends: have virtuous people for friends, have for friends the best of men.*
>
> — GEORGE SANTAYANA

In July 2012 my office received a telephone call from my chief financial officer Don Pederson. It was the end of the day and I was getting ready to head back to Fowler House where we had a reception beginning shortly. Don said he had an urgent matter and needed to see me immediately. Don came into my office and closed the door. He said that he had just been informed that our accounts at the University of

Arkansas Foundation had been frozen because of a sizable deficit in the advancement division.

It is important at this point to explain the complexity of the advancement budget. That budget comes from several different sources. The advancement division has funds appropriated from the university, which would be considered state funds, but also has budgeted funds from private gifts and income from the endowment. As we were growing the endowment considerably over the past several years, a small percentage of the income from the endowment went to pay development expenses for fundraising. This has been an acceptable practice at most colleges and universities in the country for many years.

At the end of the fiscal year, June 30, the university and the foundation settle all accounts by transferring foundation funds to university accounts to make them whole. This had been standard practice at the University of Arkansas since the foundation was founded many years ago. It is left up to the staff members in each unit to keep track of their funds, in both university accounts and foundation accounts. Throughout the year some university accounts will show a deficit, which is replaced and eliminated at the end of the fiscal year by foundation funds. This does require staff members in each unit to be diligent in watching their accounts and making certain they have enough funding in their foundation accounts to cover university accounts at the end of the fiscal year. Typically a staff member in charge of a unit budget would monitor their foundation funds closely to be certain they were not overspending and could cover any deficit. It was complicated and required due diligence on behalf of fiscal managers, but it had been the way we operated for many years.

When I was vice chancellor, I watched the budgets very carefully, both university and foundation funds. I would demand monthly reports from my budget officer to be certain we were not overspending in both state and foundation accounts. My budget manager was Joy Sharp. She had been at the university for over 35 years, and kept the books for us in our advancement division. I also demanded that each unit within the division of advancement watch their budgets very closely. Sandy and Clay Edwards were in charge of monitoring the development office budget. Never in my 10 years as vice chancellor did we experience a budget deficit.

That day in July, Don Pederson shut the door to my office and told me he was very worried that we might have a significant deficit in the advancement division's budget. At that point he did not know the extent of the deficit, but it was large enough that the foundation officers had suspended spending from any advancement accounts. I told Don that I had an event at Fowler House and was already late, and we would continue to discuss this when he had more information. Don spent most of the weekend with his budget folks trying to get a handle on the advancement deficit.

Early Monday morning Don was waiting for me in my office when I arrived at 7:30 a.m. He said he had much more work to do to determine the extent of the deficit, but he believed it could approach well over $4 million. I was flabbergasted. In those days we were operating on extremely low margins and had very little room for any kind of fiscal deficit in any unit of the university. We were not getting any new funds from the state, and we needed to do a much better job compensating our faculty and staff. While we did have reserve funds we could potentially tap to cover any deficit, that would mean some other program would have to suffer, possibly even salaries.

I immediately asked Brad Choate, vice chancellor for university advancement, and his budget officer, Joy Sharp, to come to my office and meet with Don and me. I told him we had a deficit, but at this point did not know the extent of the problem; it was most likely somewhere between $4 and $5 million. I asked him to look at his records and get back to me as soon as possible with any information he might have. Choate was very surprised and shocked to learn of the deficit. It was an absolute deer-in-the-headlights moment. Choate looked at Sharp for an explanation. Sharp pleaded ignorance and seemed surprised. I asked them to report back to me as soon as possible.

At the beginning of the next week Don Pederson and Jean Schook, the associate vice chancellor for financial affairs, came to see me. They had disheartening news. Their investigation uncovered that the operating deficit in the division of advancement was almost $4 million. They further explained that projected resources available for fiscal year 2013 would not be sufficient for paying salaries—and we could have an *additional* deficit of $3.6 million based on reasonable expectations of revenues from all sources. This was a major financial drain on scarce resources.

I asked Brad Choate to come to my office. I explained the size of the deficit to Choate, and he put his head down and said that he was completely blindsided, and had no idea he had accumulated a deficit of such magnitude. I asked him how in the world was it possible for him to overspend his budget by such a significant margin? His total operating budget for his division was not much more than $11 million, and he had overspent it by 40 percent. I told him this was a very serious matter, and that he needed to work with Don and Schook to get to the bottom of the situation. I then asked Don to conduct an internal audit to get all of the facts and report back to me.

I sent Choate an email outlining 10 directives I wanted him to initiate immediately. They included immediately implementing a drastic reduction in spending, particularly at the foundation level. I told Choate he needed to determine as soon as possible the cause of his budget overage. His budget was balanced in fiscal year 2010. The deficit began in fiscal 2011 and became even larger in fiscal 2012. Also, I told him that, not only did he overspend his budget, but Sharp improperly used an additional $1.3 million that should have been designated to the Jean Tyson Center, further compounding the problem.

I explained in no uncertain terms that failure to determine, in a timely manner, why he had accumulated such a large deficit would require me to ask the system auditors to do a complete audit of the division.

Apparently, his senior staff had not been monitoring their department budgets; in fact, Sharp had not sent them reports for some months, possibly in well over a year. I told Choate that all advancement expenditures should be signed and authorized by Choate and Sharp, at least until this deficit was cleaned up. I told them that they needed to personally monitor expenses and income on a regular basis.

Then I instructed the chancellor's office to take fiscal control and management of all of the accounts listed under Choate's authority. Under Don Pederson's direction, we would employ or assign a new fiscal manager to the division. Choate must either reassign, or dismiss from employment, Joy Sharp. She could no longer have any control over the budget. Choate should work with Don Pederson to determine a schedule of repayment of the deficit over a multi-year period—endorsed by Pederson and me—and commit it to writing.

As always happens at a major university, word got out that Choate's division was in trouble financially. Rumors spread like wildfire, and it wasn't very long before the media picked up on the issue. We started getting phone calls from the *Arkansas Democrat-Gazette,* as well as other media outlets. We tried to explain to the media that this was not a university deficit, as we had reserves of close to $50 million, but rather a deficit in one unit of the university. We clearly had plenty of funds to wipe out the deficit if we so desired, but that would mean we might have to hold back on other university programs and projects.

It would take until October 2012 to receive a full report from Pederson and Schook on the extent of the deficit. In a memorandum from Jean Schook dated October 19, 2012, she told me the total advancement operating deficit was $4,340,920! The initial conclusion, based on a review of both university and foundation accounting records and other supporting documentation, as well as interviews with key personnel, revealed that the vice chancellor for advancement provided inadequate and essentially no oversight of the financial activities of the division of advancement. Advancement staff were unable to explain the circumstances that led to the deficit balances. They were not aware of the magnitude of the deficits in both university and foundation accounts and could not propose curative steps to achieve a sound financial position. In other words, Choate had no idea how the deficit happened or what to do about it.

When we discovered the severity of the situation, we took immediate steps to address the lack of management oversight and the lack of financial management expertise of advancement staff. An advancement fiscal officer was appointed with direct reporting to Pederson. We removed all responsibility for fiscal management from Joy Sharp and Brad Choate.

The audit determined that Choate had provided his computer login credentials to Joy Sharp in direct violation of university policies and procedures. In other words, Choate was not approving any expenditures. He had abdicated that responsibility to a subordinate. What this meant was that Sharp had total authority to spend funds in the division with absolutely no oversight from her vice chancellor. Sharing credentials circumvented internal controls considered foundational to the university, as well as internal and external auditors, in ensuring proper segregation of duties and appropriate approval procedures. Choate did not exercise any oversight over the finances of his division, nor did he monitor the resources available to support operations. He delegated all of these responsibilities to his subordinate.

During the internal audit Choate was asked to show the auditors his budget. He had absolutely no documentation in his office regarding his division's budget. Apparently, he was totally ignorant on the budget of his division, and was taking absolutely no responsibility for budgetary matters. He did say Sharp had provided him with budget reports from "time to time" but he had not retained any of these reports in either electronic or hardcopy format. He had no budget documents in his office. Furthermore, the audit noted that Choate did not monitor spending of foundation funds and had virtually no idea of account balances.

We also determined that there was an intentional effort to disguise a prior year's accounts receivable balance, which had not been cleared, and that Sharp had deposited restricted funds from a sizable gift intended for capital purposes into the operating budget to cover the deficit. Obviously, this was immediately corrected when we determined what had happened. We also determined that units within the advancement division were not given sufficient information about their unit budgets to manage them individually, and were forced to rely entirely on Sharp's authorization for expenditures.

All of this, of course, was devastating information, and basically told me that Choate had been an absent manager of his budget and could give no explanation as to how he had accumulated such a sizable deficit.

During one of the sessions, Sharp finally admitted that she realized 18 months ago that the division budget was getting out of control. She said that she tried to tell her superior, Choate, that their budget margins were very thin, but she admitted that she did not push hard or raise red flags. She said she was sorry and admitted that she became embarrassed that she could no longer pay the bills and simply did not know what to do to get out of it. She just kept accumulating deficits from month to month, thinking manna from heaven would fall down upon her and save the situation. I asked her why she didn't come to me since we had worked together years ago. She had no explanation.

On the other hand, Choate did not express any remorse, and laid the blame at Sharp's feet. He basically said that he had been told by many sources that Sharp was a good budget manager, and he could rely upon her to handle fiscal affairs. I asked Choate why he did not have any documents in his office about his budget. He had no answers. He was clueless.

When I hired Choate, I made it very clear to him that he had to live within his budget. Never once did he come to me with any fiscal issues, or give me any heads-up that funding of his division was in jeopardy.

On October 20, 2012, I sent Choate a memorandum explaining to him that I had very serious concerns about his ability to manage the division. I told him that he was not approving any expenditures, and he had totally abdicated responsibility for his budget. I told him that he had no idea how much revenue he had, nor did he realize that he was overspending his budget. It was like a bunch of drunken sailors spending every dollar they had and not caring whatsoever about where the funds would come from.

A couple years after Choate came to Arkansas, I found it necessary to call him into my office and tell him that he was simply playing too much golf during the week. I told him that I thought he had a golf addiction (which, by the way, is a real affliction) and it had been reported to me that he was out of the office on multiple occasions during the work week, and could be found on the golf course. I also knew that he had been elected president of the board of the Fayetteville Country Club, which told me that he was spending an inordinate amount of time on that activity.

I do believe Choate had an addiction to golf. He would play in all types of weather, rain, snow, and any time of the day. He loved the game and made himself available for several supposed fund-raising trips throughout the country to play golf. He would always tell me they were trips associated with work, but in reviewing his travel I noticed most of his trips were to warm weather places where he could play golf multiple times. I told him that I thought it was a serious problem; I wanted him to enjoy himself in the job, but he needed to curtail his golf game as he was being adversely criticized by his peers.

Given the outcome of the internal audit, I asked my senior officers what they thought I should do? Did I need to dismiss Choate and Sharp? Every senior officer told me that if one of their employees had done what Choate had done, that person would be dismissed immediately. After giving the matter lengthy consideration I decided that I needed to ask for Choate's and Sharp's resignations.

It was one of the most difficult decisions I had ever made, but I felt in my heart that neither one of them had protected the university or their chancellor by doing an extremely poor job managing their budget. I felt betrayed. I was also angry that Choate would take no responsibility for what was clearly his negligence. Choate and Sharp had screwed up big time, and had to pay the price with their jobs.

The chancellor's fund, which came from generous unrestricted gifts that I used for special purposes, had fallen from $500,000 to $80,000 without my knowledge or authorization. They had been tapping it to pay routine advancement bills. Joy Sharp, as budget officer, had the opportunity to initiate, approve, and receive funds, and obfuscate the record with no sign-off from her supervisor, which violated basic sound practice and policy to reduce fraud.

Thank goodness we found no evidence of fraud or private inurement or anything illegal, just very poor management and business practices.

However, Choate had filed for reimbursement on a business trip and received the reimbursement twice. He claimed it was a mistake, and perhaps it was, but he did not do anything to correct the mistake until it was caught by the auditors. It was a modest amount of about $2,500, but you would think when a person got double reimbursement, they would notice it. That further told me Choate could not continue at the University of Arkansas.

Sharp had deposited gift funds meant for a capital project into a current expenditure account as a way to lessen the impact of the deficit. I did not think that was a mistake but a willful act on her part. I had lost confidence in both of them.

Then I made another huge mistake, in that I allowed them to remain at the university on full salary until the end of their appointment which was June 30, 2013. My reasoning was that neither of them did anything illegal. There was no misappropriation of funds. They were guilty of mismanagement, not anything illegal. I wanted to be as kind as I could to them, given my previous association. I wanted to give them plenty of time to find another job and leave the university with employment opportunities. While I was disappointed and even personally hurt, I didn't want to hurt them.

In retrospect I should have fired both of them immediately. I started hearing from a few board members who believed I should've fired them for cause and not allowed them to stay as long as I did. I had removed both of them from their administrative duties and placed them in other positions that had nothing to do with the budget. But I believe I made a serious error in allowing them to stay as long as I did.

Choate bragged that he would have a better job in a month. He thought he was highly marketable. I asked my friend John Glier if he would offer him a job consulting and he said he would. Choate didn't pursue the position. He decided to retire when his salary ended at the University of Arkansas. A few years later he became a semi consultant to The University of Texas where he had previously known the vice chancellor.

MEDIA FEEDING FRENZY

The media started beating me up mercilessly. Most of the damaging comments came from the editorial writer, Paul Greenberg. A couple years earlier Greenberg had written damaging articles about the university that had absolutely no basis in truth. He called the university the "sinking flagship" and pounded on our core curriculum. He said we were not "higher education but rather lower education." He had a bone to pick with the flagship institution and took aim at the University of Arkansas.

I felt it was important to take issue with his nasty columns, which were simply bogus, and corresponded with him. That was a mistake. I knew it was not wise to call out someone who buys ink by the barrel, and that he would always find time to get even. My dad used to always tell me that editorial writers make a concerted attempt to write controversial columns to spark a following and increase readership. It is just what they do, and they love sparing with readers. The more controversial and outrageous the better. Columnists hide behind their opinion pieces, as if that makes them somehow immune from the truth. Publishers will always dismiss editorial comments as just the writer's opinion, and offer a reader the opportunity to write a letter to the editor or an oped giving their side of the story. Dad would always encourage me to be careful taking editorial writers on, as they will always have the final word.

I didn't listen to my dad, and regret it now through hindsight. Judy Schwab told Jane that I just couldn't help myself and it was simply in my DNA to defend my university. I wrote Greenberg and challenged his deeply satiric prose, and pointed out all of the ways we were a major academic institution. I pointed out that we had done so many incredible things these past many years, and were building a truly great institution. It was a mistake. It simply fueled his wrath, and he continued to pound away at the university on a regular basis.

One of my colleagues told me that only 7 percent of the readers of the *Arkansas Democrat-Gazette* ever read the editorial page, and I needed to just cease any dialogue with Greenberg. He was a mean-spirited person who had a death wish for Arkansas and had been a critic of many fine programs in the state. My friend went on to say that most readers know he is hate filled, and I should not take it personally.

In one of my emails, I told Greenberg my private missives to him were not for publication. He published many of my comments anyway, as a rant against me personally. He even took a shot at my father and grandfather saying, "I suspect you know, without my having to tell you, good journalism, like a good liberal arts education, is an acquired trait, often hard won, and not the product of biological inheritance."

Greenberg used the publications of the American Council of Trustees and Alumni to support his position that we had emasculated our core curriculum. None of that was true. Besides, that organization had been discredited by many major higher education groups. A host of education writers claimed the organization was a far-right-wing effort to hurt some of the most prestigious colleges and universities across America. It had close ties to the Koch brothers.

The truth of the matter is that newspapers all across the nation are in serious jeopardy and hundreds have closed over the last 10 years. Greenberg should have taken a look at his own profession before casting stones at higher education.

I even sent a note to the publisher of the paper, Walter Hussman, asking him to explain why Greenberg was beating up on colleges and universities in several of his columns. No satisfaction from Hussman. I didn't expect to receive any.

It is important to point out that Paul Greenberg flunked his doctoral oral exams at Columbia University. He actually flunked them twice. He seemed to harbor a general hatred for higher education institutions, and his failure to make the grade at Columbia University spilled over into his serious pathological issues with colleges and universities. His hate-filled columns on so many subjects, and on so many good people, was an embarrassment to the *Arkansas Democrat-Gazette*.

Paul Greenberg would die on April 6, 2021, after months of poor health. He could do no more damage to journalism and the University of Arkansas and good people everywhere. I hope he rests in peace. The University of Arkansas lives on.

One editorial writer who was extremely supportive of me during this time was Mike Masterson. He wrote weekly columns for the *Arkansas Democrat-Gazette* and came to my defense. I knew Masterson only casually, and he had previously written numerous articles of a negative nature about John White during his time as chancellor. I was surprised that Masterson would come to my defense, but most grateful for his support. He would write numerous articles espousing the truth about the whole ordeal, and a number of my friends and associates would clip Masterson's column and mail them to me. He was a voice of reason in an otherwise spiteful newspaper looking for blood.

I could tell that President Bobbitt and the board of trustees did not like adverse publicity surrounding this deficit problem. I could not really blame them. Bobbitt started asking me for more information about the deficit. I could tell he was frustrated and not pleased. I contacted Bobbitt and told him that perhaps the only way to put an end to the negative publicity was to ask the system and the state to audit the deficit. It was not an easy decision to make, but, after consulting Don, I decided it was necessary. Bobbitt agreed.

I invited the university system auditors as well as the state auditors to come on campus and review the books of the division of advancement. They spent several months reviewing the situation, and basically concluded that no funds were spent improperly or illegally, and that it was a simple failure of Choate and Sharp to manage their budget. After the audits were released, I felt somewhat vindicated, but that didn't seem to stop the editorials by Paul Greenberg. It became apparent to me that Greenberg was on a mission to do anything he could to discredit me in the public arena.

A prominent businessman and friend of mine wrote a letter to the publisher of the *Democrat-Gazette*, Walter Hussman, about

Greenberg. I won't disclose his name since the letter was never published by the paper and I have no evidence of a response from Hussman.

He says:

Walter:

Just my two cents worth, from one friend to another—
Sunday's editorial re the Fayetteville saga was full of cheap shots, conclusions not reflective of the facts, and generally poor journalism. It was typical Paul Greenberg at the bully pulpit, and beneath the standards I know you hold dear. I have read every article published during this witch hunt, and Paul's comments are not rational based on information available. My observation is someone has a burr in their saddle that is a holdover from the F.O.1. lawsuit. I have followed Paul's career, and he often seems to enjoy bullying someone in the public sector who he dislikes. Most recently, you may recall, he took on the honorable Bob Brown, who called him "mean spirited." Actually, he seldom writes anything that I am able to follow and understand the point. He is hurting the paper and needs to be muzzled.

The *Arkansas Democrat-Gazette* appointed a tough reporter to cover the deficit. She was a barracuda who played careless with the facts. She pounded me and our university relations team day after day with unrelenting pressure. She asked for literally thousands and thousands of paper reports, many having nothing to do with the deficit. We thought it was harassment. At times she would ask for the same information multiple times.

Reluctantly I agreed to meet with her to try answer her questions. She brought an editor with her. She was caustic and rude, and I felt she wasn't interested in the truth. It was evident to me that she was looking for dirt, and specifically something to make me look bad. She had already made up her mind and the facts didn't matter. In all we had released 37 responses to the reporter and spent thousands of dollars answering her numerous inquiries, many the same ones over and over again. The prosecutors and auditors had also given her reams and reams of reports and papers about the deficit. She continued pursuing the matter into the new year. She was relentless in trying to find anything, just something the university had done that was illegal. She could never find anything of an illegal nature. Not one thing.

I received a phone call from a person who had contacts within the *Arkansas Democrat-Gazette*. The person told me that he or she had overheard a discussion that the paper had brought down other college presidents, and they could bring me down too. While not normally paranoid, that comment made me physically sick. What had happened to journalism ethics? What had happened to decency, honesty and truthful public service? The whole ordeal was despicable.

The only board member who was constantly supportive during this time was Jane Rogers. She was encouraging to me, and stayed in close touch throughout the ordeal. No other board member nor President Bobbitt made any public comments of support. Maybe they thought I was guilty of misdeeds. I just assumed they were waiting to see how it all shook out. But a word of encouragement would have helped me sleep better.

Trustee John Goodson was initially supportive of me but soon changed his mind, and I later heard that he would brag to a mutual friend that he caused me to lose my job over the deficit. Nothing was further from the truth. As I will relate later, I voluntarily retired from the chancellor's job. John Goodson had nothing to do with my decision.

Then things got much worse. After Brad Choate was hired, he basically ran off the head of university relations, our spokesperson. He hired John Diamond to be the head of our university relations office. Diamond was in charge of media relations. He had come from The University of Maine where he had served in a similar capacity, but had been let go because of apparent budget constraints. When I interviewed Diamond, I was not at all impressed. I have noticed many times in my career, with apologies for stereotyping, that some people from the east seem to think people from Arkansas are hillbillies. That was the impression John Diamond gave me when I first met him. He seemed to have all the answers and thought he was coming to Arkansas to save us. I told Choate that I was not impressed, and encouraged him to keep looking and not hire Diamond. Choate hired him anyway. I could have stopped it and should have.

Our head of university relations before John Diamond, was Tysen Kendig. I thought Tysen had done an extraordinary job for the university, as did executive officers and deans, but when Choate became vice chancellor Tysen started looking for a job. I don't really know all of the issues and probably should have intervened on Tysen's behalf, but again, I felt that I had to back my senior officers. It did not take Tysen long to find a better job, and he left the university to become a vice president at the University of Connecticut, where he remains at the time of this writing. Tysen was a good man. He was loyal, smart, and did a superb job with the media, and I hated to see him resign. I suspect there was a personality clash between Tysen and Choate. I have no doubt it was more Choate's fault than Tysen's.

After I dismissed Choate, I believed it was imperative to fill his vacant position as soon as possible. We were in a major capital campaign, and I did not have time to manage the campaign personally with all of my responsibilities as chancellor. One of the persons who I had been very impressed with was Chris Wyrick. He was the chief development officer for athletics at the University of Arkansas, and had quickly established close relationships with our most generous benefactors. He was well liked by our donors, and had a knack for cultivation. Several donors, including the president of the Donald W. Reynolds Foundation, the J.B. Hunt interests, and the Stephens family, were all impressed with Wyrick, and I received numerous compliments from many university constituents. I invited Wyrick to become the interim vice chancellor and would eventually make his position permanent.

From the very first day, John Diamond did not like working for Wyrick. In one of their sessions Diamond told Wyrick that his "management style was laughable." I'm not sure how somebody can make a statement like that to their boss and expect to keep their job. Diamond just didn't want to work for Wyrick. I feel the main reason was simply that Wyrick was not Choate, and Diamond was very upset that the person who had hired him had been dismissed.

About that time, I became very concerned about the way Diamond was handling the media during our crisis over the deficit. He seemed to be more interested in keeping the media happy than protecting the interests of the university. I also remembered that, during the Bobby Petrino episode, Diamond tried to take credit for managing the issue. It is true that Diamond did provide some prose for Jeff Long, but that's about it. In no way was he the principal manager of the Petrino dismissal.

I don't know all of the details, but things between Wyrick and Diamond deteriorated. Diamond would not take direction from Wyrick. It became clear that something had to give if Diamond was going to survive. Finally, things came to a head and Wyrick told me that he wanted to place Diamond in a different position in advancement. I told Wyrick that it was his decision to do what he thought was in the best interest of the university.

Wyrick had no choice but to dismiss Diamond. After a rather contentious meeting between Diamond and Wyrick, Diamond left the meeting and then someone called the media telling them that he was being dismissed from his position. All I know is that immediately after the contentious meeting the media started calling my office.

I contend that Diamond decided he was going to do anything he could to get back at me, Wyrick and the university, and started claiming that I had ordered my staff to destroy documents requested by the media. It was absolutely untrue and totally made up, but it was new fodder for the media. Anytime the media thinks a public official is abridging the Freedom of Information Act (FOIA), they come out swinging, and that is what they did.

Diamond asked Choate to join his crusade against me, and he readily agreed to do so. Diamond then asked Joy Sharp to join in his crusade. I had given Choate and Sharp several months to find employment and had refused to throw them out on the street, even after being advised to do so. I was flabbergasted that Choate and Sharp would sign on to Diamond's treachery. It told me a lot about their real character.

Then Diamond and Choate went to Republican members of the General Assembly claiming I had done something illegal. These were the same conservative legislators who had opposed the forum on undocumented students. My position on undocumented students, as well as LGBTQ issues, had caused some consternation among conservative Republicans in the Arkansas legislature. Diamond was enough of a schemer to know which legislators might take up his cause and Choate and Sharp joined with him.

One legislator was quite rude, and he was a Democrat: Senator Keith Ingram from eastern Arkansas. He made comments suggesting I was the cause of the deficit. Come to find out he was angry at the university over a number of matters, including football tickets. Boyce Billingsley, major donor and alumnus, published a letter to the editor taking Ingram to task for his comments. She said she would take him to the woodshed, or words to that effect.

The retired head of special collections and editorial contributor to the *Arkansas Democrat-Gazette*, Tom Dillard, also wrote Ingram a very thoughtful and supportive letter taking him to task for his mean-spirited comments. I didn't hear anything more from Senator Ingram.

LEGISLATIVE SCRUTINY

I was asked to appear before a legislative committee to explain whether or not I had broken the law by destroying documents that had been requested under the Freedom of Information Act. There was absolutely nothing truthful about Diamond's charge, but certain legislators saw an opportunity to discredit me. Both Diamond and Choate testified against me at the hearing. It was a tough day. The matter was turned over to the prosecuting attorney in Little Rock and in Fayetteville to investigate whether or not I had broken the law. The FBI also got involved, as the U.S. attorney at the time was a friend, and thought it would be helpful to me to have the FBI watch over the investigation and keep an eye on the proceedings.

Spurred on by Diamond, representative Nate Bell asked the prosecutor to investigate Don Pederson as well to see if he had made false statements to state auditors. The prosecutors totally exonerated Don, finding that he didn't break the law.

In January 2014 I appeared before a legislative committee and made brief comments before an avalanche of questions.

Below is my statement:

Thank you, Mr. Chairman:

I welcome the opportunity to be here today, to listen to your comments and to address your questions regarding the university advancement division deficit. The advancement deficit has given rise to public concern and criticism from many quarters. Members of the General Assembly, journalists, editorial writers, and others have raised questions and issues relating to the deficit that should be answered and issues clarified. In addressing those questions and issues, I am confident we share a mutual objective to separate facts from false perceptions and characterizations.

Let me begin by acknowledging that this investigation has involved the Division of Legislative Audit, the University of Arkansas System auditors, the Office of the Prosecuting Attorney for the 4th Judicial District, the Federal Bureau of Investigation, an internal investigation by campus officials, and hours and hours of staff time, all devoted to the common goal of determining exactly what happened and making recommendations for the future, to ensure it will not happen again. I am here today to offer solutions not excuses. As I told the Joint Legislative Audit Committee some weeks ago, I take complete responsibility for what has happened. It happened on my watch and under my leadership, and I accept full responsibility for any and everything that happens at the

University of Arkansas campus. While I am confident I understand the basic causes as to why it happened, it is my responsibility to alleviate the causes and ultimately fix the problem.

If I were in your shoes, I would insist on knowing if we are implementing controls and appropriate changes to insure this will not happen again. The answer is absolutely. We are implementing every single recommendation of the legislative audit and doing so on an accelerated schedule. We are strengthening oversight and responsibility and fiscal controls. We have replaced personnel and changed reporting lines of budget officers to insure more stringent accountability.

If I were you, I would want to know if the state lost any money, if there was any fraud, or any private benefit or inurement to anyone? Was a single penny misspent, misappropriated, or wasted? Did anyone steal anything? I can answer with total confidence, as confirmed by legislative audit, internal audit, the prosecuting attorney and the FBI, that *all* expenditures were for legitimate needs and there was no misspending or misappropriation of funds, and absolutely no theft or loss of state or private funds.

Further, If I were you, I would want to know if this overspending by advancement damaged the fiscal stability of the University of Arkansas. The answer is an unqualified no. This has never been about a university deficit, but rather a deficit in a relatively small unit of the institution. Your university has strong fiscal reserves and may actually be in the best financial shape in our entire history. This has always been about overspending in a unit. There has never been a deficit at the university level. That is a very important distinction.

I don't intend to get into a shouting match today with university personnel who were dismissed. They both had their day with the prosecutor, the FBI and the auditors. What Brad Choate has said here today hurts me deeply. In his heart he knows I tried to help him maintain some dignity as he looked for another job. It is true we were friends and associates for many years. The absolute hardest thing I ever had to do in my life was to dismiss him from his position. I agonized over the decision for weeks and many sleepless nights. I talked to my senior staff, to faculty leaders, to deans, to President Bobbitt and to board of trustee members. The decision was never made in a vacuum. Likewise, I had known Joy Sharp since high school. Sharp was well respected by her colleagues. She dedicated her entire life to the University of Arkansas. Making the decision to dismiss Sharp was agonizing and devastating to me.

But ultimately it was my responsibility as chancellor to make the decision. I had to admit to myself that Choate and Sharp were hired to do a job, not to be my friends. My ultimate responsibility is to the university and I'm expected to make tough, even gut-wrenching decisions regardless of personal friendships.

After an internal investigation by financial affairs, as well as my own personal discussions with Choate and his senior staff members, including Joy Sharp, we determined that the root cause of the overspending, the proximate cause, was lack of fiscal oversight by both Sharp and Choate. They had drastically overspent the budget they were directly responsible for. It was their front-line responsibility to manage their budget and ensure that something like this would not happen. I based that decision on the evidence, on the facts that have now been confirmed by auditors, internal and external, and of course the prosecuting attorney and FBI. All have arrived at that same conclusion: lack of management oversight.

To this day, Brad Choate has never taken any responsibility

for the overspending in his unit. He has never apologized to me, the faculty, the board of trustees, his staff, anyone for his lack of fiscal oversight. I believe it was Benjamin Franklin who said, "never ruin an apology with an excuse." For someone I knew and respected for many years, that too has been devastating to me personally. When I was vice chancellor, Joy Sharp did work for me and my associates, Clay and Sandy Edwards, for 10 years as budget director. We had an open and honest relationship. I never felt she was intimidated or scared to come to us with questions. We met on the budget regularly and were intimately involved in every budget decision. Sharp did not manage the budget in a vacuum, and we monitored everything she did. Sharp's job was not to make critical budget decisions. That was our job. Her job was to implement our decisions. In monitoring the budget closely, we gave budget spreadsheets to all unit heads on a regular basis. We knew exactly how much in funding we had to the penny and how much we were spending. The monthly spreadsheets monitored all spending and income. Those spreadsheets stopped the year Choate became vice chancellor. Something very important needs to be cleared up and the record set straight.

When Choate became vice chancellor, he did not inherit a deficit from me. In fact, he inherited a $600,000 surplus. I have steadfastly held that position all along, because I knew exactly how much we had in our budget. Legislative auditors made an error in the audit document, which they have since corrected. I have a copy of the corrected statement that I will make available to you if you like. It clearly shows a $600,000 surplus that Choate inherited. To my knowledge, advancement never had a budget deficit before Choate came to the UA.

Brad Choate gave his computer fiscal authorization password to Sharp, which allowed her to approve all expenditures without him. In fact, Choate did not even know how to access the university's computer system to approve budgetary transactions. Sharp could have stolen the university blind had she wanted to. He gave it to her after he was told directly by our chief financial officer not to do so. Apparently, Choate felt our fiscal oversight policies did not apply to him. He could produce no budget documents in his office when interviewed. None. His office drawers contained nothing. No spreadsheets, no budgets, no indication that he had any knowledge or engagement in budget matters. In conversations with him it became obvious he had absolutely no knowledge about his budget. I gave him several weeks to determine what had happened and give me a report on the deficit.

When questioned by me and others, he didn't know the size of his budget, or the most rudimentary information a budget executive should know. He didn't know where the cost overruns existed, what units overspent, or how the deficit could have occurred. Essentially, he was clueless. When he heard the size of the cumulative deficit, he was absolutely stunned. He had no explanation. His senior staff members were never given a budget in which to operate in the four-plus years of his leadership. Several of them told me they pleaded with him for a budget so they would not overspend, but none was ever forthcoming. He told them to see Sharp for anything concerning the budget.

Mr. Choate was paid to manage and control all aspects of the operation of the advancement division, including its financial well-being. No justifiable explanation exists for lacking basic knowledge and control of the budget that resulted in the accumulation of the deficit. Mr. Choate is accountable for failing to perform his job. He abdicated those responsibilities. And he wonders why he was dismissed? He thinks he was thrown under the bus. I told him I would give him plenty of time to find a job so he could leave with some dignity. Even after pressure mounted, from many quarters, to dismiss him immediately, I stuck with the original decision to allow him time to find a job. I actually found him a good position with a Chicago consulting firm whose president told me they would hire him, if Choate would call him to discuss the position. Choate chose not to pursue it.

And what about Mr. Diamond's continued accusations. They have been thoroughly debunked by the prosecuting attorney, and backed up by the FBI. You must reach your own conclusions about Mr. Diamond. I'm going to stick with the ones made by the prosecutor who's investigation took several months to come to his conclusions, which exonerated me from the unconscionable and baseless allegations by Mr. Diamond.

The advancement division deficit and related issues have been thoroughly investigated. The university's treasurer, who came to the university with 25 years of experience in legislative audit, conducted a review. At my request, the Division of Legislative Audit and the university system's Office of Internal Audit conducted an investigative audit that led to several recommendations, and has been accepted by the Joint Legislative Audit Committee. The Office of the Prosecuting Attorney for the Fourth Judicial District, with support from the FBI, investigated certain issues referred by the Division of Legislative Audit, including finding no basis to the sensationalized allegations that Mr. Diamond raised for the first time ever at the Joint Legislative Audit Committee conducted last September. In the final analysis, the actions and assertions of Mr. Choate and Mr. Diamond are nothing more than a desperate effort to deflect attention from the factual determinations and conclusions of each investigation. The facts and conclusions of each review and investigation are important. They *all* concluded that the primary cause of the deficit was overspending to hire personnel in the advancement division. They also determined that no theft, fraud, or misappropriation of funds occurred. The report of the Office of the Prosecuting Attorney found no wrongdoing with regard to the issues referred by the Division of Legislative Audit, and further found nothing to substantiate Mr. Diamond's allegations at the September hearing of the Joint Legislative Audit Committee. This is important because Mr. Diamond made serious allegations that were unsubstantiated during the course of a thorough investigation by the prosecuting attorney's office. In fact the FBI told me to be careful, as Mr. Diamond was out to get me. I took that threat seriously.

I encourage the members of this committee and the public to review the prosecutor's report and the interview notes that have been publicly released. The facts show that, contrary to Mr. Diamond's headline-grabbing testimony, I did not issue any directive ordering destruction of documents to impede the auditors from thoroughly reviewing the deficit. Further, the report and the investigator's interview notes show that I did not issue any directive to destroy records that were responsive to any Freedom of Information Act requests. In response to a recent erroneous media report, the Office of the Prosecuting Attorney publicly confirmed that it did, in fact, investigate these issues, and the evidence did not support the charges.

I take my responsibilities as chancellor very seriously. I am truly sorry this has happened on my watch. I am embarrassed at the continued interest in the story by some. I accept the ultimate responsibility. I truly regret that it has affected the lives of many good people. But I also know in my heart why it happened and who was the proximate cause for overspending.

I am sustained by the avalanche of support that my wife, Jane, and I have received from across the state. Legislators on both sides of the aisle, alumni, friends, faculty, staff, and students—especially the students. And, yes, even some members of the media who have also been very supportive.

For the past 15 years, I have dedicated all of my heart, soul, and energy to help the university, and I am committed to leading the university forward for the benefit of our students and the people of the State of Arkansas. As part of that effort, and with humility, I recognize there are many lessons to be learned from the events and issues surrounding the advancement division deficit. In hindsight, I recognize that I might have handled various issues and matters in a better way, and I am committed to incorporating the lessons I have learned to make the university stronger and better. I welcome input from members of this committee and the General Assembly as we move forward into the future. Thank you.

Both prosecuting attorneys and the FBI found there was absolutely nothing I did wrong, and that Diamond's charges were bogus. I was completely exonerated by all parties. In fact, the head of the FBI in Fayetteville told me that I should be careful because John Diamond was on a mission to destroy me. The FBI told me that Diamond would do anything he could to discredit me, and I should just be careful until he had left Arkansas. Diamond and Choate had lost on all attempts to destroy me and my staff.

AFTERMATH

Later John Diamond would write a book about his charges against me. I have never read it and don't plan to. I've never been particularly fond of fiction.

Diamond left the university and went to a job in Wisconsin, which lasted only a few months. He went back to Maine and started a consulting company and then landed a job as the alumni secretary at The University of Maine.

Even though all of the investigations turned out favorably toward me, it took a huge toll on me personally and my family. After the ordeal had ended, the board of trustees passed unanimously a vote of confidence resolution. That was orchestrated by Jane Rogers, which I appreciated. Unfortunately, it might've been helpful had the board done that earlier during the whole ordeal. What I regret the most was that my boss, Dr. Bobbitt, never once made comments publicly on my behalf. Privately he would tell me that he was behind me, but never made his comments known to the media or the general public. That hurt me very much. I knew I was innocent, and that John Diamond and Brad Choate were simply disgruntled employees who had a serious vendetta. I also knew that, had my president been Alan Sugg, I would've had the support from the system much earlier during my travails. In fairness to Bobbitt, perhaps he felt that he had to remain neutral until the prosecutors had reviewed the situation. But it still caused me much grief and sleepless nights that he did not come to my defense earlier.

For some time after Diamond's dismissal, he sent FOIA requests for volumes and volumes of materials, for what purpose who knows. Some suggested he was trying to find evidence of slander or libel by university officials. He wanted a copy of all print and electronic documents, correspondence, and recordings (actual as well as transcriptions) that alluded to him by name or inference for the time period of January 28, 2014 to June 17, 2014. This request included documents, correspondence, and attachments produced by and/or sent to or from over 20 individuals at the university. It would have taken hours and hours of staff time to comply with such a broad request. Fortunately he was no longer an Arkansas resident and we had no requirement to comply.

I never intend to lay eyes on Brad Choate or John Diamond again. In my opinion they were disloyal, spiteful, arrogant, and untruthful. Their true colors came through. Even though they caused me tremendous heartache, I'm not angry, just terribly disappointed, particularly in Choate, whom I gave every opportunity to be successful in his career. I'm reminded of the anonymous phrase: "There comes a point in your life when you realize who matters, who never did, who won't anymore and who always will. So don't worry about people from your past, there's a reason why they didn't make it to your future."

I also never got support from the board of trustees during the ordeal. Yes, they did give me a vote of confidence later, but while I was suffering media onslaughts and legislative hearings I was on my own. One of the only exceptions was Jane Rogers, who defended me every step of the way. Jane was vigorous in her defense, and I had many conversations with her that helped me through those tough days. I remain most grateful to her for her leadership and support. The other was Sam Hilburn, who told the *Gazette* reporter that he supported me 100 percent. When Hilburn was ending his term on the board of trustees, he wrote a very supportive letter to Jane Rogers. He said that he was unable to attend the meetings on January 24, but wanted to express his hope that the board cease any attempts to scrutinize Chancellor Gearhart regarding the legislative audit. He said in his letter that for the board to pursue the investigation is divisive and damaging to the university. He said:

> "It is time for the Board to publicly unite in backing the Chancellor, in accordance with their privately held feelings. The Board and numerous other entities have had ample opportunity to conduct an examination of these issues. Despite all such thorough inquiries, there has yet to be evidence uncovered of any illegality on the part of the Chancellor. We all know what happened. It is a shame that it happened. But we should not and cannot condone the further vilification of the Chancellor as a scapegoat. To continue on this path only serves to perpetuate the biased agenda of outsiders who seek to undermine the University. For the future good of the University, the Board must let it go and move forward. Chancellor Gearhart has been, and continues to be, a significant asset to this State and the University we love and cherish. His dedication to excellence has led to national recognition in academics, research, and job placement, as well as increased enrollment. The current position

of the U of A in the academic arena is unparalleled in our history."

I was deeply grateful to Sam Hilburn, who I found to be a thoughtful person who believed in the truth. I only wish other trustees had come to my defense earlier. I suspect Dr. Bobbitt could have made that happen.

I received literally hundreds of letters, emails and messages from friends across the state who were very supportive of the issues Jane and I were going through, and many wrote to the *Arkansas Democrat-Gazette* expressing their dismay at the pounding I was receiving from the newspaper day in and day out. One stands out, which was deeply appreciated by us, sent by Larry and Patti Brown of Dallas, Texas. Larry was a former football star for the Razorbacks, and both he and Patti knew Jane during their college days at the university. They came to my defense immediately, and Larry wrote passionate letters to the *Gazette* reporter pointing out the discrepancies in her many articles. The Browns, along with Patti's sister and brother-in-law, Ed and Bonnie Harding controlled a private foundation that had been very supportive of the university financially, and continued to support Jane and me during the ordeal. We remain close friends and their support meant the world to Jane and me.

The chairman of the trustee audit committee was Ben Hyneman. The university had accumulated two internal negative balances that had been carried forward for the past several years, which occurred before I was chancellor. The carryforwards were for two different and necessary expenditures. A new student information computer system, which was quite costly, as well as the need to shore up Garvan Woodland Gardens in Hot Springs. Neither one of these internal loans happened on my watch, and I had inherited both of them from previous administrations. Hyneman felt the internal loans should be disclosed as if they had happened on my watch. Perhaps he was correct, but I objected. I was being hammered mercilessly in the media for a deficit in advancement, and making it look like these two internal loans—which occurred long before I became chancellor

—happened on my watch, would get media attention and add insult to injury.

Sure enough, the media and Greenberg had a field day suggesting that I had caused multiple deficits on my watch. I felt that Hyneman could have been more helpful to me in the situation. We had always disclosed the internal loans in all of our financial materials, but to highlight them during this time would be deleterious to me. Because of the adverse publicity we had to pay off the internal loans immediately with surplus funds, which affected the salaries we could give faculty and staff that year.

Then the university system auditor got involved. I suspected that Hyneman turned him on to the issue of carryover accounts, but perhaps it was Bobbitt. Jacob Flournoy was the system official who strenuously objected to the carryovers, and made every attempt to link them to the advancement deficit. He claimed we had what he described as "loans" that had not been approved by the board of trustees, and had not followed any formal procedures nor created an amortization schedule. Remember, these are negative balances I inherited, the system office was totally aware of the carryforward, and they had been approved by Alan Sugg when he was president.

Don Pederson told me we had never characterized the carryforwards as loans, but rather the carrying forward of negative balances which created an accountability much like an internal loan. Flournoy seemed to be attempting to expose us, finding that we had done something wrong by not implementing a formal loan program. We immediately wondered why he was raising this issue now, as he had known about the carryforwards for years and said nothing. If we had done something improper, he was part of the problem as he never had raised it previously. Flournoy copied the legislative auditor, Hyneman, and Bobbitt, and tried to lay the blame at my feet while I was trying to deal with the advancement deficit.

I sent Flournoy an e-mail taking him to task for his issues with our carryforward accounts.

I told him that one of the carryforward accounts—the student information system—was designed to be paid back through the implementation of a fee authorized by the board of trustees. Obviously by authorizing the fee, the full board approved what he characterized as an internal loan. It was also authorized by the system president at the time. Why was he not acknowledging that fact?

I told Flournoy the other account was for Garvan Gardens, a deficit we also inherited, which was approved and also authorized by the system president and the chairman of the board at the time. But Flournoy was not acknowledging that fact at all. Both loans, as he characterized them, had clearly been stated in audited financial statements every year, yet this was the first year he and his colleagues had indicated any issues with them. Why wouldn't previous audited financial statements have flagged the issue? Was it missed by the auditors? It would seem to me that Flournoy, as chief auditor, had the principal responsibility to call these matters to the attention of all concerned many years ago. Why were they just now surfacing? Why did Flournoy not make these recommendations over a decade ago? I went on to ask how he could label these "deficits" when the UA was beginning the fiscal year with healthy reserves of almost $50 million?

I never got a reply. I knew if Alan Sugg had been president this would not have happened.

Don Pederson also found documents from FY 2000, which clearly showed that Flournoy and internal audit had reviewed the Garvan Gardens deficit many, many years earlier when I was not chancellor, and raised no issues. To this day I don't know why or who authorized him to lump it in with the advancement issue and create more problems for me.

To resolve the matter, we took funds out of reserves set aside for other projects and paid off the balances that I inherited.

Another fact worth mentioning is that, during the audits into the advancement deficit, I was never asked a single question from Flournoy, his auditors or legislative auditors on my perspective of what happened. I was never interviewed directly by any of the system or state auditors conducting the audits, specifically on the cause of the deficit. That just seemed very odd to me. More than anyone else, I had the most knowledgeable perspective on the causes of the advancement deficit, yet neither team ever reached out to me for those perspectives during the entire audit. The audits were completed having never directly interviewed the chancellor about causes and effects.

I was also extremely disappointed in trustee David Pryor. Trustees informed me that Pryor had made a comment in executive session of the board of trustees meeting that had disparaged me. Apparently, Pryor asked the question of the board if it was time to distance themselves from me because of what was happening with the advancement deficit. When I learned this I was surprised and saddened. I thought I was a good friend of Pryor's and his wife Barbara. I had put millions of dollars of university and private funds into the Pryor Center for Arkansas Oral and Visual History. I guess I should not have been surprised, as David Pryor was first and foremost a politician. Up to that time I had always thought of him as a statesman, and was disappointed that he did not rally to my defense. Later, someone very close to Pryor told me he had a great distaste for adverse publicity. I can only assume that the way I was being hounded by the media caused him to make those comments, which were very damaging to me. I never felt the same about Pryor after learning of his disparaging comments. They were very hurtful to both Jane and me.

Then, as if things were not bad enough, the media made inquiries about an alleged deficit in the Walton College. There was no deficit in the Walton College. The college's revenues had substantially exceeded its expenses for the fiscal year. No one seemed to know where the rumor came from, but a reporter told me that he had spoken to a trustee—but would not answer any of my questions as to the source of the rumor.

On January 23, 2014, I appeared before the board of trustees in open session. I told the board that the most important message I wanted to deliver was that we embraced and were actively implementing new practices gleaned from the campus-level internal review, the two extensive audits, and the detailed investigation performed by the Washington County and Pulaski County Prosecutor's offices, with the assistance of the FBI. I said we took the deficit in the advancement division and the constructive recommendations we received seriously, and we were working very hard to prevent any similar occurrence in the future. I admitted that the issue had been a humbling experience for me and for the university staff involved in the situation. I said that I was not there to make excuses for the deficit, and I was very sorry it happened. I took full responsibility for the operation of the entire university. The proverbial buck stopped here, and I embraced the overall responsibility.

At its core, the advancement division deficit resulted from the division hiring more personnel for an upcoming capital campaign than funds allowed. The advancement division failed to maintain and monitor its budget. The simple truth was that Mr. Choate failed to carry out his most basic duties and responsibilities as vice chancellor by ignoring his duty to manage and supervise budgetary matters. Mr. Choate was paid to manage and control all aspects of the operation of the advancement division, including its financial well-being, but he did not do this. Having been in that very same position for 10 years before becoming chancellor, I told the board that no justifiable explanation existed for lacking the basic knowledge and control of the budget, which resulted in the accumulation of the deficit. These facts have been confirmed by the external auditors and prosecuting attorney, who also determined that absolutely no theft, fraud, or misappropriation of funds occurred.

The prosecuting attorney also found no wrongdoing with regard to the issues referred by legislative audit, nor did he substantiate any of Mr. Diamond's claims. All of these facts confirmed exactly what I told the board a year and half ago about the deficit. I went on to say that, for the past 15 years, I had dedicated all of my heart, soul, and energy to the University of Arkansas, and I was committed to leading the university forward for the benefit of our students and the people of the State of Arkansas.

The entire ordeal took a huge toll on me. I'm reminded of the quote from George Santayana:

"Do not have evil-doers for friends, do not have low people for friends: have virtuous people for friends, have for friends the best of men."

At one point I wondered if I should retire early. I had been through the mill and wondered if my time as chancellor should come to an end. I also completely lost faith in the media. From the very beginning I felt the *Arkansas Democrat-Gazette* was trying to get me dismissed, and went on a tirade to make it happen.

About this time I heard from my pastor who sent me an email of support. I appreciated it very much. Pastor Tony Holifield of Central United Methodist Church said the following in his email:

Dear Dave,

I just wanted to let you know that you and Jane have been in my prayers regularly over these past months. I have been following closely the sequence of events surrounding the Advancement situation that you have been dealing with and cannot begin to imagine the stress and anguish you have been through as you have had to deal with this. I was so pleased to read just recently of the strong vote of confidence given to you by the Board of Trustees as they affirmed you and the excellent leadership you have given to the U of A across the years of your tenure—affirmation that is well deserved. I will continue to keep you and Jane in my prayers in the days ahead. I trust that the whole situation will soon be completely behind you, and that life will regain some semblance of normalcy. Keep faith and trust the Lord as you continue the journey. Two verses of scripture come to my mind for you this morning. They have been a great source of strength for me across the years and I trust they will be an encouragement to you. They are Proverbs 3:5–6 and Philippians 4:13.

"Trust in the Lord with all your heart and lean not on your own understanding. In all of your ways acknowledge him, and he will direct your path." (Proverbs 3:5–6)

"I can do all things through Christ who strengthens me." (Philippians 4: 13)

Dave, may God bless and guide you in the days ahead as you continue to lead the U of A into the future. Sarah and I are amongst the many who are strongly behind you.

Appreciatively,

Tony Holifield

To close out this sad chapter is one shining moment I will never forget. I felt it necessary to hire my own personal attorney during the ordeal. I simply didn't feel the system office was protecting me, and wanted someone totally on my side. I was very glad I did, as my lawyer helped me greatly with the system lawyers. After it was all over, I called my attorney to find out what I owed him. The bill was $30,000. He then shocked me and said I owed nothing.

My brother, Jeff, had stopped by my lawyer's office and paid the bill in full.

CHAPTER 84
HILLARY

> *If I want to knock a story off the front page, I just change my hairstyle.*
>
> — HILLARY CLINTON

I wrote Secretary of State Hillary Clinton in early 2013 and proposed that the university inaugurate a School of International Relations to be known as the Hillary Rodham Clinton School of International Relations. Our initial concept was to educate and train students from across the globe to succeed in an increasingly interdependent world and to promote continuing internationalization of the curriculum at the University of Arkansas. However, a major focus of the Hillary Rodham Clinton School would provide unparalleled support for women from developing countries.

Appropriately, the school would be affiliated with the J. William Fulbright College of Arts and Sciences, but would also have an interdisciplinary component, drawing from other colleges and schools at the university, including the School of Law; the Dale Bumpers College of Agricultural, Food and Life Sciences; the Sam M. Walton College of Business; and the Clinton School of Public

Service among others. I went on to say that the Hillary Rodham Clinton School would allow the university to acknowledge her as our country's preeminent Secretary of State and to serve as an educational continuation of her legacy.

I never heard from Hillary but did get a letter from her assistant many weeks later saying she was still considering it. I never heard another word, and nothing ever happened.

CHAPTER 85
SUMMER VACATION 2013

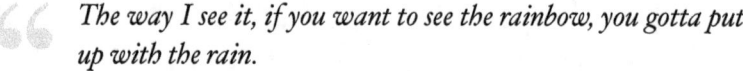

> *The way I see it, if you want to see the rainbow, you gotta put up with the rain.*
>
> — *DOLLY PARTON*

It seemed that every summer vacation was disrupted by some issue or calamity at the university. The same thing tended to happen during my time as vice chancellor. Our extended family rented a large house in Gulf Shores, Alabama for a week of rest and relaxation but it was notoriously interrupted with problems at the university.

In June 2013, right in the middle of our vacation, Don Pederson forwarded me an email he had received from Barbara Goswick, the system chief financial officer. Goswick said a board member had requested that we provide a list of former administrators who held the rank of dean or higher and had returned to teaching. She wanted each campus—except UAMS for some reason—to provide the following information about these individuals: Previous administrative position, current position, FY13 salary, 9- or 12-month appointment, number of courses taught per year, and number of hours taught per year. It was an immediate red flag for Don Pederson as well as provost Sharon Gaber. They were very reluctant to comply with the request and considered it a witch hunt. They wanted me to weigh in on the request.

I knew exactly where it was coming from, trustee Jim von Gremp. He had previously expressed dissatisfaction with the pay former chancellors and deans would receive when they went back to the faculty as a tenured full professor. Our policy was that a senior official who stepped down and returned to his or her tenured position would receive 80 percent of their administrative salary.

There was good reason for that policy. It allowed us to move a problem senior officer out of their administrative role and back to teaching and research if they knew their salary would not be too terribly diluted. I believed very strongly it had worked to our benefit, and most likely kept the institution from being sued by disgruntled academic administrators. It had the added benefit of keeping the university out of the media when we made changes in deans and vice chancellors. If they knew their compensation would not be too impaired they tended to go quietly. Besides, we were right in line with other major universities. The standard practice was 70 percent to 80 percent of salary among many institutions that we benchmarked with, particularly in the SEC. I asked provost Gaber to update information on what others were doing and she gave me a list of 25 major public institutions that had a similar or identical policy as ours.

My major concern was what looked to be a request that targeted a defined group of senior people who had, in many respects, dedicated a significant part of their lives to the University of Arkansas.

I told Bobbitt we would certainly comply, but I felt compelled to raise my concerns with this type of request from a member of the board of trustees. I went on to tell Bobbitt that this request was singling out a defined group of senior faculty and could be interpreted as the board member having an issue or problem with a particular class of faculty, many of whom had given years of service to the institution. I said that I did not believe it was in the best interests of an academic community of scholars, and it raises suspicion and doubt as to their many contributions to this campus. I went on to say, if the board member has specific questions about specific faculty members that is one thing, but to define a whole class of faculty is an abuse of authority and contrary to the principles of academic freedom. At worst, it is McCarthyesque in nature. I asked Bobbitt several questions:

- What are the reasons for such a request?
- Are there problems or issues that a board member is looking for?
- Does the board member feel this group of faculty is nonproductive?
- Is there a particular person being targeted?

I was terribly disappointed the request was going forward and did not believe it was appropriate. I told Bobbitt that I would be pleased to talk with the board member who raised the question and try to find a solution for his issues. Bobbitt would not give me the name of the board member, but I already knew who it was.

I did not receive a reply from Bobbitt to my email. I went ahead and complied with his request and sent him a long email outlining the faculty members who were affected by the request of a productivity analysis of former administrators. The report looked very good and showed Bobbitt and our unnamed board member (von Gremp) that all of the former administrators were very productive in their jobs.

FACULTY ANALYSIS

With the exception of one, all members of that defined class were teaching a full load.

Several were teaching more than the standard two classes per semester. Some were teaching three, four, or more classes, in addition to their scholarship, which, while not in the original system request, was an important faculty criteria for a major research university. To ask only for teaching hours obfuscated and diminished the other important duties of a senior faculty member in research, scholarship, advising, and service, which are all hallmarks of a land-grant institution. The request showed an overall ignorance and misconception of the type of university we are, and our unique role and mission in higher education, particularly in Arkansas.

I pointed out that some affected by the request had recently published significant books, which had received national acclaim, including Professor Randall Woods who published a book that year on William Colby that was profiled in *The New York Times* and *The Wall Street Journal*—and he did it while teaching two and three classes the last two semesters. Woods was one of our most prolific publishers and all of his books have received national acclaim. He was a former dean of Fulbright College. He had been recruited by several major universities, most recently The University of Texas, which had offered him a tenured distinguished professorship to join their faculty ranks and a significant compensation increase.

Professor Bill Schwab, also a former dean of Fulbright College, only taught one course but also published a nationally acclaimed book, *Right to DREAM*, on immigration reform. Bill had received countless accolades for his book, including mention by several members of Congress. A number of Latino organizations are using his book in the fight for fairness in immigration reform. He traveled the nation speaking on the subject, including several trips to Washington D.C. to meet with congressional officials, speak before congress, and serve as an expert witness. He resumed the standard course load the next semester.

The only former administrator and now full-time faculty member not carrying teaching responsibilities was former dean of the College of Education and Health Professions, Reed Greenwood, who was relieved of teaching to focus on issues in the education reform program. This program was funded by a $20 million gift from the Walton Foundation and Windgate Foundation during the Campaign for the Twenty-First Century. Dr. Greenwood was primarily responsible for the gift, which was the largest gift ever made to a college of education in the United States. He would resume teaching the following semester. His work with faculty in the education reform program had received high praise from the Walton family.

I pointed out that Chancellor Emeritus John White taught three courses the previous semester. He was also finishing a definitive textbook in his field. For the last five years he had refused any raise, and had asked that those funds be redistributed to younger faculty in the College of Engineering. Recently he was offered a distinguished professorship at Georgia Tech University for a salary far in excess of what we were paying him. Dr. White was the only active faculty member in Arkansas who was a member of the prestigious National Academy of Engineers. Losing him to Georgia Tech would be a huge blow to our ability to achieve our proclaimed goal of being a top-50 public research university.

Dr. Otto Loewer was the former dean of the College of Engineering. Dr. Loewer taught eight fall classes and nine spring classes. He published two research articles in 2011. He published a book in 2012, and he published another book chapter in 2012.

Professor Robert Moberly was the former dean of the School of Law. Moberly taught two fall classes and two spring classes and his scholarship was superb.

Professor Cynthia Nance was the former dean of the School of Law. Professor Nance taught two fall classes and two spring classes. She had been honored by several national organizations and was revered by former students.

As chancellor of the University of Arkansas, I stood firmly behind all these distinguished faculty and their productivity. I was terribly dismayed that such a request would emanate from the system office, and particularly without discussing it with me first, who had ultimate responsibility for the faculty at my campus. Nobody was getting rich off of the university.

Then the chancellors received an email from Bobbitt withdrawing the requested information. Bobbitt said the original purpose of this request was to better understand the application of the board policy governing the return of administrators to regular faculty ranks. He said the issue was more complicated than he first thought, and as such he was still analyzing exactly what information was required for that purpose. He asked that we suspend the request for information at this time and delete all emails.

While the request was retracted it did not diminish the impact on morale. In effect, the request was a witch hunt in an attempt to prove that a few of our faculty, who used to be administrators, were not productive citizens and did not deserve the pay they were receiving. I knew how the request came about and who perpetrated it and the motivation behind it. The main target was Chancellor Emeritus and professor John White. The board member thought he was being paid too much and wanted to take him to the woodshed.

THE ISSUE RESURFACES

The issue would not go away. About a year later it resurfaced. Bobbitt decided that the 80 percent rule was too lucrative. It was true salaries had increased markedly since the policy had been put in place, and to the public there could be a perception that we were paying our former administrators too much when they returned to the faculty.

I urged Bobbitt to reduce the percentage to 70 percent or even less. He chose to pay former administrators based on the top three salaries in the department where the former administrator would reside. That was probably OK for engineers or business faculty, where salary levels were considerably higher than faculty in education or the humanities. There existed a wide disparity among academic disciplines based mainly on supply and demand and market conditions.

Bobbitt said I could share the new proposed policy with others to gauge reaction and I did so with those affected, as well as all of our deans and vice chancellors. What I got back was borderline rage that such a policy would be implemented. Particularly offended was former chancellor John White, who felt the policy was targeting him. I was aware that White had been offered numerous faculty positions at prestigious institutions as well as Georgia Tech. White sent me an email articulating his feelings that the proposed solution was simplistic.

I asked Bobbitt and von Gremp to meet with those affected. Von Gremp refused to meet.

Personally, I took note of the proposed new policy, as it would affect me considerably if I decided to retire and join the faculty. In effect, I would lose $200,000 in salary if I retired from the chancellor position after the new policy was implemented. Basically, I knew I had a decision to make: Did I want to forgo teaching and publishing and retire from the chancellor job and get the 80 percent salary, or should I stay as chancellor for three to five more years at full salary? If the new plan was implemented and the 80 percent policy changed, I would need to move quickly to retain 80 percent of my salary. Of course this only applied to tenured faculty members, which I was, with a tenured position in the higher education program. I couldn't see remaining as chancellor for another five to seven years. The decision was an easy one to make. Maybe the system folks knew such a new policy would help me decide to step down as chancellor.

When von Gremp became chairman of the board, he immediately began questioning a number of initiatives that seemed to indicate he was acting as the system president. He would regularly come on campus and talk to faculty, asking them about my performance as chancellor. I called Bobbitt and asked him to talk to von Gremp and put a stop to his meddling and questioning of faculty and staff. Nothing happened. I soon realized that I was going to be questioned on just about everything in my administration and became quite frustrated.

GARVAN WOODLAND GARDENS

Bob Bledsoe was serving as the executive director of Garvan Woodland Gardens in Hot Springs. Bledsoe was a marvelous administrator and worked very hard to make the gardens self-sufficient. The gardens had been given to the university in the mid 1980s. Garvan Woodland Gardens is the 210-acre botanical garden of the University of Arkansas, located on Lake Hamilton. It was purchased by the Arthur B. Cook family of Malvern, Arkansas in the 1920s. Arthur B. Cook operated the Malvern Brick and Tile Company until his death in 1934. His daughter, Verna Cook Garvan, became one of the first female chief executive officers of a major southern manufacturing business after his death. I had actually called on Mrs. Garvan in 1982 when I was at the University of Arkansas the first time. Mrs. Garvan donated the 210-acre Garvan Woodland Gardens to the University of Arkansas School of Architecture in 1985, the year I left for Penn State. It was a magnificent spot, and Mrs. Garvan had been clearing the property and planting shrubs and trees for many years.

Today the gardens feature many species of azaleas and more than 100 species of ornamental and native shrubs and wildflowers. Many benefactors have given generously to make the gardens a show place for Arkansans. The Anthony family, owners of a large timber company, built the Anthony Chapel with the financial help of oil and gas executive Bob Evans and his wife Sunny, which has become a popular wedding venue. The Bob Evans Children's Adventure Gardens and the Evans Tree House were also contributed through the amazing generosity of the Evans family.

The Stella Boyle Smith Foundation was also a major benefactor of Garvan Gardens and inaugurated the Stella Boyle Smith Crescent Garden, which improved the landscape immeasurably. Philanthropists Cathy and Mike Mayton, as trustees of the foundation made that happen.

The annual holiday lights display—featuring 5 million lights over 18 acres—draws thousands of visitors each Christmas season to the gardens. Garvan Woodland Gardens is a unique and special place for Arkansas.

While many people gave generously to the gardens their gifts were not particularly for operations. The state had given some funds, but it was still experiencing money problems. Bledsoe developed a plan, with our assistance, to make the gardens self-sufficient. As an aside, most botanical gardens in the United States were not self-supporting. Maintenance and upkeep were extremely expensive, and admissions fees were simply not adequate to keep the operations going. Through philanthropy and admission fees, we thought we had a plan to move it to at least breaking even. Bledsoe was doing a remarkable job moving in that direction.

Enters board chairman von Gremp, who thought the gardens

should be immediately self-sufficient, and had no patience for adopting a plan that would take a few years to get to that point. I had heard von Gremp was concerned, and suggested to Bledsoe that he invite von Gremp to visit the gardens and see what a wonderful addition to the university we had in our midst.

Bledsoe sent him a congratulatory note when he became chairman and invited him to visit the gardens. Von Gremp responded, saying he was concerned about the continued deficit and copied Bobbitt. Bledsoe responded very politely, saying we had a plan that was indeed viable. The response was respectful and thoughtful. Somehow von Gremp took offense at the response. He said he wanted further discussion about the garden's financial position. Bledsoe called me and asked if his job was in jeopardy. Von Gremp then told Bobbitt that Bledsoe was disrespectful to him. One bit of information that seemed to quickly ameliorate Bobbitt's concerns was that Bledsoe had been recommended strongly for the directorship by former trustee and prominent banker Tommy May. Bledsoe was also related to a very powerful member of the General Assembly. Von Gremp dropped his questions about the finances.

In May 2014 von Gremp attended a meeting of the National Conference of Trusteeship and came back as an expert on colleges and universities and how they should operate. He sent a long message to all trustees and Bobbitt suggesting the campuses needed a strategic plan. We had been operating with one for years. He discussed high tuition and fees, health care expenses, retirement plans and deferred maintenance. He mentioned unacceptable retention and graduation rates and the expanding role of technology and post-tenure review. All of these were items we had struggled with for decades and were addressing with some success. All of the issues he pointed out in his three-page memo were long-standing challenges for all institutions, public and private throughout the United States. The sophomoric approach was astounding to me and I was embarrassed for him. It was as if he had pulled the items off of a web site. He looked amateurish and bush league.

I knew we were in for a year of fun with our new chairman.

CHAPTER 86
EVERSITY

> *A foolish faith in authority is the worst enemy to truth.*
>
> — ALBERT EINSTEIN

Shortly after Donald Bobbitt became president of the University of Arkansas System, it became apparent that one of his most important and really singular projects was to begin a new distance education program at the system level. When he was the provost at The University of Texas at Arlington he watched the growth of their online nursing program balloon. There was a huge shortage of nurses in the United States, and for that matter worldwide, and many institutions were expanding their nursing programs. At the University of Arkansas we had taken advantage of the great need for nurses by increasing our capacity to educate nurses and send them into the workplace. Bobbitt's program at UT Arlington was a huge moneymaker for the institution, and he believed that a completely new campus offering online degrees could also be a big profit center for the University of Arkansas System. I wasn't at all certain that his experience with online nursing education could be duplicated for a general curriculum. My senior staff also had concerns.

Soon after he became president, he called a meeting in Little Rock and invited representatives from all of the campuses. While the purpose of the meeting was not well understood by participants, it became obvious he was trying to educate the campuses on the importance of online education.

During that initial meeting, Bobbitt showed a film which suggested that higher education would be going through a huge remodeling worldwide. The film implied rather boldly that all of higher education in the future would be delivered online. The film claimed there would only be a handful of higher education institutions left in the United States, and all would be online schools, and in-person delivery would cease to exist. After watching the film my first thought was that it was much too radical. Certainly we were moving more aggressively to electronic delivery, but I still believed in-person course delivery would survive. Practically everyone in the room was surprised after viewing the video. It seemed to be promoting changes that were unlikely to happen, even in the distant future. It was pure shock value. I thought the film was outrageous and was very surprised that Bobbitt would expose university faculty and administrators to something so patently ridiculous and so soon after he arrived at the system office.

A few people spoke up with criticism of the film and naturally I opened my big mouth. I'm sure Bobbitt was not pleased with what I had to say. I told the assembled group that I thought the film was deleterious to our challenges to educate young people. I said that I didn't think it was accurate and that it was built on false pretenses. I readily admitted that distance education was extremely important to our campuses and fulfilled a great need for many students. However, I did not think all of higher education—and for that matter primary and secondary education as the film suggested—would be delivered electronically in the near future. I suggested that programs like intercollegiate athletics served as a social glue for students and alumni, and I didn't see those programs ceasing to exist anytime soon, if ever.

When I finished my remarks the assembled group gave a

resounding applause. No doubt, I angered Bobbitt early in his tenure, but he was gracious and didn't say anything to me.

Bobbitt hired an organization in Dallas, which many academics discredited, to make the case that things were going to change dramatically in the coming years, and to help him position the University of Arkansas System to launch a distance education program.

In the spring of 2012 I was called to a meeting at the system office in Little Rock. All of the chancellors were present. Bobbitt informed us he would be launching a new system campus called eVersity. The new campus would be situated at the system headquarters in Little Rock on the Cammack Village property, and would deliver online degrees exclusively.

For the first part of the meeting I was silent and just tried to listen to the rationale. Every one of the system campuses had sizable online programs. At that time our campus was delivering degrees in over 25 academic areas with well over 600 courses available for students. We had made a major effort to build our own online capacity, as were all of the other campuses, including the two-year schools.

Bobbitt explained to the chancellors and others that the campus he was suggesting would serve a different type of student. eVersity would be for older, nontraditional students who perhaps had a few hours toward a degree but never finished. He went on to say the governor was very insistent on turning out more degrees in Arkansas and he wanted the University of Arkansas System to meet the challenge.

I'm not certain to this day if Bobbitt realized that a large percentage of our students were nontraditional and many were employed while seeking a degree. We had worked very diligently to reach out to that classification of student and encourage them to pursue a degree. It was certainly true that Arkansas had one of the lowest percentages of citizens with a college education, and Bobbitt believed this new campus would make a huge difference in the state.

Then, with no discussion whatsoever, the chancellors were told they would be funding the new campus. It would initially cost the

Fayetteville campus $2 million. We would be asked to transfer those funds to the system to help in the founding of eVersity.

The decision was not to be challenged, and Bobbitt had already determined how his new program would be funded. Several of the chancellors spoke up, indicating that their budgets were already stretched very thin, and they were not certain how they would find the funds for Bobbitt's new campus. I was the most vocal among the chancellors and asked Bobbitt why he couldn't just borrow the funds, since interest rates were at an historic low. He said they had explored that option, but they wanted to have the liberty to pay back the funds over a multiple-year term.

I was never publicly opposed to eVersity per se, even though that charge was leveled at me. I was extremely surprised that Bobbitt wanted to make this a priority for the system, but I did not oppose his idea. I did believe it was wrought with extreme challenges, and frankly thought it would end in failure. Some higher education prognosticators published articles questioning the judgment of starting a new online campus.

My only issue was asking our campus to pay for it. We were on extremely thin margins, and increasing salaries for faculty and staff was our number-one priority. Giving money to another campus in the system didn't seem to make much sense to me. I couldn't understand why we would diminish the finances of the flagship campus and send those funds to an entirely new venture. It seemed counterintuitive to take scarce funds from one institution to shore up a new one. I even wondered if it was entirely legal to use funds given by parents and students for the Fayetteville campus to be used by another campus. Why would Bobbitt want to do anything that would hurt the flagship campus? We were the driver of economic opportunity for the entire state. What we accomplished made a huge difference for Arkansas.

I was extremely unhappy with the decision, and made certain Bobbitt knew of my displeasure. It didn't matter. Bobbitt had made up his mind and he decided to inform his chancellors with no discussion whatsoever. With this move, the system went against every principle of streamlining and efficiency it was created to uphold.

Then our faculty and students weighed in. On November 12, 2014, the campus faculty passed a unanimous resolution opposing the creation of eVersity.

The UA faculty had long recognized the need and value of online education for Arkansans who may not be able to attend classes on campus, and had already developed 511 high quality online courses supporting 25 degree and 5 certificate programs through the University of Arkansas Global Campus, and more than 1,300 online degree programs. Since that time the Fayetteville campus now offers over 700 courses online, with 39 degree programs.

The faculty was unanimous in believing that existing university online courses and programs were most adequate, and an additional effort was counterintuitive. We had tutoring facilities for online students, as well as major library materials that could be shared electronically. The faculty simply felt the University of Arkansas System was developing a separate online campus, eVersity, which duplicated the current and future high quality online offerings of their and other campuses within the system. It was further pointed out that UA System entrepreneurs behind eVersity had yet to articulate a clear business plan, or how that plan would avoid the expensive failures of similar initiatives in, for example, Illinois, Florida, and California.

Then there was the very real issue that neither the State of Arkansas, nor the University of Arkansas System, could afford this duplication of existing resources. This duplication would cause confusion on what was being offered and by which institution, and could ultimately compromise the quality of all online courses and degrees offered by the UA System.

On top of that, the faculty knew the eVersity initiative sought to shift most of the true cost of the program to the University of Arkansas campuses. The shift of funds from funded campuses and programs, which were appropriated by the General Assembly, paid by students and parents for tuition and fees, or accumulated from faculty research awards, should not be used for a startup venture or transferred from one campus to another.

While faculty certainly supported the inherent notion that more

Arkansans should be encouraged to complete their degrees, they remained extremely puzzled as to why—if nationally reputable faculty, experienced web designers, and robust support systems are already in place on existing campuses—the board of trustees would desire to spread a fragile revenue stream even more thinly.

In the final analysis, the faculty of the University of Arkansas, Fayetteville, requested that the UA System administration and the board of trustees delay implementation of eVersity, and proposed we all work together with our colleagues at all campuses to produce a system-wide articulation agreement for the purpose of degree completion, such that online courses taken at any of the University of Arkansas campuses would be available to students and, upon successful completion of sufficient academic work, the UA System would be empowered to grant appropriate baccalaureate degrees.

I'm sure Bobbitt suspected that I encouraged the faculty to air their objections, but it was not true. I had nothing to do with the resolution. I did invite Bobbitt to come to campus and address the faculty senate which he agreed to do. I'm sure after the session he regretted he came, as the faculty expressed anger and resentment at the creation of eVersity. But, in fairness and to his credit, he entertained all of their questions for well over two hours.

There was no further discussion or dialogue in regard to the faculty senate resolution.

Around the same time of the faculty senate resolution, the Associated Student Government weighed in with their resolution opposing eVersity with only two in opposition.

Bobbitt responded to the ASG president with a two-page letter defending his action. He stated that the system did not seize funds from the campuses, but that they are loans to be paid back.

I received telephone calls from three members of the board of trustees asking my advice about the new campus. I told them the same thing, that I was not opposed to the campus, but I was very much opposed to paying for it. I did express my opinion that I did not think it would be successful as we already had major online programs at just about every public and private institution in the state.

At a future board of trustees meeting the chairman of the board, Jane Rogers, called on me, without a heads-up, and asked me what I thought of the plans for eVersity. I had no choice but to respond, and again, I opened my big mouth and made it clear in public comments that I was very much opposed to using our campus funds to pay for the new venture. I remember clearly that sitting behind me was Daniel Ferritor, former chancellor of the Fayetteville campus. Dan was serving as an officer of the system at the time. He tapped me on the shoulder and told me I should keep quiet and not make any waves. I did not take his advice. I feel certain that my comments upset Bobbitt again. If I had been given any notice, I might have kept silent, but I felt strongly that taking our campus funds was just plain wrong. In particular, I pointed out that the logo eVersity was using in their board presentation was our logo at the Fayetteville campus.

The board of trustees approved the launching of eVersity and funding it through the other campuses. The decision had already been made. Bobbitt had convinced the trustees that it was a solid plan.

Bobbitt had told the public and the board of trustees that he expected within a very few years the new campus would have 10,000 students. I sincerely doubted it. Bobbitt had built the idea on the success of the nursing program at Texas, Arlington. I had tried to explain to him that he could not base his decision using that example. It was a false equivalency. America needed nurses and there was a huge backlog of students who wanted to be nurses. The model at Arlington had a built-in success factor that eVersity did not have. I believed in my heart that the whole project would be an abject failure.

There were many good reasons why older Arkansans did not return to college later in life. Many of the reasons centered around family matters and the need to hold a job and support their family. I did not believe this new campus would make much of a difference in the governor's desire to populate the citizenry of Arkansas with baccalaureate degrees. Frankly, I thought the whole thing was nonsense.

I became friends with one of the staff members of eVersity. That person kept me confidentially informed about the new campus. From the very beginning the campus struggled to get up and running. Later, it would be necessary to ask the campuses for more funding. We would end up giving eVersity more money from campus coffers. The funds were to be paid back within 10 years. To date none of the funds have been returned to the campuses.

My friend told me eVersity had never exceeded an enrollment headcount of 700 students. Bear in mind that is not full-time equivalency, but rather the number of students who might be taking only one course. He further told me the number of people who had actually graduated with a baccalaureate was extremely small, if not minuscule.

Bobbitt was able to convince the General Assembly that his new campus did not have to comply with various reports on enrollment, which are submitted annually to the state. It was virtually impossible to get any information about finances or enrollment on eVersity. One of our faculty members in the College of Education and Health Professions was doing an academic study and tried to get information about the new college, but he was ignored.

Dr. Javier Reyes was serving as our vice provost for distance education. He was doing a marvelous job. He was well respected and well liked by everyone. He had received rave reviews from students who had taken his classes in the Walton College. He was on a track to become a leader in higher education. I was very fond of him, and knew he could provide our Global Campus with leadership as we were expanding our online programs. We needed an aggressive and highly qualified executive to take those programs to the next level. Javier was the person the provost and I selected to manage the ever-expanding distance learning for our campus.

I received a call from Don Bobbitt soon after the launching of eVersity. He was livid. He accused our Global Campus of launching an advertising program designed to hurt eVersity and denigrate their efforts. He was extremely upset with Javier, who he blamed for the ads. I tried to explain to the system president that Javier had done nothing wrong. The accusations were completely bogus and far from the truth.

Javier had simply contracted with an outside agency to have Google list our Global Campus programs first, whenever anyone did a search online for distance education programs and degrees. Anytime you run a search on any subject you can pay Google to have your programs listed first in the search. They appear as advertisements and everyone knows from their designation as ads that you were paying for the service. Thousands of people across the world pay for this service, and it was standard in the business and still is. Javier had never said a discouraging word about eVersity, and was not opposed to the launching of Bobbitt's pet project. But Bobbitt saw him as a pariah and his purchase of the ads as hurting eVersity.

Bobbitt told me I should replace Javier as head of our distance education programs. I was flabbergasted. I tried to explain that Javier was simply doing his job, and had no intent to do any harm to eVersity. Bobbitt had previously praised Javier to me as a first-class administrator, and I reminded Bobbitt of that, but he said he had a change of mind.

I thought his criticisms were unconscionable and terribly unfair. I reminded Bobbitt that he had said himself, many times, that online programs at practically every institution in Arkansas would not compete with students enrolling at eVersity, because they were trying to reach a totally different audience. If that were in fact accurate, why would Bobbitt care what we were doing with our very significant and healthy online efforts, which had existed for years before eVersity was ever conceived?

Javier was hurt and despondent that the system president would call him out as a troublemaker. He was a thoughtful soul and everyone thought highly of him.

Not long after the criticism, Javier decided to leave the University of Arkansas for greener pastures. He has enjoyed a brilliant career. He left to become dean of the West Virginia University College of Business and Economics, and just recently became the provost of the University of Illinois, Chicago. I suspect before long he will be a college president if he so desires. He is a good man who was chased away for no good reason at all.

Another valued staff member of the Global Campus also left university employment because of this blatant overreach. Anselm Lambert got caught up in the witch hunt too. He was a valued and talented employee and handled many IT issues for the Global Campus. On March 30, 2015, he received a call from Jacob Flournoy, UA System auditor asking for a meeting. Anselm had no idea what he wanted, but readily agreed to the meeting thinking it might be about some of the concepts he was pushing on campus that would help IT problems. The meeting took place on April 2, and Flournoy brought a senior auditor with him to take notes. Flournoy explained that Anselm could leave at any time and he could refuse to answer any questions. I'm sure that was intimidating to an employee of his rank. The first questions were about Anselm's participation in software agreements for Global Campus. Anselm explained that software agreements went to legal for approval.

Flournoy then explained that a complaint was made to them about how internet search results would produce an advertisement for a Global Campus website when a query was entered into Google for eVersity. Anselm went into detail about his expertise with search engine optimization (SEO) and IT security, and how the search results were an understandable occurrence due to branding and search optimization, but done without nefarious intent. At that stage, the tone became somewhat accusatory in nature because Flournoy alluded to IT security involvement in the process and that nefarious activity would null and void his certification, clearly a threat from the system auditor.

Anselm told them he had had enough of their questioning, and insisted it was a non-issue, but they were making it an issue. He told them they had labeled the meeting completely differently from what had actually happened, and their intent, he now knew, was a poor attempt to discredit him and the Global Campus.

In a memo to Javier Reyes, Anselm articulated his frustration, saying he was disappointed in the system office for being made to feel he had done something wrong. He said his unit was run with high integrity, and he had always worked with eVersity as a partner and did not appreciate the accusations against him.

I was in disbelief that the system auditor would be called into a matter to threaten an employee regarding an issue on which the auditor was completely ignorant and had absolutely no expertise. He's an auditor for heaven's sake, but he was being used as the inquisition.

Not long after the incident, which, by the way, went nowhere, Anselm resigned from the university for greener pastures.

Soon after eVersity was up and running, which took some time, we began seeing tweets from eVersity that we believed were directed at our campus and other four year, predominately in-person institutions. The tweets were pithy. A few examples:

- "The average American student now graduates $25,000 in debt and unprepared to enter the workforce. eVersity says that is unacceptable."
- "Went to College and became a statistic."
- "The expense of higher education is just not viable."
- "Nothing against 'beer and circuses,' but eVersity is here for those who are more concerned with degrees and jobs."

I could not for the life of me understand how tearing down traditional education was helpful to a system that should be promoting our four-year institutions. It seemed antithetical to me.

I wasn't sure where the reference to "beer and circuses" came from, but there was a book published by Murray Sperber in 2000 titled *Beer and Circus: How Big-Time College Sports Is Crippling Undergraduate Education*. I suspect it came from that book, which is highly critical of big-time university athletics as well as the focus on research at colleges and universities. Bobbitt suggested it came from a 2014 documentary, *Ivory Tower*, which questioned the value of higher education in an era when the price of college had increased more than any other service in the United States. Not sure that was helpful either. While college and university presidents and chancellors were fighting every day to shore up the advantages of higher education, many others, including lawmakers, were tearing it down. Why would a system campus, eVersity, join the crowded field of dissent?

In late December 2014 I received an email from an Arkansas state senator questioning an ad that ran in the *Arkansas Democrat-Gazette* about our distance education program, Global Campus. We had run multiple ads over many years, but this one apparently caught the senator's eye. The senator also asked several questions about our online programs and its interference with eVersity. The questions made it very evident that he did not understand the basic issues at hand, and had been asked to make the inquiries. He then called Randy Massanelli, my vice chancellor for government relations, and demanded through voice mail that he be given answers to his questions before a legislative hearing to take place the next Friday morning. We determined he was going to hold up a software contract for the global campus.

We learned that the senator had a relationship with one of our major donors. I asked the donor to call the senator and try to slow him down. The donor asked the senator to "Lay off the UA and my dear friend David Gearhart." The state senator then revealed that he was asked to "monkey" with the UA by trustee von Gremp, and thought he was just following orders from trustees. We explained to the senator that our campus has enjoyed distance education, in one form or another, for 60 years, and that we advertise in multiple venues and publications throughout the year.

I approached von Gremp at commencement and told him what we had heard. He seemed shocked that we knew, but proceeded to deny any involvement. Perhaps he was being truthful, always hard to tell. But, if accurate, a trustee has a fiduciary responsibility to support the campus, not hurt it. Going to a member of the General Assembly to cause pain and anguish would be unforgivable.

Fast forward to 2021 when Bobbitt asked the board of trustees for approval to purchase a campus in the Kansas City area. The board approved the purchase, and the University of Arkansas System bought Grantham University for a reported one dollar. Grantham is a for-profit school founded in 1951. In the announcement from the system office it indicated that the bargain price comes with "certain discrete liabilities." Grantham has 170 full-time and 200 part-time faculty, and has a student body head count of 4,000 online students. I received a number of telephone calls from former board members and university administrators. All we could conclude was that this was a way to shore up eVersity and the purchase was needed to right-size the campus in Little Rock.

I was baffled that the board of trustees of the University of Arkansas System would endorse eVersity, not to mention the purchase of Grantham University. The media reported that the purchase of Grantham would cost the system $1. Later, at a board of trustees meeting, Bobbitt told the board that startup costs for acquiring Grantham could be much higher. Rumors were that the startup costs could be as much as $8 million.

Grantham University has a 38 percent graduation rate, a typical student debt of $24,806, and a 21 percent student loan repayment rate by the institution's own account. Grantham University is nationally accredited by the Distance Education and Training Council (DETC), not by the Higher Learning Commission (HLC), which has rigorous standards. Some universities do not accept credits for courses not accredited by the HLC.

Then, suddenly in 2022, with the rumor mill rampant, Bobbitt announced that eVersity would close down. After eight years in existence, and millions of dollars spent from the coffers of other system campuses and taxpayer funds, with very few students and fewer still that graduated, Bobbitt was finally realizing the whole effort was an abysmal failure. Many of us tried to tell him that in the beginning. Faculty, students, administrators all tried to caution him not to pursue what we felt would end up in total failure. He would not listen. His mind was made up. He knew better than anyone else.

When Bobbitt first mentioned the idea of eVersity to the chancellors, he tolerated no discussion, no input. He did not want the chancellors to weigh in on his idea. Now eVersity was closing and not one penny of the funds he took from the campuses had been paid back. He has said the funds will be paid back, but when?

I was called by media outlets to comment on the eVersity

closure, but decided not to. I did receive a number of phone calls from faculty and staff, and a few from former board of trustee members, all wanting to know if I was gloating. I was not. The expenditure of our campus funds to pay for what ended in complete failure is sad to me and an unconscionable blunder.

When eVersity was first concocted I casually asked Bobbitt what would happen if it ended in failure. Bobbitt said, he supposed if it did fail he would be looking for a job!

I hope the other campuses will not find it necessary to one day bail out Grantham University.

CHAPTER 87
STAFF RETIREMENTS

> *Don't cry because it's over, smile because it happened.*
>
> — DR. SEUSS

In 2014 two of my most trusted advisors and vice chancellors announced their retirements.

Richard Hudson, who had worked under three chancellors during his 20-year career at the University of Arkansas, announced plans to retire July 31. He had been hired by Chancellor Dan Ferritor and then worked for John White. As vice chancellor for government and community relations, he represented the U of A to state and federal lawmakers, as well as to political and community leaders in Northwest Arkansas and around the state. He had been a respected voice for the university and higher education at the state capital and helped initiate many programs and services to benefit higher education in Arkansas. Richard had worked with almost 600 state legislators, five governors, and over a dozen members of the Arkansas Congressional delegation during his career in government relations.

Richard would turn 70 soon after his retirement announcement, and he wanted to travel with his lovely wife, Joanna, I had great respect for Richard and found him to be very effective with legislators. In 2010 he received the Marvin M. "Swede" Johnson Achievement Award as the nation's top higher education government relations official.

The Arkansas General Assembly was changing from a balanced Republican/Democrat assembly to mostly Republican. Conservative politics was the game of the day and I was convinced my more centrist views were not as accepted by Republican leadership as they had been with Democrats. Many Republicans did not like my views on undocumented students, protection of LGBTQ students and what some perceived as my liberal leanings. Richard got along with both sides of the aisle and I hated to see him retire. He had actually wanted to retire earlier, but I convinced him to stay a year longer.

I launched a national search, realizing it was most likely we would hire someone from Arkansas who had a connection to state politics. I formed a search committee and set out to find the best person possible. The committee narrowed the search down to three people. Mac Campbell, Arkansas native who had worked in Senator Blanche Lincoln's office; Senator Johnny R. Key, a term-limited legislator who had served in both the Arkansas State House and Senate and was well liked by his colleagues; and Randy Massanelli, UA alumnus and state director for U.S. Senator Mark Pryor. We held intensive sessions with all three candidates, but it was obvious from the interviews that Massanelli was the leading candidate.

The search committee and my executive committee were unanimous in wanting Massanelli for the position.

Before we had even conducted the interviews I started getting heavy pressure from Republicans in the legislature to hire Key. Some of the calls didn't even mince words but told me who I should hire, and if I didn't there could be consequences. Bobbitt weighed in and told me I should hire Key. He said that Key was leaving the senate as a very powerful member and he still had many friends in power, and if we did not hire him we would have many very unhappy legislators. I resisted Bobbitt's request to hire Key. Massanelli was the first choice of the search committee and my senior staff.

I asked Bobbitt if he was ordering me to hire Key and he said no.

He would leave it up to me to make the final decision. I selected Massanelli.

Immediately I started getting snarky comments by legislators who were unhappy with my decision. Justin Harris, a Republican from West Fork beat me up in the media, saying I continued to disregard the legislature. Not long after his comments Harris would choose not to run for re-election following an embarrassing investigation that found he gave away adopted children to another family. Reports showed Harris was concerned about the adopted children being possessed by the devil.

Senate Republican whip Jonathan Dismang was critical of the appointment, even though he admitted that he didn't even know Massanelli.

Within a matter of days, and before we could even announce the Massanelli appointment, Richard Hudson informed me Bobbitt was going to offer a system job to Johnny Key as a consolation. Key became an associate vice president for university relations of the system working alongside Melissa Rust, the system lobbyist. Frankly, I can't really say that I was surprised. I knew Bobbitt wanted me to hire Key, and when I didn't he created a job for him in the system office. I didn't have anything against Key. He seemed a decent enough fellow, but we thought Massanelli would be a better choice.

Unfortunately, Key didn't last long. Within seven months he resigned his position with the university system and became commissioner of the Arkansas Department of Education. He would later become a cabinet secretary for the Department of Education.

The next person I would lose was Don Pederson, who announced his plans to retire effective June 30, 2014. Pederson was vice chancellor for finance and administration and had played an integral role in the transformation of the University of Arkansas, serving during his tenure as both vice chancellor for academic affairs and later financial affairs. He was the longest serving senior administrator in University of Arkansas history, having served as vice chancellor a total of 29 years, working under Chancellors Daniel Ferritor, John A. White and me.

Don Pederson joined the University of Arkansas faculty as an assistant professor of physics in 1972 and published 60 scientific papers in the field of condensed matter physics. From 1978 to 1983 he was chairman of the department. I found him to be honest, hardworking, extremely intelligent and committed to the growth and prosperity of the University of Arkansas. Once again I had talked Pederson out of retiring earlier, but he told me that he felt the time had come. Although he never said it, I suspected that he was just tired of the misguided criticism over the advancement deficit. Some trustees had laid the blame at Pederson's feet, looking for a scapegoat. Bobbitt had not been helpful in protecting him, and Bobbitt's vice president for finance had come down hard on Pederson for a minor issue in his financial reporting. I knew Pederson had done more for the university than most any other administrator. I could not blame him for wanting to retire, but I hated to see him go. It would be a huge loss for the university and me personally. He had been a friend and colleague and I had relied on his advice, support and wise counsel.

I found myself needing a new chief financial officer. I appointed Tim O'Donnell as interim. Prior to joining the U of A in 2013, O'Donnell's experience in financial management and administration included a 22-year career with Southwestern Energy Company, where he rose to the position of vice president and served as treasurer. His name had come to me from Charles Scharlau, a former CEO of Southwestern Energy and a former trustee. We were looking for a number two person in the finance area and hired Tim. We thought he might work out for the top finance job and would later be appointed to that position after I retired. He only stayed in the position a short time, working with Joe Steinmetz. He left to be the chief financial officer for the Northwest Arkansas Regional Airport.

CHAPTER 88
WHITE HOUSE SUMMIT ON EDUCATION

" *There's nothing like white trash at the White House.*

— *DOLLY PARTON*

In early 2014 I received an invitation from President Barack Obama to come to the White House for a day-long summit meeting. The purpose of the event was to discuss ways to make a college education more accessible to low-income and underrepresented students, and to help them succeed and graduate. I suspected my position on undocumented students was the reason I was selected. President Barack Obama and First Lady Michelle Obama hosted the event. The Obamas would lead the summit, along with members of the National Economic Council and the Federal Department of Education. The White House issued a media release that said higher education leaders were invited based on their institutions' commitment to increasing access and academic success for this student population.

At that time the University of Arkansas had four programs specifically aimed at preparing low-income, underrepresented students for college. The ACT Academy was a five-day residential summer program that prepared high school students for the ACT exam and the college admissions process while living on the U of A campus. The Academic Enrichment Program provided academic support through tutoring, workshops, early intervention advising, peer and faculty mentoring, and experiential learning opportunities. The iBridge program was a two-week academic program offering an intensive orientation to college-level literacy and STEM courses to ease the transition to college for incoming freshmen. The Engineering Career Awareness Program was another transitional bridge program that also provided gap funding support, and used rigorous academic retention strategies for each year's group of incoming freshmen. In addition, the university was in the process of developing three new programs to further its efforts to recruit, retain and graduate low-income and underrepresented students.

The Commitment to College Completion Program was a pilot program funded with a $2.1 million gift from the Walton Family Foundation. The program provided first generation and low-income Arkansas students with financial resources to help meet the cost of attending the university, as well as to giving them opportunities for study abroad. The program also offered academic enrichment and peer and faculty mentoring. The Expanded Summer Bridge Program represented the U of A's commitment to establish a six-week summer program that provided transitioning freshmen an in-depth introduction to college life and learning. Students lived on campus while taking two credit-bearing classes. And finally, the Targeted University Perspectives Course was a first-year course focusing on the special concerns of first-generation and low-income students. The course curriculum included intensive advising and career coaching while addressing topics such as financial aid literacy and cultural sensitivity. Students also received enhanced tutoring support for select academic areas.

I was flattered and honored to be invited to the White House by the President and First Lady of the United States, along with a select group of scholars and government officials.

CHAPTER 89
FINDING A NEW SEC COMMISSIONER

> *If you hire good people, give them good jobs, and pay them good wages, generally something good is going to happen.*
>
> — STEVE JOBS

In October 2014 the Southeastern Conference launched a national search to name its next commissioner following the announcement that Mike Slive would retire in July, after 13 years in the position. Nicholas S. Zeppos, chancellor of Vanderbilt University and chair of the SEC's presidents and chancellors, appointed a committee to search for the eighth commissioner in the history of the league. He asked me to serve as chairman of the committee. I in turn invited others to join me in the search for a new commissioner: Dr. Judith Bonner, president of The University of Alabama; Dr. Eli Capilouto, President of the University of Kentucky; Dr. Mark Keenum, president of Mississippi State University; and Dr. R. Bowen Loftin, chancellor of the University of Missouri. Interestingly enough, John White served as the head of the search committee that hired Slive 13 years previously.

Mike Slive had done a brilliant job as commissioner, and our league had enjoyed an unprecedented period of growth during his tenure. At that time our conference was the most lucrative in college football and we were the envy of the other conferences.

Mike Slive was considered to be the most powerful person in college sports, and we knew we wanted someone to replace him who could carry on with no interruptions. Finding the right person to carry on the leadership of the Southeastern Conference, an unquestioned leader in intercollegiate athletics, was a major undertaking as the position would be vital to the continued positive transformation of the conference and intercollegiate athletics as a whole. I was honored to have been selected by Nick Zeppos to lead the search committee.

Our committee began the task immediately and we worked closely with athletics directors, faculty representatives, senior women administrators and student-athletes in the search. Our goal was to have a new commissioner in place to allow a transition period before Slive's retirement on July 31, 2015.

The committee knew we had a very viable candidate in the number-two person at the SEC, Greg Sankey. I believed it was his to lose. Sankey had been at the SEC for 13 years, and was the chief operating officer. Previously he was the commissioner of the Southland Conference.

The committee decided we needed to run a legitimate search, even though we knew Sankey was already a top candidate. We reviewed a large number of résumés from across the nation. We had some very good candidates and narrowed the search down to 10. We conducted phone interviews and then narrowed the search down to five, including Sankey. We interviewed all five candidates. All of the candidates were worried about media exposure during the search, and believed that if the press got a hold of the list it could damage their current positions. We kept the search and candidate names very confidential and fortunately nothing got in the hands of the media.

We also hired a search firm to assist us with appropriate names as well as the vetting process.

We decided to interview three of the candidates a second time,

Greg Sankey was one of the three. The committee selected Sankey as the finalist and proposed his name to the entire group of SEC presidents and chancellors. The vote was unanimous.

At the time we were in Nashville at the SEC meetings when we confirmed Sankey. We were holding our meetings at the Vanderbilt chancellor's home. I learned later that, when we called Sankey into a room to offer him the job, he had no idea he was going to be selected. He was hopeful, but thought maybe Nick and I were letting him down easy by telling him privately that he didn't get the job.

Sankey has confirmed our expectations and has done an extraordinary job as the commissioner.

CHAPTER 90
CRAZIES

" *Do you know what's cheaper than therapy? Admitting you're batshit crazy and running with it.*

— DAN PEARCE

" *We are all born mad. Some remain so.*

— SAMUEL BECKETT

During my time as chancellor I received a number of emails and letters from what my office staff began to call "the crazies." They actually labeled the file folder "crazies" where we kept their letters and emails.

One came from a lady in Fayetteville who was harping about our football coaches needing to lose weight. I replied to her email by saying we hire people not based on their weight or girth but on the content of their character! (With apologies to Dr. Martin Luther King, Jr.)

Another person wrote to tell me her 19-year-old son should be allowed to drink alcohol on campus and state laws should not apply to him because he has always been allowed to drink at home and is a responsible drinker!

I received a number of emails, presumably from parents, extolling the virtues of smoking marijuana and allowing its use on campus.

One person was extremely upset that we had residence halls occupied by both men and women. It was true that male and female students did occupy the same residence facilities, but were separated by closed doors and partitions, with rules about hours students could congregate. That had been in existence for many years. The person said that "Fornication is a sin," and I should be ashamed. I wrote her back and said that she should not assume the students were "fornicating"! What else could I say?

I would receive numerous letters about our smoking ban on campus, and one in particular stood out: Their kids "had a constitutional right to smoke in campus buildings and if they got cancer that was their God given right"!

Perhaps the funniest one I received is worth sharing. Enjoy:

Dear Dr. Gearhart:

I was in Fayetteville, AR for a mother/daughter sorority event at the University of Arkansas last weekend. I was tuned into the weather and made plans to leave early Sunday morning, March 2. At 7 a.m., Fayetteville was already under ice, but I saw trucks on the city streets putting down sand. At 8:30 a.m., I headed down Razorback Road to I-540 south which was covered in ice and sleet and still plummeting down like a rainstorm. For 20-25 miles, there was not any sand truck or any other type of transportation vehicle putting anything on that dangerous stretch of interstate. I was dismayed at how poorly the state of Arkansas was in preparing their roads. I live in Memphis, TN and proud to say that our state does a much better job during bad weather in preparing roads, bridges and interstates. I drove 5 hours on I-40 east bound and never saw any type of sand truck or any truck putting down anything on that stretch to help the incoming ice. Shame on your state! My daughter is in her third year at The University of Arkansas. We will be very happy when she graduates and returns to Memphis, so we don't have to drive on your poorly maintained interstates. For the past three years, there has always been road construction which has caused huge (1-3 hours) traffic delays. If we had known how poorly your interstate system is maintained, we would have considered choosing a different university for our daughter. Over a three-year period, your lack of consideration for those paying tuition in your state and using your roads has been inexcusable. I hope the bad publicity that you receive on the media helps you reconsider your plan for better preparation for the next ice storm and for everyday use. We hope to stay in Memphis or travel to other areas, so we won't have to deal with such incompetent transportation issues.

Sincerely, [Name withheld]

I replied thusly:

Dear [Name]:

Thank you for your message.

I do hope your daughter has otherwise had a good experience at the University of Arkansas. We work very hard to support our students in their educational pursuits.

As for our interstate highways, well, that does not fall under my jurisdiction, but I am truly sorry you have not been pleased. This has been a tough, tough winter on everyone.

Warm wishes for better travels.

G. David Gearhart
Chancellor, University of Arkansas

I shared the letter with Jane, and she said, "David, you're going to heaven."

CHAPTER 91
RETIREMENT LOOMING

> *Tough times never last, tough people do.*
>
> — DR. ROBERT SCHULLER

In late 2014 I was tired. Perhaps the advancement deficit ordeal had taken more out of me than I realized. But a major factor of concern and discontent was that Bobbitt would not bring closure to renewing my contract, which I had been given in 2008 by Dr. Sugg. The contract had expired in 2013 after five years. I had asked for a new contract a full 6 months before the expiration date but got no answer. Nothing!

I didn't actually need a contract to be chancellor, as no chancellors had one until I came to the job and insisted on one.

I wrote Bobbitt a number of times inquiring about the matter but no reply. I did speak with a couple trustees who told me renewal should not be a problem, but still nothing happened. I was getting angry that Bobbitt would not come to closure on renewing my contract. I decided to make an appointment to see Bobbitt and discuss my contract. I had even gone to the effort of drafting a new document, very similar to the original contract, to make it easy on his lawyers.

I did ask for a change in my compensation. Through the SEC presidents and chancellors, the Grenzebach Glier firm's benchmark salary studies, and the Chronicle of Higher Education's published public university salaries, I determined that I was the lowest paid SEC president or chancellor, with the exception of Mississippi State University. I gave the list of executive compensation to Bobbitt. It was the first time I had asked for enhanced compensation since coming to the University of Arkansas in 1998.

I took my attorney, Alan Lewis, with me to see Bobbitt, which I later learned was very upsetting and intimidating to Bobbitt. Perhaps it was not very wise of me to take an attorney, although I did not blindside Bobbitt and had told him my lawyer would accompany me to the meeting. I assumed the UA lawyer would meet with us and outline the contract. Bobbitt met with us alone. I could tell when we sat down in his office that he was not pleased. He had no paper in front of him and said very little during the meeting. As we left I asked him to please get back to me. He just nodded. I never heard from him again about a new contract or compensation package.

I was tired. Perhaps I was just tired of working for the system. Perhaps I was just tired of the daily grind.

Molly Corbett Broad, a former University of North Carolina system president and former president of the American Council on Education, said:

> "University governing boards have become much more politicized. They're wrapped up in power struggles with campus presidents who can't—or won't—always mollify the competing interests of board members while also remaining attentive to students, parents, donors, professors and politicians forced to cut public spending on higher education as many states struggle to emerge from the recession. A president really cannot succeed in leading unless she has a working majority of those constituencies, and their interests are not typically aligned."

On May 1, 2014, my son, Brock, sent me an e-mail, which I printed off and kept in my desk drawer and referred to many times in the coming weeks and months. He said:

> Dad—
>
> A few random thoughts. You sounded a little stressed when we talked earlier. Not sure what it is about but whatever it is I wouldn't let it bother you. This is all the final little remnants and the press's last opportunity to get a jab in. They lost and you won ... and they know it. However, as long as you are in this role there will be other times where you will have to endure negativity. It won't fully stop.
>
> I think you should really consider a firm date to retire and stick to it. You need an "end in sight" mentality. Find the 3–5 key things you want to accomplish and then move on.
>
> We (Mom, Katy, me, Lindsey, and Justin) don't like you having this much stress at this point in your life. When I was sitting across from Nathan Reed today I couldn't help but think about the death of his dad at an early age. Your best years are ahead of you with grandkids and leisure. You need to think about your health with our family history. Life is too short to put up with this much longer.
>
> Just my unsolicited thoughts to think about ...
>
> Love, Brock

Financially I was in very good shape. I had exceeded my financial goals for retirement by several million dollars and could live very comfortably in retirement or as Brock said, "retire a rich man." I had been an inveterate saver all my life and made a lot of money in consulting, which Jane and I tended to invest in the stock market.

Brock had taken over my investments and was doing double-digit returns.

I also was most interested in teaching and writing as the denouement to my career. I had taught in the Graduate School at Penn State years previous and enjoyed it very much. I thought that would be a fine way to end my career in higher education: spending quality time with students and fellow faculty members by activating my tenured faculty appointment in the College of Education and Health Professions. I certainly realized that I would have to publish and be engaged in scholarship in addition to teaching. I decided to drop by to see the dean of the college, Dr. Tom Smith. I told Tom that I was considering retiring from the chancellor position and wanted to know his thoughts. He was most supportive and gave me an idea of what I would be getting into if I came full time to the college. I asked him to keep our conversation confidential as I wasn't quite ready to make the leap, and said I would continue to talk about the possibility.

I was 63 years old, but thought perhaps rounding out my career as a tenured faculty member might be fun and rewarding. At the time I was thinking I would teach for a few years and maybe retire for good when I was 68 or 70. I didn't want to work past 70. I have known too many people who worked into their 70's only to experience poor health. My health was excellent, but you never know what awaits you around the corner. I was hoping the good Lord would give Jane and me a good ten to fifteen years of excellent health in retirement so we could travel and enjoy our grandkids.

I must admit, I was a little concerned that if I retired too soon after the debacle in advancement, people might speculate that I was dismissed. So I waited patiently for time to pass so speculation would be dormant. Truth was, I thought of retirement even earlier, but the deficit fiasco kept me from pulling the trigger. I did not want any speculation that I had been asked to step down.

POLITICS, BOTH STATE AND COLLEGE

State government had changed rather dramatically in a few short years. Arkansas elected a very conservative Republican as governor, Asa Hutchinson, and the legislature was turning bright red. Governor Beebe had protected me to a certain extent while he was in power. When I was having the advancement deficit issues, Beebe showed up at Fowler House during a reception for the Chancellor's Society. Out of the corner of my eye, here comes the state police and Beebe's limo. Beebe got out of the car, walked up to Jane and me at the front door with several people milling around and said, "Gearhart, I'm here for one reason, to show my support for you." I was deeply grateful to him.

But now things were very different. I didn't have anything against Hutchinson, although our political views were not too similar. I had never had a run-in with him. When he was running for office he stopped by the chancellor's box during a football game with Mrs. Hutchinson.

I also felt some board support was slipping away, and I was not being protected at all by Bobbitt. The fact that I could not get Bobbitt to answer me on a new contract was concerning. Having a contract was not required to continue as chancellor but it became an issue of principle for me. I began to feel like Bobbitt would be OK if I decided to retire. Our communication was at an all-time low. In fact, Bobbitt was a terrible communicator, and I felt kept in the dark on many issues of concern for our campus. I longed for the days of Dr. Sugg, who had marvelous communication skills and approached the job as a partnership with his chancellors.

I don't remember the issue, but something came up and I felt it important to talk with each trustee to inform them about the issue. It must not have been earth shattering or I would have remembered it. What I do remember is that one trustee, Mark Waldrip, refused to speak with me on the phone without Bobbitt on the phone as well.

I had heard rumors that Bobbitt had issued an order that chancellors, faculty and staff were not to speak to trustees, as that was

Bobbitt's job. In fairness, Bobbitt never directly told me that, but several people did confirm the directive to me while I was chancellor, and even again most recently. I never felt a gag rule was necessary or helpful. It just made the implementer look weak and paranoid. But, true or not, Waldrip had refused to talk with me. I had known Waldrip and generally had gotten along well with him, or at least I thought I did. When his daughter was homecoming queen I made a special effort to let him crown her at halftime. I took his declining to speak with me as a signal that perhaps I had lost some board support and concluded it was over the advancement deficit. Perhaps it was something else altogether I didn't even recognize. But it was a blow to me and one I couldn't understand. A trustee refusing to talk with the head of the flagship campus is just dangerous!

We had done some truly great things for the university. Our endowment was approaching $1 billion. We had an all-time high enrollment. We had invested millions of dollars in the campus renovation program. I felt very good about my record. But to some people your record doesn't really matter. We live in a world of "What have you done for me today?" Politics is fickle.

I did run afoul of David Pryor again around that time, at a board meeting where he beat on me about our selection of a bond company for an upcoming bond issue. Of course, Pryor had already made damaging comments about me over the advancement deficit. This time he was not happy with the selection of bond counsel and bond floaters we made for a bond issue. Our campus had selected Stephens Inc. and Crews & Associates, as well as Friday, Eldredge & Clark as bond counsel. We had always been given the authority to select the company that would float bonds for construction projects, as well as the law firm that would handle the legalities of the transaction. We had regularly used Stephens and Crews. (Crews is owned by Reynie Rutledge, who was a trustee at the time).

Pryor wanted a different company and a new law firm to handle the bonds. His son, Mark, had been defeated for his third term as U.S. Senator, and the Stephens and Rutledge clans had not supported Mark because he voted for the Dodd–Frank Act that placed harsh regulations on banking. (In 2018 the Senate and the House passed the Economic Growth, Regulatory Relief and Consumer Protection Act exempting dozens of U.S. banks from the Dodd–Frank Act's banking regulations. President Trump signed the partial repeal into law).

I saw David Pryor's move at the board meeting as an act of revenge against Stephens and Rutledge because they did not support his son. Pure political theater. I held my ground. We had always operated under the understanding that the campuses should choose companies headquartered in Arkansas for our bond issues. The only companies at the time headquartered in Arkansas were Stephens and Crews. On top of that I explained to Pryor, in open session, the board of trustees had given the campuses the authority to decide bond issues. If the board wanted to take that authority away they could certainly do so. But until then I felt it was our prerogative.

During Sugg's time he felt it was important to give the bond business to local in-state companies. He also felt that giving the authority to the campuses to choose bond companies, as well as construction companies, lessened the possibility of the board turning the selection process into a political nightmare. The board remained silent as Pryor pounded on me during the public board meeting. I told him both of those companies had hired hundreds of our students and supported the university with philanthropy, and were the only Arkansas companies in the mix.

Bobbitt didn't say a single word in my defense.

On another occasion, our campus had selected a construction company to build a new facility. Mike Johnson had a very professional selection process to come up with the best construction team for the particular project. Multiple interviews were held with a team of professionals who would recommend to me the best construction company for that project. I always accepted the professionals' recommendation. Bobbitt called me and said he felt we had discriminated against a company that was owned by two Black gentlemen who he was friends with. I was aghast and most disappointed in Bobbitt. I asked Johnson to send me the process used to make the selection and forwarded it on to Bobbitt. I was very angry that we would be accused of discrimination by the president of the university. It was a totally bogus accusation. I never quite got over that comment by Bobbitt.

After I retired the board would take over the selection process from the campuses for bond issues and construction projects. Politics won out rather than professional decision making.

In late 2014 Arkansas played in the Texas Bowl against The University of Texas. We won the game decisively, 31–7. Everyone was happy, or at least I thought so. Early in the new year Jeff Long called me to say that he had received a call from Don Bobbitt, who asked him if I had consciously put trustees in poor seats for the bowl game. Jeff told Bobbitt I had nothing to do with ticket allocation and that the trustees got the best seats available. He told Bobbitt that the inquiry was ridiculous and wanted to know who raised it. Bobbitt told Jeff, "Trustees were asking." Jeff determined that one trustee had inquired: John Goodson had called Bobbitt and wondered if Gearhart was teaching the board a lesson as to who was in charge. It was an outrageous accusation, and I was furious. How a trustee could stoop to something so low was beyond me.

The absolute truth was that I did not have anything to do with ticket allocations for bowl games or any other games. I called Bobbitt and asked him point blank why he had not called me instead of Jeff Long about the matter. He had no explanation. I was terribly disappointed in Don Bobbitt that he would for a single second think I would do something like that, and I told him of my disappointment. He basically said nothing, which was Bobbitt's modus operandi when he didn't have an answer. It was complete crap.

Some of my close associates tried to comfort me by offering an explanation. One friend said that type of behavior by a board generally happens when you have a power vacuum. Board members feel free to make bogus and outrageous accusations when they know that no one will take them to task for their comments. Poor leadership allows boards to create their own agendas. All I know is that it would never have happened under Alan Sugg's leadership. He would have shut it down immediately and would never have called one of my subordinates behind my back.

In February 2014 another issue concerning athletics was raised by

Bobbitt and the trustees. Apparently some of the trustees wanted more perks for post-season basketball games. They wanted transportation to and from the games as well as more and better tickets. When Jeff Long arrived in 2008 he felt it was very important to develop a policy for post-game participation in bowls and tournaments. The University of Arkansas was very close to becoming the only NCAA Division IA institution not to be certified. The NCAA Certification Report indicated that the Certification Committee felt some UA board of trustee members were too involved in management of Intercollegiate Athletics on this campus.

In light of this information, Jeff recommended to Chancellor White, and subsequently to me, that we formalize what we do for our board members. Jeff developed a postseason bowl game policy and established guidelines for the SEC Men's Basketball Tournament. Upon request, board of trustee members would receive the following to the Men's or Women's SEC Basketball Tournament: Two complimentary tickets and two additional tickets available for purchase next to the two complimentary tickets for the entire SEC tournament. (This included sessions where the UA is not participating). Based upon availability there was a supply of additional tickets, but with no guarantee they would be in the same section as the other seats. In addition, if requested the athletics department would reserve a hotel room at the team hotel subject to availability. This room was at the board member's expense.

Jeff provided Bobbitt with a list of multiple institutions and what they did regarding post-season games and all were in line with our policy—some even more restrictive. Some board members pushed for air transportation to the game.

It was becoming obvious to me that change was in the wind. I could feel it.

On February 9, 2015, I had meetings in Little Rock and took the UA plane. About 25 miles from Fayetteville one of our excellent pilots came back to the cabin and informed me they had experienced a total electrical failure and were returning to the Fayetteville Executive Airport. We landed without incident. Several fire trucks and ambulances were on the runway waiting for us to land. All I could think of was what a kick in the head if my tenure ended with a tragic crash. It reminded me of the same experience years before when Frank Broyles and I had a similar occurrence when we were raising funds for the library. At that time I thought if something tragic happened, the papers the next morning would say, "Frank Broyles in a plane crash and other personnel believed to be on board!"

PART IX
RETIREMENT

2015–2022

It's paradoxical that the idea of living a long life appeals to everyone, but the idea of getting old doesn't appeal to anyone.

— ANDY ROONEY

CHAPTER 92
SOME THINGS DONE—SOME THINGS NOT

> *You can do anything, but not everything.*
>
> — DAVID ALLEN

Jane and I worked very hard for the university, a 24/7 job that literally tires and exhausts you and can age you considerably. Nothing would have happened without a very dedicated staff and faculty and wonderfully supportive student body. A few of the items I am most proud to mention include:

University of Arkansas enrollment reached 27,000 a 37 percent increase since 2008. We had a 43 percent increase of students with an ACT of 30 or higher, and a 60 percent increase in the number of students with GPAs of 3.75 or above. The University of Arkansas has added more than 6,000 students since 2008 and we could say without any exaggeration that it was the most academically qualified and diverse student body we had ever had.

The six-year graduation rate reached 64 percent, the highest in the state among public institutions, and highest in the U of A's history.

We were recently identified by the Chronicle of Higher Education as being the seventh-fastest-growing university in the country.

While growing in size and in academic quality, the diversity of campus had increased by more than 80 percent since 2008.

The greatest single area of enrollment growth was online enrollment with 7,444 students taking at least one online class during the fall 2014 semester, a 506 percent increase since 2008.

We had added 300 faculty in five years to meet student growth needs.

The university was in the best financial shape it had been in for years, perhaps in its entire history, due in large measure to exploding enrollment. The university is in excellent financial condition and has worked hard to build healthy reserves for unforeseen problems and challenges.

We had a record 52 invention disclosures, and we broke $120 million in research expenditures for the third straight year.

The University of Arkansas was elevated to the highest possible classification by the Carnegie Foundation for the Advancement of Teaching during its last reclassification of the nation's 4,633 universities and colleges. The University of Arkansas is one of just 108 schools with this distinction, bestowed for increased accomplishments in research and productivity.

Businessweek.com ranked the Sam M. Walton College of Business in the top 50 among public undergraduate business programs in its latest report. Walton College placed 48th among public schools and 105th in the 2013 rankings of public and private business schools. Those rankings were up from 55th among public business schools and 108th among all the top business schools in 2012. The college also received an A-plus grade for job placement.

We had Initiated the first tuition freeze in 24 years for the 2009–2010 academic year. Tuition remains lower than at many institutions not only in the SEC, but in the nation, and the university is consistently ranked as a "best bargain" in higher education.

We had implemented a set of 15 institutional goals under the heading of Providing Transparency & Accountability to the People of Arkansas, a triennial report chronicling progress toward goals.

Recent recognition by the Chronicle of Higher Education as

being one of the best universities in the country for which to work.

We had created the first Commission on Women, a panel advisory board focusing on issues such as work and family balance, mentoring among faculty and staff, campus safety and environment, and other issues that may have an impact on women.

During my tenure as vice chancellor and chancellor the endowment increased from $119 million to $920.6 million.

Research expenditures increased markedly and reached $124 million, up from $113.8 million in 2008.

Annual fundraising surpassed $100 million for five consecutive years, with $113.3 million raised in fiscal year 2014.

We oversaw the expansion, renovation, or addition of more than 1.5 million square feet to our campus space, an investment of approximately $600 million and impacted more than 40 buildings.

We were among the first institutions in the country to submit a long-range Climate Action Plan to reduce greenhouse gas emissions on campus to zero by the year 2040 in response to the American College and University Presidents Climate Commitment.

We established the Commission on Affordability and Cost Containment, which led to more than $62 million in savings and containment over a period of three years.

We began strong support for students who were serving or had served in the military by founding an office to support veterans and their families. We were recognized as a "Military Friendly School" in the *Guide to Military Friendly Schools* every year for the past six years.

We had made progress in increasing salaries for assistant professors to move them 3.6 percent above the university's peer public institutions in the Southeastern Conference.

We had dramatically increased the number of our students who were studying abroad to close to 1,000 students in more than 42 countries, mainly through private gifts.

Greek Life was flourishing. Alpha Chi Omega, Phi Mu, Delta Gamma, Kappa Alpha Order, and Beta Theta Pi all established chapters to meet the demand. All other houses were full to capacity.

We were one of the first 50 signatories on the Presidents' Commitment to Food and Nutrition Security, an historic effort by universities declaring their commitment toward fighting global hunger. Through Jane's efforts we established a food pantry on campus, one of the first in the nation, to fight food insecurity for students and staff.

In 2008 we began our time in the chancellor's office with literally no fiscal reserves. In 2015 we ended the fiscal year with reserves of $70 million.

MORE TO DO

But when I was contemplating retiring from administration in 2014, I wasn't satisfied with this legacy of accomplishment. I knew that much, much more needed to be done. Some of the regrets I have remain a part of me to this day:

We should have done more to support students of color and increase diversity among faculty, staff and students.

We should have helped more undocumented students gain access to college.

We should have done a better job raising faculty and staff salaries.

We should have raised more funds for scholarships for students.

We had several more facilities to renovate and refurbish, including iconic buildings in the center of campus.

We were never able to convince the governor or the Arkansas General Assembly of the worthiness of supporting increases in our appropriation, even though their own information showed our campus was underfunded by $50 million annually.

Our football program never reached the heights expected by fans under Petrino, Smith and Bielema.

Our men's and women's basketball program never took off like we had hoped.

We desperately needed to improve our intramural playing fields for students.

While making some progress on improving the aesthetics of our campus we never accomplished the pristine and second-to-none campus I dreamed of, due mainly to funding. I wanted more plantings, flower beds, fountains, and outdoor sculpture.

Campus parking was a source of real frustration for faculty, staff, and students, and still is.

We needed more on-campus hotel space and felt that an on-campus conference center would have served us well, especially the Walton College of Business, which could have sponsored large academic and business conferences.

During my tenure I desperately wanted to become known as a top-50 public research university. We got to 62 in 2015, the best ranking we would achieve even to this day. In 2022 we have unfortunately fallen to 78.

Graduate enrollment lagged behind undergraduate enrollment. Again, we needed more funding to bring in more high-level grad students, and, in particular, we should have paid our graduate assistants a much higher stipend.

We probably needed a much larger, or even new, student union facility, as well as a new student recreation facility. Cost projections were prohibitive.

We had explored the potential founding of several new schools, some within existing colleges and some even free standing. We discussed schools of international relations, art, retail, entrepreneurship and sustainability.

We should have done more to create additional faculty offices for the burgeoning size of our faculty, even though we needed more faculty for the size of the student body.

Mullins Library needed a whole renovation and addition. The renovation would finally be accomplished in 2021.

We had very serious IT needs, but could not afford the changes without a large fee on our students.

We had proposed to the Walton family that we establish a School of Art in Alice Walton's name. We had received encouragement and submitted a proposal for over $100 million in late December 2014. It would not be funded until after I retired as chancellor. I had hoped it would happen on my watch, although I did get a call from a Walton staff member in late 2016 asking me to resend them the proposal.

In the coming years some of these bucket list items would be addressed. But I regretted that I was unable to make them happen on my watch.

One project we did begin, or at least begin the initial stages, was a place for indigent and homeless people to congregate and sleep. For many years Northwest Arkansas has experienced a rather severe homeless population. In Arkansas as a whole the predictions were that there were in excess of 2,500 homeless people, basically living on the streets. Northwest Arkansas was believed to have about 500 of those. Many of the homeless would congregate on a wooded area in south Fayetteville on land owned by the university. It was a serious issue that needed attention. Several stabbings and deaths, and even murders, had occurred on our property. We saw it as a potential legal liability and social issue that was in need of a solution. It would not be easy.

The land was not productive for us and we had no plans for its usage. Professor Kevin M. Fitzpatrick, Jones Chair in Community, director of the Community and Family Institute and an expert on homeless issues, approached me in 2014 about turning the property into a secure location for the homeless with a safe, positive living environment, combined with support services that would at least give them a secure and warm environment to live until they could reestablish stable housing. Kevin was a super-star faculty member and I wanted to help him as much as possible.

We naturally had some hurdles that needed to be jumped, including funding, city and state approvals, as well as board of trustees authorization. It would not be easy, but most necessary. I threw my support behind Kevin. In 2020, my son, Brock, became involved in the effort and volunteered to raise funds for the project. Jane and I were very proud of Brock taking on such a massive and complicated effort. With the help of others he managed to raise over $3 million in private support. A major gift came from Jane Hunt and the Hunt family of J.B. Hunt fame, a large trucking and transportation company. The facility was opened in 2021 and received national acclaim.

In March 2015 Provost Sharon Gaber accepted the position of president of The University of Toledo. It was a big-deal job with a medical school, a law school and an excellent reputation as a first-class institution. I was very proud of Sharon. She had been a superb provost and the campus would miss her.

Her replacement would be appointed in January 2017, but resigned in May 2020 to accept a similar post at The University of North Carolina, Greensboro. Jim Coleman would resign from that post in December 2020. The *Triad City Beat* reported that an email sent out to faculty indicated the university had "removed Jim Coleman from the office of provost due to behavior that did not meet expectations for senior leaders at UNCG." Rumors flew as to what Steinmetz's appointee had done to be unceremoniously removed from his position.

Jane and I were encouraged by faculty and staff to have a large dinner in our honor as we retired. We opted instead to have an afternoon ice cream social for anyone on campus. It was bittersweet as we said goodbye to so many folks we had worked with through the years. Jane and I had tears in our eyes.

Just a few weeks before my time was up as chancellor, Mike Johnson informed me that Bobbitt told him to take out part of the wall from the chancellor's football box and have an opening into the president's box. I was told the board of trustees were asking for this to be done. I told Mike to just make Bobbitt happy.

In May 2015 the board of trustees was making decisions about the upcoming fall tuition. I was told that the board wanted our tuition increase to be the lowest of all the campuses. UAPB, UAMS and UAM would all receive larger increases in tuition. How was I going to explain to faculty and staff that we would only be able to give nominal raises when health care premiums would increase dramatically and other campuses got a higher percentage tuition increase? One of the trustees explained to me that I was quitting the job and faculty would be upset with me and not the board or Bobbitt. That was the reality of the situation. I would serve as the scapegoat. I raised an objection, but as the lame duck I had no more clout.

CHAPTER 93
RETIREMENT AS CHANCELLOR

> *When it's time for me to walk away from something, I walk away from it. My mind, my body, my conscience tell me that enough is enough.*
>
> — *JERRY WEST*

I had often told Jane throughout my entire career that I would never stay in a job that I didn't enjoy. Life was too precious and short. Jane and the kids were pushing hard for me to retire. Both Katy and Brock talked to me about coming to closure with a decision and urged me to call it quits. I had done well financially and we had always been savers. Brock called me and said, "Dad, retire a rich man and enjoy life."

I was only 63 and not completely ready to move into the life of a man of leisure. I also felt that I had so much more to accomplish. There were parts of the job I really enjoyed. Then there was the prestige of being chancellor, which is difficult to give up. My life's work culminated in a university presidency and relinquishing the job was a tough decision. I debated and debated the pros and cons but was having difficulty pulling the trigger. My health was excellent; I still had the vigor for the job and felt my energy level was still high. No doubt the job could be grueling and sometimes almost too demanding. You never got away from it. It was 24/7. There was always another problem just around the corner, and staff, faculty, legislators, system officials, alumni and parents of students always needed your attention.

So why retire so relatively young? Was there an overriding reason calling me to make the move? Was I giving up too soon? Could better days be ahead? I decided to call a few friends to get their analysis. The first person I called was my dear friend Roy Shilling. I respected his thinking more than anyone. Roy was sympathetic. He wouldn't tell me what to do, and we debated the various issues for well over an hour on the phone. He finally said no one should have to beat their head against the wall, and he could verify life does indeed go on after retirement. He said something that resonated with me: "Dave, we are all ultimately judged by who we are, not by what we are."

Next I called Alan Sugg to get his advice. He had been a mentor to me, and more than anyone was responsible for my being chancellor. He urged me to stay in the job and thought things would get better in the coming months. When I told him that I was thinking of going on the faculty to close out my tenure in higher education, he didn't think that would be fulfilling enough for me. He wanted me to remain as chancellor. I appreciated his advice as I did Roy's, and knew nobody could make the decision for me.

I also thought about my staff, especially those who had just joined the administration. Chris Wyrick and Randy Massanelli had not been in their respective jobs too long and I didn't want to upset their lives. That weighed on me greatly.

I decided to drive up to our place in Winslow, which we had acquired when I became chancellor. We had sold our home on Razorback Road right next to Fowler house to my brother. We didn't think we wanted to live next to the chancellor's home after retirement. The Winslow house had a beautiful view, and it was a perfect place for a getaway, just 30 minutes from campus. Jane had named it Camp David! I decided it was time to make a decision one way or another and headed to Winslow by myself to contemplate the future.

I made a conscious decision not to call any trustees and get their opinions. Not even the ones I respected and had a good relationship with. I knew they would try to talk me out of it, and the decision had to be mine and my family's. Besides, phoning a trustee would just come across as wanting them to beg me to stay. I needed to be definitive on my own. I did call Jane multiple times, as well as Katy and Brock, while ensconced in our house with a view. They all were adamant about retiring. They told me that they could see the stress of the job and the toll it was taking on me. Brock said, "Dad, these kind of jobs don't always have a good way of ending. Retire on a high note." I knew my life partner, Jane, was ready to let someone else do the job. She had had enough of the constant entertaining and being in the limelight. She was ready for a different lifestyle. I smoked a few cigars and tried to clear my head.

One thing that was really on my mind was our grandkids. We had four sweet grandchildren, and thought Brock and Lindsey wanted more children. Jane and I really enjoyed watching them grow up. Often I could not attend their activities because of my schedule, and that disturbed me. I thought of all the activities I missed with our children through their early years because of my job. I was determined to not let that happen again with the grandkids.

So, why retire so relatively young?

I suppose all of these factors played a part, but one overriding reason was my inability to obtain a new contract. I had waited two years for some indication from Bobbitt, but none came. I had even gone to Little Rock with my attorney to discuss the parameters of a new contract. Nothing happened. Bobbitt was stalling and gave me no indication if he would renegotiate a contract with me. I knew that was his style: say nothing, remain silent, don't address the issue head on, no communication. I thought that style was sneaky, underhanded, perhaps crafty, and even devious. I had always believed in recognizing the elephant in the room. I knew I had some support from the board of trustees, but also knew there were more than a couple who just as soon I retire.

So retire I did. I did not bring up the contract anymore to anyone, especially Bobbitt. I did not start calling benefactors or trustees or the governor or any legislators. I was entirely ready to let someone else do the job. I was tired and worn out and never looked back.

From our place on the mountain, Camp David, I called Bobbitt early on a Monday morning in January 2015 and informed him that I had decided I was going to retire but remain on the faculty. The retirement as chancellor would take effect June 30 to give him 6 months to conduct a search. He made a comment that it was not a call he was expecting, and I could tell, even over the phone, that he was taken aback. He said he needed to inform the trustees and I said that was fine. He was most polite. We discussed the terms of my retirement and he said he would be back in touch with me in five to seven days. I then called two trustees to let them know of my decision. Jane Rogers and Reynie Rutledge had both been most supportive of our efforts to become a top 50 public university, and I wanted them to hear it from me. Both tried to talk me out of it, but my mind was made up.

Bobbitt didn't need five to seven days and called me back the very next morning, and all was approved. I felt a huge sense of relief that the decision had been made. Strangely I wasn't sad or regretful for one second like I thought I might be. I was ready to do something new and different. Back on campus I told my senior staff of the decision. That was most difficult to say the least. Word across campus spread fast and we put out a public statement.

I sent Bobbitt a resignation letter and mentioned two names in the letter, Alan Sugg and Stanley Reed, thanking them for giving me the opportunity to serve as chancellor. Stanley was board chair when I was elected chancellor. I concluded the letter by saying this would give me more time to spend with my kids and grandkids.

My letter follows:

Dear President Bobbitt:

As we discussed recently, it is my desire to retire from my

position of chancellor of the University of Arkansas on July 31, 2015. I do this after much discussion with my family. I have four main reasons for making this difficult decision. They are our four grandchildren: Ben, age 5; Caroline, age 4; Ellie, almost 2; and soon to be born, Lily Jane. Going forward, I hope to spend more quality time with each of them, as well as with our children and their spouses, Katy and Justin and Brock and Lindsey.

The most difficult part of this transition will be giving up my daily contact with our superb faculty and staff, extraordinary students, loyal and generous alumni and benefactors and campaign volunteers. We have a tremendous team at the University of Arkansas, and that team has made these past seventeen years, ten as vice chancellor, and seven as chancellor, both exciting and memorable.

I would be remiss if I didn't also mention the commitment my dear wife, Jane, has given the university every step of the way. The hundreds if not thousands of events she has planned and attended, not to mention her deep involvement in the Northwest Arkansas community and the incredible support she has afforded so many people, all on her own time, is simply breathtaking. Jane has been an amazing partner in this venture.

I hope you will express to members of the board of trustees that it has been my absolute privilege to serve as the chancellor of the flagship campus. As you know, I never applied for the position nor sought it, but had the good fortune to be tapped for the honor by then President B. Alan Sugg and then chairman of the board of trustees, the late Stanley Reed.

I wish you and all associated with the University of Arkansas the very best.

Sincerely,

G. David Gearhart
Chancellor

A few days before I resigned, I learned that *The Northwest Arkansas Times* newspaper would cease to exist. It was the end to a long and celebrated era. *The Democrat* was founded in 1860 and operated under that name until 1893. The paper was then renamed the *Fayetteville Daily Democrat*. In 1911, it was purchased by Jay Fulbright, and upon his death in 1923 it went to his wife, Roberta Fulbright. She became president and publisher, renaming the paper *The Northwest Arkansas Times* in 1937. From 1940 until 1977 my grandfather and then father ran the paper for the Fulbright family. My family's newspaper and my time as chancellor ended at the same time.

A few days later I began receiving letters from each member of the board of trustees. They were laudatory and thoughtful and appreciative. Alan Sugg got phone calls from a few trustees wondering why I had retired and telling him they were shocked by my announcement. Sugg told them they shouldn't be shocked, as I had been trying to get a new contract for some time. They expressed no knowledge of that fact.

Jane and I received literally hundreds of thoughtful letters from donors, students and alumni after the announcement of my retirement. Three letters that touched us greatly were from Mack McLarty, Becky and Bob Alexander and Will Roth.

Mack was the former chief of staff to the president of the United States and chairman of McLarty Associates, an international strategic advisory firm headquartered in Washington, DC, and chairman of the McLarty Companies in Little Rock, Arkansas. I had known him since my time at Hendrix College. He was always a perfect gentleman. He told me in his letter that it was a bittersweet moment for him. He mentioned the students-first philosophy and my commitment to diversity and fundraising success. He then thanked Jane and me for our leadership to Arkansas.

Bob and Becky Alexander were major donors to the university

and benefactors of Razorback athletics. Becky's parents were Bob and Marilyn Bogle, who were also very significant benefactors to the university and so many other philanthropies.

Bob and Becky's words touched us:

> Thank you, thank you, thank you! Becky and I are so happy for you guys and feel so fortunate and appreciative for your time and accomplishments at the helm of the U of A. And I say "you guys" because you two truly are a team. They say everybody's replaceable but they are wrong. Under your watch our flagship University has gone to new heights in fundraising, enrollment, academics, research, facilities, athletics, and national recognition. The U of A, Northwest Arkansas, and the entire State of Arkansas is in a better place because of your hard work, dedication, and vision. Dave and Jane Gearhart are irreplaceable.

Will Roth was an intern in the athletics department and subsequently became a senior member of the staff. he is a remarkable young man:

> From the time you announced your upcoming retirement to your last actual day as Chancellor, I am sure you two will be flooded with congratulatory letters, e-mails and phone calls. I am writing to you today to add to this flood. I vividly remember my first few encounters with you. The cliche is correct: "You never get a second chance to make a first impression." You both were so interested in what I was doing as a student and as an intern in the athletic department. You immediately said, "Hey, aren't you the guy who shoots the t-shirts at the basketball games?" And you were correct. That was me. How many Chancellors and "first ladies" do you think know who shoots the t-shirt gun at basketball games? My guess is one, and it's the Gearharts. I graduated May 9, 2009. My phone rang a few hours before the ceremony began. I answered—and much to my surprise—it was you,

Chancellor Gearhart, calling to congratulate me on the significance of this day. You will never know what that meant to me then and still does today. The "You of A" tagline, more public art on campus, increased efforts for sustainability, your campus update videos, your welcome videos on the first day of each semester, and your unwavering support of athletics, just to name a few ... It is no wonder our campus on the hill is rising so fast in seemingly every college category in the country.

After the announcement of my retirement as chancellor I received a call from Naccaman Williams of the Walton Family Foundation. I had worked very closely with Naccaman and respected him greatly. He asked me to remain a board member of the UA Campus Foundation, the sub entity that managed the $300 million gift. I told Naccaman I was really flattered to be asked to remain a board member, but didn't think it was the right thing to do. A new chancellor would be coming on board and I needed to get out of the way. I suggested Chris Wyrick for the vacancy. I said my time in that role was done and I was moving on to new adventures. I told him I would miss working with him, Rick Chapman and Buddy Philpot, and offered sincerest best wishes.

My retirement was effective July 31, 2015. The very last act of my tenure on the very last day as chancellor was a sexual harassment case involving two student-athletes. The athletes had been accused of sexual assault and harassment by a female student. The female alleged victim accused the male alleged perpetrators of taking her back to their apartment to engage in sex without her consent. The judicial board on campus voted to discipline the students by expelling them from school. That action can be appealed to the chancellor for a final decision. The appeal is based totally on audio tapes of the hearing without any chance to interview the persons involved. I had one duty, which was to affirm the action of the judicial board or overturn it. It was an important responsibility that had to be given time and taken seriously.

I carefully listened to the tapes, which went on for several hours.

What struck me immediately was that the female involved was acting very much like the sex acts were of mutual consent. Liquor was involved, to which I had to give special attention, to be certain she was able to give consent.

After reviewing the tapes twice I called Dr. Charles Robinson to my office to listen to them as well. I did not tell him that I had reservations about the students being found guilty. Dr. Robinson listened to the entire recording. It was about 5:30 PM on my last day in office. I had alerted university counsel Scott Varady that my decision could go into the evening. I officially went out of office at midnight.

Dr. Robinson looked at me and immediately said "I think there was mutual consent. In fact, I'm certain of it."

I agreed, and we both sat in my office and listened to parts of the tapes again. It was now 8:00 p.m. Both Dr. Robinson and I felt strongly that the decision of the judicial board should be reversed. I called Scott and told him of the decision, and he said he would put together a document and come to Fowler House for my signature. I called our student services staff and told them to inform the various parties to the alleged infraction of my decision. I also let Jeff Long know.

It was rare that I would reverse a decision of the judicial board, but after a thorough review and the backup review by Dr. Robinson, I felt clearly that an injustice had been done. At 10:15 p.m. I signed the document reversing the decision. It was not appealable any further. It was my last act as chancellor.

Through the good efforts of Chris Wyrick, Jane and I were the beneficiaries of three wonderful and deeply appreciated honors.

As mentioned, the food pantry was named after Jane for being the founder of the pantry.

The Graduate School and Honors College building was named after me by the board of trustees.

A scholarship fund was given by friends and family. The largest contributors were Bob and Marilyn Bogle. The fund now has over $2 million.

Chris shepherded all of those very thoughtful tributes for which we are most grateful.

I have never regretted early retirement, not for one second. In some ways it was the smartest thing I ever did. I lost a little weight, which I needed to do, spent much more time attending grandchildren's events and slept much better. The stress and strain was more evident than I had realized. My family saw the strain, but I didn't really admit to it until after retirement. The final chapter in my professional life was about to unfold.

CHAPTER 94
OFF TO THE FACULTY

> *I touch the future. I teach.*
>
> — CHRISTA MCAULIFFE

On July 1, 2015, I became a full-time faculty member in the College of Education and Health Professions. The dean of the School of Law wondered why I had not joined their faculty instead of education and invited me to teach a class in the law school. My tenure appointment was in education, and on top of that, I really didn't feel qualified to teach in the law school. It had been almost 40 years since I got my law degree, and I had never practiced as an attorney. How in the world could I teach law classes? The dean told me it would be a course in philanthropic management as many lawyers were going into the field of public/private sector service. As I had already decided to join the education faculty I politely declined, and said maybe later. I did, however, make a guest appearance and conduct a few classes for faculty in the law school.

Part of my agreement upon retirement as chancellor was a period of time on sabbatical to redeploy my skills to teach and put my classes in order. I would be a nine-month appointee, so classes would not begin until the following August. The dean of the College of Education and Health Professions was Dr. Michael Miller. He could not have been more supportive or more helpful. He was welcoming and expressed excitement for my arrival in the college. He immediately gave me tons of materials and syllabi to help me get started as a full professor in the college. He also got me started on publishing, and during my time as a professor I published 13 journal articles and four books, mostly with Miller as co-publisher. Miller and I became close friends during this time and collaborated on a number of projects and publications.

Miller decided to return full-time to the faculty after having served as dean for three years. We created and founded the National Lab for the Study of the College President and served as co-editors. The first edition was published in December 2017. I must give Miller credit for getting that up and going. I played a less valuable role than he did, but his kindness and ego-free personality allowed me to get more credit than deserved. I enjoyed working with Miller, and he helped me greatly in getting my courses in line. He was a mentor to me, a brilliant writer, accomplished publisher and amazing teacher. I will miss working with him on a daily basis. In September 2018 Miller was invited to visit Beijing Normal University to discuss collaboration on education projects. BNU is one of the oldest and most prestigious universities in China. He invited me to accompany him. I was invited to give an address to faculty and students at BNU. I was amazed that all who asked questions did so with fluent English. They asked informed questions about American higher education, and were polite and respectful.

Mike Miller asked me to teach two courses a semester, which is standard, and of course have a robust scholarship and publishing agenda as well. Publishing is expected and keeping up with the latest trends in higher education helps your teaching responsibilities to remain on the cutting edge.

I had five graduate courses I would rotate from semester to semester: 1) University Advancement, 2) College and University Presidency, 3) Governance of Higher Education Institutions, 4) Leading Change, 5) Non-Profit Management.

Truth is I loved it! I truly loved it!

The students for the most part were bright and eager to participate and rarely missed class. Of course, they were all graduate students, so they wanted to be there working toward a master's or doctorate degree. I must say, I think it was the most enjoyable job I had ever had. I served on numerous doctoral dissertation committees and was assigned as advisor to a ton of students. I graded exams for master's students every semester. I got to know most of the students in the program and I'm still in touch with them today. It seemed to me that I moved almost seamlessly from chancellor to faculty member, but the truth is that none of it would have been possible without Mike Miller.

Two other people were key to my making the move with virtually no hassle. Dr. Michael Hevel was head of our college division and head of the higher education program, and he was superb. Totally supportive of all faculty and a real scholar himself. I greatly enjoyed working for him.

The new dean, Dr. Brian Primack, came in July 2019 and continued Miller's very helpful and thoughtful support. Primack was a renowned scholar with quite a pedigree. He earned a B.A. in English and mathematics from Yale University, a master's degree in education, human development, and psychology from Harvard University, an M.D. from Emory University, and a Ph.D. in clinical and translational science from the University of Pittsburgh. Academic credentials don't get any better than that, and we were very lucky to have him at Arkansas. He came to the University of Arkansas from the University of Pittsburgh, where he was the dean of the honors college and holder of an endowed chair. I liked him the first time I met him, and he has been a marvelous dean.

Then, in January 2022 word came that Primack was leaving the university and going to Washington State University to be a dean. I was surprised, as he had been at the University of Arkansas only about two years. Word on the grapevine was Primack was unhappy about the education reform program, and didn't feel he was getting the proper support from the administration after he replaced Jay Green as head of the program. I hated to see it, as Primack had a national reputation and stellar credentials, which brought renown to our college and university. He was likely the highest-paid dean of a college of education in the nation, but that didn't seem to weigh in his decision to go elsewhere.

When I was staring 70 years of age squarely in the face, I started thinking about total retirement. Frankly, I could tell that my memory in class was not as sharp as I would have liked. It was not a serious problem like having dementia by any means, but I just was not as quick as I wanted to be when answering student questions and lecturing. No doubt it was the aging process taking hold, and I could feel some of my basic abilities being compromised. I have known so many people who stayed past their prime and taught into their late 70's or even 80's. I remember Robert Leflar of the law school, who taught into his 90's and even without compensation his last several years. He was the exception.

I informed my classes that I would retire from the faculty in June 2022. When asked why by one of my students I said, "I don't want to be accused of drooling when I'm speaking or having students tell me my fly is open."

CHAPTER 95
QASSIM UNIVERSITY

> *It's important to reach out to moderate Arab nations, like Jordan and Egypt, Saudi Arabia and Kuwait.*
>
> — GEORGE W. BUSH

In November 2015 I was invited to be a member of an international advisory committee for Qassim University. Qassim is a public university in the Al-Qassim Province of Saudi Arabia. The institution was relatively young, having been founded in 2004. Within four years the enrollment had grown to 40,000 students. Today it has 75,000 students. When you have virtually unlimited resources one can accomplish much in a very short time. I was selected for the advisory committee along with five other American university presidents. The Saudis were working very hard to establish universities in their homeland so they would not have to rely as much on universities around the world, particularly the United States and the United Kingdom. It is estimated that about 40,000 Saudi students study in the United States annually.

The King Fahd Center for Middle East Studies was founded at the University of Arkansas in the mid 1990's. President Clinton was primarily responsible for securing the gift, which was situated in the J. William Fulbright College. The Saudi government contributed approximately $22 million to endow the center so we had a substantial tie to the Saudi government.

David Gearhart in Saudi Arabia with the president and vice president of Qassim University.

I was informed by the Qassim University representative that all of my expenses would be paid, including a first-class ticket to Riyadh as well as a stipend. I accepted the offer to join the advisory committee.

I spent a week in Saudi Arabia in multiple meetings, luncheons, and dinners. It was an amazing experience. The president of Qassim was most accommodating and thoughtful, as were other members of his team. We discussed curriculum issues for the 21st century and talked a lot about their economy and the building of colleges and universities in an attempt to keep students in Saudi Arabia rather than going abroad. I learned the Saudis expected their oil and oil reserves to last for many more years, but at some point depletion is a given. They are trying desperately to prepare the nation for the time when they have no more oil to pump up the economy. They need to move into other industries or face an economic crisis down the road.

We also spent some leisure time when not in meetings. We visited several historic attractions and even went on a camel ride, much to the delight of the Saudis, who got a kick out of our attempts to ride a camel. The whole experience was phenomenal, and our hosts were most gracious.

At the end of the week one of the university officials approached me and said they would like to pay our stipend in cash. I asked my other committee members, and everyone was fine with it. Just before we were scheduled to leave for the airport each of the committee members was handed $30,000 in cash. Three hundred $100 U.S. bills. I had a layover in London for 24 hours and walked around the city with $100 bills stuck in all my pockets! When I arrived at the airport in Dallas I went immediately to the counter to declare the cash as the law said you had to declare anything over $10,000. That meant I would be taxed on the stipend and I was. It broke my heart, but if I had not declared it and got caught, my heart would have been broken much more! I had to obey the law. The agent at the counter looked at me and said, "Mister, you did the right thing." That did not make me feel any better.

CHAPTER 96
A NEW CHANCELLOR

> *There's a new sheriff in town and his name is Reggie Hammond.*
>
> — EDDIE MURPHY IN THE MOVIE 48 HRS.

> *Outstanding leaders go out of their way to boost the self-esteem of their personnel. If people believe in themselves, it's amazing what they can accomplish.*
>
> — SAM WALTON

The search for my replacement didn't begin immediately. The delay caused the necessity of naming an interim chancellor. Bobbitt called me and said that he was going to appoint a former chancellor, Dan Ferritor—chancellor before John White—to serve until a new person was selected. That made good sense to me. Dan was well respected and popular in the community and would fill in beautifully.

Dan was also a real person, savvy, engaging and honest. We got along well, at least from my perspective. He had been a good chancellor.

Four chancellors and spouses: Chancellor Emeritus Willard Gatewood, Lou Gatewood, Patsy Ferritor, Chancellor Emeritus Dan Ferritor, Chancellor David Gearhart, Jane Gearhart, Mary Lib White, Chancellor Emeritus John White

From the very beginning, it was most obvious that Don Bobbitt wanted Joe Steinmetz to be the next chancellor. Bobbitt was enamored with Steinmetz, and pushed his candidacy at every opportunity. Steinmetz was serving as provost at The Ohio State University. I was not involved in the search for a new chancellor, but watched it from afar. Several trustees and members of the search committee kept me informed of the leading candidates, and told me Bobbitt wanted Steinmetz and had no real interest in anyone else. Steinmetz is who he got!

I had many friends at Ohio State from my days at Penn State and my stint in consulting. My former firm was serving as the fundraising consultant to Ohio State at the time of the search. So I knew more than I probably should have about Joe Steinmetz. He had been a candidate for a number of presidencies before he landed the job at

Arkansas, including Iowa State University, The University of Texas and Ohio State University, where he was passed over.

Not all of the trustees were enamored with his selection, but they quickly fell in line since Bobbitt was so favorable for him. The trustees approved his appointment unanimously, even though I was told there were a few quiet objections during the discussion. One of the trustee wives who met with his wife, Sandy Steinmetz, pleaded with her husband to object to his appointment. Apparently, she found Sandy to be a somewhat bland choice for first lady.

Be that as it may, Steinmetz succeeded me as chancellor of the University of Arkansas. I began getting phone calls from senior staff the very first week. They told me that he was a bully and difficult to work for. One prominent staff member even said he was "a son of a bitch." Apparently he would excoriate senior staff in front of others, and even in executive committee meetings, and cause them great embarrassment. One staff member was so upset that he walked out of the meeting after being thoroughly trashed by Steinmetz. Folks were afraid of him and had reason to be. I had heard that he could be callous from friends outside the UA circle, but the stories from colleagues painted a disconcerting situation. If someone would make a casual statement when advising Steinmetz that, "This is how we used to do it," Steinmetz would tell them he never wanted to hear that phrase again. He was now the chancellor and the past would remain in the past.

I only had one official meeting with Steinmetz in the five-plus years of his tenure. I was contacted by the chancellor's office with an invitation to lunch three months into his tenure. I thought that was a nice gesture, and we had lunch at Carnall Inn. Later I found out that it was not Steinmetz's idea, but was suggested to him by Dean Mike Miller. We exchanged chit-chat. Nothing definitive or important. I learned he did not like wine and only drank beer. The only positive statement he made to me was, "You left things in good shape." I thanked him.

We mainly talked about his family and I did most of the talking, asking him questions. He asked no questions about anything at the university. He asked no questions about my family or background.

We had a few long, awkward silences at the table that day. As faculty or staff would come into the dining room, I made a point of introducing him to folks, but I noticed he didn't ask them any questions either and a couple times didn't even get up from the table. Maybe I was being too critical of him. I mean he had been at the university for less than three months and was still learning the ropes. Give him a break! Or maybe it was prescient for how things would turn out for him.

Jane and I would occasionally run into the Steinmetzes on campus and exchange pleasantries. As indicated previously, we were never invited to sit in the chancellor's box for any game of any sport, the entire five years of his tenure. We had given a million dollars to the university before we left the job, but that didn't even qualify us to be his guests for a single solitary game. We thought it odd. We thought the vice chancellor, Mark Power, might put us on the list, but he never did. It didn't really matter to us, as we would attend the games and sit in our son's skybox. But out of simple courtesy you would think he might include us. Never once.

One of the senior folks told me he was intimidated by us. I couldn't imagine that. I made it a point to never criticize him or his agenda publicly, that is, until this book. I figured that I had my time as chancellor, and being public with criticism of his initiatives would not be productive. He was the chancellor now and I should keep my opinions to myself, as difficult as it would be.

His signature project was a building he would label the Student Success Center. At first, few understood what the facility was to be used for and why it had become a priority. It would be built in the center of campus and would unite a number of student functions in one building. Perhaps it will turn out to be a building that is needed. I will give him the benefit of the doubt. But there were so many other needs, that many felt it wasn't first on the list. In fairness I suppose he thought it would help with student retention, but it seemed to me and others that student scholarships and advising personnel would be a much better investment.

Another project that gained momentum and financial support was a School of Art. That was not a Steinmetz creation by any means. We had submitted the proposal to the Walton family two years before he became chancellor. In fact, after I left office, I received a call from a Walton executive asking if I had a copy of our original proposal, which I sent to her. But the project happened on his watch so at least credit should be given for that fact.

Then in August 2016, I got an early morning call from Chris Wyrick, who said he had been asked to resign his position as vice chancellor for university advancement. I was stunned. I knew that Chris had made some comments that appeared to be taken out of context, which upset two female members of his staff. Chris could be brash, and his athletics and sports background sometimes showed through. Rough-and-tumble could manifest on occasion. But he had a marvelous relationship with major donors and he was honest and forthright. I liked him very much and felt he did an amazing job for the university. But did he deserve to be fired or just disciplined? Was that a fireable offense? From what I was told—and I was knowledgeable about most of the incidents leading up to his dismissal—firing was an over-the-top reaction. In fact, Chris Wyrick and Steinmetz were scheduled to play golf the weekend after he was fired on a Friday.

I hired Chris into the job after the debacle caused by Choate and Diamond. I needed someone who had close relationships with our major donors, and Chris was the only one I felt had those special relationships. He was extremely well liked by major benefactors, and I knew him to be an aggressive fundraiser. I needed someone to take hold of the program and keep our campaign moving forward.

I had contemplated asking Mark Power, associate vice chancellor, to take the job, and talked to many people on campus and off about his candidacy. I just didn't feel he was strong enough for the job, even though I liked him very much and had worked with him for several years. I felt he had a tough time making decisions. I was also concerned that he was one of the chief lieutenants in development when the deficit accumulated. I didn't blame Mark for the deficit, but he was clearly one of the senior staff members who should have been engaged in monitoring the budget. I also had considered Bruce

Pontious, another senior staff member in advancement, but had the same concerns.

Then I learned that Mark was involved in advising Steinmetz to dismiss Chris. I was shocked, as they seemed to have a very close relationship. Chris had given Mark a sizable raise, and they seemed to be compatriots and even close friends.

Later Steinmetz would dismiss Jeff Long as vice chancellor and director of athletics. When he fired Long, he told him that he didn't deserve to be fired, then proceeded to dismiss him anyway. I could not have fired someone who didn't deserve to be fired.

Long's dismissal was all about winning football. The board of trustees had tired of Coach Bret Bielema as had the fan base. They wanted and were demanding more wins and Bielema had been under fire for some time. The irony was that Long had already decided to dismiss Bielema, but the decision was taken out of his hands.

Long's firing surprised me greatly. He had been a great athletics director and had accomplished a great deal. It is true he did not suffer fools and could be dismissive of the everyday fan, but he raised a lot of resources, improved facilities—and most importantly —graduated students in all sports. When I retired as chancellor the board of trustees asked me to give him a new contract, as they were concerned he might leave for another AD position. He was the first chairman of the College Football Playoff selection committee, and had received national attention for doing the right thing by firing Bobby Petrino. Now two years after giving him a new contract, he was fired. Could Bobbitt and Steinmetz have exercised some good old-fashioned guts to keep it from happening. They didn't!

I learned early in my tenure there are dos and don'ts in managing athletics. A president should not even think about running athletics day-to-day, and should avoid getting into the weeds in making decisions about athletics. A president's job is to monitor compliance with NCAA rules for sure, but not to try to hire coaches or attempt to be a jock and become a close friend of a sitting coach. A president should monitor the athletics budget, like all units, but not measure success by the win/loss record completely. And a president should never try to compete with coaches or the athletics director for public attention.

Steinmetz had made a huge change by having the development officers placed on the deans' budgets rather than centrally. No longer did the development officers, the main fundraisers for the university, have any allegiance to the central office. What was a perfect model of joint supervision had been destroyed.

Then Steinmetz decided to break up the central fundraising staff and send them packing from University House. Only problem was, they had no place to go when he gave the house to another entity. They were told to work from home. So dozens of development personnel were sent home to work remotely. Then, months later, many were crammed into Hembree Alumni House where they were packed like sardines. No planning and no regard for the human contact element so important for any administrative organization. My phone rang off the hook with calls from dissatisfied staff members. No one, and I mean no one, could understand the decision. Apparently, Steinmetz was looking for a campus space and, with Mark Power's agreement, gave up University House and displaced a large number of professionals. No one could explain the reasoning. Not even the senior staff of the institution. Mark Power also was moved from the fourth floor of the administration building to the second floor. Most all major senior officers reside on the fourth floor with the chancellor and provost. That is where my office was located as vice chancellor. Moving Power to the second floor was viewed as a demotion.

The chancellor's residence, The Wallace W. and Jama M. Fowler House, was built with private gifts from the Fowlers. They had been extraordinarily generous to the university, as well as Razorback athletics, contributing well over $10 million. I had approached them to build a residence that could be used for entertaining alumni, friends, students and faculty. Previously, the chancellor's house was woefully inadequate for any large group functions. Jane and I used the house to capacity, holding literally hundreds of events during our time in the job. About two years into the position Steinmetz decided he didn't want to live in Fowler House and purchased a private home in Springdale, about 15 miles from campus. My contract required Jane and me to live on campus in the Fowler House. I assume Steinmetz had the same provision. It is required by the IRS so a chancellor does not have to pay taxes on the benefit to him of university housing. Bobbitt and the trustees looked the other way. I could not believe they would allow him to essentially vacate the beautiful Fowler House and move off campus, but they did. I'm told very few events were held in the house during his tenure. I'm the first to admit that it is like living in a fishbowl, but that is part of the job. Besides, a very generous donor had given the house and expected it to be used for the benefit of the institution. I thought it was despicable he would move out and not use the house for its intended function. It sat empty most of his tenure and he was quietly criticized by faculty and staff. Not long after Steinmetz moved out, I got a call from Wallace Fowler extremely upset about the matter. He questioned why he had given $6 million when the house was not being used. I had no answer for him. He said he was going to call Bobbitt.

About a year and a half after Steinmetz arrived, I began to get calls from deans, staff, faculty, legislators, former employees, and others about Steinmetz's performance. In fact, a few deans told me they had been interviewed by the chairman of the board, John Goodson, and were told Steinmetz would be gone by the middle of the summer. Summer came and went, and he was still chancellor. Bobbitt convinced the board to give him a contract extension, much to the surprise of the many folks who the board chair had spoken to. Bobbitt was his protector. He defended him through thick and thin and told the board he was doing a great job.

It was about that time we began hearing very unsettling things about Steinmetz. A staff member told us that compromising, provocative photos of an intimate nature had been circulated and seen by a number of students and staff members. We discounted it as just nasty rumors, but they kept coming. Rumors spread that provocative photos had been discovered. Jane and I again dismissed the notion that a chancellor would be so careless as to post a compromising photo of himself or put his name on a hookup site.

We just couldn't get our arms around something so egregious by a sitting senior executive with tons of big college experience. Could it be true? To our utter and total shock we were sent provocative photos of Steinmetz. Were they real or fake?

Then on June 17, 2021, it was announced that University of Arkansas Chancellor Joe Steinmetz had resigned. In an email to students, faculty, and staff, Steinmetz said his resignation would be effective the next day Friday, June 18. No reason was given. In a statement he did say, "I still strongly believe in the mission of higher education, yet given the many challenges found trying to manage a university in today's polarized society, I need to do what's best for my family and I feel ready to make way for others." Steinmetz's resignation came just hours after a special meeting held by the UA board of trustees, during which members went into executive session, which is typically done when discussing personnel matters.

Then members of the General Assembly weighed in. They had seen the provocative photos and some were interviewed by the media. Steinmetz claimed the photos were Photoshopped and bogus, but he resigned immediately after they became public. I was sent some of the photos and if they are real—and many believe they are— they are indeed disturbing. It was a most embarrassing chapter in the history of the university.

If they were indeed bogus as suggested by Steinmetz, then why didn't he fight it. Modern technology can determine if a photo is bogus, or Photoshopped. The photos I saw appeared real enough and no effort was made to verify their validity.

Apparently, Bobbitt was going to allow Steinmetz to keep his tenured faculty appointment until some trustees and legislators intervened. The university paid him to relinquish his tenure and he was gone for good in 24 hours. Why Bobbitt stood by him, even when the evidence was overwhelming, is a question many would ask. Just recently I'm told that Bobbitt still defends him to this day.

His appointment was a colossal mistake that will reverberate for years to come.

In late 2021 Steinmetz accepted a position as executive director of the PCSAS at Indiana University Bloomington.

Soon after Steinmetz resigned, Bobbitt named Bill Kincaid as acting chancellor. He was in that job for about five weeks when Bobbitt named Charles Robinson interim chancellor. No one really knows why he had two chancellors in a month's time. It is a mystery that Bobbitt didn't explain, but it caused quite a stir on campus. Any time a new chancellor is appointed—even acting or interim—there are many procedures in fiscal management that have to be tended to. Folks on campus were scrambling to change all of the approval processes and procedures.

The major issue during the writing of this book was the terrible problem of so many senior interim positions in the administrative ranks. Chancellor, provost, vice chancellors, all deans but two, vice provosts are all interim. Not good for any university. Just recently the UA lost a very effective longtime dean and faculty member, Todd Shields, who became chancellor of Arkansas State University in Jonesboro. It is a huge loss for the University of Arkansas. I attended his going-away function, and was inundated with a large number of faculty and staff exclaiming how bad things are with so many interim positions.

SENATOR J. WILLIAM FULBRIGHT

Toward the end of Steinmetz's tenure, there was a significant push to remove Senator Fulbright's statue on campus because of his untenable civil rights record. Fulbright signed the Southern Manifesto, which was a document written in 1956 opposing racial integration of public places. Over 100 members of Congress signed the manifesto, most of them Democrats from southern states that had fought for the Confederacy. While Fulbright did work to soften the wording, it was still a black mark on him as a respectable member of Congress, and would haunt him for the rest of his life. He would tell people that, had he not signed it, he would have been defeated for re-election. He also opposed civil rights legislation in the 1960s. A number of students and faculty called for the immediate removal of his statue on campus because of his terrible legacy on civil rights. They also wanted his name removed from the college. Steinmetz agreed with their feelings and recommended to the board of trustees that the statue be removed, but allow Fulbright's name to remain on the college. Ultimately the board did not allow the statue to be removed and Steinmetz's recommendation was not heeded.

I'm not sure Steinmetz really understood the impact Fulbright's life had on Fayetteville and the University of Arkansas. If he had, I cannot imagine he would have made the recommendation to take down his statue. One cannot forgive Fulbright's unconscionable stand on civil rights to be sure, but one must take his entire life into context before rendering judgment.

Among the great joys of living in Fayetteville and working at the University of Arkansas are the constant reminders of Senator J. William Fulbright. Even though he had been gone for many years, his presence was still palpable and he was still seen as one of Arkansas' icons. You can still sense Bill Fulbright everywhere. His bust, created by sculptor Hank Kaminsky, graces the Fayetteville Square. The Fulbright family home on Mount Nord, purchased on the eve of World War I, stands as a monument to their central presence in this community for many decades. Bill Fulbright's life came full circle on our campus. He did his primary and secondary schooling in Peabody Hall, which still graces our campus near Old Main. Only a short distance from Peabody Hall, across the Old Main greensward, he lies buried in the family plot in Evergreen Cemetery. What a legacy he left on campus. He was here as a student, a star scholar and athlete, graduating in 1925 and winning a Rhodes Scholarship to Oxford. He later returned and served the university as president from 1939 to 1941, at age 34 the youngest college president in America.

In this town, on this campus, Senator Fulbright is remembered in statues, fountains, the many buildings he lived and worked in—but most of all in the hearts of so many people in this community who hold his memory dear. His most valuable bequest to the University of Arkansas, however, is not material but metaphysical—a philosophy that guides the institution to this very day.

"The highest function of higher education," he said, "is the teaching of things in perspective, toward the purposes of enriching the life of the individual, cultivating the free and inquiring mind, and advancing the effort to bring reason, justice, and humanity into the relations of men and nations." That philosophy suffuses the university in general but more particularly its core college of arts and sciences. Senator Fulbright's true legacy is global, not local. And it is the cornerstone of that global legacy. The Fulbright Scholars Program seeks to promote academic excellence and cultural understanding between the United States and other nations throughout the world. It has succeeded handsomely since it was inaugurated by Congress in 1946. In 1945, Senator J. William Fulbright proposed a bill to use the proceeds from selling surplus U.S. government war property to fund international exchanges between the U.S. and other countries.

In the half century since, the impact of the program has been extraordinary. There have been more than 300,000 Fulbright grantees from about 140 nations in all. Since the catastrophe of September 11, The Fulbright Program has become more important than ever. One of the best ways for building greater understanding among nations is by exposing individuals to foreign ideas, the animating principle of Senator Fulbright's life.

CHAPTER 97
THE FINAL CHAPTER

> *I have no regrets at all. None. I consider myself to be the luckiest old broad on two feet.*
>
> — BETTY WHITE

On January 1, 2022, Jane and I decided to treat our extended family to the Outback Bowl in Tampa, Florida. We leased a sky box and entertained 22 family members. All of our kids and grandkids, as well as my brothers in Florida and their families attended. Since Arkansas was playing Penn State, the first time in our history for football, we thought it appropriate to be present for the matchup. It was one of the best times we have ever had in our lives. We also were hoping to see our dear friends, Dave and Sharon Lieb, and their family. As it turned out, the Penn State president decided to forgo the trip because of Covid concerns. The next in line to manage the skybox for the president of Penn State was Dave Lieb. And, on top of that, their box was right next to ours! What were the chances of that happening?!

It was a once in a lifetime opportunity and then Arkansas beat Penn State 24 to 10.

With the David and Sharon Lieb family and their kids: Dillon (youngest boy), Lauren and Adam.

As Jane and I sat in the box watching the Penn State Blue Band perform before the game, memories came flooding back of all the experiences we had at Penn State, the good ones and the not so good. It was a nostalgic moment for both of us. It had been 27 years since we had left Penn State, but it didn't really seem that long. The magnificent Penn State band played their alma mater, and we could still remember the words and sang along with our daughter. I thought of all of the faculty and staff we had known, and the many dear friends we had made during the 13 years we lived in State College. I thought about the Penn State friends we had lost through the years. I thought about Joe Paterno and the many contributions he made to Penn State only to be dismissed after 50 years coaching the Nittany Lions. I thought about Bill Schreyer, Merrill Lynch CEO and our campaign chairman, and how wonderful he and his wife Joan had been to Jane and me. I thought about the Campaign for Penn State and our amazing staff who worked so hard for the institution.

Then the Arkansas alma mater began to play, and I looked over at Jane and she had big tears streaming down her face. They were happy tears. Besides thinking of all of the memories, she was also focusing on our family all being together that day in Tampa. Arkansas and Penn State, the two institutions where we had worked the longest by far, were playing each other and it was a momentous occasion for us. Then it hit me how lucky in life Jane and I have been. We worked for great institutions, public and private and lived in wonderful communities and met so many marvelous people along the way. We have been blessed by reasonably good health and a good standard of living. We have traveled the world and been in every state in the United States except North Dakota. (It is on my bucket list). We have tried to live a life of faith and goodness.

Surely the ultimate reward we get in life, for a life well lived, is the blessing of family. We have been blessed beyond what we deserve.

The Gearhart family at the Outback Bowl, January 1, 2022.

As I'm entering the cusp of old age I have some regrets for sure. There are people who I should have been kinder to through the years. I should have been more engaged with my children in their younger years. I should have been more willing to just go along and get along with folks I worked for. I should have listened more to the words of Bill Schreyer, "Life is a journey, not a destination."

I officially retired from the faculty June 30, 2022. If you count my student time beginning in 1970 at Westminster College, I have been in higher education 52 mostly glorious years. My entire professional life has been in the academy.

Jane and I plan to travel, enjoy some cruises and spend much more time with the grandkids and with dear friends who have blessed our lives. Whatever time we have left on this earth, God willing, will be devoted to a simple, uncomplicated, volunteer-driven, faith-based, blessed life with family and friends.

Curvahedra sculpture at the UA Honors College.

I've played golf since I was a little boy. I stopped playing for 50 years but took it back up after I retired from being chancellor. I'm not very good, but am enjoying it immensely with a wonderful group of guys who try to play twice a week. The crew consists of John Vitale, Brock's father-in-law; Joe Dickinson from Ft. Smith, who drives over to play at the Fayetteville Country Club; his brother, Brian Dickinson; and Mark Curlett, the former golf pro at Hardscrabble Country Club and former golf coach at the University of Arkansas, Ft. Smith, who graciously gives me tips on my game.

Dedication of the Gearhart Curvahedra art sculpture donated by David and Jane Gearhart to the Honors College at the UA. David ("Pa") with Ellie, Caroline, Lily Jane, and George.

In 2021 Jane and I made a gift to the Honors College to build a steel sculpture on the grounds of Gearhart Hall. Dean of the college Lynda Coon and development director Autumn Lewis Spicher proposed the idea to us, and we were taken by their plans to enhance the courtyard at the facility. The sculpture is called Curvahedra. The Curvahedra sculpture originated from a 2018 Honors College seminar, Place in Mind, where honors students from a wide range of disciplines investigated ways to activate the dormant courtyard space. Led by mathematics professor and artist Edmund Harriss and landscape architecture professor Carl Smith, the students ultimately proposed a sculpture inspired by Harriss' system of Curvahedra paper models.

Over the last 10 years the world has become a very dangerous place. The list of challenges for citizens of the United States is longer than at any time in our history. Just mentioning a few of the critical issues facing our nation leaves one breathless: racism, sexism, immigration, climate change, federal budget deficits, college affordability, health care issues, drug addiction, alcohol addiction, terrorism, international diplomacy and foreign policy, and Congress's inability to get anything done.

In spite of the many challenges ahead of us, I still fervently believe in the power of education. I still believe in the academy. I still believe in our colleges and universities.

A dear friend of mine sent me a statement, which I kept framed on my desk my entire career. It was written by John Edward Masefield, an English poet and writer and poet laureate of Great Britain from 1930 to 1967. He wrote this poem for the June 25, 1946, inauguration of the chancellor of the University of Sheffield in the aftermath of World War II:

> There are few earthly things more splendid than a university.
> In these days of broken frontiers and collapsing values, when
> every future looks somewhat grim and the dams are down and
> the floods are making misery, when every ancient foothold
> has become something of a quagmire, wherever a university
> stands, it stands and shines; wherever it exists, the free minds
> of men, urged on to full and fair enquiry, may still bring
> wisdom into human affairs.
>
> There are few earthly things more beautiful than a university.
> It is a place where those who hate ignorance may strive to
> know, where those who perceive truth may strive to make
> others see; where seekers and learners alike, banded together
> in the search for knowledge, will honor thought in all its finer
> ways, will welcome thinkers in distress or in exile, will uphold
> ever the dignity of thought and learning, and will exact stan-

dards in these things. They give to the young in their impressionable years, the bond of a lofty purpose shared, of a great corporate life whose links will not be loosed until they die.

They give young people that close companionship for which youth longs, and that chance of the endless discussion of the themes which are endless, without which youth would seem a waste of time.

There are few things more enduring than a university. Religions may split into sect or heresy; dynasties may perish or be supplanted, but for century after century the university will continue, and the stream of life will pass through it, and the thinker and the seeker will be bound together in the undying cause of bringing thought into the world. To be a member of these great societies must ever be a glad distinction.

REFERENCES

PREFACE

Kerr, Clark. *The Uses of the University*. Cambridge, MA: Harvard University Press, 1994.

"125 Successful People Who Didn't Graduate College." Praxis. Accessed August 27, 2022. https://discoverpraxis.com/125-successful-people-who-didnt-graduate-college/.

Joubert, Shayna. "10 Benefits of Having a College Degree." Northeastern University. January 9, 2020. https://www.northeastern.edu/bachelors-completion/news/is-a-bachelors-degree-worth.

Whitford, Emma. "Survey Shows Americans Are Divided over Value of a Degree." *Inside Higher Ed*. September 13, 2021. https://www.insidehighered.com/news/2021/09/13/survey-shows-americans-are-divided-over-value-degree.

"American College President Study 2017." American Council on

Education. Accessed August 27, 2022. https://www.acenet.edu/Documents/American-College-President-VIII-2017.pdf.

HERITAGE

Berry III, Arthur Yell. "The Gearharts & Constantinos." *Fort Smith Historical Society Journal*, September 2008. University of Arkansas Fort Smith. Boreham Library. https://uafslibrary.com/fshsj/32-02_Complete_Issue.pdf.

SMALL COLLEGE EXPERIENCE

Carver, Nancy. *The Inspiring History of a Special Relationship*. St. Louis: Binding Solutions, 2020.

BACK TO FAYETTEVILLE

"University of Arkansas at Little Rock." Encyclopedia of Arkansas. Last modified January 13, 2022. https://encyclopediaofarkansas.net/entries/university-of-arkansas-at-little-rock-1157/.

UNIVERSITY SYSTEMS AND THE FLAGSHIP CAMPUS

Berdahl Robert, Steven Sample, and Raquel M. Rall. "Are State Systems Endangering Our Public Flagship Universities?" *Inside Higher Ed*, March 7, 2014. https://www.insidehighered.com/views/2014/03/07/are-state-systems-endangering-our-public-flagship-universities-essay.

Svrluga, Susan. "U. Missouri President, Chancellor Resign over Handling of Racial Incidents." *The Washington Post*, September 9, 2015. https://www.washingtonpost.com/news/grade-point/wp/2015/11/09/missouris-student-government-calls-for-university-presidents-removal/?utm_term=.d5d090025f8d.

Savidge, Nico. "UW-Madison Faculty Declare 'no Confidence' in Board of Regents, UW System President." *Wisconsin State Journal*, May 3, 2016. http://host.madison.com/wsj/news/local/education/university/uw-madison-faculty-declare-no-confidence-in-board-of-regents/article_bf7e7864-7ea6-54f1-8dfc-edbba2e14c59.html.

Lewin, Tamar. "University of Oregon President Is Ousted." *The New York Times*, November 29, 2011. https://www.nytimes.com/2011/11/29/education/richard-w-lariviere-university-of-oregon-president-is-ousted.html.

Whittaker, Richard. "UT Chancellor to President: Resign, Or I'll Fire You." *The Austin Chronicle*, July 8, 2014. https://www.austinchronicle.com/daily/news/2014-07-08/ut-chancellor-to-president-resign-or-i-ll-fire-you/.

Watkins, Matthew. "A&M Chancellor Requests Resignation Letters at Flagship Campus." *The Texas Tribune*, April 16, 2015. https://www.texastribune.org/2015/04/16/sharp-requests-resignations-all-m-vice-presidents/.

Gluckman, Nell. "Red, Yellow, or Green? A University System Color-Codes Its Presidents' Political Speech to Try to Regulate It." *The Chronicle of Higher Education*, April 3, 2018. https://www.chronicle.com/article/red-yellow-or-green-a-university-system-color-codes-its-presidents-political-speech-to-try-to-regulate-it/.

Flaherty, Colleen. "AAUP Will Investigate UNC System Governance and Climate." *Inside Higher Ed*, September 30, 2021. https://www.insidehighered.com/quicktakes/2021/09/30/aaup-will-investigate-unc-system-governance-and-climate.

UNDOCUMENTED

McGuire, Patricia. "Colleges Share the Blame for Assault on Democracy." *The Chronicle of Higher Education*, January 8, 2021. https://www.

chronicle.com/article/colleges-share-the-blame-for-assault-on-democracy.

Hubbard, Jon Michael. *Letters To The Editor: Confessions Of A Frustrated Conservative.* Bloomington, IN: iUniverse, 2009: 183-89, 9.

LEGISLATORS

Hu, Winnie. "Many State Legislators Lack College Degrees." *The New York Times*, June 12, 2011. https://www.nytimes.com/2011/06/13/education/13legis.html.

"Degrees in the Statehouse: Arkansas." *The Chronicle of Higher Education*, June 12, 2011. https://www.chronicle.com/article/degrees-in-the-statehouse-arkansas/.

Brantley, Max. "18 Legislators Object to Free Speech by UA Chancellor." *Arkansas Times*, November 28, 2014. https://arktimes.com/arkansas-blog/2014/11/28/18-legislators-object-to-free-speech-by-ua-chancellor.

GOOD NATIONAL PR

Masterson, Kathryn. "From Fund Raiser to President: An Uncommon Path Pays Off." *The Chronicle of Higher Education*, July 4, 2010. https://www.chronicle.com/article/from-fund-raiser-to-president-an-uncommon-path-pays-off/.

PENN STATE, PATERNO, SANDUSKY, SPANIER

"The Freeh Report: Report of the Special Investigative Counsel Regarding the Actions of The Pennsylvania State University Related to the Child Sexual Abuse Committed by Gerald A. Sandusky" Freeh Sporkin & Sullivan, LLP, July 12, 2012. https://archive.nytimes.com/

www.nytimes.com/interactive/2012/07/12/sports/ncaafootball/13pennstate-document.html?ref=ncaafootball.

FRIENDS

Edited by Carolyn Kousky, Billy Fleming, and Alan M. Berger. *A Blueprint for Coastal Adaptation: Uniting Design, Economics, and Policy*. Washington, DC: Island Press, 2021.

FOOD PANTRY

Cady, Clare L.. "Food Insecurity as a Student Issue." *Journal of College and Character*, November 2014: 265

ARKANSAS DEPARTMENT OF HIGHER EDUCATION (ADHE)

Britt, Bill and Susan Britt. "Serious Questions Remain over ACHE Funding Methodology for Colleges and Universities." *Alabama Political Reporter*, September 12, 2019. https://www.alreporter.com/2019/09/12/serious-questions-remain-over-ache-funding-methodology-for-colleges-and-universities/.

OPEN DOOR

"Obstacles Facing International Pre-Medical Students." Missouri State. Accessed August 27, 2022. https://www.missouristate.edu/bms/cmb/Obstacles.htm.

Virji, Azan Zahir. "As a Non-U.S. Citizen, I Faced Hurdles Applying to U.S. Medical Schools. Now That I've Made It, I Want to Help Others like Me." Association of American Medical Colleges, July 29, 2021. https://www.aamc.org/news-insights/non-us-citizen-i-faced-hurdles-applying-us-medical-schools-now-i-ve-made-it-i-want-help-others-me.

"Important Information for International Students Intending to Study Medicine." Amherst College. Accessed August 27, 2022. https://www.amherst.edu/admission/apply/international/pre-med/node/29005.

SOME THINGS DONE—SOME THINGS NOT

Green, Jordan. "Jim Coleman Removed from Provost Position at UNCG." *Triad City Beat*, December 23, 2020. https://triad-city-beat.com/jim-coleman-removed-provost-position-uncg/.

ACKNOWLEDGMENTS

I am indebted to my editor, Karen Long, for her substantial skill and expertise in editing this book. Her efficiency, organizational skills and work ethic contributed greatly to the completion of the manuscript.

Dr. Brian Primack, dean of the College of Education and Health Professions, gave me time off from my teaching duties to write this book, and I am deeply grateful to him. Professor and department chair Michael Hevel also approved my time off, which allowed me to dedicate myself to finishing the book on time. Professor Michael Miller contributed thoughts and revisions to the book and was kind enough to read the manuscript in draft form. I am also deeply grateful to Judy Schwab for reading the manuscript and making very helpful suggestions along the way. The library staff at the Mullins Library were kind enough to loan me an office while I was painstakingly going through my chancellor papers, and to give me access to a computer, copy machine and other helpful aids, which made it much easier to complete the task. I thank my two attorney brothers, Van Gearhart and Jeff Gearhart, who read the manuscript and provided their legal expertise.

Finally, I'm deeply grateful to my wife of 50 years, to whom this book is dedicated, for putting up with me throughout our life together. I know it wasn't always easy for her and she has my eternal love and gratitude.

INDEX

AAMC. *See* Association of American Medical Colleges
AAUP. *See* American Association of University Professors
Abernathy, Ralph David, 23, *23*, 24
Academic Enrichment Program, 562
ACHE. *See* Alabama Commission on Higher Education
ACT Academy, 561–62
Adams, John Quincy, 375
Adams, Sally, 202
ADEQ. *See* Arkansas Department of Environmental Quality
ADHE. *See* Arkansas Department of Higher Education
Adkins, Homer, 393
advancement budget deficit, 498–531
    accounts at UA Foundation frozen, 498–99
    aftermath, 522–31
    internal audit, 501, 503, 505
    investigation of, 500–501
    legislative audit, 514–22
    management of, steps for, 502–503

    media in, role of, 507–14
    memorandum from Schook, 502
AGB. *See* Association of Governing Boards
Alabama Commission on Higher Education (ACHE), 391
alcohol consumption, in University of Arkansas, 357–60
Alexander, Becky, 595–96
Alexander, Bob, 595
Alfaori, Loy, *409*
Alfaori, Qusay, 408, *409*, 410, 411
Alice L. Walton Foundation, 413
Allen, Charles, 390
Allen, David, 583
Alpha Gamma Rho (AGR), 322–24
Altman, Dana, 253–55, 401
    going back to Creighton, 253, 254–55
    performance of, 254
American Airlines Flight 11, 175
American Association of University Professors (AAUP), 314
American College President Study,

636 INDEX

xxiii, 370
American Council of Trustees and Alumni, 508
American Council on Education, xxiii, 370
American Farmland Trust, 107, 138
American Institute of Architecture, 302
American opportunity system, xviii, xix, 377, 421
American Stock Exchange, 100
Americans with Disabilities Act, 290
Ameritech, 102
Amherst College, 412
Anderson, Marcheita, 406
Anderson, Mike, 212
 become St. John's University head coach, 406
 fired in 2019, 406
 hired as basketball coach of UA, 404–6
Anderson, Stephen L., 301
Angelou, Maya, 1
Anthony, John Ed, 436–41
anti-anti-discrimination bill, 470–75
APPA (Association of Physical Plant Administrators), 214
Appalachian State University, 494
Arkansas, 205, 375–79
 Department of Higher Education *see* Arkansas Department of Higher Education
 economy of, 205–6
 General Assembly *see* Arkansas General Assembly
 Latinos in, 416–17
 Poll, 277
 rankings of educational and economic indicators, 204
 Supreme Court, 473
 World Trade Center, 210
Arkansas Alumni Association, 83, 298, 324
Arkansas Democrat-Gazette, 348, 427, 510, 511, 530, 554
 acceptance of presidency by David, 439
 editorial page, readers of, 508
 and Mike Masterson, 509
 reporter, Larry's letters to, 525
 "Statement of Core Values," 427
 story of Nugent's marriage, 85
 and Tom Dillard, 514
 and university deficit, 502
 Walter Hussman and, 13, 427
Arkansas Department of Environmental Quality (ADEQ), 451
Arkansas Department of Health, 451–52
Arkansas Department of Higher Education (ADHE), 351, 387–92
 allowed undocumented students to pay in-state tuition, 414–15
Arkansas Gazette, 81
Arkansas General Assembly, 205, 206, 376, 466, 473, 547, 550, 558
 capital improvements, support for, 275
 criticism of higher education, 393
 Higher Education's funding formula, 351
 lack of support for higher education, 280
 leadership of, 465
 letter from members of, 472
 members of, 78, 79, 166, 274, 280, 353, 354, 515, 554, 615
 Republican members of, 514
 respect for Richard Hudson, 281
 Speaker of the House of, 350
 underfunding of flagship campus, 219
Arkansas Razorbacks, 492
Arkansas State Legislature, xiv
Arkansas State University, 128–29, 493
 College of Business, 316
 playing football, 171–72
 presidency of, 129

Sustainability Consortium, 304
Arkansas Symphony Orchestra, 306
Arkansas Union, 300
Army ROTC building, 299
Associated Student Government
    (ASG), 337, 548
Association of American Colleges and
    Universities, xxii
Association of American Medical
    Colleges (AAMC), 412
Association of American Universities,
    362
Association of Governing Boards
    (AGB), 271–72
Atwood, Margaret, 145
Auburn University, 88, 391
Auerbach, Red, 370
Augusta National Golf Club, 255
Augusta National Golf Course, 169

B
Bacon, Francis, 177
Baker, Gilbert, 468–69
Ballinger, Bob, 466, 472
Balzer Family Clock Works, 194
basketball program
    change of coaches, 401–6
    hiring Mike Anderson as coach,
        404–6
Bates, Daisy, 146
Bates Elementary School, 245
Baughn, Charles, 336–37
Baylor University, 362
Beckett, Samuel, 566
Beebe, Mike, 280, 281, 355, 371, 391,
    414, 419, 435, 485, 574
Beechcraft King Air, 222
Beer and Circus (Sperber), 553
Beijing Normal University (BNU), 601
Beker, Jeanne, 16
Bell, Nate, 515
Bell, Raquel M., 310
Bell Engineering Center, 300
Sister Benita, 28–29

Bentley, Mary, 472
Berdahl, Robert, 309, 310
Berger, Manny, 256
Berra, Yogi, 143
Berry, Artie, 10–11
Bev Lewis Women's Center, 214
Biden, Joe, 173, 316, 474
Bielema, Bret, 492–94, 586, 612
Big Ten universities, 4, 117, 198, 261
Billingsley, Boyce, 308, 370, 514
Bipartisan Policy Center, xxii
Bittle, Larry, 4, 334, *335*
Bittle, Nancy, 334, *335*
Black Lives Matter movement, 24
Black Monday, 103
Black people, 23–24
    police shootings of, 24
Black students, 109–10, 384, 418
    Hubbard on, 424–25
Bledsoe, Bob, 540, 541–42
Bledsoe, Cecile, 472
*A Blueprint for Coastal Adaptation:
    Uniting Design, Economics, and
    Policy*, 338
blue-ribbon committee, 147–48, 198
Bluff, Pine, 448
Bobbitt, Donald, 212, 307, 348, 442–43,
    458, 464, 469, 538, 539
    accused David for discrimination,
        576–77
    during advancement budget deficit,
        509, 511, 517, 523
    agreed on offer new contract to
        Long, 491
    ban on speaking with trustees,
        574–75
    eVersity, 543–56
    information about deficit, 509
    named Kincaid as acting chancellor,
        616
    and Pederson, 560
    program at University of Texas,
        Arlington, 543
    raised issue concerning athletics,

577–78
renewal of David's contract, 570–71, 574, 592
resignation letter to, 593–95
support to Steinmetz, 615
and targeted defined group of senior faculty, 535, 536
termination of Petrino, 479, 481
wanted Steinmetz as chancellor, 608, 609
working with Tyson, 489
Bob Evans Children's Adventure Garden, 541
Bodenhamer, Beverly, 308
Bodenhamer, Lee, 212, 308
Bodenhamer Fellowship program, 212
Bogle, Bob, 596, 598
Bogle, Marilyn, 308, 596, 598
Bogner, Tori Pohlner, xiii
Bonner, Judith, 563
Bookhout, Mattie, 338
Boozman, John, 468
Boss, Steve, xiii
Bostock v. *Clayton County*, 474
Boyer, Tommy, 211–12, 405
Bozynski, Cathy Oxford, 335
Bradley, Bill, 470, 471
Brand, Myles, 403
Brantley, Max, 237, 238, 439, 472
Brazzel, Johnetta Cross, 179
Britt, Bill, 391
Britt, Susan, 391
Broad, Corbett, 571
Broadway, Shane, 425
Brockmann, Bob, *49*
Brockmann, Jane. *See* Gearhart, Jane
Brockmann, Katsy, *49*
Brockmann clan/family, 5, 6
Brown, H. Jackson, Jr., 463
Brown, Janet Estes, 43
Brown, John, III, 237–38
Brown, Karilyn, 472
Brown, Larry, 525
Brown, Patti, 525

Broyles, Barbara, 188, 189
Broyles, Frank, xxiii, 79, 81–83, *82*, 167, 212, 579
  at Augusta National Golf Club, 255
  friendship with Jack Stephens, 169
  hired Chuck, 330, 331, 332
  and Little Rock football games, 168, 170
  opposed to playing in-state teams, 172
  relationship with Nolan, 183
  replacement of, 260–63
  retirement of, 188–92
  and soft drink contract, 153
  wife diagnosed with Alzheimer's, 189
Bryant, Bear, 124, 185, 361
Buchanan, James, 447
Buchanan-Droke Hall, 303
Bud Walton Arena, 184, 253, 255, 403, 405, 431
Bud Walton Hall, 303
Bumpers, Dale, 210
Bumpers College of Agricultural, Food and Life Sciences, 454
Burke, Edmund, 3
Burris, Sidney, 431, 432
Bush, George, 108
Bush, George W., 432, 604
Butterfield Residential Care Center, 19
Butterfield Trail Village, 7

C
Campaign for the Twenty-First Century, xii, 155–56, 195, 204–14, 279
  donors participated in, 213
  first order of business for, 207
  impact of, 224, 307–8
  milestones achieved by, 222–24
  and Old Main clock, 193–94
  public announcement of, 213
  size and success of, 219
  staff celebration, *214*
  success of, 209

INDEX   639

tool for building university's endowment, 234
Campbell, Earl, 460
Campbell, Mac, 558
Capilouto, Eli, 563
"capital campaign," 216
Capone, Al, 345
Carnall Hall, 158–61
   spending night at, 9
   in teardown condition, 158–59, *159*
   transforming into Carnall Inn, 160–61
Carnall Inn, 464
Carnegie Foundation for the Advancement of Teaching, 204, 289, 297
   reclassification of universities and colleges, 396–97
Carrier, Ronald, 86, 87–88
Carroll Hall, 427
Carroll, Lewis, 95
Carter, Davy, 350
Carter, Jimmy, 146
Cartwright Mountain, 19
Carver, Nancy, 34
CASE. *See* Council for Advancement and Support of Education
Cate, Laura, 202
Catholicism, 26–27, 28
Cato Springs Research Center, 302
Center for Educational Access, 290
Champions Hall, 460
chancellor of University of Arkansas, David as, 272–76
   challenges in higher education, 273–74
   diversity at university, 274
   faculty and staff salaries, 275
   intercollegiate athletics, 274
   management style, 274–75
   philosophy, vision, mission and plans, 272–74
   priorities of administration, 283–84
   "Providing Transparency and Accountability to the People of Arkansas," 284–85
   renovation of facilities, 275, 284
   research as scholarship, favored, 273
   technical infrastructure, 275
Chapel, Anthony, 541
Chapman, Rick, 217, 218–20, 221, 237, 239–40, 597
charitable remainder trusts (CRT), 198
Chavez, Jonathan, 415–16
Children's Hospital in Philadelphia, 130–31
Childers, Ron, 405
Chi Omega Greek Theatre, 156
Choate, Brad, 308, 430, 500–506, 511, 517–20, 611
   addiction to golf, 505
   and Diamond, 512, 513–14
   disgruntled employee, 523
   failed as vice chancellor, 529
   failure to manage budget, 509
   filed for reimbursement, 506
   gave computer fiscal authorization password Sharp, 518–19
   during internal audit, 503
   memorandum to, 504
   overspending, 517–18
Choctaw Nation, 10
The Chronicle of Higher Education, 339, 369–70, 419–20, 467, 571, 583–85
Churchill, John, 441–42
Churchill, Winston, 34, 195
   Iron Curtain speech, 32, 33, 59
   memorial in Westminster College, 33, *34*
Civil Rights Act
   of 1964, 433, 474
   of 1975, 474
Clark, Bill, 169
   and retirement of Broyles, 188, 189, 190–91
Clark, Steve, 471
Cleveland Clinic and Washington Regional Medical Center, Fayetteville, 413

Climate Action Plan, 585
Clinton, Bill, 72, 89, 101, 467, 604–5
    David with, *101*
    as governor in 1985, 25
    on law faculty, 45, 156
    listed as reference in résumé, 91
    meeting in Philadelphia, 108
    murder of John R. Locke, 163
    Old Main clock, 193
    planning on being in Princeton, 100
    taught constitutional law and admiralty law, 45
    thinking about running for president, 101
Clinton, Hillary, 45, 108, 156, 532–33
Clinton School of Public Service, 338, 532–33
Coca-Cola, 152–53
Cochran, Mark, 452
Cogdell, Joe, 30–31
Colby, William, 537
Coleman, Jim, 589
College and University Food Bank Alliance, 382
College Champions for Change, 382
College Football Playoff Selection Committee, 481
College of Education and Health Professions, 302, 550, 573, 600
College of Engineering, Georgia Tech University, 139
Columbia Tribune, 61
Columbia University, 508
Commission on Affordability and Cost Containment, 585
Commission on Coordinating Higher Education Finance, 387. *See also* Arkansas Department of Higher Education
Commission on Women, 585
Commitment to College Completion Program, 562
Conner, Bob, 308
Conner, Sandra, 308

Constantino, Maria Theresa, 10, 15, 159
    hired as bookkeeper, 11
    relationship with, 14
Continuing Education, 326, 327, 496
Cook, Arthur B., 540
Coon, Lynda, xiv, 234, 235, 623
Cooper, John, 472
Copeland, Donnie, 472
Copenhaver, Harold, 425
Coppersmith, Mimi Barash, 126
Cordell, Roy, 322
Council for Advancement and Support of Education (CASE), 127, 197–200
Courtway, Tom, 469
Covid pandemic, Arkansas legislature during, 466
Crews & Associates, 575
Critchlow, Paul, 104
CRT. *See* charitable remainder trusts
Curlett, Mark, 623
Curley, Tim, 372, 373
Curvahedra sculpture, UA Honors College, *622, 623,* 623–24

D
Dalai Lama, 371, 431–34
    Congressional Gold Medal to, 432
    honorary degree to, 433
    Nobel Peace Prize to, 431–32
    visited University of Arkansas, 431
Dale Bumpers College of Agricultural, Food and Life Sciences, 532
Dallas Cowboys, 191
Dalton, John, 32–33
Dame, Notre, 260–61
Dart, David, 21
Dart, Nelly, 21–22, 23
    sustenance for provided to, 24
Davidson, Robert L.D., 33
Davies, David, 242–43, 464
Davis, Andy, 472
Davis, Butch, 493

Davis, Wylie, 46
Davis Hall, 299
Dead Man Walking (Prejean), 432
The Death of Innocents (Sister Helen), 432
Delta Gamma sorority house, 149–51
Delta Schools College Completion Consortium, 294
Department of Curriculum and Instruction, 302
Derek, Bo, 16
DETC. *See* Distance Education and Training Council
Diamond, John, 430, 511–15, 520–23, 529, 611
Dickinson, Brian, 623
Dickinson, Joe, 623
Dirksen, Everett, 215
Dickson Street Champions Hall, 302, 358, 365, 495–97
Dicus, Chuck, 330–32
Dillard, Bill, 308
Dillard, Tom, 514
Dismang, Jonathan, 559
Distance Education and Training Council (DETC), 555
Distinguished Lecture Series, 431
TheDivine Comedy, 329
Division of Agriculture, 447–59
  directives, 451
  Fayetteville campus relationship with, 448–51, 453, 454, 546
  issue between campus and, 451
  problems with, 449, 453
  property of, hazardous waste site, 451
  staff from, 454
  structural relationship, 455
  vice president for, reporting of, 450
Division of Legislative Audit, 520
Dodd, Michael, 339
Dodd-Frank Act, 575
Donald W. Reynolds Foundation, 301, 512
Donald W. Reynolds Razorback Stadium, 214
Doolittle, James H., 385
Dorjee, Geshe, 431
Dorrell, Jessica, 478, 479
Dotson, Jim, 472
Douglas, Hal, 13
Dow Jones Industrial Average, 103
Dream Act, 422, 428–29
Drowning America (Fleming), 338
D rule, 185–87
Duke, Mike, 371

E
Earhart, Amelia, 113
Ecclesia College, in Springdale, Arkansas, 467
Edwards, Clay, 107, 151, 207–9, *209*, 220, 499–500, 518
Edwards, Sandy, 107, 151, 207–9, *209*, 220, 499–500, 518
EEOC. *See* Equal Employment Opportunity Commission
Einstein, Albert, 543
Ellis Island, 10
Engineering Career Awareness Program, 562
Engineering Research Center, 300
Epley, Donna, 346
Epley, Lewis, 196, 346
Epley Center for Health Professions, 299
Equal Employment Opportunity Commission (EEOC), 478
Erdman, Warren, 362
Evans, Bob, 541
Evans, Sunny, 541
Evans Tree House, 541
Evarts, Mac, 118
Evergreen Cemetery, 617
eVersity, xviii, 307, 543–56
  board of trustees approved, 549
  enrollment on, 550, 551
  funding for, 545–46, 549

642 INDEX

Google for, 552
launching of, board of trustees approved, 549
logo of, 549
for older, nontraditional students, 545
resolution to oppose, 547, 548
shift of funds, 547
staff members of, 550
system headquarters in Little Rock, 545
UA System entrepreneurs, 547
University of Arkansas System and, 545, 547, 548, 555
Expanded Summer Bridge Program, 562

F
faculty analysis, 536–39
Faculty Athletics Representative (FAR), 398–400
FAR. *See* Faculty Athletics Representative
Farm Bureau of Arkansas, 452
Farmington High School, 296
Farmington Public Schools, 296
Faubus, Orval, 383
Faulkner, Jim, 195–96, 305, 366
Faulkner, Joyce, 305, 366
Faulkner and Associates, 196
Fausett, Elbert, 71
Faust, Drew Gilpin, 256–59
Fayetteville, Arkansas, 18, 77–79
  Chamber of Commerce, 365, 470, 471
  City Council, 470, 473
  community, 367
  Fayetteville Public Library, 52
  University of Arkansas, 77–78 *see also* University of Arkansas
  Walton Arts Center, 365
Fayetteville Board of Education, 245
Fayetteville Country Club, 505, 623
Fayetteville High School, purchase of, 244–52
  negotiations for, 245–46
  property, 245
  utilization of property, 246–47
  withdrawing offer, 251–52
Fayetteville Square, 463, 464
Federal Bureau of Investigation, 515
Federal Department of Education, 561
Feltmeier, Bob, 42
Ferritor, Dan, 247, 262, 471, 549, 557, 607–8, *608*
  administration, 278, 471
Ferritor, Daniel, 559
Ferritor, Patsy, *608*
Finch, Robert H., 59
First National Bank Building, 328
First United Methodist Church, 67
Fite, Charlene, 472
Fitzgerald, F. Scott, 357
Fitzpatrick, Kevin M., 588
Flack, Roberta, 162
Fleming, Billy, xiv, 338–39
Flournoy, Jacob, 526–27, 552
FOIA. *See* Freedom of Information Act
food pantry, 380–82
Football Center, 299
Foote, Tad, 11–12
Ford, Carter, 338
Ford, Gerald R., 59
Ford, Joe, 168, 169
Founders Hall, 303
Fowler, Jama, 265–67
Fowler, Wallace, 265–67, 614
Fowler Conservatory, 266
Fowler House, 264–68, 423, 437, 498, 500, 598, 613, 614
  art collection for, 307
  artwork in, 305
  screened-in porch at, 373, 480
Fox, Jeanie, 335
Franklin, Benjamin, 193
Fred and Mary Smith Golf Center, 214
Freedom of Information Act (FOIA), 237, 238, 513, 514, 523

INDEX   643

Freeh, Louis, 372
Friday, Eldredge & Clark, 575
Ft. Smith, Arkansas, 6, 10–11, 19
   campaign event in, 82–83
Ft. Smith Historical Society, 10
Fulbright, Bill, 393, 394, 617
Fulbright, Jay, 595
Fulbright, J.W., 6, 12, 616–18
   signed Southern Manifesto, 616
Fulbright, Roberta, 6, 393, 595
Fulbright College, 277, 328
Fulbright family, 6, 11–12, 13, 595
   The Northwest Arkansas Times owned by, 14
Fulbright Program, 618
Full Circle Campus Food Pantry, 380–82
   Jane B. Gearhart, 381–82
Fulton Country Club, 58
Fulton Sun Gazette, 61
fundraising, 81, 83, 212, 370, 585
   and John White, 206–7
   and Lippincott, 199
   staff, 211
   volunteers for, 195
"Futures Campaign," 56

G
Gaber, Sharon, 293, 307, 453, 454, 458, 459, 535
   president of University of Toledo, 588–89
   replacement of, 589
Gamboa, Erika, 385–86
Garban, Steve, 105, 106, 114
Garland Center project, 302
Garner, John Nance, 387
Garner, Trent, 466
Garvan, Verna Cook, 540–41
Garvan Woodland Gardens, 525, 540–42
Gates, Bill, xxi
Gatewood, Lou, *608*
Gatewood, Willard, 88–89, 145–47, *608*

Gauger, Tim, 420–21
Gearhart, Brock, *98*, 373, 572, 573, 588, 590, 592
Gearhart, Caroline Louise, 50, *50*, 594
Gearhart, David, xi, xii, xiv, 7, *49*, *69*, *301*, *312*, *608*
   Abernathy with, *23*
   attended high school in Fayetteville, 30–31
   with best friends from State College, *141*
   with Bill Clinton, *101*
   at Campaign for Penn State committee meeting and dinner, *102*
   and Catholicism, 26–27
   college presidency or chancellorship, 39
   consultant for American Farmland Trust, 138–39
   date with Ross, 27
   drug use and alcohol abuse during college, 35–37
   elected chancellor of UA, 272–76
   emails and letters received while chancellor, 566–69
   enrolled in law school, 41–47
   experience at St. Joe, 28
   family of, *620*
   financial goals for retirement, 572
   with Frank Broyles, *82*
   friendship with Whillocks, 128–29
   friends in Conway, Arkansas, 68
   full-time faculty member, 600–603
   with Greg and Hannah Lee, *367*
   interview in Penn State University, 91–92
   legislative audit of advancement deficit, 524–26
   Life in Ozarks, 18
   married to Jane, 41–42
   Meeting Jane in high school, 26–27, 31
   move back to Fayetteville (1998), 140–41

644 INDEX

Pastor Holifield's email, 530–31
and patriotism, 37–38
received education at St. Joseph, 26–27
regrets, 586–87
relationship with Dicus family, 332
relationship with James Major, 71–72
research as scholarship, views on, 273
resignation letter to Bobbitt, 593–95
retirement as chancellor, 590–99
reunited with mother, 19
in Saudi Arabia, 605
search for college president job, 129–30, 140
second book, 197–200
small college experience, 32–40 see also Westminster College
time with students, 337–41
traveled to recruit volunteers, 212
trip east with Greg and Hannah Lee, 442
Twitter account draft governor, 461–62
at Westminster College, 60
Gearhart, Doug, 7, 19–20
career, 16
visited Oxford, 126
Gearhart, George Anthony, 5–7
death of, 7, 13
family heritage, 10
family of, 15
heart problems, 12, 13
nature of, 13–14
newspaper career, 6, 7, 12
races, views on, 22
sense of humor of, 14
Sigma Nu fraternity, member of, 6
trip to Dallas, Texas, 13
Gearhart, George Brockmann, Jr., 50, 50
Gearhart, Jane, 4, 5, 17, 44–45, 48–52, 67, 69, 301, 525, 590, 608

APB (all-points bulletin), 201
with best friends from State College, 141
at Campaign for Penn State committee meeting and dinner, 102
cub reporter, 61
and food pantry, 380–82, 586
with Frank Broyles, 82
with Greg and Hannah Lee, 367
interview in Penn State University, 91–92
introduced as "interim wife," 89
invited Bill Nugent, 84
meeting in high school, 31
as mother and grandmother, 50–51
worked at Springdale High School, 42
Gearhart, Jeff, 7, 218–19, 367, 531
baptism, 15
lived in Northwest Arkansas, 440
worked for Walmart, 16
Gearhart, Katy, 49, 50, 590, 592
Gearhart, Lily Jane, 50, 50, 594
Gearhart, Lindsey, 50, 592
Gearhart, Sam, Jr., 290
Gearhart, Sam E., 6, 10, 11
Gearhart, Van, 7, 253
as country lawyer, 15–16
enrolled in law school, 41
lived in Mountain Home, 287
Gearhart family, 6, 14, 15, 23
in Gulf Shores, Alabama, 51
at Outback Bowl, 621
reunion of, 15
Gearhart Hall, 623
George, Gary, 180, 190
Georgia Tech University, 538, 539
Gibson, Cliff, 458–59
Gibson, Gaston, 195, 482–84
Gilchrist, Ellen, 77, 146
Gladson-Ripley Hall, 303
Glier, John, 130, 136–38, 140, 369
about Big Ten universities, 117

INDEX   645

advised about salary in Penn State, 96
competent staff of, 137
supported David for fundraising, 98
worked with Penn State, 90, 131
Goldman Sachs, 101
Goldwater scholarship, 222, 223, 291
good faculty, xix
Goodson, John, 511, 577, 614
Google, 136
Goswick, Barbara, 534
Grantham University, 554–55, 556
Gravette High School, 336
Great Depression, 9
"Greatest Generation," 22
Greek life, 177, 178, 179, 180, 585
Greek Theater, 303
Green, Anne, 210
Green, Ernest, 383
Green, Jay, 602
Green, Lothaire Scott, 383–83
Greenberg, Paul, 507–10, 526
Greenwood, Reed, 345, 537
Greenwood and Associates, 49
Greenwood Gearhart, 49
Grenzebach, Martin, 131, 140
developed friendship with, 137
GrenzebachGlier (consulting firm), 131, 140, 256
benchmark salary studies, 571
clients across the United States, 135
joined, 135
time with, 137–38
GrenzebachGlier and Associates, 11
Gretzky, Wayne, 330
Grise, Stephanie, 339
Guide to Military Friendly Schools, 585

H
Hall, Derek, 349
Hallowell, Thomas, 119–20
Halter, Bill, 234
Hamilton, Andrew, 371
Hannah-Jones, Nikole, 427–28

Harding, Bonnie, 525
Harding, Ed, 525
Harding, Vincent, 432–33
Hardscrabble Country Club, 623
Harlech, Lord, 59
Harrington, Cordia, 298
Harris, Jim, 210
Harris, Justin, 472, 559
Harrison, William, 157
Harriss, Edmund, 623
Harvard University, Cambridge, Massachusetts, 256–59
Hatcher, Joe B., 70–71
Havens, W.R. (Pat), 7–8
Hayakawa, S.I., 342
Heath, Stan, 402
Hembree Alumni House, 151, 613
Hendren, Jim, 472
Hendrix, Dan, 210
Hendrix College, Conway, Arkansas, xii, xxii, 3, 64, 66–73
administration building fire in, 71
benefactors, 68, 77
donor, 72
leadership of, 73
reputation of, 67–68
Herrmann, Bob, 121
Herrmann, Carol, 121, 122
Hershey Entertainment Corporation, 101–2
Hershey Foods, 101
Hershey Medical Center, 118
Hester, Bart, 472
Hevel, Michael, 602
Higginbotham, Bicky, 335
Higginbotham, Spencer, 335
Higher Education Coordinating Board, 281, 389
Higher Learning Commission (HLC), 555
high school, in Fayetteville, 30–31
new friendships, 30
teachers in, 31
Hilburn, Sam, 347–48, 524, 525

Hillary Rodham Clinton School of International Relations, 532–33
Hillary Rodham Clinton School of Law, 338
Hillside Auditorium, 300
historical markers, in Penn State University, 154–57
  $300 million challenge gift, 154–55
  advances in nutrition, 155
  Campaign for the Twenty-First Century, 155–56
  Chi Omega marker, 156
  Clintons on law faculty, 156
Hitler, Adolf, 424
HLC. *See* Higher Learning Commission
Hodges, Kaneaster, 210
Holifield, Tony, 530–31
Holmes, T.J., 298
Holtz, Lou, 182
honorary degrees, 370–71
Honors College, 217, 218, 239, 275, 329, 623
  donation for, 221
  success and reputation of, xiv, 226
Hot Springs, 19
Hotz, Henry, 264
Hotz Hall, 300–301
Houseman, John, 41, 43
Howard University, 494
Hubbard, Jon, 424–25
Hudson, Joanna, 557
Hudson, Richard, 281, 349–50, 419, 468, 469, 559
  Marvin M. "Swede" Johnson Achievement Award, 558
  retirement announcement, 557–58
Human Rights Campaign, 470–75
Hunt, Benjamin David, 50, *50*, 594
Hunt, David, 49, *301*
Hunt, Ellen Kathryn, 50, *50*, 594
Hunt, Jane, 588
Hunt, Johnelle, 212, 308, 371
Hunt, Sharon, 49, *301*, 399–400

Hunt, Silas, 306, 418
Hunt Transport Services Company, 212
Hussman, Walter, 13, 427–28, 508, 509–10
Hussman family, 12–13
Hutchinson, Asa, 62, 466, 474, 574
Hyneman, Ben, 491, 525, 526

I
Ian L. McHarg Center, 338
iBridge program, 562
ice storms, in Northwest Arkansas, 318–19
Inaugural Scholars Program, 319–20
Ingalls, Wally, 6
Ingram, Keith, 514
Inside Higher Ed, 310
intercollegiate athletics, 274
international students, 407–13
  accessing American medical schools, 410
  difficulty in accessing American medical schools, 410–12
  meeting with, 408–9
Ivory Tower (documentary), 553

J
Jackson, Keith, 191
Jacobs, Jane, 149
James H. Faulkner Advertising, 196
James Madison University, 86, 87
  board of trustees of, 88
  Carrier leaving, 88
  Willard Gatewood as chancellor of, 88–89
James Patterson Teacher Education Scholarship, 494
J.B. Hunt Company, 79, 371
J.B. Hunt Transport Services Building, 214
Jean Tyson Child Development Study Center, 299, 501
Jefferson, Thomas, 447

Jeffress, Jimmy, 393, 394
Jim & Joyce Faulkner Performing Arts Center, 196
Jobs, Steve, xxi, 563
John Findley Green Lectures, 59
Johns Hopkins University, 125
Johnson, Carl, 433
Johnson, Jeff, 298
Johnson, Marcia, 298
Johnson, Mike, 158, 249–50, 318–19, 381, 464, 497, 576, 589
Johnson, Randy, 14, 42
Johnson Fellows program, 298
Johnson & Johnson, 101
Joint Legislative Audit Committee, 515, 520
Jones, Belinda, 315
Jones, Fay, 208
Jones, Jerry, 191
Jones, Nikole Hannah, 314
Jordan, Bryce, 91, 92, 95–98, 104–5, 109, 110, 113–21, 130
   basketball facility named after, 152
Jordan, Jonelle, 96, 121
Jordan, Michael, 283
J. William Fulbright College, 229, 431, 532, 605

K
Kaminsky, Hank, 617
Kappa Sig, 495
Keenum, Mark, 563
Keller, Helen, 53
Kelly, James Easton, 162–63
Kendig, Tysen, 321, 512
Kennedy, Jackie, 158
Kennedy, J.F., 29, 59, 126, 256
Kennedy, John, Jr., 29
Kerr, Clark, xvii–xviii
Key, Johnny R., 558–59
Kik, Marinus C., 155
Kimmel, Jimmy, 133
Kimpel Hall, 299
Kincaid, Bill, 616

King, Martin Luther, Jr., 18, 24, 25, 433
King, Tom, 42
King Fahd Center for Middle East Studies, 604
Kingsfield, Charles W., Jr., 41
Kissinger, Henry, xvii
Klaich, Dan, 392
Knight, Bobby, 403–4
Knight, Phil, 483
Kohler, Peter, 345, 346
Kopp, Wendy, 414
Kral, Tim, 286
Ku Klux Klan, 393
Kutak Rock, 218–19

L
Ladyman, Jack, 472
Lambert, Anselm, 552–53
Land Grant Act, 447
Learfield Directors' Cup, 289
Lee, Greg, 334–35, 367, *367*, 442
Lee, Hannah, 334–35, *367*, 442
Lee, Robert E., 24, 25
Lee, Spike, 467
Leflar, Robert A., 394, 603
legislators, 465–75
   and anti-anti-discrimination bill, 470–75
   Arkansas, 466, 467
   education and experience of, 466–67
   gender-confirming treatments for transgender youth, 466
   senator Gilbert Baker, 468–69
Leroux, Maggie, 137
Letters to the Editor (Hubbard), 424
Lewis, Alan, 571
Lewis, Bev, 262
Lewis, C.S., 334
Lewis, Harley, 210
LGBTQ people, xiv, 466, 474, 558
LidaBaday, 16
Lieb, Dave, 106–7, 619
Lieb, David, 126, 142
Lieb, Sharon, 107, 619, 620

648 INDEX

Lincoln, Abraham, 269, 445, 447
Lincoln, Blanche, 558
Lindsey, Jim, 189, 190, 332
Lippincott, John, 199
Little Rock, 18–19, 78, 439, 440
   football games in, 167–72
   medical campus in, 296
   public schools, 383
   Razorback baseball game in, 404
   senior leadership in, 427
   Stella Boyle Smith Foundation of, 305
   University of Arkansas at *see* University of Arkansas, Little Rock (UALR)
Little Rock Country Club, 195
Little Rock Nine, 383
Little Rock School District, 383
Little Rock University (LRU), 78
"Living in the Shadows in America," 421
Locke, John R., 162–64
Loewer, Otto, 538
Lofe, Donald, 58
Loftin, R. Bowen, 563
Lombardi, Vince, 401
Long, Jeff, 153, 160, 170, 212, 251, 483, 577
   academic culture in athletics during, change in, 490
   an change in FAR, 390
   and Bielema, 492
   on changing coach, 402
   criticism of, 485
   fired by Steinmetz, 612
   hiring as athletics director of UA, 261–63
   on hiring of Mike Anderson, 405
   leadership, 486
   mistake of hiring John L. Smith, 487, 489–90
   opposed hiring of Bobby Knight, 404
   Petrino's accident, 477
   policy for post-game participation, 578
   and Razorback Foundation, 330–32, 333
   termination of Petrino, 478–81
   transferring athletics revenue to academics, 460
Looney, Nate, 338
Low, Sara Elizabeth, 175
LRU. *See* Little Rock University
Lunsford, Scott, 326–27
Lunstrum, Robin, 472

M

Macechko, Kris, 210
Macechko, Mike, 210
Maggio, Michael, 469
Magness, C.R., 335
Magness, Kay, 335
Major, James, 67, 71–72
Malone, David, 211
Malvern Brick and Tile Company, 540
Malzahn, Gus, 493
Mandela, Nelson, 396
Manning, Clara, 84–85, 86
Marathon Oil, 102
Marshall, Thurgood, 383
Martin, Jim, 78–79, 87, 88
Martin, Steve, 197
Martinelli, Ricardo, 371, 452
   elected president of Republic of Panama, 342–44
   left office, 343
Marx, Karl, 165
Masefield, John Edward, 624
Mason Dixon, 99
Massanelli, Randy, 554, 559, 591
Massey, Bryan, 306
Masterson, Kathryn, 370
Masterson, Mike, 509
May, Tommy, 542
Mayton, Cathy, 305, *306*, 541
Mayton, Mike, 305, *306*, 541
Mcauliffe, Christa, 600

McCray, Suzanne, xiii, 292, 341
McDaniel, Dustin, 425
McFadden, Darren, 487
McFarland, Daniel, 339
McGuinness, Aims, 388–89
McGuire, Patricia, 420
McKennon family, 5
McLarty, Mack, 298, 595
McLarty Associates, 298
McMath, Bob, 234, 454
McMillion, Doug, 308
McMillion, Shelley, 308
McNair, Ron, 472
Melhorn, Jodi, *209*, 405
Melhorn, Mel, *209*, 405
Mellon Bank, 104
Mercury, Freddie, 188
Merrill Lynch, 49, 98, 99, 100
   Campus, 100
   World Headquarters, 174–75
Merton College, Oxford University, 126
Methodist Church, 66, 67
Metropolitan Life Insurance Company, 102
Michigan State University, 494
Sister Mildred, 29
military-affliated students, 386
Miller, Michael, 601
Miller, Mike, 601, 602, 609
Minnesota Medical Foundation, 308
Mississippi State University, 571
Moberly, Robert, 538
Modaffare, Mark, 142
Moeser, James, 112
Moorer, W.B., 393
Morissette, Alanis, 87
Morrill, Justin Smith, 447
Morrill acts of 1862 and 1890, 447
Morrison, Toni
Morton, Michael, 469, xviii
"Mothers Against Drunk Driving," 36
Mt. Nittany Society, 196
Mullins Library, 83, 213, 300, 303, 587

murder-suicide, in Kimpel Hall, 162–64
Murray State University, 129

N
NACUBO. *See* National Association of College and University Business Officers
Nance, Cynthia, 538
Nanoscale Materials Science and Engineering Building, 299
National Academy of Engineers, 538
National Association of Black Journalists, 428
National Association of College and University Business Officers (NACUBO), 197–98, 199
National Association of College Stores, 302
National Association of Collegiate Directors of Athletics, 289
National Center for Higher Education Management Systems (NCHEMS), 388, 389, 391, 392
National Conference of Trusteeship, 542
National Economic Council, 561
National Lab for the Study of the College President, 601
National Merit Scholars, 353
National Merit Scholarship, 353
Naturally Blue, 338
NCAA, 406
   Certification Report, 578
   Division IA institution, 578
   imposed fine on Penn State, 373
   institutions, 398
   probation, 490
   rules, 262, 404, 479, 489, 612
NCHEMS. *See* National Center for Higher Education Management Systems
Neighbors, Mike, 398
Nelson, Bob, 407

Nevada System of Higher Education (NSHE), 392
New, Bobby, 244, 245, 246, 249, 250
New Arkansan Scholarship Award, 350, 353, 354, 389, 390
New York University (NYU), 123
Nicklaus, Jack, 99
Nittany Lions, 620
Niven, David, 38
Noland, Paul, 343
North Carolina State University, 123
Northeast Oklahoma, 353
Northeastern University, xxi
Northwest Arkansas, 13, 27, 42, 168, 175–76, 588
  arts scene in, 367
  vs. Central Arkansas, 439
  economic power of, 78, 79
  health outcomes across, 413
  ice storms in (January 26, 2009), 318–19
  Katy came back to, 50
  Medical Sciences campus in, 413
  qualified staff in, market for, 296
  trustees in, 190–91
Northwest Arkansas Community College (NWACC), 247–48, 315–18
Northwest Arkansas Gridiron, 485
The Northwest Arkansas Times, 6, 11, 12
  sale of, 14
NSHE. *See* Nevada System of Higher Education
Nugent, Bill, 77–78, 79, 80–86, 449
  administration of, 86
  "The Campaign for Books, Incunabula to the Future," 81, 83
  and Clara, 84–85
  divorced, 85
  invited by Jane and David, 84
  resignation, 86
nursing program, 345–46
Nutt, Houston, 487, 493
NWACC. *See* Northwest Arkansas Community College

O

Obama, Barack, 561
Obama, Michelle, 561
O'Donnell, Tim, 560
Ohio State University, 127
Ola, Benjamin, 58
Old Main, 86, 108, 109, 617
  clock, 193–94
  original bell, 194
  volunteers and Towers members of, 195–96
Old Main Society, 196
Oliva, Jay, 123
open-door policy, 407–13
Open University of Arkansas, 291
Outback Bowl, Tampa, Florida, 619
out-of-state students, 349–54
  advantages of, 354
  discount, 354
  scholarship award program for, 353
Overby, Marcia, 202
Ozark Hall (Gearhart Hall), 299

P

Pacific-10 Conference, 261
Palazzo Taverna, 329
Paneitz, Becky, 247, 316, 317, 318
panty raids, 38–39
Parents Fund, 98
Parton, Dolly, 534, 561
Paterno, Joe, 91, *98*, 99–101, 106, 372–74, 620
Paterno, Sue, 100
patriotism, 37–38
Patterson, Cam, 466
Patterson, Hugh, 81
Patterson, James, 493–94
Pat Walker Health Center, 213–14, 359
Paul, Aaron, 355
Peabody Hall, 302, 617
Pearce, Dan, 566
Pederson, Don, xiii, 150, 248, 279, 284, 289, 340, 527
  and Bobbitt, 560

on carryforwards, 526
deficit in advancement budget, 500–501, 502
head back to Fowler House, 498
investigation of, 515
Open UA, 291
red flag for, 534–35
retirement announcement, 559–60
Pelphrey, John, 401–3, 404
fired, 402
winning percentage as coach, 402
Penn State Alumni Association, 114, 209
Penn State University, xii, 3, 58, 78, 90–92, 372–74
Alumni Association, 374
applied for vice president, 90
award honorary degrees, 370–71
Campaign for, 107, 119
contract with Pepsi and Coca-Cola, 152–53
$30 million gift to, 216
former staff members, 128
Graduate School at, 573
historical markers, 154–57
last year at, 128
Mt. Nittany Society, 196
NCAA imposed fine on, 373
salaries in, 96
Pentagon, 175
Pepsi, 111, 152–53
Peter, Lily, 72
Petit Jean Mountain, 241, 242, 476
Petrino, Bobby, 477–81, 482, 486–88, 513, 586
hired Dorrell against policy, 478
lied about motorcycle accident, 477–78
Smith replaced, 487
termination of, 478–81
Petty, Rebecca, 472
Pew Hispanic Center, 416
Phi Delta Theta, 323
fraternity, 357

Philpot, Buddy, 218, 597
Pi Beta Phi, 6
Centennial Gate, 303, 323
sorority, 323
Pittman, Sam, 172
Pohlner, Tori, 339
Pontious, Bruce, 611–12
Power, Mark, 210, 267, 610, 611, 612
agreement, 613
Prejean, Sister Helen, 432
Presbyterian Church, 66
Presidents' Commitment to Food and Nutrition Security, 585–86
Primack, Brian, 602–3
Prince, Bernie, 107
"Providing Transparency and Accountability to the People of Arkansas" (TAP), 284–308, 476
competitive packages for faculty, staff, and graduate students (goal 6), 295–96
diversity and minority enrollment (goal 4), 293–94
enrollment growth (goal 3), 291–93
establish and market quality brand reputation for university (goal 12), 304–5
expand distance education and partnerships with other institutions (goal 14), 307
foster arts on campus and throughout region (goal 13), 305–7
goals published in, 286–308
grow public support and endowments (goal 15), 307–8
grow state's knowledge-based economy and to address major issues (goal 8), 297–98
improve graduation rates and degree-completion times (goal 5), 294–95
improvement of institution's libraries and technology resources (goal 10), 303

652 INDEX

increase funding in research (goal 7), 297
promote environmental sustainability (goal 11), 303–4
renovation of existing facilities (goal 9), 299–303
"Students First" (goal 1), 286–91
transparent and accountable to people of Arkansas (goal 2), 291
Pryor, Barbara, 326–28, 528
Pryor, David, 210, 326–28, 437, 528, 575–76
Pryor, Mark, 575–76
Pryor Center for Arkansas Oral and Visual History, 326–28
Pugh, Danny, 287, 385
Purcell, James, 317, 388, 390–92

Q
Qassim University, 604–6

R
Rahn, Dan, 345
Rall, Raquel M., 309
Razorback Athletics, 253
Razorback Basketball, 253
Razorback Bridge Scholarship Program, 294
Razorback football game, 89, 167
Razorback Foundation, 81, 83, 189, 192, 195, 330–33
  funding, 330–31
  marketing strategy, 333
  modernization of, 333
RCRA. *See* Resource Conservation and Recovery Act
Reagan, Ronald, 103
Reed, Stanley, 260, 442, 593, 594
Regan, Donald, 103
Renner, James "Bo," 339
Resource Conservation and Recovery Act (RCRA), 451
Reyes, Javier, 307, 550–51, 552
Rhodes scholarships, 291

Rice University, Houston, Texas, 115–17
Richardson, Bill, 125
Richardson, Nolan, 182–84, 404, 484
  criticizes university administration, 183
  relationship with Broyles, 183
Right to DREAM (Bill Schwab), 537
Rivarolo, Italy, 10
Roberts, John, 127
Robertson, Chip, 42, *60*
Robinson, Charles, 293–94, 384, 598, 616
Rockefeller, John D., 138
Rockefeller, Winthrop, 241, 242
Rockefeller Institute, 476
Rogers, Jane, 511, 524, 549, 593
Rome Center, 329
Rooney, Andy, 581
Roosevelt, Theodore, 32, 257
Rosa, Jana Della, 472
Rose Law Firm, 219
Ross, Robert, 78–79
Roth, Will, 595–96
Ruby, Jack, 29
Ruffner, Roy, 56
Rushing, Laurie, 472
Rust, Melissa, 468, 559
Ruth, Babe, 271
Rutledge, Leslie, 473
Rutledge, Reynie, 308, 593

S
Sam M. Walton College of Business, 223, 226, 532
  MBA program, 285
  ranking by Businessweek.com, 584
Sample, Steven, 309, 310
Sanders, Bernie, 347
Sandusky, Dottie, 372
Sandusky, Jerry, 111, 372–74
Sankey, Greg, 564–65
Santayana, George, 498, 529
Saunders, Harvey, 59–61, 63, 64–65

administration, 61
  legacy, 60
Savage, JaQuay, 486
Saxena, Ashok, 410
Sayre, Wallace S., xvii
Scharlau, Charles, 560
Schenke, Joe, 337
Schenke, Judi, 337
Schook, Jean, 501, 502
Schreyer, Bill, 98, 98–104, 117, 130, 217, 620
  at Campaign for Penn State, 102
  gift to Penn State, 216
  at Oxford university, 127
Schreyer, Joan, 127
Schuller, Robert, 570
Schultz, Gary, 372, 373
Schwab, Bill, 328, 420, 429, 537
Schwab, Judy, 194, 220, 283, 425, 507
  in charge of preparing annual report, 239
  fundraising campaign, contribution in, 210
  Pryor Center, managing, 328
  recruited by Fayetteville Public Schools, 201–2
Schwarzenegger, Arnold, 495
Scottoline, Lisa, 26
Selective Service, 37
September 11 attacks (9/11), 173–76
Sevareid, Eric, 135
Shakespeare, William, 154
Shankly, Bill, 167
Sharp, Joy, 499–506, 513–14, 517
  and advancement budget deficit, 500–506
  authority to spend funds, 503
  authorization for expenditures, 503
  as budget manager, 504
  Choate gave computer fiscal authorization password to, 518–19
  deposited gift funds, 506
  failure to manage budget, 509
  resignation, 505

Sherman, William T., 10
Shields, Brooke, 16
Shields, Todd, 454, 616
Shilling, Margaret, 69, 69
Shilling, Nancy, 69
Shilling, Roy B., Jr., 65, 66–71, 69, 437, 591
  accepted presidency of Southwestern University, 70
  tenure in Hendrix, 68–70
Shult, Milo, 439–40, 452, 453
Sig, Kappa, 180
Sigma Alpha Epsilon, 323
Sigma Chi, 358
Sigma Nu, 6, 178, 323, 343, 482
Silas Hunt Hall, 157
Slive, Mike, 309, 361, 362–63, 481, 563–64
Smith, Bob, 166
Smith, Carl
Smith, John L., 487–88, 489
Smith, Stella Boyle, 306
Smith, Tom, 454, 573
Snowden, Judy, 266
Soames, Lady Mary, 60
Sonnier, Patrick, 432
Sorrentino, Mary, 137
Southeastern Conference (SEC), 198, 251, 291, 293, 302, 362, 363, 402, 492
  administrators, 310
  Basketball Tournament, 578
  commissioner, 309
  expansion of, 361–63
  finding commissioner for, 563–65
  institutions, vice presidents of, 199
  institutions/schools, 293, 295, 310, 349, 398, 421
  invited Texas A&M University, 362
  leading program in, 307
  presidents and chancellors, 362
  rules, 167, 262, 404
Southwestern University, 70
Spanier, Graham, 106, 111, 127, 130,

654 INDEX

372–74
Sperber, Murray, 553
Spicher, Autumn Lewis, 623
Springdale High School, 493
Springfield, Stewart, 217–18
Springfield, Yvonne, 217
Stafford, Stewart, 236
Stanley Works, 102
Starr, Ken, 362
state appropriation
   budget challenges and, 278–82
   cut to 2009-2010, 355–56
   increase in, 278, 280–81
State College, Pennsylvania, 91, 92, 95, 207
   candidacy for presidency at, 129
   decided to remain in, 136
   friends in, 141–42
   leaving, 141–42
   real estate in, 97
Steele, Marty, 298
Steinmetz, Joe, 264, 267, 285, 560, 608–17
   change in development officers by, 613
   dismiss Jeff Long, 612
   official meeting with, 609
   performance, 614
   provocative photos of, 614–15
   purchased private home in Springdale, 613–14
   resigned, 615
Steinmetz, Sandy, 609, 615
Stella Boyle Smith Concert Hall, 305
Stella Boyle Smith Crescent Garden, 541
Stella Boyle Smith Foundation, 305–6, 541
Stephens, Jack, 168, 169
Stephens Inc., 168, 575
Stephenson, John, 30
Stewart, Julian, 212
St. Joe, 27, 28, 30
St. Joseph Catholic School, Fayetteville, xxii, 11, 26, 27
St. Mary the Virgin Aldermanbury, London, *33*, 33–34
Stoltz, Drew, 68
Stoltz, Steve, 68
Stoltz, Susan, 68, *209*
St. Scholastica Convent, 27, 29
Stucker, Bill, 41–47, 55, 56–57
Student Assistance Program, 359
"Students First," xiii–xiv
Student Success Center, 610
Sugg, Alan, 129, 139, 186, 251, 594, 595
   agreed not to increase tuition, 348
   asking advice from, 591
   board meeting in Fayetteville, 168
   board of trustees awarded, 433
   carry forward approved by, 526
   communication skills, 574
   and criticism of higher education, 393
   discussion of chancellor position with David, 256, 257, 258, 271, 272
   discussion on financial situation with, 278, 279
   and Division of Agriculture, 452–53
   four-year degree program at NWACC, 316, 318
   and hiring of Chuck, 332
   and lawsuit by Waltons, 237
   leadership of, 86, 169, 577
   meeting in Little Rock, 248
   meeting with White and David (summer of 2003), 188
   meeting with UAMS administrators, 345, 346
   president of University of Arkansas System, 128, 311–12, *312*
   pressured David, 140
   Purcell's comments on NCHEMS report, 390
   and resignation letter by David, 593
   retirement, 435, 436–37
   and retirement of Broyles, 188, 189, 190, 191

and search for system president, 442–43
supported facilities fee, 299
systems *vs.* campus administration, 311–12
and undocumented students issue, 419
and Winthrop Rockefeller Institute, 242
wrote letters to board of trustees, 147
Summer ACT Academies, 294
Sure, Barnett, 155
Sustainability Consortium, 304
Sutherland, Gloria, 202

T
Taft, J. Richard, 63–64
Targeted University Perspectives Course, 562
Task Force for the Enhancement of Greek Life, 178, 179–80
Taylor, Jim, 210
Texas A&M University, 313–14, 352, 362
Texas Tech University, 411
Tharp, Twyla, 364
Thiel, Peter, xxi
Thomas, Joab, 108, 123–24
  leadership, 127
  as scratch golfer, 125
Thomas, Marly, 123–24
Thompson, Kirk, 317
Thompson, Sandy, 107
Thomson, Lord, 12
Thomson Newspapers, 12
Thornton, Ray, 80, 89
TIAA Institute, xxiii
Tolleson, John, 210, 323
Tri Delta sorority, 264
Trinity Washington University, 420
Truman, Harry, 32, 55
Truman award, 291
Trump, Donald, 475

tuition increase, 347–48, 589
Turner, George, 290
Twain, Mark, 38, 277, 465
Tyson, Don, 148, 327, 371
Tyson, John, 190, 213, 489
Tyson Foods, Inc., 79, 148, 334–35, 371
  acquired IBP Inc, 221–22

U
UALR. *See* University of Arkansas at Little Rock
UAMS. *See* University of Arkansas for Medical Sciences
unauthorized immigrants, 415
undocumented immigrants, 421, 422, 425–26
undocumented students, 414–30
  allowed to pay in-state tuition, 415
  disallow to obtain in-state tuition, 419–21
  discussion with trustee on, 414
  and Dream Act, 422, 428–29
  existing U.S. law for, 417
  fact about, 417–18
  fair treatment to, 416
  as honors students, 416
  immigration issue, 421–26
  meeting with, 429
  out-of-state tuition, 421
  right to attend public school, 417
  as "unauthorized immigrants," 415
University Advancement, 308
University House, 151, 299
University of Alabama, 353, 354
University of Arkansas (UA), xii, 3–4, 32, 89, 139
  and Arkansas' economy, 204–5
  benchmarking, 325–26
  Bill Nugent, 77–78
  board of trustees, 191, 248, 249
  brain drain, 352
  Campaign for the Twenty-First Century *see* Campaign for the Twenty-First Century

Carnegie classification of, 396–97, 584
change of basketball coach, 401–6
Climate Action Plan, 304
closing Dickson Street for campus safety, 495–97
consumption of alcohol in, 357–60
contract with Pepsi and Coca-Cola, 152–53
criticism by Carrier, 87
Delta Gamma sorority house, 149–51
director of development at, 72
$300 million donation by Waltons, 217, 221, 224–35
and D rule, 185–86, 187
Economic Development Institute, 352
enrollment, 39, 81, 83, 583–84
Fayetteville campus, 77–79
flagship campus, 438
fundraising, 81, 83
Global Campus, 547, 550–51, 552, 554 *see also* eVersity
goals published TAP report, 286–308
Greek system, 180
Hendrix benefactors ties with, 77
hiring new athletics director, 260–63
interviewed for director of development, 77
law school, 41–47
lawsuit against, by Max Brantley, 237–40
military-affiliated students, 386
"Military Friendly School," 585
murder-suicide in Kimpel Hall, 162–64
national scholarships and fellowships, 222
NCAA Division IA institution, 578
new logo of, 321–22, 322
Police Department, 163
Press, 145–48
product of sorority at, 33
professional salaries at, 278
Pryor Center, 326–28
ranking of, 285–86
Rome Center, 329
R-1 Carnegie status, xiii
seven-figure gift to, 169
transferring athletics revenue to academics, 460
two-year program at, 247
University of Arkansas Libraries, xii
University of Arkansas, Little Rock (UALR), 78–79, 311
  interest in chancellor position at, 128–29
  interview for, 129
  tuition increase, 348
University of Arkansas for Medical Sciences (UAMS), 345–46, 410, 413, 466, 534
University of Arkansas Foundation, 211, 498–99
University of Arkansas System, 128, 296, 307, 311–12, 413, 435, 448, 543
University of Central Arkansas, 394, 468, 469
University of Connecticut, 138, 512
University of Florida, 127
University of Hawaii, 137
University of Illinois Foundation, 85
University of Maine System, 314
University of Massachusetts, 382
University of Miami, 11
University of Michigan, 127
University of Mississippi, 293
University of Missouri, 6, 313
  Press, 148
University of Nebraska, 112
University of North Carolina, 112, 428, 493
  investigation of, 314
  journalism faculty at, 427
University of Northwest Arkansas, 388

INDEX 657

University of Oklahoma, 353, 354, 362
University of Oregon, 313
   football team, 483
University of Pittsburgh, 362, 363
University of Sheffield, 624
University of South Carolina, 308
University of Tennessee, Knoxville, 312–13
University of Texas, 352
   Arkansas played in Texas Bowl against, 577
   at Arlington, 543
   Austin campus, 313
   built college of business, 463
   SEC and, 362
University of Toledo, 293, 459
University of Tulsa, 128, 182, 336
University of Wisconsin, 313, 494
university systems, 309–14
   vs. campus administration, 311–12
   and flagship campus, 310–11
   inherent weakness of, 311
   Texas A&M University, 313–14
   University of Arkansas System, 128, 242, 296, 307, 311–12
   University of Maine System, 314
   University of Missouri, 313
   University of North Carolina system, 314
   University of Oregon, 313
   University of Tennessee, Knoxville, 311–12
   University of Texas, Austin campus, 313
   University of Wisconsin, 313
Uptown Campus, 300

V
Van Hoose, Joan Inman, 5–7
   articles of clothing, 20
   death of, 7
   family heritage, 8–9
   family of, 15
   interaction with sons, 21

Pi Beta Phi, member of, 8–9
   as prude, 21
   races, views on, 22
   remarried to Pat, 7
   social skills of, 20
   suffering from dementia, 19–20
   trip to Dallas, Texas, 13
Van Hoose, Louise Inman (Lulu), 9, 20, 159
Van Laningham, Kathy, 325
Varady, Scott, 479, 598
Veach, Randy, 452
veterans, 385–86
Veterans Resource and Information Center, 289, 385
Vietnam War, 37–38, 39
Virginia Tech, 362, 363
Virji, Azan Zahir, 412
Vitale, John, 49, 623
Vitale, Nancy, 49
Vivona, Ross, 27, 27–28
   construction company in Oklahoma, 28
   date with David, 27
Vol Walker Hall, 299, 301
von Gremp, Jim, 535, 539–40, 542–43, 554
Vonnegut, Kurt, 30

W
Waldrip, Mark, 574, 575
Walizer, John, *141*, 141–42
Walizer, Karen, *141*, 141–42
Walker, John, 183, 184
Waller, Matt, 464
Walmart, 18, 78, 79
Walter, Hal, 287, 288
Walter, Raymond, 287–88
Walton, Alice, 371, 413
Walton, Helen, 216, 365
Walton, Jim, 212, 215
Walton, Rob, 212, 215
Walton, Sam, 80, 215, 364, 366, 607
Walton Arts Center, 364–68

658   INDEX

governance model of, 367–68
original concept of, 366
placed on Dickson Street, 365
Walton College, 216, 464
   deficit in, 528
   ranking of, 584
   supply chain program, 223
Walton College of Business, 463, 587
Walton family, 12–13, 215–24, 537, 587, 611
   appealling program for, 216–17
   approaching, for funds, 218–20
   contribution to College of Business, 215–16
   $200 million donation by, 221
   $300 million donation by, 217, 224–35
   requested for proof of impact of gift, 236–37
Walton Arts Center, 365, 367
Walton Family Charitable Support Foundation, xi, 154, 155, 190, 211, 234–35, 236, 366–37, 562, 597
Walton's $300 million gift, to University of Arkansas, xi, 217, 221
   component of, 329
   Distinguished Doctoral Fellowships, $24 million, 231–32
   endowed chairs, $30 million, 225
   endowed dean's chair, $3 million, 224
   Endowed Distinguished Professorships, $10 million, 225–26
   endowed Honors College Academy student scholars, $24 million, 227–28
   endowed Honors College student fellows, $75 million, 226–27
   graduate assistantship endowment fund, $40 million, 232
   Graduate Faculty Endowed Research Chairs, $24 million, 230–31
   graduate student research fund, $8 million, 232–33
   international experience endowment, $4 million, 229
   library acquisition fund and endowment, $24 million, 229–30
   library support endowment for graduate school, $4 million, 233–35
   matching funds for endowed faculty positions, $15 million, 226
   student research grant endowment, $10 million, 228–29
   technology upgrade fund, $5 million, 230
War Memorial Stadium, 168, 171, 172
Washington, Treopia, 383–84
Washington Gridiron Club, 485
Washington Regional Hospital, 345
Washington Regional Medical System, 413
Washington State University, 602
Weaver, Sigourney, 16
Webb City, Missouri, 6, 9
Weber State, 487
Weiler, Karen, 107
Weiler, Peter B., 107
Welch, Jack, 123
West, Jerry, 590
Westminster College, xii, xxii, 3, 14, 32–40, 55–65, 66, 622
   board of trustees, 58
   capital campaign by, 56
   dedication of memorial to Churchill, 33, *34*
   director of development at, 61
   drug usage and alcohol abuse in, 35–37
   "Futures Campaign," 56
   leadership, 64
   liberal faculty members of, 36
   panty raids, 38–39
   Selective Service for deferments, 37
   Sigma Alpha Epsilon fraternity at, 179
Whillock, Carl, 128–29

Whillock, Margaret, 128–29
Whipple, Allen, 8
White, Betty, 619
White, John, xiii, 139–40, 162, 169, 188, 199, 215–18, 239, 449, *608*
   administration, 349
   and Altman, 253–55
   articles about negative nature of, 509
   at Bud Walton Arena, 253
   Chancellor Emeritus, 538, 539
   closed University of Arkansas Press, 146–48
   decided to step down as chancellor, 321
   and D rule, 186
   establishing honors college, 217
   fundraising, 206–7
   hiring of new athletics director, 260–63
   interviewed by agency regarding Walton Foundation, 235
   leadership, 276, 297
   met Helen Walton, 216
   murder of professor Locke, 163
   negotiations for high school, 245, 248
   offered lucrative salary, 140
   opposed Greek life on campus, 178
   Purcell's comments on NCHEMS report, 390
   and ranking of UA, 285
   retirement of, 271
   and retirement of Broyles, 188–91
   Task Force for the Enhancement of Greek Life, 178
   transformation of Carnall Hall, 160
   traveled to recruit volunteers, 212
   2010 Commission, 165–66
   views on Judy Schwab, 202
White, Mary Lib, 276, *608*
Whitehead, James, 157
White House summit on education, 561–62
Whiteside, Charlie, 180
Whitworth, Bryan, *301*
Whitworth, Donna Axum, *301*
Whole Health Institute, 413
Whole Health School of Medicine and Health Sciences, 413
Wilkins, Beth, *49*, 335
Wilkins, Larry, *49*, 335
Wilkins, Roy, 157
Willard Walker Hall, 214
Williams, Doyle, 215, 463–64
Williams, Miller, 145, 157
Williams, Naccaman, 597
Williams, Roger, 154, 160, 207, 209, 221
   and murder of professor Locke, 163
   "Quantum," 220
William Woods College, 42
Willie, Robert, 432
Wilson, William R., 184
Wilson, Woodrow, 461
Wilson Sharp-Darby Hall, 303
Windgate Foundation, 238
Winfrey, Oprah, 16
Winrock International, 242
Winslow, 591–92
Winthrop Rockefeller Charitable Trust, 242
Winthrop Rockefeller Foundation, 242
Winthrop Rockefeller Institute, 241–43, 284
Wolfe, Tom, 39
Womack, Steve, 410
Woods, Jon, 467
Woods, Randall, 537
Woolf, Virginia, 48
World Trade Center, 174, 175
Wyrick, Chris, 512–13, 591, 597, 598, 611

X

Xiaogang Peng, 224

Y

Yoffe, Avraham, 59

Young, Elizabeth, 419
Young, Neil, 38
Yurachek, Hunter, 406

Z
Zahedi, Ardeshir, 59
Zeppos, Nicholas S., 563, 564, 565
Ziglar, Zig, 90

Zuckerberg, Mark, xxi

ABOUT THE AUTHOR

DR. G. DAVID GEARHART, CHANCELLOR EMERITUS,
UNIVERSITY OF ARKANSAS

Dr. G. David Gearhart was chancellor of the University of Arkansas from 2008 to 2015, following 10 years of service to the university as vice chancellor for the Division of University Advancement. Prior to being appointed chancellor, Dr. Gearhart oversaw the Campaign for the Twenty-First Century, the most successful capital campaign in Arkansas history, which raised more than $1 billion for academic programs. That campaign included a $300 million gift, which established the Honors College and endowed the Graduate School.

With enrollment topping 28,000 students during his tenure and an 80 percent increase in diversity since 2008, the University of Arkansas was recognized by *The Chronicle of Higher Education* as the seventh-fastest growing public research university in the country and by *U.S. News and World Report* as an "up and comer" public institution. In 2011 *The Chronicle* named the university to its list of "Great Colleges to Work For," and in 2011 the Carnegie Foundation awarded the university its highest research classification.

In 2015 Dr. Gearhart retired as chancellor, and the board of trustees named an iconic academic building on campus the G. David Gearhart building. The board also named the on-campus Full Circle Food Pantry after his spouse, Jane Brockmann Gearhart.

He and Jane have been married 48 years and have two children and five grandchildren.

ALSO BY G. DAVID GEARHART

Also by G. David Gearhart

The Capital Campaign in Higher Education: A Practical Guide for College and University Advancement

Philanthropy, Fund Raising, and the American Capital Campaign: A Practical Guide

By G. David Gearhart and Michael T. Miller:

Case Studies in Higher Education Fundraising

Case Studies in College Leadership: The American College President

Handbook of Research on the Changing Role of College and University Leadership

www.ingramcontent.com/pod-product-compliance
Lightning Source LLC
Chambersburg PA
CBHW070743060526
44119CB00098B/469/J